Critical Topics in an Aging Society

Editorial Adviser, Toni C. Antonucci, PhD

- *Using Technology to Improve Care of Older Adults*
  Diane Chau, MD, FACP, and Thomas F. Osborne, MD, Editors
- *Homeless Older Populations: A Practical Guide for the Interdisciplinary Care Team*
  Diane Chau, MD, and Arnold P. Gass, MD, FACP, Editors
- *The New Politics of a Majority-Minority Nation: Aging, Diversity, and Immigration*
  Fernando M. Torres-Gil, PhD, and Jacqueline L. Angel, PhD
- *Social Isolation in Older Adults: Strategies to Bolster Health and Well-Being*
  Lenard W. Kaye, DSW, PhD, and Clifford M. Singer, MD, Editors
- *Elder Justice, Ageism, and Elder Abuse*
  Lisa Nerenberg, MSW, MPH

Social Isolation of Older Adults

Lenard W. Kaye, DSW, PhD, is professor of social work at the University of Maine School of Social Work and Director of the University of Maine Center on Aging. A prolific writer in the field of healthcare and aging, he has published more than 150 journal articles and book chapters and 14 books on specialized topics in aging. Dr. Kaye is the director of the Encore Leadership Corps (ENCorps), codirector of evaluation of the Penquis Regional Linking Project, and was the principal investigator of the National Institutes of Health (NIH) funded research project Balancing Act: Impact on Falls in Older Adults With Vision Impairment. Dr. Kaye is also the lead organizer of the International Symposium on Safe Medicine, and a founding board member of the International Institute for Pharmaceutical Safety. Dr. Kaye was the 2010 recipient of the Career Achievement Award of the Association for Gerontology Education in Social Work (AGESW). He has served on the National Advisory Committee for Rural Health and Human Services of the U.S. Department of Health and Human Services as well as the advisory boards of a wide range of national and local health and human service programs for older adults. He is a national research mentor for the Hartford Geriatric Social Work Scholars Program, a research scientist at Eastern Maine Medical Center, and past president of both the Maine and New York State gerontological societies. He is the past chair of the National Association of Social Worker Section on Aging, sits on the editorial boards of the *Journal of Gerontological Social Work* and *Geriatric Care Management Journal*, and is a fellow of the Gerontological Society of America.

Clifford M. Singer, MD, is a psychiatrist and geriatrician who has been a physician, teacher, and researcher for more than 30 years. He carries with him memories of the thousands of older adults he has known and with whom he has had the privilege of working over that period of time. He currently serves as chief of geriatric mental health and neuropsychiatry at Acadia Hospital and Eastern Maine Medical Center (EMMC) in Bangor, Maine and an adjunct professor at the University of Maine. He leads a multidisciplinary team in the Mood and Memory Clinic at Acadia Hospital and is the principal investigator for the Acadia/Eastern Maine Medical Center's Alzheimer's disease clinical trial program. He trained in general psychiatry and geriatric medicine at the Oregon Health and Science University and Portland VA Medical Center and served on the psychiatry and neurology faculty from 1988 to 2005. He was the founding president of the Oregon Geriatric Society and received an award in 2005 from the Oregon Department of Human Services for service to older adults in Oregon with mental illness and dementia. He moved to the University of Vermont in 2005 and then to Maine in 2010 to start the geriatric program at Acadia Hospital. Dr. Singer is vice president and president-elect of the Dirigo Maine Geriatrics Society. He was named "Teacher of the Year" by the EMMC Family Medicine residents in 2016. He has made national and regional television and radio appearances speaking on topics related to aging. He has published 38 papers and 18 book chapters and given more than 330 presentations at regional and national meetings.

Social Isolation of Older Adults
Strategies to Bolster Health and Well-Being

Lenard W. Kaye, DSW, PhD
Clifford M. Singer, MD
Editors

SPRINGER PUBLISHING COMPANY

Copyright © 2019 Springer Publishing Company, LLC

All rights reserved.

No part of this publication may be reproduced, stored in a retrieval system, or transmitted in any form or by any means, electronic, mechanical, photocopying, recording, or otherwise, without the prior permission of Springer Publishing Company, LLC, or authorization through payment of the appropriate fees to the Copyright Clearance Center, Inc., 222 Rosewood Drive, Danvers, MA 01923, 978-750-8400, fax 978-646-8600, info@copyright.com or on the Web at www.copyright.com.

Springer Publishing Company, LLC
11 West 42nd Street
New York, NY 10036
www.springerpub.com

Acquisitions Editor: Sheri W. Sussman
Compositor: Exeter Premedia Services Private Ltd.

ISBN: 978-0-8261-4698-4
ebook ISBN: 978-0-8261-4699-1
DOI: 10.1891/9780826146991

18 19 20 21 22 / 5 4 3 2 1

The author and the publisher of this Work have made every effort to use sources believed to be reliable to provide information that is accurate and compatible with the standards generally accepted at the time of publication. The author and publisher shall not be liable for any special, consequential, or exemplary damages resulting, in whole or in part, from the readers' use of, or reliance on, the information contained in this book. The publisher has no responsibility for the persistence or accuracy of URLs for external or third-party Internet websites referred to in this publication and does not guarantee that any content on such websites is, or will remain, accurate or appropriate.

Library of Congress Cataloging-in-Publication Data

Names: Kaye, Lenard W., editor. | Singer, Clifford M., editor.
Title: Social isolation of older adults: strategies to bolster health and well-being / Lenard W. Kaye, Clifford M. Singer, editors.
Other titles: Critical topics in an aging society.
Description: New York, NY: Springer Publishing Company, LLC, [2019] | Series: Critical topics in an aging society | Includes bibliographical references and index.
Identifiers: LCCN 2018038955 | ISBN 9780826146984 | ISBN 9780826146991
Subjects: | MESH: Social Isolation | Aged | Interpersonal Relations
Classification: LCC RA564.8 | NLM WT 145 | DDC 362.19897—dc23
LC record available at https://lccn.loc.gov/2018038955

Contact us to receive discount rates on bulk purchases.
We can also customize our books to meet your needs.
For more information please contact: sales@springerpub.com

Publisher's Note: New and used products purchased from third-party sellers are not guaranteed for quality, authenticity, or access to any included digital components.

Printed in the United States of America.

Contents

Contributors ix
Preface xiii

PART I. Setting the Context

1. The Scourge of Social Isolation and Its Threat to Older
   Adult Health 3
   Lenard W. Kaye and Clifford M. Singer

2. Historical Perspectives on the Research of Social Isolation,
   Loneliness, and Social Support 17
   Mary Lou Ciolfi

3. Making the Case: The Clinical Value of Assessing Older Adults'
   Social Isolation, Loneliness, and Social Relationships 35
   Sarah Pillemer, Chelsea Schoen, and Sloane Sheldon

4. International Perspectives on Social Relationships,
   Social Isolation, and Well-Being Among Older Adults 49
   Howard Litwin

**PART II. Proven Strategies and Programs for Promoting Social
Integration and Health**

5. Friend Power—A View From the Front Lines:
   The Importance of Relationships in the Lives of the Disabled,
   People With Dementia, and Older Adults 67
   Hope Reiner

6. Physical Activity for Older Adults: Supporting Social Integration 71
   *Marilyn R. Gugliucci, Erica Robertson, Susan Wehry, and
   Shirley A. Weaver*

viii Contents

7. Designing Age Friendly Communities as a Strategy for Enhancing Social Connectedness   89
   Patricia Huffman Oh

8. Healthy Places and the Social Life of Older Adults   103
   Keith Diaz Moore, Ivis Garcia, and Ja Young Kim

9. Volunteering as a Strategy for Combatting Social Isolation   119
   Jennifer A. Crittenden

10. Using Technology to Advance Social Health   135
    Hiroko H. Dodge

11. Spirituality and Religion in the Lives of Elders   149
    Kenneth J. Doka

12. Involving Our Pets in Relationship Building—Pets and Elder Well-Being   161
    Aubrey H. Fine and Erika Friedmann

PART III. Special Challenges Influencing Social Connectedness in Later Life

13. Social Networks and Social Isolation Among LGBT Older Adults   181
    Sandra S. Butler

14. Family and Intergenerational Relationships   197
    Donna M. Butts and Kristin Bodiford

15. Rethinking Love, Intimacy, and Sexual Relationships in the Later Years   219
    Nicholas Velotta and Pepper Schwartz

16. The Gendered Nature of Later Life Relationships   235
    Edward H. Thompson, Jr. and Kate de Medeiros

17. The Social Implications of Growing Old in Small Towns and Rural Communities   253
    Kristina M. Hash, Deana F. Morrow, and Mandana R. Weirich

Appendix: Resources on Older Adult Social Isolation and Relationships   271
   Lisa Dezso

Index   *281*

Contributors

Kristin Bodiford, PhD, MBA, United Nations Representative, Generations United; Consultant, Community Strengths, Portland, Oregon

Sandra S. Butler, PhD, MSW, BA, Professor and MSW Coordinator, School of Social Work, University of Maine, Orono, Maine

Donna M. Butts, Executive Director, Generations United, Washington, D.C.

Mary Lou Ciolfi, JD, MS, Assistant Director of Thesis Advising, Graduate Programs in Public Health, University of New England, Bath, Maine

Jennifer A. Crittenden, MSW, Assistant Director, University of Maine Center on Aging, Bangor, Maine

Kate de Medeiros, PhD, Associate Professor, Robert and Nancy Blayney Professor, Miami University, Oxford, Ohio

Lisa Dezso, LMSW-cc, CADC, Substance Use and Mental Health Counselor, Discovery House, Waterville, Maine

Hiroko H. Dodge, PhD, Professor of Neurology, Oregon Health and Science University, Portland, Oregon

Kenneth J. Doka, PhD, Professor, The College of New Rochelle and Senior Consultant, The Hospice Foundation of America, Poughkeepsie, New York

Aubrey H. Fine, EdD, Professor, Education Department, California State Polytechnic University, Pomona, California

Erika Friedmann, PhD, Associate Dean for Research, University of Maryland School of Nursing, Baltimore, Maryland

Ivis Garcia, PhD, AICP, Assistant Professor, University of Utah, Salt Lake City, Utah

Marilyn R. Gugliucci, PhD, MA, Professor and Director, U-ExCEL Older Adult Fitness Program, Division of Geriatrics, University of New England College of Osteopathic Medicine, Biddeford, Maine

Kristina M. Hash, PhD, LICSW, Professor and Director, Gerontology Program Professor, West Virginia University School of Social Work, Morgantown, West Virginia

Lenard W. Kaye, DSW, PhD, Professor, University of Maine School of Social Work and Director, University of Maine Center on Aging, Orono, Maine

Ja Young Kim, MCP, Doctoral Candidate, University of Utah, Salt Lake City, Utah

Howard Litwin, PhD, Professor Emeritus, Paul Baerwald School of Social Work and Social Welfare, The Hebrew University, Jerusalem, Israel

Keith Diaz Moore, PhD, Dean of the College of Architecture and Planning, University of Utah, Salt Lake City, Utah

Deana F. Morrow, PhD, LICSW, ACSW, Director and Professor, West Virginia University School of Social Work, Morgantown, West Virginia

Patricia Huffman Oh, MS, MSW, PhD Candidate, University of Massachusetts, Boston, Massachusetts

Sarah Pillemer, PhD, Postdoctoral Fellow, Warren Alpert Medical School of Brown University, Providence, Rhode Island

Hope Reiner, Geriatric Care Manager, Certified Dementia Practitioner, Founder, Hope Cares, New York, New York

Erica Robertson, MPH, BS, Fitness Director, U-ExCEL Older Adult Fitness Program, Division of Geriatrics, University of New England College of Osteopathic Medicine, Biddeford, Maine

Chelsea Schoen, PhD, Postdoctoral Fellow, Rusk Rehabilitation, New York University Langone Health, New York, New York

Pepper Schwartz, PhD, Professor, Department of Sociology, University of Washington, Seattle, Washington

Sloane Sheldon, PhD, Postdoctoral Fellow, Columbia University Medical Center, Department of Neurology, New York, New York

Clifford M. Singer, MD, Chief, Geriatric Mental Health and Neuropsychiatry, Northern Light Acadia Hospital, Bangor, Maine

Edward H. Thompson, Jr., PhD, Professor Emeritus, Sociology and Anthropology, College of the Holy Cross, Worcester, Massachusetts

Nicholas Velotta, BA, Professional Assistant, Department of Sociology, University of Washington, Seattle, Washington

Shirley A. Weaver, PhD, Retired, Former Assistant Dean, University of New England College of Osteopathic Medicine, Biddeford, Maine

Susan Wehry, MD, Chief of Geriatrics, Division of Geriatrics, University of New England College of Osteopathic Medicine, Biddeford, Maine

Mandana R. Weirich, LSW, MSW, Randolph County Housing Authority and West Virginia University School of Social Work, Elkins, West Virginia

Preface

THE PRECIPITATING EVENT

This book project was conceived during the planning of the 2016 University of Maine Clinical Geriatrics Colloquium, which convened in Orono, Maine, the home of the flagship campus of the University of Maine System, on October 7, 2016. The theme of the 11th Annual Colloquium was "Relationships in Later Life." It drew more than 200 health and human service providers, educators, and students from across the state. The sense of urgency regarding the challenge of social isolation that pervaded that day's presentations and discussions and the call that was heard to mobilize meaningful responses to this troubling social issue were undeniable. This volume aims to continue inquiry into the evolving nature and all too frequent fragility of late life relationships and the grand challenge of social isolation. We do this by documenting our current understanding of the complex and multidimensional nature of the interrelated issues of social relationships and health in late life, and the promising health and human service practices that have emerged to lessen the negative impacts of weakened relational ties for older adult health and well-being.

ABOUT THIS VOLUME

In this collection of chapters, we explore from multiple disciplinary perspectives the characteristics and significance of a wide range of social relationships that, when taken together, can determine the extent to which older adults will be at risk of being socially isolated, disengaged, lonely, and otherwise at risk in late life. We consider the influence on older adult social health of trends in multigenerational family relations, friendships, grandparenting, love, intimate and sexual relationships, divorce and widowhood, and interactions with community and healthcare providers and other public entities. We highlight innovative and alternative forms of community and later life relationships that can serve to forestall or prevent altogether social isolation and loneliness. Creative programs and intervention techniques that help maintain the integrity of an older adult's individual, group, and community relations, communication pathways, and a sense of belonging are showcased, as are multidisciplinary and integrated best practices for minimizing the risk of late life social isolation. Special cases are offered that highlight the issues that arise in practice and service delivery and proven responses for successfully addressing them.

With explicit intent, contributors to this volume have been drawn from a diverse range of disciplines and professions as well as from multiple practice perspectives including those of direct service providers, administrators, researchers, and educators. As a result, the reader benefits from a series of well-informed, yet different, voices and experiences and bodies of research pertaining to the changing nature of late life relationships.

Time and attention are given to both the long-standing and evolving influence that diversity in all its forms including gender, sexual preference, marital status, personality traits, race, ethnicity and culture, physical and behavioral health, housing and living arrangements, and geographic location plays in impacting the quality of our social lives and the changing nature of the relationships we maintain or else newly establish in the later stages of life.

Given the significance placed on the quality of our social lives in preparing us for a satisfying old age, we explore as well a variety of strategies for bolstering older adult social health and community engagement. While one's physical health status in late life may not be able to be dramatically altered for the better, we argue that one's social health and the relationships that constitute one's social life can. Whether you are an older adult yourself or a professional or family caregiver of an older adult, you have the capacity to shore up potential gaps in the integrity of your own or another person's social world.

THE INTENDED AUDIENCE

Health and human service professionals working in the fields of aging, healthcare, long-term care, and the human services will find this book relevant as will practitioners in a range of allied professions including medicine, social work, nursing, and public health. Clinicians, administrators, planners, researchers, educators, care managers, supervisors, and even community first responders are appropriate targets for this content as are students enrolled in professional health and human service programs.

Readers will gain a better understanding of the ways in which the quality of late life relationships can be influenced by physical, behavioral, environmental, social, and economic forces. They will also develop an enhanced understanding of preferred assessment and treatment techniques that will be most beneficial in helping older adults and their significant others address the challenges to the integrity of their personal and public lives. Finally, readers will expand their knowledge of available resources and specialized interventions that are available to help older adults minimize their isolation and disengagement from others and maintain healthy and mutually satisfying personal and public relationships while remaining integrated in their communities.

Lenard W. Kaye, DSW, PhD
Clifford M. Singer, MD

PART I

Setting the Context

1

The Scourge of Social Isolation and Its Threat to Older Adult Health*

Lenard W. Kaye and Clifford M. Singer

INTRODUCTION

Increasing numbers of socially isolated older adults have caught the attention of social and health organizations as well as the federal government. In the spring of 2017, the U.S. Senate Special Committee on Aging held a hearing on the risk of isolation for older adults who may become disconnected in virtually all respects from other individuals and communities. Testimony presented by Kaye (2017a) and other experts underscored the alarming rates of social isolation and loneliness confronting older adults in today's world. The facts speak for themselves. Fueled by a 40% increase in the number of individuals living alone between 1980 and 2010, the prevalence of social isolation and loneliness may be as high as 43% among older adults living in the community (Nicholson, Molony, Fennie, Shellman, & McCorkle, 2010). The stoicism and resistance to seeking help of particular subgroups of older adults (e.g., individuals residing in small towns and rural communities) may place them at even higher risk of becoming isolated (Kaye, 2017b).

---

*Selected content for this chapter has been drawn from: Kaye, L. W. (2017a, April). *Aging without community: The consequences of isolation and loneliness*. Testimony presented before the U.S. Senate Special Committee on Aging. Washington, DC; Kaye, L. W. (2017b). Older adults, rural living, and the escalating risk of social isolation. *Public Policy & Aging Report, 27*(4), 139–144; Kaye, L. W. (2018). Relational fragility and the isolational trajectory in the latter stages of life. *Journal of Aging Life Care*. https://www.aginglifecarejournal.org/guest-editors-message-2; and Singer, C. M. (2017). Health effects of social isolation and loneliness. *Journal of Aging Life Care*.

The escalating risk of isolation has put too many older adults on a troubling trajectory with potentially life-threatening consequences. The need to reduce social isolation and loneliness has been designated as one of 12 great challenges (Lubben, Gironda, Sabbath, Kong, & Johnson, 2015). As an underaddressed social issue in contemporary society, it is argued that we are in immediate need of new ideas, scientific inquiry, and bold innovation for reducing the negative impacts of this pervasive social problem. Both the World Health Organization and the National Institutes of Health have highlighted the need for this issue to receive greater attention. Likewise, the American Association of Retired Persons (AARP) has prioritized social isolation as an issue warranting greater attention (Lubben et al., 2015).

Closely associated with the downward trajectory in social connectedness that many older adults find themselves moving along are the increasingly fragile relationships that exist between them and family, friends, neighbors, and other members of the communities in which they reside. The threat posed by the weakening of one's social network is increasingly recognized as a threat to health. Social relationships provide not only social support but increase our access to resources, create a buffer against stress, and serve as a trusted social influence. Research suggests that social relationships have as much influence on our health as a number of lifestyle factors including obesity and smoking.

Older adults at greatest risk of becoming socially isolated are lesbian, gay, bisexual, transgender, and questioning (LGBTQ) elders, as well as those with physical, sensory, and functional impairments; those who live alone, are 80 years of age and older, are geographically isolated, live on limited income, or lack instrumental supports (access to transportation, the Internet, telephones, etc.); and those with poor mental health, weak social networks, and who face critical life transitions (divorce, death of a spouse or partner, an abrupt retirement, a health crisis, children moving out, etc.); see Lubben et al. (2015). This high risk pool includes older men who, as a group, may be more likely to have fragile and sparse social support networks, and are less likely to engage with informal support networks.

Social isolation can shorten your life. Socially isolated individuals have both higher morbidity and mortality rates including increased rates of disability, dementias, hospitalizations, falls, poor health practices, psychological distress, neglect and exploitation, and lower self-reported health and well-being (Lubben et al., 2015). Social isolation was found to increase the relative risk ratio of being a current smoker compared to having never smoked by 67%, and this risk was found to be greatest among males and non-Hispanic Whites. Similarly, social isolation was also found to increase the relative risk ratio of being depressed by 13% (Choi & Dinitto, 2015). These are associations and not cause-and-effect relationships, but the strong correlations between social isolation and ill-health are startling.

SOCIAL HEALTH: A CRITICAL PART OF HEALTH AND WELL-BEING

Social health is the critical third leg of the stool that combines with physical and psychological health to determine late life well-being. How communal and connected we are ultimately predicts the extent and quality of our personal relationships. Research has firmly established that social contact and committed relationships promote physical and emotional health. Conversely, social isolation is a major risk factor for multiple chronic illnesses and earlier death. While the most important contributor to social health in older adults is close personal ties, the quality of relationships with others in public settings also plays a significant role in determining overall well-being and especially timely access to needed assistance and support from both professional and nonprofessional helpers.

Inevitably, regardless of who you are and no matter how socially connected you are to the world, aging is likely to be accompanied by alterations in the integrity of your social network. Relatives, friends, and neighbors move away, die, or lose their connection to you for any variety of reasons. Marriages may dissolve and rifts arise in relationships with even close confidants and significant others. At the same time, people may be fortunate enough to meet other individuals who become extremely meaningful participants in their life story. And so, the size, strength, and intensity of one's social network naturally wax and wane over the years.

While social isolation can occur at any stage of life, older adults may be especially at risk of finding themselves cut off from personal and public ties. For them, social isolation, characterized by a lack of consistent, reliable, and meaningful social relationships, can be lethal.

Social isolation, the consequence of a compromised and weakened network of social supports, has been associated with an exceedingly wide range of health problems and dangerous life situations (discussed in greater detail later in this chapter) including: risk of dementia and cognitive impairment; nonadherence to good health practices; risk of elder abuse, neglect, and exploitation; challenges surviving natural disasters; risk of depression and anxiety; and ultimately, heightened mortality. Even our susceptibility to the common cold has been associated with being socially isolated, suggesting an effect on immune function. Socially isolated individuals do not maintain as balanced a diet or other sound healthcare practices, nor visit their primary care practitioners on as regular a schedule as their socially connected counterparts.

Appreciating the association between compromised personal and public ties in later life and the potential for finding yourself enmeshed in inequitable, manipulative, and even abusive relationships is also important. A deeper understanding of the implications of this troubling relationship can be expected to further reinforce the call for more concerted steps that will reduce the all too common fragility of personal ties and the weakening of social networks in the lives of older adults. In this chapter, we explore the evidence supporting the connection between social isolation and ill-health and try to clarify whether it is isolation itself or loneliness that is the critical factor affecting health in people who are isolated.

HEALTH EFFECTS OF SOCIAL ISOLATION AND LONELINESS (ADAPTED FROM SINGER, 2018)

Social connectedness is in our genes. Throughout our history, social networks (families, tribes, communities, etc.) have enabled us to survive. Our survival was served by the evolutionary development of behaviors and physiologic mechanisms (neural, hormonal, cellular, genetic) that support social interactions (J. T. Cacioppo, Hawkley, Norman, & Berntson, 2011). But as with all human traits, there is variation in our social behaviors and needs. The fact is, most of us are driven to seek social connection. Social networks not only provide us with social support but are socially influential, creating a buffer against stress and increasing our access to resources. It is not surprising, therefore, that social isolation may impose stress on our minds and bodies, which has a significant impact on health.

Since social isolation and loneliness are common in older adults, much attention has been paid to clarifying their adverse effects on health in old age. The challenge is that it can be difficult to distinguish the effects of social isolation and loneliness on health when preexisting health conditions, such as immobility and depression, can themselves contribute to ill-health as well as increase isolation and loneliness. It is also challenging to distinguish social isolation and loneliness from one another; not all who are isolated are lonely and not all who are lonely are alone.

DEFINING SOCIAL ISOLATION AND LONELINESS

Not all people experience "aloneness" in the same way. Social scientists who study isolation and loneliness have attempted to define these terms in specific ways, since a person is considered socially isolated if he or she lives alone, has less than monthly contact with friends or family, and does not belong to a group (religious congregation, club, work or volunteer organization, etc.); see Ciolfi and Jimenez (2017). Of course, some choose isolation as a preferred lifestyle. Others, likely far more in number, have isolation imposed on them through the death of loved ones, family and friends moving away, remote rural housing, recent moves to an unfamiliar city, impaired mobility, and other situations leading to depleted social networks and isolation. People in these situations may be more likely to experience loneliness and to feel isolated ("perceived isolation"). We can quantify social isolation and loneliness in terms of number and frequency of social contacts, but defining isolation in quantitative terms may not always be valid. The quality of our social interactions, more than the number of our relationships, determines loneliness.

Researchers have also approached these issues using qualitative methods. Cornwell and Waite (2009) use terms such as *social disconnectedness* and *perceived isolation* to define social isolation and loneliness using the objective and subjective nature of these states. Social disconnectedness is defined as lack of contact with others. Perceived isolation is defined as the subjective experience of lack of companionship and support. Loneliness may be part of that, although people can still experience subjective isolation around others. The assumption is that social disconnectedness without perceived isolation (i.e., isolation without loneliness) would be less stressful than states of loneliness and depression, thereby having less impact on health. Research has not always supported this assumption (Cornwell & Waite, 2009). Social isolation, with or without loneliness, can have as large an effect on mortality risk as smoking, obesity, sedentary lifestyle, and high blood pressure (J. T. Cacioppo et al., 2011).

CORRELATIONS OF ISOLATION AND LONELINESS ON HEALTH

Several indicators of social isolation have been associated with poor health. Several studies, in particular, can help us better understand the relationships of social networks, perceived isolation, health, and mortality. From a methodological perspective, these studies assume that health status contributes to one's ability to be socially engaged. Therefore, health status can contribute to loneliness and isolation, thereby creating a "cause-and-effect" dilemma when attempting to define the relationships between loneliness, social isolation, health, and mortality. Investigators have to control for baseline health status in the design of their studies and in the analysis of their data. Despite this, the effects of social isolation and loneliness on health are a strong enough force that they consistently emerge as unambiguous risk factors for ill-health and mortality in the many studies that have examined these relationships through various methodologies, including longitudinal cohort studies and meta-analyses (quantitative analysis of the combined results of carefully selected studies).

It is natural to assume that loneliness has a greater effect on health than isolation itself and some studies support that conclusion. Adverse effects on health from loneliness are seen at every stage of the life cycle (Hawkley & Capitanio, 2014). But older adults may be at particular risk both for loneliness and the health consequences of loneliness. For example, in a study involving a large number of older adults in Finland, 39% suffered loneliness at least some of the time; 5% "often or always." Loneliness was statistically associated with several demographic variables, including rural living, older age, living alone or in residential care, widowhood, low level of education, and low income. Subjectively, the people in this study attributed their loneliness to illness, loss of spouse, and lack of friends. Poor health status and poor functional status were also associated with greater feelings of loneliness (Savikko, Routassalo, Tilvis, Strandberg, & Pitkalla, 2005). A study done by J. T. Cacioppo and Cacioppo (2014) found loneliness to be associated with ill-health to a greater degree than just social isolation. They examined two elements of social isolation independently (social disconnectedness and perceived isolation) on both physical and mental health. Stronger relationships were shown between loneliness and worse health, including cardiovascular disease, inflammation, and depression, than social isolation itself. Loneliness in older adults was shown to significantly increase risk of functional decline and death in a recent longitudinal cohort study of 1,604 individuals followed over 6 years. Some 43% of the cohort reported loneliness and they were at higher risk for both functional decline (activities of daily living, mobility) and death. The authors of this study found that loneliness was associated with these poor outcomes even after adjusting for baseline health status and depression, but did not compare those who were isolated to those who were lonely (Perissinotto, Cenzer, & Covisnky, 2012).

On the other hand, many investigators have found social isolation itself to be a risk factor for ill-health. In a meta-analysis of studies examining the magnitude of the effect of social isolation and loneliness on mortality in which important baseline health variables were controlled in the analysis, Holt-Lunstad, Smith, and Baker (2015) found a 29% increased risk of mortality over time from social isolation and 26% increase in mortality risk from loneliness. Interestingly, they found a 32% increased risk from just living alone, independent of social isolation. That is, they found no correlation of objective versus subjective social isolation. This finding is counterintuitive, in that we would think that the stress of loneliness would be a driving factor for ill-health, yet "aloneness" seems to be at least as strong, if not a stronger influence on health. Steptoe, Shankar, Demakakos, and Wardle (2013) investigated whether the health impact of social isolation was "caused by loneliness" in 6,500 men and women more than 52 years of age participating in the English Longitudinal Study of Aging. They quantified contact with family, friends, and community organizations and administered a loneliness questionnaire. They monitored mortality for an average of 7.25 years per subject. After adjusting for demographic variables, *social isolation* increased mortality whereas *loneliness* did not. Those with the highest social isolation (least social contact) had an even higher risk. Although there was an increased mortality risk in lonely people, they also had higher baseline mental and physical health problems that may have accounted for the increased risk. That is, loneliness in this study was associated with higher baseline levels of depression, arthritis, and mobility impairment than the social isolation without loneliness cohort, so when baseline health variables were factored out, the cohort who expressed loneliness did not seem to have as high a mortality rate. In an effort to clarify the relative effect of loneliness and social isolation on cardiovascular mortality risk, Valtorta, Kanaan, Gilbody, Ronzi, and Hanratty (2016) conducted a meta-analysis of 11 cardiac and eight stroke studies. Poor social relationships in general (social isolation and loneliness) were associated with a 29% increase in risk of coronary heart disease and 32% increase in stroke risk. This increased risk is comparable to the risk of obesity and lack of physical activity and whether isolated people were lonely or not did not appear to make a difference. Across all studies, both social isolation and loneliness appear to increase the risk of premature death (Steptoe et al., 2013).

POTENTIAL MECHANISMS INFORMING SOCIAL SUPPORT AND HEALTH

Many potential mechanisms have been proposed to account for the relationships between social integration, perceived social support, and health outcomes. First of all, spending time with people who exhibit healthy habits may reinforce healthy behaviors, improve access to health-related information, maintain better nutrition, achieve more physical activity, arrange transportation to healthcare providers, and even increase financial resources. Of course, peer relationships can easily lead to unhealthful behaviors or interpersonal stress as well, but in the literature pertaining to older adults, the health-promoting benefits of social relationships seem to outweigh the negative effects

(Cornwell & Waite, 2009). But changing health behaviors is likely not the only mechanism by which social contacts protect health and well-being.

Loneliness is known to be a major risk factor for depression, which itself accelerates functional decline and increases mortality rate (Mehta, Yaffe, & Covinsky, 2002). Even subclinical depression may increase risk of all-cause mortality (Culjpers & Smit, 2002), so depression may have contributed to the increased mortality and cardiovascular diseases found in the loneliness cohorts of those studies cited previously. Depression may increase mortality and illness through several mechanisms. Depression can increase platelet aggregation through diminished serotonin function and thereby increase risk for myocardial infarction and stroke. There may also be increased heart rate variability (unstable autonomic nervous system) and increased release of adrenaline, both leading to increased risk of cardiac arrhythmia (Seymour & Benning, 2009). Whatever the mechanism, the effect of depression on mortality is significant in size. In a large cohort study (Cardiovascular Health Study), investigators found that depression increased mortality risk by 24% when they accounted for all important covariables (Schultz et al., 2000).

Social isolation can have direct effects on cardiovascular disease risk factors. Perceived isolation and loneliness are associated with increased sympathetic nervous system activity, increased inflammation, and decreased sleep, all of which can accelerate brain and cardiovascular aging (J. T. Cacioppo et al., 2011). Loneliness increases risk for dementia, likely through these mechanisms; however, the absence of social interaction itself may also be a primary factor in that social stimulation can help maintain brain health (J. T. Cacioppo & Hawkley, 2009; S. Cacioppo, Capitanio, & Cacioppo, 2014). Grant and colleagues examined key metabolic risk factors for cardiovascular mortality, looking at blood pressure, lipids, and cortisol responses to stress. Using a measure of social integration ("Close Persons Questionnaire"), they found dysregulated blood pressure and cortisol responses to acute stress in people (238 middle-aged men and women) with few close friends. They also saw increased cholesterol in the socially isolated men, but not women. These physiologic changes increase risk of heart attacks and stroke. The authors note that these changes in cardiovascular risk factors in isolated individuals were independent of whether they expressed feelings of loneliness (Grant, Hamer, & Steptoe, 2009).

Finally, there is some evidence that loneliness can affect immune function, increasing susceptibility to infection (Cohen, Doyle, Skoner, Rabin, & Gwaltney, 1997). Loneliness is also associated with disrupted sleep. Insomnia affects immune function, glucose regulation, cardiovascular risk, dementia risk, mood, and daytime function (Hawkley, Preacher, & Cacioppo, 2010; Wilson et al., 2017).

SOCIAL PROGRAMMING TO REDUCE ISOLATION

The evidence linking social isolation in old age with poor health is strong enough that efforts to reduce cardiovascular disease need to consider social interventions aimed at reducing isolation (Valtort et al., 2016). There are studies that do suggest increasing social networks can improve health. In one such study, conducted over a 10-year period of follow-up, men (aged 42–77) with lower levels of "social integration" (by a standard social network index) were, as expected, found to be at greater risk of total mortality than those with more social connections. What was surprising in this study was that in a subanalysis of the older men of the sample who showed increasing social network size over the 10 years of study, an increased number of close friends or increased attendance at religious services were both associated with a reduced risk of death. The effect size was robust. Those reporting having more friends over time showed a reduction of 29% in mortality risk per year (Eng, Rimm, Fitzmaurice, & Kawachi, 2002). This does not prove causality; perhaps improvements in health for other reasons promoted behaviors that lead to more friends. Nevertheless, the finding is encouraging.

Although the stress of being a caregiver to a disabled family member is not the same kind of stress as social isolation, caregivers consistently describe the isolation of the caregiver's role as one of the most stressful aspects of the caregiving role. Caregivers consistently report higher levels of stress than noncaregivers, and chronic stress is associated with poorer health outcomes and higher rates of mortality. But caregivers, overall, have a lower mortality rate. The important variable is the level of stress a person experiences in the caregiver role. Not all caregivers experience significant stress, and those who do not may experience health benefits from the caregiving relationship. In fact, in one study, nonstressed caregivers had 43% lower rates of mortality relative to noncaregivers. In previous studies, caregivers experiencing significant emotional stress showed a 60% increase in mortality rate (Fredman, Cauley, Hochberg, Ensrud, & Doros, 2010). These findings are relevant to considerations of interventions for social isolation. Nonstressed caregivers are more likely to experience positive emotions from the person they are providing care for and to gain strength from having a vital role to play in another person's life. To be a caregiver and not feel some reciprocal caring from your partner is a special form of isolation that is particularly demoralizing, stressful, and unhealthy. Even small efforts to make isolated people feel appreciated and useful may reduce the stress of loneliness and thereby improve health.

Innovative ways to help depressed, isolated people may also have positive effects on health. In a 12-month multimodality, home-based intervention, randomized controlled trial for older adults with depression, those receiving a home-based (as opposed to usual, office-based) treatment had significantly better responses. The home-based treatment group was more likely to be in remission from depression, had greater quality of life improvements, and displayed greater gains in functional well-being and emotional well-being (Ciechanowski et al., 2004).

Given the mobile nature of our society, social relationships frequently are maintained at a distance through telephone contact, email, and social media when physical contact is not practical. Interventions relying on technology to reduce isolation may be better than no intervention at all, but they are not the same as in-person visits. A large cohort study has recently revealed that different methods of contact are not equal in reducing feelings of loneliness and depression. These investigators found a higher risk of depression in those with less than once-a-month face-to-face contact with children, family, or friends. People with once- or twice-a-week contact had the lowest rates of depression. However, older age, interpersonal conflict, and depression at baseline decreased the effect of physical contact. That is, if a person is prone to depression, is physically frail, or the relationship causes tension, a phone call may be as good as (or better than) in-person contact (Teo et al., 2015).

There is an increasing amount of evidence that pets, especially dogs and cats, are associated with health benefits and reduced mortality. Research into whether animal companions can offset the deleterious effects of social isolation on health is needed.

IMPLICATIONS FOR THE PROVISION OF GERIATRIC CARE

Geriatric care providers may be in a better position than any other member of the healthcare team both to recognize social isolation and to organize interventions. Based on current evidence, they can justify increased focus on social relationships in the multidisciplinary healthcare treatment plan and in their individual efforts to reduce isolation in their clients. An understanding that social isolation is a significant risk factor to health, of similar magnitude to obesity and diabetes, may be persuasive for some of their clients who are able to increase social contact with others, either in person or through social technologies.

SUMMARY

Many older adults feel isolated and lonely. There are compelling data that these states are associated with poor health and higher rates of mortality. The effect of social isolation (with or without subjective loneliness) on health appears to be of a similar magnitude to other risks to health, such as high blood pressure, smoking, and obesity. Whereas these other health risk factors have stimulated major public health interventions in recent decades, efforts to reduce isolation and loneliness have not been made on a level of population health. We also have to keep in mind that being in toxic relationships may be even more stressful and unhealthy than loneliness (Birmingham, Uchino, Smith, Light, & Butner, 2015). Nevertheless, there is enough evidence to consider social isolation and loneliness among older adults a significant public health issue. There are also compelling hypotheses and some experimental data to explain the physiologic mechanisms by which social isolation increases the risk of disease. There is also an emerging body of evidence that interventions to reduce loneliness may improve health. Although there are no simple prescriptions to address isolation and loneliness, population-health authorities should take this issue as seriously as other known health risk factors. It is very likely that social interventions provided at relatively modest costs will result in cost savings in public health. At the very least, such efforts provide a safe, humane approach to a common cause of suffering in older adults.

REFERENCES

Birmingham, W. C., Uchino, B. N., Smith, T. W., Light, K. C., & Butner, J. (2015). It's complicated: Marital ambivalence on ambulatory blood pressure and daily interpersonal functioning. *Annals of Behavioral Medicine, 49*(5), 743–753. doi:10.1007/s12160-015-9709-0

Cacioppo, J. T., & Cacioppo, S. (2014). Social relationships and health: The toxic effects of perceived social isolation. *Social and Personality Psychology Compass, 8*(2), 58–72. doi:10.1111/spc3.12087

Cacioppo, J. T., & Hawkley, L. C. (2009). Perceived social isolation and cognition. *Trends Cognitive Sciences, 13*(10), 447–454. doi:10.1016/j.tics.2009.06.005

Cacioppo, J. T., Hawkley, L. C., Norman, G. J., & Berntson, G. G. (2011). Social isolation. *Annals of the New York Academy of Science, 1231*(11), 17–22. doi:10.1111/j.1749-6632.2011.06028.x

Cacioppo, S., Capitanio, J. P., & Cacioppo, J. T. (2014). Toward a neurology of loneliness. *Psychological Bulletin, 140*(6), 1464–1504. doi:10.1037/a0037618

Choi, N. G., & Dinitto, D. M. (2015). Role of new diagnosis, social isolation, and depression in older adults' smoking cessation. *The Gerontologist, 55*(5), 793–801. doi:10.1093/geront/gnu049

Ciechanowski, P., Wagner, E., Schmaling, K., Schwartz, S., Williams, B., Diehr, P., . . . LoGerfo, J. (2004). Community-integrated home-based depression treatment in older adults: A randomized controlled trial. *Journal of the American Medical Association, 291*(13), 1569–1577. doi:10.1001/jama.291.13.1569

Ciolfi, M. L., & Jimenez, F. (2017). *Social isolation and loneliness in older people: A closer look at definitions. Issues and insights in disability and aging.* Portland: University of Southern Maine, Muskie School of Public Service.

Cohen, S., Doyle, W. J., Skoner, D. P., Rabin, B. S., & Gwaltney, J. M. (1997). Social ties and susceptibility to the common cold. *Journal of the American Medical Association, 277*(24), 1940–1944. doi:10.1001/jama.1997.03540480040036

Cornwell, E. Y., & Waite, L. J. (2009). Social disconnectedness, perceived isolation, and health among older adults. *Journal of Health and Social Behavior, 50*(1), 31–48. doi:10.1177/002214650905000103

Culjpers, P., & Smit, F. (2002). Excess mortality in depression: A meta-analysis of community studies. *Journal of Affective Disorders, 72*(3), 227–236. doi:10.1016/S0165-0327(01)00413-X

Eng, P. M., Rimm, E. B., Fitzmaurice, G., & Kawachi, I. (2002). Social ties and changes in social ties in relation to subsequent total and cause-specific mortality and coronary heart disease incidence in men. *American Journal of Epidemiology, 155*(8), 700–709. doi:10.1093/aje/155.8.700

Fredman, L., Cauley, J. A., Hochberg, M., Ensrud, K. E., & Doros, G. (2010). Mortality associated with caregiving, general stress and caregiving-related stress in elderly women: Results of caregiver-study of osteopathic fractures. *Journal of the American Geriatrics Society, 58*(5), 937–943. doi:10.1111/j.1532-5415.2010.02808.x

Grant, N., Hamer, M., & Steptoe, A. (2009). Social isolation and stress-related cardiovascular, lipid and cortisol responses. *Annals of Behavioral Medicine, 37*, 29–37. doi:10.1007/s12160-009-9081-z

Hawkley, L. C., & Capitanio, J. P. (2015). Perceived social isolation, evolutionary fitness and health outcomes: A lifespan approach. *Philosophical Transactions of the Royal Society B: Biological Sciences, 370*(1669), pii. doi:10.1098/rstb.2014.0114

Hawkley, L. C., Preacher, K. J., & Cacioppo, J. T. (2010). Loneliness impairs daytime functioning but not sleep duration. *Health Psychology, 29*, 124–129. doi:10.1037/a0018646

Holt-Lunstad, J., Smith, T. B., & Baker, M. (2015). Loneliness and social isolation as risk factors for mortality. A meta-analytic review. *Perspectives on Psychological Science, 10*(2), 227–237. doi:10.1177/1745691614568352

Kaye, L. W. (2017a). *Aging without community: The consequences of isolation and loneliness* [Video]. Testimony presented before the United States Senate Special Committee on Aging, Washington, DC. https://www.aging.senate.gov/hearings/aging-without-community-the-consequences-of-isolation-and-loneliness-

Kaye, L. W. (2017b). Older adults, rural living, and the escalating risk of social isolation. *Public Policy & Aging Report, 27*(4), 139–144. doi:10.1093/ppar/prx029

Kaye, L. W. (2018). Relational fragility and the isolational trajectory in the latter stages of life. *Journal of Aging Life Care.* https://www.aginglifecarejournal.org/guest-editors-message-2

Lubben, J., Gironda, M., Sabbath, E. Kong, J., & Johnson, C. (2015). *Social isolation presents a grand challenge for social work* (Grand Challenges for Social Work Initiative Working Paper No. 7). Cleveland, OH: American Academy of Social Work and Social Welfare.

Mehta, K. M., Yaffe, K., & Covinsky, K. E. (2002). Cognitive impairment, depressive symptoms and functional decline in older people. *Journal of the American Geriatrics Society, 50*(6), 1045–1050. doi:10.1046/j.1532-5415.2002.50259.x

Nicholson, N., Molony, S., Fennie, K., Shellman, J., & McCorkle, R. (2010). *Predictors of social isolation in community living older persons.* (Unpublished PhD). New Haven, CT: Yale University.

Perissinotto, C. M., Cenzer, I. S., & Covisnky, K. E. (2012). Loneliness in older persons: A predictor of functional decline and death. *Archives of Internal Medicine, 172*(14), 1078–1083. doi:10.1001/archinternmed.2012.1993

Savikko, N., Routassalo, P., Tilvis, R. S., Strandberg, T. E., & Pitkalla, K. H. (2005). Predictors and subjective causes of loneliness in an aged population. *Archives of Gerontology and Geriatrics, 41*(3), 223–233. doi:10.1016/j.archger.2005.03.002

Schultz, R., Beach, S. R., Ives, D. G., Martire, L. M., Ariyo, A. A., & Kop, W. J. (2000). Association between depression and mortality in older adults: The Cardiovascular Health Study. *Archives of Internal Medicine, 160,* 1761–1768. doi:10.1001/archinte.160.12.1761

Seymour, J., & Benning, T. B. (2009). Depression, cardiac mortality and all-cause mortality. *Advances in Psychiatric Treatment, 15,* 107–113. doi:10.1192/apt.bp.107.004770

Singer, C. M. (2018). Health effects of social isolation and loneliness. *Journal of Aging Life Care.* https://www.aginglifecarejournal.org/health-effects-of-social-isolation-and-loneliness

Steptoe, A., Shankar, A., Demakakos, P., & Wardle, J. (2013). Social isolation, loneliness, and all-cause mortality in older men and women. *Proceedings of the National Academy of Sciences, 110*(15), 5797–5801. doi:10.1073/pnas.1219686110

Teo, A. R., Choi, H. J., Andrea, S. B., Valenstein, M., Newsom, J. T., Dobscha, S. K., & Zivin, K. (2015). Does mode of contact with different types of social relationships predict depression in older adults? Evidence from a nationally representative survey. *Journal of the American Geriatrics Society, 63*(10), 2014–2022. doi:10.1111/jgs.13667

Valtorta, N. K., Kanaan, M., Gilbody, S., Ronzi, S., & Hanratty, B. (2016). Loneliness and social isolation as risk factors for coronary heart disease and stroke: Systematic review and meta-analysis of longitudinal observational studies. *Heart, 102,* 1009–1016. doi:10.1136/heartjnl-2015-308790

Wilson, S., Jaremka, L. M., Fagundes, C. P., Andridge, R., Peng, J., Malarkey, W. B., . . . Kiecolt-Glaser, J. K. (2017). Shortened sleep fuels inflammatory responses to marital conflict: Emotion regulation matters. *Psychoneuroendocrinology, 79,* 74–83. doi:10.1016/j.psyneuen.2017.02.015

2

Historical Perspectives on the Research of Social Isolation, Loneliness, and Social Support

Mary Lou Ciolfi

INTRODUCTION

Social isolation and loneliness are distinct concepts with a research history that evolved separately over many decades in the disciplines of sociology, psychology, psychiatry, and epidemiology. This chapter provides a historical overview of highlights from the research on social isolation, loneliness, and social support, and considers the implications of that research on current practice. Even though use of the term *social support* is less common in public discourse than *social isolation* and *loneliness*, it is included here because its definition in the research includes many of the functions that supportive relationships fulfill in preventing or reducing isolation and loneliness.

Awareness of how and what we have learned about the defining characteristics of these concepts fosters an appreciation of the many differences in the human experience of relational disconnectedness. It also explains the diversity of perspectives in the way we analyze human social engagement and allows for more personalized assessment of social needs and more targeted delivery of social programs and services. This is critical to achieving the goal of helping individuals maintain strong, meaningful, and functional social bonds throughout the aging process.

Viewing the long arc of research in this area also prevents oversimplification of complex human experiences and supports more nuanced recognition of an individual's social reality. It prevents us from applying one-size-fits-all solutions to the growing number of isolated older people and expands our analytic and creative capacity to brainstorm interventions and preventive approaches that will support the well-being of all people across the life span, not just those who fit in the most common categories of social disconnection.

The use of several other terms representing various aspects of the social lives of humans has complicated the scientific and lay discussions of social disconnection. The social science literature includes references to *social contacts, social engagement, social cohesion, social participation, social integration, social network,* and *social ties*. Some of these concepts have been independently studied and have a deep research history of their own. Yet, as a result of commonalities in human social experiences and the various disciplines building on the work of one another, there is still conceptual confusion within the scientific community. This lack of clarity has made it challenging to translate research and theory into practice. The entangled research history includes views on human social needs from the perspective of evolution, genetics, personality, and social environment, at the individual, community, and cultural levels, and considering both objective factors and the subjective view (Rook, 1984).

In the domain of empirical research, identifying the characteristics and contours of human behavior and phenomena is the precursor to testing hypotheses and developing theories (Peplau & Perlman, 1982). Understanding characteristics, concepts, and theory provides us with ways to organize information and make it useful in practice. Concepts and theory have predictive capacity and provide a platform for planning, problem solving, and developing interventions and best practices (Fishbein & Yzer, 2003). When social isolation and loneliness became popular research topics in the mid-20th century, the different disciplines were challenged to understand and define their respective unique characteristics, articulate their relevance, and distinguish themselves from the other, more extreme manifestations of human disconnection such as grief, depression, and severe forms of mental illness (Weiss, 1973). From their respective angles, the different disciplines first wanted to understand the human drives behind social disconnection. Intertwined with this work was mapping the many ways in which humans are—and feel—socially disconnected, and the physical, mental, or environmental circumstances that pose risk factors for, or result from, disconnection. With this knowledge in hand, researchers developed a variety of isolation and loneliness assessment tools to test their theories (see, for instance, Valtorta, Kanaan, Gilbody, & Hanratty, 2016). Finally, and more recently, researchers have been motivated to prevent or alleviate isolation and loneliness, and there are current efforts to create interventions and align them with the many ways in which individuals experience periods of social disconnection (see, for instance, Gardiner, Geldenhuys, & Gott, 2016).

This research agenda took place in overlapping ways over several decades. Figure 2.1 shows the view across the long-range continuum from understanding the phenomena to crafting interventions and preventive measures. Along this continuum, individual disciplines and individual researchers have continued to refine concepts, theories, and research questions.

Our attention in this chapter is at the left side of Figure 2.1, looking at how the early research, in different disciplines with differing but overlapping interests, focused on understanding, defining, and mapping causal factors for social isolation, loneliness, and social support. This foundational work can, and should, be used for activity at the right side of the continuum—the development and use of analytic and practical tools to create interventions and social programs for isolated or lonely people. As a result of the ongoing focus on understanding substantive aspects of social engagement in the various disciplines, there has been less effort to translate the decades of theoretical research into guidance for health and social service providers and community agencies in their daily work of finding socially isolated and lonely persons and providing support. This work remains to be done now that the health risks and quality of life impact of social disconnections have caught the attention of the healthcare community and the public.

HISTORICAL OVERVIEW

Paul Halmos's 1952 text, *Solitude and Privacy: A Study of Social Isolation, Its Causes and Therapy*, is one of the earliest on the topic of social isolation. Halmos quotes Wilfred Trotter's 1916 publication, *Instincts of the Herd in Peace and War*, "[t]here exists a law . . . which renders the concept of association inseparable from the concept of existence." In the immediate post–World War II environment, Halmos and other social scientists identified with post–World War I existentialism and struggled to integrate the widespread destruction and the fractured global relationships wrought by a second world war into their understanding of the necessity of meaningful human

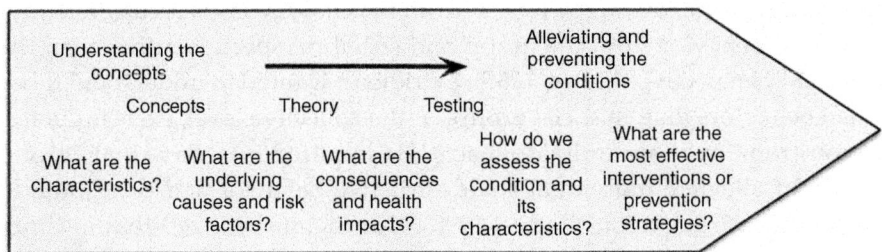

FIGURE 2.1 The continuum from understanding to intervening and preventing.

connection. Halmos's reference to the direct link between human "association" and human existence demonstrates the research community's alarm over how an increasingly individualistic, bordered, mistrustful society might maintain sufficiently strong bonds to ensure its long-term survival.

Across the scientific disciplines, researchers suspected that the human longing for social engagement arose from an evolutionary drive to be connected to the safety and security of the "herd" (Bowlby, 1973; Cacioppo & Hawkley, 2003; Harlow, 1945). Midcentury thinkers interested in this topic were divided into two groups: those who viewed social disconnection as the result of societal changes and those who viewed it as individual pathology (Halmos, 1952). This diversity of approach reflected the differences in the disciplines. The sociologists and anthropologists were primarily interested in the behavior of social groups and tended to speak the language of *social isolation*. The psychiatrists and psychologists were primarily interested in the individual pathology of socially disconnected patients and tended to speak the language of *loneliness*.

Finally, as the discipline of epidemiology matured in the early 20th century from its 19th century beginnings with London's cholera epidemics (Newsom, 2006), epidemiologists began to look beyond the transmissibility of disease among individuals, asking wider ranging questions about how infectious agents might be impacted by the social environment of those infected (Cassel, 1976). In their effort to understand how individuals and communities supported one another in times of illness, stress, and adversity, the epidemiologists working on the impact of human relationships on health tended to speak the language of *social support* in the emerging field of social epidemiology (Berkman, Kawachi, & Glymour, 2014).

The Lines of Research

Social Isolation

The early social isolation research grew out of the work of Émile Durkheim in the late 19th century. Durkheim gained recognition of sociology as an independent discipline, distinguishing it from psychology in its focus on studying human behavior from the group and social perspective rather than the individual perspective (Lukes, 1985). Durkheim wanted to understand those human behaviors that, in social groups at the collective level, exert influence and constraint over our individual acts. He inquired into ways that "group life" might alleviate individual self-destructive behavior and contribute to greater civic participation (Portes, 1998). Durkheim theorized that in times of societal upheaval and social stress and change, societal values and social norms shift, disrupting the extent to which they guide and check individual behavior, causing reduced social cohesion (Berkman, Glass, Brissette, & Seeman, 2000). He developed the concept of *social integration* and studied the social and behavioral consequences of varying levels of social involvement (Rook, 1984). For instance, in his work on suicide and religion (Durkheim, 1951, 1995), he explored how one's social environment, and level of integration with it, triggered feelings of aimlessness or despair, or alternatively, feelings of belonging and connection.

As society modernized in the early decades of the 20th century, worker tasks became more differentiated and individualized, people moved into cities in large numbers, and social spaces became more influential in our lives. Our individual and collective behavior had to accommodate the many "others" around us; we had greater need for social coordination in a more complex, "organized society" (Weber, 1947). Scientists tracked social movement in modern communities and studied the development, structure, and function of social networks, as well as the impact that network characteristics had on social integration (Hughes & Gove, 1981). Engagement with social network connections were the vehicles for meeting human needs, ensuring safety, and accomplishing life goals (Machielse, 2006). As the research on social networks progressed beyond midcentury, networks were defined according to objective measures of size, composition, and diversity, and by the functions served by network connections. Individuals lacking meaningful and functional social networks, disconnected from those who helped meet their needs, were socially isolated (Meeuwesen, 2006). Scientists developed a body of research linking these low network measures to increased mortality risk (Berkman, 1986).

Curious about network characteristics beyond size, composition, and function, scientists expanded the scope of their research perspective to explore social connections at several social levels and whether and how individuals experienced adverse consequences when they were disconnected from engagement at these different levels. Lin (1986) and others looked at connections at the community level, with its attendant sense of belonging to a larger group; at the level of work, friendship, or kinship, and the accompanying close bonding with other individuals; and at the most familiar level of confidante and intimate, with its binding, reciprocal, and caring expectations and exchanges. Biordi and Nicholson (2013) added the life span, duration dimension of social isolation, defining characteristics of isolated individuals as "early," "recent," or "lifelong."

Sociologists were also trying to sort out the emotions and feelings that resulted from social isolation and it was in this area that their work intersected with research of the psychiatrists and psychologists who were primarily concerned with the human feeling of loneliness. The interrelatedness of the concepts and characteristics of social integration, social networks, and social isolation, and the emotional, feeling aspects of disconnection, resulted in a lack of conceptual certainty and the absence of a widely used definition (Meeuwesen, 2006; Nicholson, 2009; Valtorta & Hanratty, 2012).

Nicholson (2009) recognized this "conceptual ambiguity" and the lack of an accepted, consistent definition for social isolation. To gain greater clarity, he deconstructed the social isolation research up to that point to find the most commonly noted social isolation attributes that had emerged in the preceding decades. Nicholson suggested that these attributes might be incorporated into a fixed definition. He looked at objective attributes such as number of social contacts, as well as more subjective factors such as a sense of belonging, inadequate relationships, level of engagement, and quality of network members, and arrived at the current, most commonly accepted definition of social isolation:

> A state in which the individual lacks a sense of belonging socially, lacks engagement with others, has a minimal number of social contacts, and is deficient in fulfilling and quality relationships. (Nicholson, 2009, p. 1346)

This definition reflects the theoretical roots of the sociologist's perspective by focusing on the objective qualities of structure and function of the network; it defines social isolation according to network contacts and acknowledges the primary network function of facilitating social engagement. However, it also incorporates some subjectivity by considering the extent of engagement with one's network and whether relationships with network contacts are of sufficient quality and sufficiently fulfilling to the individual. This definition suggests that to determine whether someone is socially isolated, we must look at several factors: the structure of the network, the extent of engagement with the network, and some characteristic of "quality" or "fulfillment," typically understood to mean an analysis of whether the network is meeting an individual's support needs (Meeuwesen, 2006). This tripartite analysis—structure, quality, and function—provides a framework for understanding and recognizing the many ways that an individual may be socially isolated or at risk for becoming isolated.

To achieve the ultimate goal of crafting effective interventions and prevention strategies, some researchers have focused on assessing whether social isolation exists and identifying those who are most at risk. Effective assessment, particularly assessment targeted at potential risk factors, requires an understanding of causes, precursors, and other variables that will most likely lead to a socially isolated status. Berkman et al. (2000) developed a model that contemplated "upstream" and "downstream" factors. The upstream factors are those that might lead to isolation, including cultural factors (e.g., racism), socioeconomic factors (e.g., poverty), political factors (e.g., disenfranchisement), and social change factors (e.g., civil unrest, urbanization). The downstream factors are those pathways by which social isolation might impact our health, including health behavior (e.g., substance use), psychological well-being (e.g., self-efficacy, self-esteem), or physical wellness (e.g., immune function, cardiovascular health). Between these upstream and downstream factors is the network itself, defined, as we have seen, by size, diversity, and function. Berkman's model is depicted along a continuum that includes those factors that lead to a limited social network and those that flow from it.

Berkman's model inspired subsequent refinement by Iredell, Grenade, Nedwetzky, Collins, and Howat (2004), whose slightly simpler model retained a continuum approach with upstream and downstream factors, but condensed the center of network characteristics into a list of *relational deficits* that we typically associate with social isolation, such as a lack of social contacts, minimal engagement with others, and a diminished sense of belonging. Iredell's model also recategorized potential precursors to social isolation into five domains: physical (e.g., vision/hearing, comorbidities), psychological (e.g., depression), economic (e.g., retirement status), change in family (e.g., death of relative), and environmental (e.g., living alone or in unsafe living conditions).

These domains have been recently reworked to contribute to a typology, or classification, of socially isolated individuals. Machielse (2015) acknowledged the lack of demonstrated effectiveness in most current social isolation research and the corresponding need for improved matching of individuals with more targeted, personalized interventions. Her research describes a social isolation typology according to the *persistence*, or duration, of the isolation, as well as the level of an individual's *coping strategy*, or motivation, to address one's isolation. Machielse determined that social isolation that has persisted for many years (e.g., resulting from personality type or poor mental health) often has *structural* aspects that are fundamentally different from isolation that is more *situational* and results from life circumstances in the near term (e.g., moving to a new community). She further noted that whether an individual has an active or passive coping strategy for life adversity is also a factor in the type, method, or level of support needed to alleviate isolation. These typology domains are then bisected by consideration of whether the

TABLE 2.1 Practice Tips: Social Isolation

Concepts	Questions to Consider
Network factors	
Network structure	What is the size and diversity of the individual's social network?
Network function	Are the individual's needs for support being met?
Individual factors	
Situational factors	Are there recent life events that impact social engagement?
Structural factors	Are there long-standing factors that impact social engagement?
Integration with network	Is the individual engaged with his/her network?
Desire for social interaction	What is the individual's level of need for social engagement?
Environmental factors (e.g., home, neighborhood)	How does the individual's environment impact socially isolated status?
Coping skill	What is the individual's coping style or extent of coping skill?

individual's personality is oriented toward greater or lesser social engagement. Some individuals want to be around people more often or in greater numbers, and others do not; knowing where an individual falls along this spectrum helps align proposed interventions.

This social isolation research overview provides context for the diversity of circumstances and experiences associated with isolation and a framework for thinking about the ways in which oneself, or one's family, friends, or service providers, can help relieve it. Table 2.1 provides some theory-based questions that practitioners can consider when talking with people at risk.

Loneliness

The early psychiatrists interested in loneliness approached the topic from the perspective of psychiatric and psychoanalytic pathology, and much of the published writing on the topic, prior to the midcentury rise in research interest, was clinical observation of patients (Peplau & Perlman, 1982). In one of the earliest and most widely cited texts on the topic, *Loneliness: The Experience of Emotional and Social Isolation* (1973), Robert Weiss sought to develop an approach to research beyond the clinical setting. Weiss noted that earlier scientists (Reichmann, 1959) bemoaned the shortage of scientific literature and theories of loneliness; indeed, there was so little research on loneliness that Weiss and his contemporaries wondered whether something inherent in the experience of loneliness made it unappealing to researchers. Was it so painful an experience that "it baffles clear recall" (Sullivan, 1953) or that we avoid it entirely? Even more recent scientists have noted the research challenges and underreporting associated with the tendency for individuals to avoid admitting that they feel lonely (de Jong Gierveld, van Tilburg, Dykstra, Vangelisti, & Perlman, 2006).

While Weiss brought much to the understanding of loneliness in subsequent decades, the very title of his text reflects the conflating of social isolation and loneliness. Weiss, then an associate professor of psychiatry at Harvard Medical School, wanted to understand why humans evolved to have an emotional response pattern that included the "gnawing" feeling of loneliness. He included in his text a chapter reprinting the work of psychiatrist John Bowlby (1969), who was studying attachment theory and disruptions in the affectional bonds between mother and child. Bowlby, building on the work of Harry Harlow observing the consequences of prolonged separation of baby rhesus monkeys from their mothers (Harlow & Harlow, 1965), had identified "proximity-promoting mechanisms" that supported human survival by motivating people to remain physically close to one another for food, shelter, safety, and care. Bowlby's research confirmed the innate alarm and stress responses when humans were separated from a primary attachment figure and the severe pathology that results from long periods of separation. Based on Bowlby's theory, Weiss proposed that the distressing feeling associated with loneliness drives humans to return to the safety of their significant and meaningful emotional and social relationships.

Some separations do not produce feelings of loneliness but, when they do, each person's triggers for distress and threshold for alarm are unique. As a result, the research on loneliness has always focused on an individual's subjective experience of despair associated with certain separations. This subjective quality forms the foundation of the definition of loneliness and is the primary factor distinguishing loneliness from social isolation. In another important contribution to the field, Peplau and Perlman's 1984 text, *Loneliness: A Sourcebook of Current Theory, Research, and Therapy*, examined 12 definitions of loneliness looking for the common ground among them. These "points of agreement" contribute to the definition of loneliness that is still most commonly used today:

> Loneliness is a subjective experience that is unpleasant and distressing and results from deficiencies in a person's social relationships.

The "deficiencies" referenced in this definition are the product of Weiss's research. He suggested that the physical discomfort and feelings of distress and despair associated with loneliness indicate a "relational deficit," and his research explored the diverse ways in which humans perceive and experience deficiency in relationship. To understand these deficits, he mapped the types of relationships that typically bring meaning to an individual's life, and in what ways, such that when these relationships are absent, we feel lonely. Despite that the study of loneliness emerged from the realm of pathology, Weiss was most interested in the ordinary human experience of loneliness, as distinct from extreme relationship disturbances resulting in social alienation, grief, or major depression. He and others (Davies, 1996; de Jong-Gierveld, 1987) also distinguished one of the positive states of aloneness that humans experience as *solitude.*

As indicated by the book title, Weiss divided loneliness into two categories: emotional isolation and social isolation. Within those categories, he further defined situational and characterological causal factors based on the then-current understanding that the cause of loneliness could either be external to oneself or related in some way to one's character. Perlman and Peplau (1981) later characterized them as either precipitating or predisposing factors. This external–internal categorization of the precursors to loneliness aligns with the social isolation distinction between situational and structural factors.

Weiss understood that there was a difference between what our emotional and social relationships provided in our lives and, accordingly, he developed a framework that outlined six *social provisions* (Weiss, 1974). These social provisions are attachment, social integration, nurturance, worth, alliance, and guidance. Each of these provisions corresponds to a different interpersonal need that is most often associated with a particular type of relationship. Attachment needs are most often fulfilled by a spouse or intimate partner; social integration needs are most often fulfilled by friends; nurturance needs are usually fulfilled by our children; our need for worthiness is most often met by our coworkers and colleagues; our need for alliance is often met by our family and kin; and our need for guidance typically is met by our teachers and mentors. According to Weiss, when loneliness results from the loss or absence of an emotional attachment, we are *emotionally isolated,* and when loneliness results from disconnection from our social network, we are *socially isolated.* Social isolation as defined earlier is broader than Weiss's use of the term, but this is the area of overlap: when we are isolated or disconnected from those with whom we feel an emotional or social attachment, we feel lonely.

Weiss's theoretical work on social provisions is particularly helpful in understanding the diverse spectrum of relationships that can trigger feelings of loneliness. It is a reminder, for instance, that the loss of a close attachment figure, such as an intimate partner, and the resulting feelings of loneliness are unlikely to be fully resolved by interactions with other types of relationships. While loneliness resulting from social or emotional disconnection may feel similar in the human body, very different interventions may be necessary to alleviate that feeling. Later work on Weiss's social provisions focused on creating scales to assess and measure loneliness and gain a better understanding of this spectrum of individual relational needs and desires (see, for instance, Russell, Cutrona, Rose, & Yurko, 1984).

As the psychiatrists and psychologists continued their work in the latter decades of the 20th century, they were challenged in the same ways as the sociologists: how do we define and categorize attributes of loneliness; how do we incorporate a duration component; and how do we view it across the life span or in relation to an individual's societal or environmental surroundings? In work that predated their text, Perlman and Peplau (1981) identified the importance of one's social context in an individual's experience of loneliness. Their *discrepancy–attributional* approach emphasized an individual's perceptions of self in relation to others, and perceived control over one's situation, as important characteristics of the experience of loneliness. Because feelings of loneliness occur when there is a discrepancy between our actual and our desired relationships, Peplau and Perlman recognized that an individual's cognitive processes—the way one thinks about one's own state of loneliness—will influence the likelihood that one's loneliness will be relieved and the type of intervention that is most appropriate. For instance, if one attributes loneliness to an internal, "stable" factor such as perceived unattractiveness, then this suggests more long-term, chronic loneliness. This is contrasted with someone who attributes loneliness to a recent move and feels competent and confident about developing new friendships in a new community.

Collecting the many attributes of loneliness helped further define it. Rokach (1989) interviewed 526 individuals about their experiences of loneliness. Her analysis revealed "clusters" of loneliness causes, which she categorized as relational deficits, traumatic events, and characterological and developmental variables. Rokach's model cast a wide causal net and illustrates the many individual circumstances, including relationship loss or separation, inadequate social supports, being physically uprooted, childhood trauma, social skill deficits, or physical disabilities; any one or more of these might contribute to feelings of loneliness. This long list highlights the considerable overlap in circumstances that might lead to both social isolation and loneliness and in part explains why many people who are socially isolated are also lonely.

The distinction between isolation and loneliness has recently been articulated as *perceived social isolation* and *objective social isolation*. Hawkley and Cacioppo

(2010) suggested that "[l]oneliness is synonymous with perceived social isolation, not with objective social isolation" (p.218). This objective–subjective distinction reflects the different orientations of sociology and psychology and establishes that loneliness, while defined according to entirely subjective criteria, can be impacted and attenuated by external, environmental factors.

de Jong Gierveld et al. (2006) is one of several social scientists who wrote about social isolation and loneliness together. She acknowledged the objective and subjective continuum of each and the importance of viewing loneliness in a social context in addition to an individual context. One's physical and social environment can significantly impact whether and to what extent we feel lonely. For instance, citing other research (Thomese, Van Tilburg, & Knipscheer, 2003), she notes that when one's neighbors and community members display an attitude of *mutual concern*, there is a corresponding decrease in levels of individual loneliness. In this reference to neighborhood and community characteristics that impact loneliness, she hints at the emerging research on the relationship between social capital and increased amounts of social engagement (see Keating, Swindle, & Foster, 2005).

As noted, while there is overlap in some of the factors that might indicate the presence of social isolation or loneliness, the research confirms that risk assessments for each are not interchangeable and they should be considered separately (Holt-Lunstad, Smith, Baker, Harris, & Stephenson, 2015). Table 2.2 provides some general questions to consider in determining possible loneliness, and the individual and environmental factors that might suggest appropriate interventions.

Social Support

The foundations of the concept of social support include identifying who helps us in times of adversity or stress, in what ways, and with what beneficial impact. Social support theory intersects with social isolation and loneliness theories primarily around the *function* of our important social

TABLE 2.2 *Practice Tips: Loneliness*

Concepts	Questions to Consider
Subjective feelings	Does the individual admit to feeling lonely?
Social provisions	What relationship needs are not being met?
Attribution	To what does the individual attribute the loneliness?
Character or situation	Is the loneliness longstanding or the result of recent life events?
Motivation	Is the loneliness motivated to alleviate the loneliness?
Environmental factors	How does the physical or social environment impact loneliness?

relationships; when adversity inevitably strikes, what kind of support do we need and want, from whom, and what specific characteristics of that support contribute to our well-being?

Once the epidemiologists better understood the transmissibility of infectious disease in the early-to-mid–20th century, their curiosity extended to the impact of environment on disease susceptibility. Not everyone who was exposed to a pathogen got sick, and others got sick only later when environmental conditions changed (Cassel, 1976). Which environmental factors, particularly in one's social environment, produced physiologic stress and increased the likelihood of disease? Zoologists and biologists confirmed that social environments such as overcrowding in animal environments, and marginal social status and lack of social contact in humans, impacted health status, though the exact physiologic pathways were as yet undefined (Cassel, 1976).

Public health scientists considered how to use the research on social environment to further understand poor health and disease prevention (Cobb, 1976). As society modernized and we became more mobile, our social networks spread, diversified, and included greater numbers of shallow and weak ties and fewer family and close community members which, despite geographic distances, were easier to maintain given growing communication options (Berkman et al., 2000). The epidemiology community concerned itself with these changes in network structure and function and the impact they might have on population health.

Social support theorists were challenged to create clarity for their ideas in the same way as other disciplines. While they recognized the obvious link between small network size and the inability to get one's needs met, they sought to clearly define other influential factors. For instance, they questioned the subjective perceptions of the parties to the support relationship, the connection between social network characteristics and social support, support activity that had harmful effects for the recipient or provider, the short- and long-term effects of receipt of social supports, and social support impact in the absence of stress (Shumaker & Brownell, 1984).

Over the past several decades, there have been several articulations of a definition of social support. Cobb (1976) defined social support in terms of *information* from one's social network that communicated certain aspects of belonging to an individual. He expressed these aspects of belonging as feeling loved and cared for, feeling esteemed and valued, and feeling part of a network of communication and reciprocal exchange. Cobb specifically distinguished social support from direct, compensated services that help people in difficult times, such as healthcare services. Articulated in terms of love and belonging, the concept of social support was akin to some of the relationship provisions described by Weiss in the loneliness research being conducted in the same time period, but it is distinct in one important way: Social support focuses specifically on *helpfulness* in times of need or distress.

Rook (1984) described the primary areas where there was a lack of consensus among social support researchers as *objective versus subjective support, types and function of support*, and whether social supports have *buffering or direct effects*—that is, whether they buffer against adversity or whether they produce a direct beneficial effect on well-being. Shumaker and Brownell (1984) defined social support with an emphasis on exchange and without regard to the perceptions of the recipient: an exchange of resources between at least two individuals perceived by the provider or the recipient to be intended to enhance the well-being of the recipient. Gottlieb (1985) defined social support as the feedback provided by way of contact with similar and valued peers, and later (Gottlieb & Bergen, 2010), recognizing that not all intended help is perceived to be helpful, included the subjective aspect and expanded the definition to include

> the social resources that persons perceive to be available or that are actually provided to them by nonprofessionals in the context of both formal support groups and informal helping relationships. (Gottlieb, 2010, p.512)

Krause (1995, 2007) studied those who had negative perceptions of social support and found, unsurprisingly, that when recipients of help were criticized or when the helper was inconsiderate or acted upset, individuals were more likely to feel that future help would be unreliable. While the focus of social support remains on helpfulness in times of need, it now includes the perception of helpfulness by the recipient, and the informal (unpaid), nonprofessional (unlicensed) nature of the support.

As noted, the most important component of the research on social support has been around the functional aspect of social help and resources. Although researchers have arrived at the types of social support from differing perspectives, there has been consistent categorization of supports into four primary areas: instrumental support (physical assistance, money); informational support (advice, information, suggestions); appraisal support (affirmation, feedback); and emotional support (trust, concern) (Holt-Lunstad & Uchino, 2015; House, 1981; Rook, 1984). This categorization has particular implications for practitioners and provides a practical framework to assess an individual's social network to determine the types of critical functional needs that are absent in times of social disconnection or when one's social network is small and insufficient to support well-being.

Some of the most current research in social support is particularly relevant to providing services and support to older people. Feeney and Collins (2015) take a longitudinal view of socially supportive relationships and investigate how social support within a relationship can be used to enhance wellness and contribute to thriving under ordinary, nonstressful life circumstances. They borrow the safe haven concept from Bowlby's attachment theory and describe helpful and supportive relationships as a *source of strength* (SOS) and significant contributors to thriving. In addition to providing more traditional social support, these SOS individuals can assist with newly identified approaches to wellness such as reframing adverse events. Feeney and Collins also contemplate the benefit of SOS in ordinary, nonstressful life circumstances through expansion of opportunities for engagement and growth and through the celebration of successes.

Evaluating how individuals can be helped using the social support framework will typically follow a determination of whether they are socially isolated, lonely, or both. If someone is isolated or lonely and has an identifiable support need, social support theory can help direct the appropriate intervention. Lonely individuals are likely to need emotional or appraisal support, while isolated individuals are likely to need instrumental or informational support. Table 2.3 provides some questions to consider.

SUMMARY

This overview of research history of social isolation, loneliness, and social support concepts and theory demonstrates the complexity of how social connections shape and are shaped by our individual predispositions and perceptions, our physical and mental health, the events in our lives and our ability and skill to cope with adversity, the availability of people and services to support us when we are in need, and our physical and social environments. While the conceptual fundamentals described in much of the research apply across the life course, some have particular applicability to older people who

TABLE 2.3 *Practice Tips: Social Support*

Concepts	Questions to Consider
Need for functional support	What is the need for instrumental, informational, appraisal, or emotional support?
Perception factors	Does the individual perceive that the support that is or will be provided will be helpful?
Negative factors	Is there a perception of negative interaction from previous helpers?
Reciprocity	Is there an opportunity for a reciprocal exchange?

often have naturally occurring smaller social networks as a result of the illness or death of a spouse, partners, and close friends; or their own physical or cognitive limitations; or life circumstances such as retirement or relocation. Practitioners are encouraged to approach isolated or lonely individuals or those in need of supportive services—or at risk for any of those conditions—in ways that reflect the diversity of the life situations and experiences. Researchers continue in their efforts to find effective interventions for social isolation and loneliness and for effective delivery of social support, and while we await further guidance, we can use the concepts and theories developed over decades to inform our practice. Awareness of the long research history will result in more targeted and effective help for individuals who need it.

REFERENCES

Berkman, L. F. (1986). Social networks, support, and health: tTaking the next step forward. *American Journal of Epidemiology, 123*(4), 559–562. doi:10.1093/oxfordjournals.aje.a114276

Berkman, L. F., Glass, T., Brissette, I., & Seeman, T. E. (2000). From social integration to health: Durkheim in the new millennium. *Social Science & Medicine, 51*(6), 843–857. doi:10.1016/S0277-9536(00)00065-4

Berkman, L. F., Kawachi, I., & Glymour, M. M. (Eds.). (2014). *Social epidemiology* (2nd ed.). New York, NY: Oxford University Press.

Bowlby, J. (1969). *Attachment and Loss, Vol. 1: Attachment. Attachment and Loss.* New York: Basic Books.

Bowlby, J. (1973). Affectional bonds: Their nature and origin. In R. Weiss (Ed.), *Loneliness: The experience of emotional and social isolation* (pp. 38–52). Cambridge: Massachusetts Institute of Technology Press.

Biordi, D. L., & Nicholson, N. R. (2013). Social isolation. In I. M. Lubkin (Ed.), *Chronic illness: Impact and intervention* (pp. 85–115). Burlington, MA: Jones & Bartlett Learning.

Cacioppo, J. T., & Hawkley, L. C. (2003). Social isolation and health, with an emphasis on underlying mechanisms. *Perspectives in Biology and Medicine, 46*(3), S39–S52. doi:10.1353/pbm.2003.0049

Cassel, J. (1976). The contribution of the social environment to host resistance: The Fourth Wade Hampton Frost Lecture. *American Journal of Epidemiology, 104*(2), 107–123. doi:10.1093/oxfordjournals.aje.a112281

Cobb, S. (1976). Social support as a moderator of life stress. *Psychosomatic Medicine, 38*(5), 300–314. doi:10.1097/00006842-197609000-00003

Davies, M. G. (1996). Solitude and loneliness: An integrative model. *Journal of Psychology and Theology, 24*(1), 3–12. doi:10.1177/009164719602400101

de Jong Gierveld, J., van Tilburg, T., Dykstra, P. A. (2006). Loneliness and social isolation. In Vangelisti, A., & Perlman, D. (Eds.), *Cambridge handbook of personal relationships* (pp. 485–500). Cambridge, UK: Cambridge University Press.

de Jong-Gierveld, J. (1987). Developing and testing a model of loneliness. *Journal of Personality and Social Psychology, 53*(1), 119–128. doi:10.1037/0022-3514.53.1.119

Durkheim, E. (1951). *Suicide: a study in sociology* (J. A. Spaulding & G. Simpson, Trans.). Glencoe, Illinois: The Free Press. (Original publication 1897)

Durkheim, E. (1995). *The elementary forms of religious life* (pp. 1–30; K. E. Fields, Trans.). New York, NY: New York Free Press. (Original publication 1912).

Feeney, B. C., & Collins, N. L. (2015). A new look at social support: A theoretical perspective on thriving through relationships. *Personality and Social Psychology Review, 19*(2), 113–147. doi:10.1177/1088868314544222

Fishbein, M., & Yzer, M. C. (2003). Using theory to design effective health behavior interventions. *Communication Theory, 13*(2), 164–183. doi:10.1111/j.1468-2885.2003.tb00287.x

Gardiner, C., Geldenhuys, G., & Gott, M. (2016). Interventions to reduce social isolation and loneliness among older people: An integrative review. *Health and Social Care in the Community, 26*(2), 147–157. doi:10.1111/hsc.12367

Gottlieb, B. H. (1985). Social networks and social support: An overview of research, practice, and policy implications. *Health Education Quarterly, 12*(1), 5–22. doi:10.1177/109019818501200102

Gottlieb, B. H., & Bergen, A. E. (2010). Social support concepts and measures. *Journal of Psychosomatic Research, 69*(5), 511–520. doi:10.1016/j.jpsychores.2009.10.001

Halmos, P. (1952). *Solitude and privacy: A study of social isolation, its causes and therapy*. London, UK: Routledge & K. Paul.

Harlow, H. F. (1945). Studies in discrimination learning in monkeys: V. Initial performance by experimentally naive monkeys on stimulus-object and pattern discriminations. *The Journal of General Psychology, 33*(1), 3–10. doi:10.1080/00221309.1945.10544491

Harlow, H. F., & Harlow, M. K. (1965). The affectional systems. *Behavior of Nonhuman Primates, 2*, 287–334. doi:10.1016/B978-1-4832-2821-1.50008-2

Hawkley, L. C., & Cacioppo, J. T. (2010). Loneliness matters: A theoretical and empirical review of consequences and mechanisms. *Annals of Behavioral Medicine, 40*(2), 218–227. doi:10.1007/s12160-010-9210-8

Holt-Lunstad, J., Smith, T. B., Baker, M., Harris, T., & Stephenson, D. (2015). Loneliness and social isolation as risk factors for mortality: A meta-analytic review. *Perspectives on Psychological Science, 10*(2), 227–237. doi: 10.1177/1745691614568352

Holt-Lunstad, J., & Uchino, B. N. (2015). Definition and conceptualizations of social support. In K. Glanz, B. K. Rimer, & K. Viswanath (Ed.), *Health behavior: Theory, research, and practice* (5th ed., pp. 183–204). San Francisco, CA: Jossey-Bass.

House, J. S. (1981). *Work stress and social support*. Reading, MA: Addison-Wesley.

Hughes, M., & Gove, W. R. (1981). Living alone, social integration, and mental health. *American Journal of Sociology, 87*(1), 48–74. doi:10.1086/227419

Iredell, H., Grenade, L., Nedwetzky, A., Collins, J., & Howat, P. (2004). Reducing social isolation amongst older people-implications for health professionals. *Geriaction, 22*(1), 13–20.

Keating, N., Swindle, J., & Foster, D. (2005). The role of social capital in aging well. *Social Capital in Action: Thematic Policy Studies*, 24–51.

Krause, N. (1995). Negative interaction and satisfaction with social support among older adults. *The Journals of Gerontology Series B: Psychological Sciences and Social Sciences, 50*(2), P59–P73. doi:10.1093/geronb/50B.2.P59

Krause, N. (2007). Longitudinal study of social support and meaning in life. Psychology and aging, 22(3), 456.

Krause, N. (2007). Longitudinal study of social support and meaning in life. *Psychology and Aging, 22*(3), 456–469. doi:10.1037/0882-7974.22.3.456

Lin, N. (1986). Conceptualizing social support. In N. Lin, A. Dean, & W.M. Ensel (Ed.), *Social support, life events, and depression* (pp. 17–30). Waltham, MA: Academic Press.

Lukes, S. (1985). *Emile Durkheim, his life and work: A historical and critical study.* Redwood City, CA: Stanford University Press.
Machielse, A. (2006). Theories on social contacts and social isolation. In R. Hortulanus, A. Machielse, & L. Meeuwesen, *Social isolation in modern society* (pp. 13–36). Abingdon, UK: Routledge.
Machielse, A. (2015). The heterogeneity of socially isolated older adults: A social isolation typology. *Journal of Gerontological Social Work, 58*(4), 338–356. doi:10.1080/01634372.2015.1007258
Meeuwesen, L. (2006). A typology of social contacts. *Social Isolation in Modern Society, 37*–59.
Newsom, S. W. B. (2006). Pioneers in infection control: John Snow, Henry Whitehead, the Broad Street pump, and the beginnings of geographical epidemiology. *Journal of Hospital Infection, 64*(3), 210–216. doi:10.1016/j.jhin.2006.05.020
Nicholson Jr., N. R. (2009). Social isolation in older adults: An evolutionary concept analysis. *Journal of Advanced Nursing, 65*(6), 1342–1352. doi:10.1111/j.1365-2648.2008.04959.x
Peplau, L. A., & Perlman, D. (1982). *Loneliness: A sourcebook of current theory, research, and therapy.* New York, NY: John Wiley & Sons.
Perlman, D., & Peplau, L. A. (1981). Toward a social psychology of loneliness. *Personal Relationships, 3*, 31–56.
Portes, A. (1998). Social capital: Its origins and applications in modern sociology. *Annual Review of Sociology, 24*(1), 1–24. doi:10.1146/annurev.soc.24.1.1
Reichmann, F. F. (1959). Loneliness. *Psychiatry, 22*(1), 1–15. doi:10.1080/00332747.1959.11023153
Rokach, A. (1989). Antecedents of loneliness: A factorial analysis. *The Journal of Psychology, 123*(4), 369–384. doi:10.1080/00223980.1989.10542992
Rook, K. S. (1984). Research on social support, loneliness, and social isolation: Toward an integration. In L. Wheeler & P. Shaver (Eds.), *Review of personality and social psychology* (vol. 5, pp. 239–264). Beverly Hills, CA: Sage.
Russell, D., Cutrona, C. E., Rose, J., & Yurko, K. (1984). Social and emotional loneliness: An examination of Weiss's typology of loneliness. *Journal of Personality and Social Psychology, 46*(6), 1313. doi:10.1037/0022-3514.46.6.1313
Shumaker, S. A., & Brownell, A. (1984). Toward a theory of social support: Closing conceptual gaps. *Journal of Social Issues, 40*(4), 11–36. doi:10.1111/j.1540-4560.1984.tb01105.x
Sullivan, H. S. (1953). *The interpersonal theory of psychiatry.* New York, NY: W. W. Norton.
Thomese, F., Van Tilburg, T., & Knipscheer; C. P. M. (2003). Continuation of exchange with neighbors in later life: The importance of the neighborhood context. *Personal Relationships, 10*, 575–550. doi:10.1046/j.1475-6811.2003.00064.x
Trotter, W. (1916). *Instincts of the herd in peace and war.* London, UK: T Fisher Unwin Ltd.
Valtorta, N., & Hanratty, B. (2012). Loneliness, isolation and the health of older adults: Do we need a new research agenda? *Journal of the Royal Society of Medicine, 105*(12), 518–522. doi:10.1258/jrsm.2012.120128
Valtorta, N. K., Kanaan, M., Gilbody, S., & Hanratty, B. (2016). Loneliness, social isolation and social relationships: What are we measuring? A novel framework for classifying and comparing tools. *BMJ Open, 6*(4). doi:10.1136/bmjopen-2015-010799
Weber, M., Henderson, A. M., & In Parsons, T. (1947). *The theory of social and economic organization.* New York, NY: Oxford University Press.
Weiss, R. S. (1973). *Loneliness: The experience of emotional and social isolation.* Cambridge: Massachusetts Institute of Technology Press.
Weiss, R. S. (1974). The provisions of social relationships. In Z. Rubin (Ed.), *Doing unto others.* Upper Saddle River, NJ: Prentice Hall.

3

Making the Case: The Clinical Value of Assessing Older Adults' Social Isolation, Loneliness, and Social Relationships

Sarah Pillemer, Chelsea Schoen, and Sloane Sheldon

INTRODUCTION

In community health settings, the opportunity for primary care including the prevention of social isolation in at-risk groups has the potential to make the biggest difference through early assessment. This practice includes administration of a risk profile. For example, when older adults are admitted to a visiting nurse service, community health nurses are tasked with addressing a specific diagnosis or diagnoses with their skilled nursing care. However, during these visits, the nurses have a unique opportunity to provide primary care prevention of social isolation. (Nicholson, 2012, p. 137)

Social relationships are fundamentally important to the health of older adults. However, measuring this variable is challenging. In the fields of medicine and psychology, methodological approaches to measurements of social relationships are diverse. While many measurements focus on the structure or composition of an individual's social network, there are also the emotional aspects of these relationships, which can be difficult to measure. Social relationships incorporate quantitative factors including size of social networks, degrees of social engagement, number of and time engaged in activities, and amount of social support. But there are qualitative elements to all these factors that require different methodological approaches to assessment. Recent reviews have suggested that social networks and social activity represent more *structural* aspects of social relationships, whereas social support represents more *functional* aspects (Kuiper et al., 2015; Kuiper et al., 2016). It is, therefore, important that service professionals working with older adults use a measurement technique that would systemically examine a broad range of aspects of social relationships, including structure/social network, social engagement, and perceived support.

SECTION I: DEFINING ISOLATION, LONELINESS, AND THEIR HEALTH-RELATED EFFECTS

Social Networks

One way to collect data on social relationships is by focusing on the composition of an individual's social structure. In defining "social networks," we follow Wrzus, Hanel, Wagner, and Neyer (2013), who proposed that "social networks comprise a person's social relationships, that is, the set of people with whom an individual is directly involved with, such as family members, friends, and acquaintances." Social network characteristics are measured in various ways. Characteristics of a social network include variables such as the range or size of a network (i.e., number of members in the network), the extent to which members are connected to each other, frequency of contact with network members, and the multiplexity of the network (i.e., the number of unique social connections between individuals of the network) (Berkman, Glass, Brissette, & Seeman, 2000).

Measuring the number of individuals in an older adult's social network in isolation, however, is incomplete given the absence of an affective component that can assess the quality of relationships. Therefore, additional approaches to measuring social relationships that focus on both the structure and the pattern of interactions is favored as they also assess qualitative variables that impact well-being (Hampton, 2007; Smith & Christakas, 2007).

Social Integration, Engagement, and Activity

Social integration, which is an overarching concept encompassing the extent to which an individual has social connections, is also used as a measure of social relationships (Berkman et al., 2000). Social integration is often considered the opposite of social isolation (Seeman, 1996), and is typically thought of as the extent to which an individual participates in private and public social interactions. Social engagement and activity are additional components of social relationships and consist of the promotion of participation in social activities, such as getting together with friends, attending social gatherings, group recreational activities, and membership in organizations (Berkman et al., 2000). Measuring social integration/engagement in combination with social network characteristics would be a useful method to capture a wide range of variables that affect social relationships.

Perceived Social Support

Another important area to assess is perceived social support, which indicates the social resources that an individual perceives to be available, or that are actually provided, by other individuals. Multiple facets of this construct have been identified, including emotional, instrumental, appraisal, informational, and affectionate support, and are typically categorized by the type of aid provided. Briefly, *emotional support* reflects the expression of positive affect and empathetic understanding. *Instrumental support* reflects the amount of aid or assistance one receives. *Appraisal support* relates to receiving help with decision making/deciding on actions and providing feedback. *Informational support* is the receipt of information, feedback, or advice. Lastly, *affectionate support* includes feelings of being loved and receiving affection.

Taken together, it is important to capture both received and perceived support, assess the different types of support (e.g., informational, emotional, affectionate), and consider the composition of an individual's social network. Time permitting, it would be beneficial to evaluate the support provided by particular people in the network as they may serve different functions, as opposed to asking general questions about support from the social network as a whole.

Importantly, social relationships have historically been measured by self-report questionnaires or brief questions regarding composition of an individual's network (e.g., marital status, number of children, etc.). Less used, but perhaps more informative, are interview methods whereby the individual is prompted to provide more thoughtful, detailed, and relevant information about this intricate structure. Ideally, a combination of interview and self-report measures of social relationships would be helpful in considering the multidimensionality of social support.

Measuring Social Relationships

Examples of commonly used self-report measures of social relationships to incorporate into clinical practice include:

- *Berlin Social Support Scale:* measures both cognitive and behavioral aspects of social support by assessing perceived, provided, and received

support, need for support, support seeking, and protective buffering (Schwarzer & Schultz, 2013)
- *Duke-UNC Functional Social Support Questionnaire:* measures an individual's perception of the amount and type of support (Broadhead, Gehlbach, De Gruy, & Kaplan, 1988)
- *ENRICHD Social Support Inventory:* measures how frequently emotional, informational, and practical supports are available (Mitchell et al., 2003)
- *Inventory of Socially Supportive Behaviors:* evaluates the frequency of receipt of emotional, informational, and practical support, and companionship from network members (Stokes & Wilson, 1984)
- *Lubben Social Network Scale:* a measure of social engagement, including with family *and* friends (Lubben, 1988)
- *Norbeck Social Support Questionnaire:* measures quantity, source, and functional types of support available (Norbeck, Lindsey, & Carrieri, 1981)
- *Medical Outcomes Study Social Support Survey:* measures an individual's perceived level of the availability of positive social interaction, and emotional, informational, tangible, and affectionate support (Sherbourne & Stewart, 1991)
- *Multidimensional Scale of Perceived Social Support:* measures perceptions of emotional and instrumental support, and measures both the support available and support actually received (Zimet, Dahlem, Zimet, & Farley, 1988)
- *Perceived Support Scale:* measures perceived levels of tangible, emotional, and informational support from family and friends, as well as satisfaction with support and negative social interactions (Krause, 1995)
- *Social Network Index:* measures the number of people that an individual has contact with and the total number of people in his or her social network (Cohen et al., 1997)
- *Social Provisions Scale:* measures six types of provisions available from an individual's social network: practical help, informational support, emotional support, social integration, esteem support, and providing support (Cutrona & Russell, 1987)
- *Social Support Questionnaire:* measures (a) the number of social supports in an individual's life, and (b) the degree to which these relationships are personally satisfying (Sarason, Levine, Basham, & Sarason, 1983).

Loneliness and Social Isolation

Loneliness is subjective distress over perceived unmet social needs and/or the perceived lack or loss of fulfilling relationships. *Social isolation* refers to the objective absence or paucity of social contacts and lack of interactions between an individual and a social network (Townsend, 1957; Weiss, 1982). Central components of social isolation have been identified, including *social disconnectedness*, or the lack of contact with others indicated by situation factors (e.g., small social network, infrequent social interaction, and lack of participation in social groups), and *perceived isolation*, or the subjective experience of a lack of social resources, such as companionship and support. *Loneliness* and *social isolation* are terms often used interchangeably; however, they are distinct constructs. An individual can be socially isolated but not experience loneliness. Conversely, an individual with a robust social network can still feel lonely.

Older adults are especially vulnerable to feelings of loneliness and social isolation because of multiple factors, including shrinking social networks owing to death or relocation of family members/friends, limited mobility, and age-related physical changes (e.g., hearing loss and visual difficulties). In fact, living alone, health problems/disability, sensory impairments, and stressful life events have been identified as risk factors for social isolation and loneliness.

Both loneliness and social isolation are associated with poor health, morbidity, and mortality. For example, loneliness and social isolation have been linked to increased cardiovascular risk over time (Hawkley & Cacioppo, 2007). They have also been associated with an increased risk of Alzheimer's disease. Given these associations, it is important to identify older adults with subjective and objective deteriorations in their social networks to reduce risk of disease. Treatment providers are encouraged to recommend lifestyle changes aimed at promoting socialization. Some examples of this include attendance at a senior center, volunteering, or visiting family members or friends more regularly. In addition, treatment providers may promote services and activities that are intended to alleviate social isolation and loneliness, for example, through the implementation of home-based support for older people who live alone.

In addition, poor mental health, particularly depression, has been shown to be a predictor of loneliness and social isolation in older age (Bowling, Edelmann, Leaver, & Hoekel, 1989). This provides further support for the utility of psychological assessment and intervention in this context, as comorbid psychiatric symptoms may play a unique role in the manifestation of late-life social isolation.

As social isolation and loneliness are distinct concepts, they should be measured and assessed differently. Therefore, a person-centered approach consisting of initial screening to assess whether the primary issue is social isolation or loneliness and to gather more information is appropriate. Similar to the measurement of social relationships, loneliness and social isolation have been historically measured either as related constructs or with one or two indicators of isolation or loneliness. It is, therefore, difficult to assess how these factors present day to day in an older adult's life without a more comprehensive assessment. As such, a more *person-centered* approach would be useful through a combination of self-report and a detailed interview with the patient and collateral informant, if possible. Further, service providers should also measure an older adult's progress over time to monitor for improvement or to change recommendations. As mentioned earlier, treatment providers should also assess for modifiable factors and barriers to combat social isolation, such as psychiatric issues and lack of resources (e.g., transportation issues), to treat these factors with hopes of promoting social engagement.

In sum, given that social isolation and loneliness are different, treatment targets would also differ. Research suggests that fostering opportunities that promote social interaction, such as attending social programs, even over the telephone, may help reduce isolation. For loneliness, interventions targeted at changing maladaptive perceptions and enhancing social supports have been proven effective (Hawkley & Cacioppo, 2010). If care providers suspect an individual they are treating is socially isolated, they should be made aware of programs available to mitigate isolation and loneliness, such as active living plans and senior center activities. If transportation is a barrier to social interactions, the availability of transportation options may also help increase engagement. Those individuals who express feelings of loneliness may be better served by referral to mental health services, especially if they appear to have access to social opportunities.

Measuring Social Isolation and Loneliness

Examples of commonly used self-report measures of loneliness and social isolation to incorporate into clinical practice include:

- *Gierveld Loneliness Scale:* measures overall loneliness, as well as emotional loneliness (feeling of lacking an intimate relationship) and social loneliness (feeling of lacking a social network) (Gierveld & Tilburg, 2006)
- *Perceived Isolation Scale:* measures social isolation through subjective (perceived) social isolation (Cornwell & Waite, 2009)
- *Social Disconnectedness Scale:* measures two central factors related to social isolation: a lack of social network robustness and lack of participation in social activities (Cornwell & Waite, 2009)

- *Three-Item Loneliness Scale:* brief measure of how often individuals feel they lack companionship, feel left out, or feel isolated from others (Hughes, Waite, Hawkley, & Cacioppo, 2004)
- *UCLA Loneliness Scale:* measures subjective feelings of loneliness and social isolation (Russell, Peplau, & Cutrona, 1980).

Given that loneliness is not a direct reflection of the availability or frequency of social contact, measurement should inquire about maladaptive thoughts, feelings of rejection, and low self-worth. Additional risk factors for social isolation or loneliness include:

- Living alone
- Being unmarried
- Possessing a small social network
- Infrequent contact with members in one's network
- Lack of diversity in social network
- Lack of perceived social support
- Low participation in social activities
- Emotionally distant relationships
- Subjective feelings of loneliness or not belonging

Care providers should also be sure to ask the following questions during routine visits:

1. Do you feel that you lack support or companionship? How often?
2. Do you feel left out? How often?
3. Do you feel isolated from others? How often?

SECTION II: IMPLEMENTING ASSESSMENT OF LATE-LIFE SOCIAL RELATIONSHIPS IN CLINICAL PRACTICE

A growing body of literature demonstrating the significant impact of social relationships on the health and functioning of older adults has fostered the continued development of self-report measures, such as those listed earlier. However, despite the availability of such tools, conducting an effective, comprehensive assessment of social relationships in late life may still present a variety of challenges. First and foremost, service providers must be made aware of the utility and clinical implications of routinely incorporating an assessment of social relationship factors into their care practices. Moreover, given the diversity of measurements across both *structural* and *functional* dimensions of social relationships (Kuiper et al., 2015; Kuiper et al., 2016), providers must be educated on appropriate scale selection, the differential effects of social relationship constructs on health outcomes, and effective methods to integrate both quantitative (i.e., self-report scales) and qualitative (i.e., clinical interview questions) approaches.

Screening and Scale Section: Where Do We Start?

To effectively conduct an assessment of social relationships in work with older adults, several key factors should be considered. While the specific setting and type of healthcare provided may inherently determine the nature of the aforementioned assessment, clinicians should nonetheless be encouraged to specifically tailor their evaluation to the unique background and presenting problem(s) of the patient. As such, a qualitative clinical interview including open-ended questions related to life events, composition of social networks, nature of social interactions or emotional response to role transitions, and/or loss may be a crucial first step to determining the course of the remaining assessment. In fact, existing research provides support for combined use of qualitative and quantitative data collection methods in the assessment of social relationships, as it provides an opportunity for deeper exploration of clinically relevant issues (Drageset, Eide, Dysvik, Furnes, & Hauge, 2015). Alternatively, clinicians may choose to utilize initial screening measures, such as a single-item (Anderson, 1984) or three-item (Hughes et al., 2004) loneliness scale, aimed to increase the probability of early detection of risk factors, as well as facilitate subsequent selection of quantitative scales. These less-comprehensive screening measures may be more practical in fast-paced, high-volume practices where completing a clinical interview regarding the quality of social networks with every patient is unrealistic.

With regards to selection of validated self-report measures of social relationships, it is important to keep in mind that, as mentioned earlier, a thorough understanding of both the *quantity* and *quality* of social ties is essential. As such, providers may begin by selecting one or more relevant self-report measures of social network, integration/engagement, and/or support, such as those mentioned herein. A two-step assessment is recommended in the event of a positive screen. That is, if the initial screening or clinical interview reveals issues of new onset social withdrawal, relationship disruption or dissatisfaction, and/or feelings of loneliness, a scale of perceived social isolation or disconnectedness may be important to include, either at the initial or subsequent visit (Cornwell & Waite, 2009). As in any formal clinical assessment, measure selection should also consider relevance to the clinical population of older adults at hand (e.g., age, ethnic background, diagnosis, etc.), composition of the normative sample to which they will be compared, and practicality of the measure in the context of the type/length of evaluation.

Data Collection and Interpretation: Important Considerations

An array of medical, psychological, social, and cultural factors may significantly influence an individual's understanding of, and response to, his or her own social relationships. Thus, in order to more accurately interpret both quantitative and qualitative data collected during an assessment, potential interactions/effects of these factors must be considered. In general, higher prevalence rates of psychiatric and medical illness in older compared to younger adults contribute to a more challenging process of teasing apart the unique effects of social relationship factors on mood, physical symptoms, and overall functioning. For example, research has demonstrated that late-life depression and loneliness involve a variety of overlapping concepts, which may considerably impact the way in which older adults describe and interpret their unique personal experience. In fact, one study found that loneliness was highly salient to older adults who were asked to describe themselves when depressed. Notably, interpretations of loneliness with respect to depression were diverse, as some older adults viewed it as a precursor to depression, others as self-imposed withdrawal, and others as a natural expectation of the aging process (Barg et al., 2006).

From a sociocultural perspective, constructs of social network, integration, and support may have unique implications for older adults from different racial, ethnic, and socioeconomic backgrounds. For example, research has suggested that African Americans generally place greater importance on extended family ties compared to White Americans, so the absence of these significant social and familial relationships may be experienced as a more profound loss (Dressler, Hoeppner, & Pitts, 1985). Furthermore, cultural as well as other demographic and personality factors may impact an individual's willingness to discuss his or her social life. As questions along these lines may feel intrusive and might not be perceived as necessary information for service providers, the honesty of responses may be limited. It is sometimes helpful to introduce the topic gently and explain why social factors are important to assess in order to establish trust between provider and client, and to facilitate an open dialogue.

SECTION III: IMPORTANCE OF ASSESSMENT OF LATE-LIFE SOCIAL RELATIONSHIPS IN CLINICAL PRACTICE

Associations Between Social Relationship Factors and Major Health Outcomes

Clinicians should be aware of the proven associations between social relationships and specific psychological and medical outcomes. For example, a study of community-dwelling older adults found that low perceived social support was associated with greater risk of cognitive impairment (Pillemer & Holtzer, 2015). With knowledge of empirical findings such as these, healthcare providers may be better able to detect people at higher risk of cognitive decline, frailty, falls, and physical disability (see also Chapter 1).

The earlier low social connectedness is detected, the easier it is to intervene and reduce the likelihood of adverse outcomes like morbidity and mortality (Nicholson, 2012). Once those who are at risk of social isolation are identified, service providers can deliver targeted support prior to the onset of negative health and lifestyle outcomes. At these earlier stages, intervention is often easier and more effective. For example, as stated earlier, social isolation has been associated with worsening cognition. Memory impairment may lead to embarrassment and avoidance of social settings and frontal lobe–executive problems may lead to apathy and low motivation for social interaction. Yet, isolation itself may accelerate the cognitive decline. As people with poor cognition have greater barriers to engaging in social activities, improvements to social isolation will be more difficult. Another example in which early detection may be more effective is sensory impairment. Hearing loss can lead to social isolation and even increase risk of cognitive decline. Early detection of social isolation may lead to more effectual intervention, resulting in better health outcomes.

Importance of Measuring Various Factors of Social Relationships

As there are various structural and functional factors in social relationships, it is critical that these different components are measured when assessing patients and clients. When only one component is considered, at-risk individuals can easily be overlooked. Let us consider an example. "Bob" is a 76-year-old man who lives with his wife in an active community where his son, daughter-in-law, and four grandchildren also live. He plays tennis once a week and regularly attends book club meetings. His physician, who understands the importance of identifying and exploring social isolation, may hear

Bob's description of his marriage, weekly dinners with his grandchildren, and regular interactions with peers, and reasonably come to the conclusion that Bob is doing well from a social perspective. However, it is possible that Bob is superficially connected while still having the subjective experience of loneliness. This may be due to a lack of meaningful relationships with openness, positive interactions, and intimacy with those around him (e.g., poor social support). If Bob develops symptoms of depression, such as insomnia, irritability, or suicidal ideation, both family and provider may be taken by surprise. Through proper assessment of all aspects of social relationships, those experiencing social loneliness can be more clearly identified. Since Bob's physician only asked about two specific aspects of social life, social network (e.g., "Who do you live with?") and social activity ("What do you do in a typical week?"), it was assumed that Bob was socially connected. Therefore, his physician did not make recommendations or provide additional support, leaving Bob at risk for a variety of negative outcomes.

Proper assessment also has significant implications for treatment planning. By understanding which aspect of one's social life is deficient, intervention can be better directed to improve one's connectedness. While social skills or couples therapy may be appropriate for Bob to improve his perceived social support and ability to experience intimacy and meaningful relationships, behavioral activation interventions or providing education on local community centers may increase social activity levels. Once the specific needs are identified, appropriate program planning can begin.

Beyond identifying the presence or severity of social isolation, the unique way in which it manifests in late life can also have a significant impact on critical health outcomes. For example, it is important to assess an individual's level of social support as certain subtypes (emotional, instrumental, and informational) may influence health via access to resources and material goods (Cohen, 2004). While emotional support is important for many aspects of one's well-being, it may be critical that a patient with physical disabilities, for instance, has strong instrumental support to help him or her attend appointments and receive medications. Providers must understand the specific social resources available to their patients to understand what is possible for each individual, and then adapt treatment plans accordingly.

Impact for Individuals and Families

In addition to assisting providers to (a) conceptualize each client's case, (b) identify those who may be at risk for social isolation and associated negative health outcomes, and (c) create targeted treatments for each person's specific needs, proper assessment of social factors can be more immediately impactful for the individual and family members. With proper assessment, patients may gain awareness into their own level of social connectedness that they might otherwise overlook. Consider Bob described earlier. Just like his physician, Bob may consider himself to be well connected as he is married with family nearby (i.e., adequate social network) and is involved in his community (i.e., adequate social activity). Without taking the time to consider and discuss all aspects of his social life, Bob may have ignored or placed less emphasis on his subjective experience of distance between himself and his wife, or isolation at the book club, or on the tennis court, for example. Through thorough assessment, awareness can be raised for the clinician as well as the individual.

Following proper psychoeducation on the role social relationships play on nearly all aspects of one's well-being, individuals and their families may aim to spend more time fostering relationships and encouraging activities. Simply going through the process of assessing one's social connectedness can serve as a bonding activity. As social relationships are best created and nurtured in the community, rather than in a doctor's office, educating and encouraging families will have the most direct impact on improving one's social life and reduce isolation.

SUMMARY AND NEXT STEPS

Once a thorough assessment of social relationships is conducted, healthcare providers have the unique opportunity to integrate the information they have collected into their plan of care. Detailed information about the quality and quantity of late-life social relationships may be advantageous for a multitude of reasons as it can facilitate diagnostic formulation, aid treatment planning, increase understanding of a patient's receptivity to intervention(s), and elucidate the likelihood of treatment adherence. Moreover, clinicians are encouraged to routinely provide feedback to patients, their families, and other healthcare providers about the potential implications of unique social relationship factors on health. These practices promote transparency and communication between provider and patient, as well as between treatment team members, resulting in more effective delivery of care to the fast-growing older adult community.

REFERENCES

Anderson, L. (1984). Intervention against loneliness in a group of elderly women: A process evaluation. *Human Relations, 37*(4), 295–310. doi:10.1177/001872678403700402

Barg, F. K., Huss-Ashmore, R., Wittink, M. N., Murray, G. F., Bogner, H. R., & Gallo, J. (2006). A mixed-methods approach to understanding loneliness and depression in older adults. *The Journals of Gerontology, Series B, Psychological Sciences and Social Sciences, 61*(6), 329–339. doi:10.1093/geronb/61.6.S329

Berkman, L. F., Glass, T., Brissette, I., & Seeman, T. E. (2000). From social integration to health: Durkheim in the new millennium★. *Social Science & Medicine, 51*(6), 843–857. doi:10.1016/S0277-9536(00)00065-4

Bowling, A. P., Edelmann, R. J., Leaver, J., & Hoekel, T. (1989). Loneliness, mobility, well-being and social support in a sample of over 85 year olds. *Personality and Individual Differences, 10*(11), 1189–1192. doi:10.1016/0191-8869(89)90085-8

Broadhead, W. E., Gehlbach, S. H., De Gruy, F. V., & Kaplan, B. H. (1988). The Duke-UNC Functional Social Support Questionnaire: Measurement of social support in family medicine patients. *Medical Care, 26*, 709–723. doi:10.1097/00005650-198807000-00006

Cohen, S. (2004). Social relationships and health. *American Psychologist, 59*(8), 676. doi:10.1037/0003-066X.59.8.676

Cohen, S., Doyle, W. J., Skoner, D. P., Rabin, B. S., & Gwaltney, J. M., Jr. (1997). Social ties and susceptibility to the common cold. *Journal of the American Medical Association, 277*, 1940–1944. doi:10.1001/jama.1997.03540480040036

Cornwell, E. Y., & Waite, L. J. (2009). Social disconnectedness, perceived isolation, and health among older adults. *Journal of Health and Social Behavior, 50*(1), 31–48. doi:10.1177/002214650905000103

Cutrona, C. E., & Russell, D. W. (1987). *Social provisions scale*. Retrieved from https://www.unc.edu/depts/sph/longscan/pages/measures/Ages12to14/writeups/Age%2012%20and%2014%20Social%20Provisions.pdf

Drageset, J., Eide, G. E., Dysvik, E., Furnes, B., & Hauge, S. (2015). Loneliness, loss, and social support among cognitively intact older people with cancer, living in nursing homes—A mixed-methods study. *Clinical Interventions in Aging, 10*, 1529–1536. doi:10.2147/CIA.S88404

Dressler, W., Hoeppner, S. H., & Pitts, B. J. (1985). Household structure in a southern black community. *American Anthropologist, 87*, 853–862. doi:10.1525/aa.1985.87.4.02a00070

Gierveld, J. D. J., & Tilburg, T. V. (2006). A 6-item scale for overall, emotional, and social loneliness: Confirmatory tests on survey data. *Research on Aging, 28*(5), 582–598. doi:10.1177/0164027506289723

Hampton, K. N. (2007). Neighborhoods in the network society. *Information, Communication & Society, 10*, 714–748. doi:10.1080/13691180701658061

Hawkley, L. C., & Cacioppo, J. T. (2007). Aging and loneliness: Downhill quickly? *Current Directions in Psychological Science, 16*(4), 187–191. doi:10.1111/j.1467-8721.2007.00501.x

Hawkley, L. C., & Cacioppo, J. T. (2010). Loneliness matters: A theoretical and empirical review of consequences and mechanisms. *Annals of Behavioral Medicine, 40*(2), 218–227. doi:10.1007/s12160-010-9210-8

Hughes, M. E., Waite, L. J., Hawkley, L. C., & Cacioppo, J. T. (2004). A short scale for measuring loneliness in large surveys: Results from two population-based studies. *Research on Aging, 26*(6), 655–672. doi:10.1177/0164027504268574

Krause, N. (1995). Negative interaction and satisfaction with social support among older adults. *Journal of Gerontology: Psychological Sciences, 50B*, 59–73. doi:10.1093/geronb/50B.2.P59

Kuiper, J. S., Zuidersma, M., Voshaar, R. C. O., Zuidema, S. U., van den Heuvel, E. R., Stolk, R. P., & Smidt, N. (2015). Social relationships and risk of dementia: A systematic review and meta-analysis of longitudinal cohort studies. *Ageing Research Reviews, 22*, 39–57. doi:10.1016/j.arr.2015.04.006

Kuiper, J. S., Zuidersma, M., Zuidema, S. U., Burgerhof, J. G., Stolk, R. P., Oude Voshaar, R. C., & Smidt, N. (2016). Social relationships and cognitive decline: A systematic review and meta-analysis of longitudinal cohort studies. *International Journal of Epidemiology, 45*(4), 1169–1206. doi:10.1093/ije/dyw089

Lubben, J. (1988). Assessing social networks among elderly populations. *Family & Community Health: The Journal of Health Promotion & Maintenance, 11,* 42–52. doi:10.1097/00003727-198811000-00008

Mitchell, P. H., Powell, L., Blumenthal, J., Norten, J., Ironson, G., Pitula, C. R., . . . & Berkman, L. F. (2003). A short social support measure for patients recovering from myocardial infarction: The ENRICHD Social Support Inventory. *Journal of Cardiopulmonary Rehabilitation and Prevention, 23*(6), 398–403. doi:10.1097/00008483-200311000-00001

Nicholson, N. R. (2012). A review of social isolation: An important but underassessed condition in older adults. *The Journal of Primary Prevention, 33*(2–3), 137–152. doi:10.1007/s10935-012-0271-2

Norbeck, J. S., Lindsey, A. M., & Carrieri, V. L. (1981). The development of an instrument to measure social support. *Nursing Research, 30,* 264–269. doi:10.1097/00006199-198109000-00003

Pillemer, S. C., & Holtzer, R. (2015). The differential relationships of dimensions of perceived social support with cognitive function among older adults. *Aging & Mental Health, 20*(7), 727–735. doi:10.1080/13607863.2015.1033683

Russell, D., Peplau, L. A., & Cutrona, C. E. (1980). The revised UCLA Loneliness Scale: Concurrent and discriminant validity evidence. *Journal of Personality and Social Psychology, 39*(3), 472. doi:10.1037/0022-3514.39.3.472

Sarason, I. G., Levine, H. M., Basham, R. B., & Sarason, B. R. (1983). Assessing social support: The social support questionnaire. *Journal of Personality and Social Psychology, 44*(1), 127. doi:10.1037/0022-3514.44.1.127

Schwarzer, R., & Schultz, U. (2013). Berlin Social Support Scales (BSSS). Retrieved from http://www.midss.org/content/berlin-social-support-scales-bsss

Seeman, T. E. (1996). Social ties and health: The benefits of social integration. *Annals of Epidemiology, 6*(5), 442–451. doi:10.1016/S1047-2797(96)00095-6

Sherbourne, C. D., & Stewart, A. L. (1991). The MOS Social Support Survey. *Social Science & Medicine, 32*(6), 705–714. doi:10.1016/0277-9536(91)90150-B

Smith, K., & Christakas, N. (2007). Social networks and health. *Annual Review of Sociology, 34,* 405–429. doi:10.1146/annurev.soc.34.040507.134601

Stokes, J. P., & Wilson, D. G. (1984). The inventory of socially supportive behaviors: Dimensionality, prediction, and gender differences. *American Journal of Community Psychology, 12*(1), 53–69. doi:10.1007/BF00896928

Townsend, P. (1957). *The family life of older people.* London, UK: Routledge and Kegan Paul.

van Baarsen, B. (2002). Theories on coping with loss: The impact of social support and self-esteem on adjustment to emotional and social loneliness following a partner's death in later life. *Journal of Gerontology: Social Sciences, 57*(1), S33–S42. doi:10.1093/geronb/57.1.s33

Weiss, R. S. (1982). Issues in the study of loneliness. In L. Peplau & D. Perlman (Eds.), *Loneliness: A source book of current theory, Research and therapy* (pp. 71–80). New York, NY: Wiley.

Wrzus, C., Hanel, M., Wagner, J., & Neyer, F. J. (2013). Social network changes and life events across the life span: A meta-analysis. *Psychological Bulletin, 139*(1), 53–80. doi:10.1037/a0028601

Zimet, G. D., Dahlem, N. W., Zimet, S. G., & Farley, G. K. (1988). The multidimensional scale of perceived social support. *Journal of Personality Assessment, 52*(1), 30–41. doi:10.1207/s15327752jpa5201_2

4

International Perspectives on Social Relationships, Social Isolation, and Well-Being Among Older Adults

Howard Litwin

INTRODUCTION

The interpersonal environment in which older adults are embedded strongly influences their health and well-being (Berkman, Glass, Brissette, & Seeman, 2000; Kawachi & Berkman, 2001). However, it is also a complicated construct to study. This is because the interpersonal realm is composed of a variety of interconnected phenomena that include the social relations that one maintains, or their absence, and the range of activities in which one engages. Are people who are more socially connected in late life, indeed, happier and healthier? Do active older persons enjoy a better state of well-being than those who are less active? This chapter explores these questions through recent research findings to shed light on this topic.

The findings that are reported all stem from the Survey of Health, Ageing and Retirement in Europe (SHARE), a longitudinal study that currently follows persons age 50 and older in 28 countries, revisiting the same respondents every 2 years (Börsch-Supan et al., 2013). The SHARE queries a wide range of areas, spanning financial and social matters as well as physical and mental health. The largest data infrastructure of its kind, SHARE introduced a unique method to measure the interpersonal environment of its participants in 2011 (Litwin, Stoeckel, Roll, Shiovitz-Ezra, & Kotte, 2013) and then again in 2014. The information thus retrieved allows us to gain new insights into the correlates of social relations in later life and their outcomes.

After presenting some important theoretical and methodological distinctions, this chapter looks at the association between several key aspects of the interpersonal realm, on the one hand, and selected positive and negative well-being outcomes, on the other. It then examines the contribution of the construct of network type, a composite measure of social relations, to the study and the understanding of the interpersonal domain of older people, and its role in well-being. This is followed by consideration of yet another indicator of social relations—this time, a scale of social connectedness—and how this measure disentangles the effects of social relations and social activity on well-being. Finally, the chapter presents findings on the implications of changes that occur in the interpersonal environment on the mental health of older people.

THE SOCIAL NETWORK

The interpersonal environment encompasses both prescribed social ties, such as family relations, as well as ties of choice, like friends and colleagues. These may include either primary or "strong" ties with meaningful others, or secondary or "weak" ties with people who are less meaningful on a day-to-day basis. The interpersonal realm also reflects the domains of financial and social exchange, that is, the giving and/or the receipt of money and time among individuals. Social relations are also inherent in activity performed in the company of others. A state of social isolation can be defined as the absence of a meaningful interpersonal environment. Such isolation may be objectively driven, as in the case of older people who live alone, or subjectively experienced, as in the case of elders who feel lonely regardless of their residential arrangements. However, not all persons who live alone are lonely, and not all lonely persons live alone.

Given the complexity of the interpersonal environment, social scientists have coined the term *social network* to reflect the variety of social relations that people of all ages have, and the term *personal social network* to indicate the immediate and the most important of the social ties that they maintain (Litwin, 1996). Specifically, the personal social network reflects the collection of close ties that are the most significant to a given individual and from which he or she may derive a variety of supports, such as tangible assistance, emotional nurturance, cognitive guidance, and social companionship. Personal social networks may also be the source of stress, especially if the ties in question are perceived as negative (Krause & Rook, 2003).

MEASURING THE PERSONAL SOCIAL NETWORK

Networks are measured in various ways. Some studies employ indirect measures, also known as *sociodemographic proxies*. An example of such would be family members who are seen as being part of one's social network regardless of how the focal network member feels about them. A more direct measurement methodology asks focal network members to name the people who are most important to them, or with whom they discuss matters of importance. Known as name generators, these inventories ask only for the first names, nicknames, or initials of the people mentioned in order to preserve confidentiality. Once the list of names is completed, the respondent is generally asked to give additional information about each of the individuals named, for example, the nature of the relationship, contact frequency, and so on. SHARE, noted earlier, employed just such a name-generating inventory for the measurement of the personal social networks of its participants, limiting the number of persons in the roster to a maximum of seven. The use of the direct approach to network identification is based on the supposition that personal social networks are essentially subjective phenomena and their measurement thus requires direct input from the person whose network is being queried.

Another methodological distinction is whether the personal social network is viewed in terms of disparate network indicators, such as size or average contact frequency, or in terms of composite measures that capture a wider range of network properties. The disparate network variables are usually divided among indicators that variously reflect the structure of the network, its dynamics (that is, the interactions that take place within it), and its quality. In comparison, the composite measures are generally summary scales or network typologies. Both of these composite indicators are explained in detail and illustrated later.

NETWORK CHARACTERISTICS AND WELL-BEING

The first set of findings reported is from a study that examined disparate network indicators in relation to mental health, using SHARE data from 2011 (Litwin, Stoeckel, & Schwartz, 2015). The study focused exclusively on the respondents age 65 and above who participated in the SHARE project. The analytical sample numbered some 26,784 respondents who reported having had at least one social tie. They came from 16 countries: Austria, Belgium,

Czech Republic, Denmark, Estonia, France, Germany, Hungary, Italy, Netherlands, Poland, Portugal, Slovenia, Spain, Sweden, and Switzerland.

The network indicators were from the three network domains mentioned earlier—structure, interaction, and quality. Structure was tapped by *network size* (0–7). Interaction was measured by three variables: *geographical proximity*, *frequency of contact*, and *emotional closeness*. Quality was indicated by *satisfaction with the social network*, a self-report measure. The average social network in the study sample numbered two to three meaningful persons with relatively high mean scores for proximity, contact, and emotional closeness. Respondents also reported a high level of satisfaction with their social network, on average.

Mental health was measured on the EURO-D scale as the number of depressive symptoms experienced (higher scores reflect poorer mental health). The EURO-D was developed specifically to compare depression across European countries (Prince et al., 1999). The average number of depression symptoms was 2.7 out of a possible 12 symptoms. The statistical analysis employed a log transformation of the depression score.

Several sociodemographic and health-related variables were controlled in the analysis as well. The sociodemographic controls were gender, marital status, number of children, education, financial status, and country. The health-related controls were physical symptoms, mobility dependence, functional dependence (activities of daily living [ADL]), and cognitive functioning (memory). About one-fifth of the study sample was 80 years or older, a bit more than half was female, two-thirds were married, and the average number of children per respondent was two. Almost one-half had only primary education. Respondents reported having two to three symptoms, difficulty in performing two to three mobility tasks, less than one limitation (ADL), and a midrange level of cognitive functioning.

Figure 4.1 presents a graph of the main statistical findings. The dark bars show the correlation between the network characteristics and the mental health measure before taking the control variables into account (Model 1). As may be seen, network size, proximity, emotional closeness, and satisfaction were all negatively related to depressive symptoms. That is, larger, higher quality social connections were associated with fewer depressive symptoms. Curiously, contact frequency was associated with more symptoms, a finding that raises interesting questions. All the coefficients were statistically significant.

The light gray bars in the figure show these same correlations after controlling for country, sociodemographic, and health controls (Model 2). The graph shows that the significant associations between most of the social

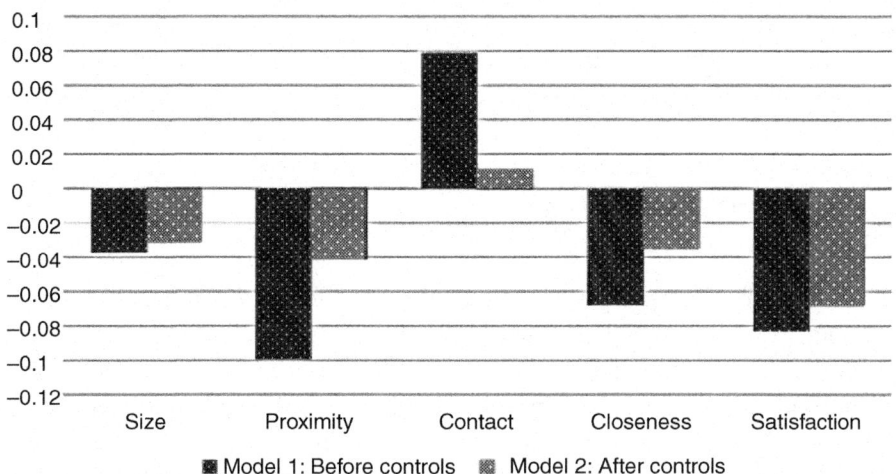

FIGURE 4.1 Social network correlates of well-being among older Europeans (age 65+): before and after controlling for country and background characteristics: Beta weights.

Note: Model adjusted for country, age, gender, marital status, education, household income, number of children, physical symptoms, mobility dependence, ADL difficulties, and memory. Negative correlation implies variable is associated with fewer depressive symptoms.

network variables and the EURO-D symptoms in the previous model remained, although to a slightly lesser degree. However, the contact frequency variable lost its significance. Of note is that the network quality variable (satisfaction with the network) emerged as the strongest predictor, after entry of the controls.

Interaction terms were also entered into the analysis to consider how age and each of the social network characteristics jointly intersect with the mental health outcome (not shown in the figure). The age interaction terms revealed that relationship quality was equally important for the mental health of respondents of all ages. However, network structure showed some variation by age. Specifically, while larger network size was beneficial for those under age 80, the association was even stronger among those age 80 and older. The three network interaction variables revealed even more complicated age differences. This suggests that age variously nuances the effect of different aspects of social network on depression, all else considered.

The study demonstrated that social networks are a potentially significant factor for the promotion of good mental health in late life. However, as was also shown, the findings revealed that different aspects of the social network work in different ways. To make social network data more accessible to practitioners and more relevant for their work, there is a need for singular measures that capture the essence of the interpersonal environment. The next section describes the application of one such measure—a typology of social networks.

SOCIAL NETWORK TYPE AND WELL-BEING

First coined by Wenger (1991), *social network type* is a composite characterization of the nature and the extent of one's interpersonal environment (Fiori, Smith, & Antonucci, 2007). The construct permits analysis as to how social interconnectedness can interplay with well-being in late life. Network types have been shown to predict morale (Litwin, 2001), anxiety, loneliness and happiness (Litwin & Shiovitz-Ezra, 2011), depressive symptomatology (Fiori, Antonucci, & Cortina, 2006), physical health (Litwin, 1998), functional dependency (Doubova, Perez-Cuevas, Espinosa-Alarcon, & Flores-Hernandez, 2010), and mortality (Litwin & Shiovitz-Ezra, 2006b).

A recent study derived network types from the SHARE data, focusing again on respondents age 65 and older (Litwin & Stoeckel, 2014a). Cluster analysis was applied to eight network variables. Five of the variables characterized the composition of the network: Who is in the network? As you would expect, the networks consisted of the following five relationship groupings, respectively, (a) spouse or partner, (b) children, (c) other family (e.g., siblings, grandchildren), (d) friends, and (e) others (e.g., neighbors, colleagues, formal helpers). The remaining three variables in the clustering procedure took interaction into account: proximity, contact frequency, and emotional closeness.

The results of this procedure are shown in Figure 4.2 in a graph that illustrates mainly the compositional character of the network. As may be seen, six network types were derived. The "spouse and children" network averaged two to three members; had high proximity, contact, and emotional closeness; and accounted for almost one-quarter of the study sample. The "children" network had three confidants, on average, and high emotional closeness, but somewhat lower proximity and contact frequency. Almost one-fifth of the sample fell in this grouping. The "spouse" network numbered one member only (the spouse). It exhibited the highest proximity, contact, and emotional closeness, and accounted for a bit more than one-sixth of the sample.

The "other family" network had an average of three members, with somewhat high emotional closeness, but only moderate proximity and somewhat lower frequency of contact. Less than one-sixth of the sample belonged to this network type. The "friend" network had three members, of which more

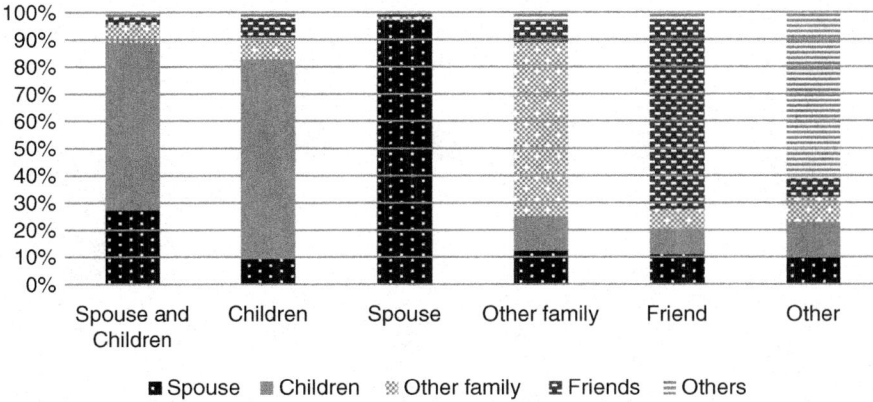

FIGURE 4.2 Social network types among older Europeans (age 65+).

than two-thirds were friends, with moderate proximity and emotional closeness but low contact frequency. A bit less than one seventh of the sample were in the friend network type. Finally, the "other" network also reported having about three confidants who, while in moderate proximity, were low in contact and emotional closeness. Six percent of the study sample fell into this network grouping.

Unlike the study described earlier, this particular analysis also took into account the respondents who had no network at all, that is, those who did not name anyone when asked: "Who are the people with whom you discuss important matters?" Six percent of the study sample fell into this grouping and are classified here as having "no network." They may be considered socially isolated in that they do not share important thoughts and/or feeling with others. Thus, the network typology encompassed the entire SHARE study sample of persons age 65 and older ($n = 28{,}697$), including those having no confidants at all.

Also, unlike the previous study which considered negative well-being (depressive symptoms), this analysis looked at positive well-being as measured by the CASP scale, a measure of quality of life (Wiggins, Netuveli, Hyde, Higgs, & Blane, 2008). It used the validated 12-item version of CASP that is employed in SHARE. The scale reflects four quality-of-life domains: control (C), autonomy (A), self-realization (S), and pleasure (P). Together, they offer an inclusive measure of the state of well-being.

Figure 4.3 shows a graph of the results of the regression analysis, using the respondents' well-being scores on the respective network types, controlling for country, age, gender, marital status, education, and mobility. As in the previous study presented, the graph shows two statistical models. The first

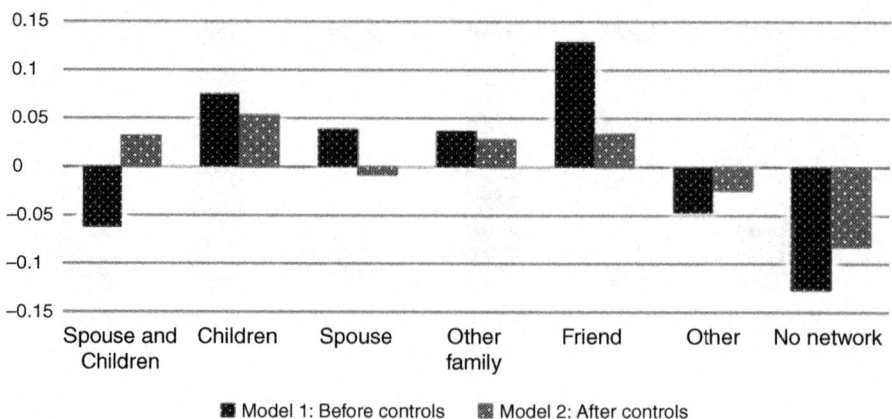

FIGURE 4.3 Social network type correlates of well-being among older Europeans (age 65+) before and after controlling for country and background characteristics: Beta weights.

Note: Model adjusted for country, age, gender, marital status, education, and mobility.

reflects the association between network type and well-being. The second presents the same after taking into account the respective effects of the control variables.

The dark bars (Model 1) show that two network types in the unadjusted analysis had the dominant effects on well-being. "Friend" networks were the most strongly positively related, and having "no network" (the socially isolated) was the most negatively related. "Children," "spouse," and "other family" networks were positively associated with well-being (albeit more modestly) while "spouse and children" and "other" networks were negatively related. All the associations were statistically significant.

However, this picture changed somewhat after taking the control variables into account (Model 2). As may be seen in the graph, the "children" network emerged as the network type that was the most positively related with well-being. The "friend" and "spouse and children" networks were the second and third most positively related network types, respectively. The "other family" network type had a somewhat lower but still positive correlation with the well-being score. In contrast, the "spouse" network type became unrelated to the well-being measure, perhaps because of having adjusted for marital status in the second model. Respondents in the "other" network retained a modest negative correlation with the well-being outcome. Most importantly, those having no confidants (the "no network" grouping) had the strongest and the most negative association with the well-being indicator, all else considered.

This analysis underscored that a composite measure of the interpersonal environment—network type—can effectively distinguish between older people having better and worse well-being. It shows, moreover, that those with greater social capital, as reflected by the different network types, have better well-being as well. In addition, the study underscores that social isolation, or lack of a social network, is a strong correlate of poor well-being, beyond the effects of several other predictor variables. This supports the face validity of the model and CASP as an outcome measure when employing social interventions to improve networks, especially in those lacking any meaningful social ties.

ACTIVITY, SOCIAL CONNECTEDNESS, AND WELL-BEING

Activity is another important part of the interpersonal environment insofar as it fosters one's engagement with others. In fact, the successful aging paradigm sees sustained engagement with life as one of the three key determinants of aging well (the others being disease avoidance and the maintenance of high functioning; Rowe & Kahn, [1997]). According to the paradigm, engagement with life is composed of two complementary aspects: interpersonal relations and productive activity. An interesting question is whether interpersonal relations and productive activity contribute equally to well-being in late life.

A study addressed this issue using data from the entire SHARE dataset, that is to say, from all respondents in the survey age 50 and older. The study in question not only compared the relative effects of social relations and activity on well-being, it also developed a summary social connectedness scale for the measurement of the social relations component (Litwin & Stoeckel, 2014b). The scale, based on the name-generated data from the SHARE social network inventory in 2011, provides a composite score for each respondent that reflects the extent of his or her social connectedness.

The scale score was calculated on the basis of the number of persons cited (network size), as well as the number of them residing within 25 kilometers (15.5 miles), having at least weekly contact and close emotional closeness, respectively. A fifth component was the diversity of relationship types within each network, insofar as the greater the diversity (spouse, child, other family, and friend or other), the greater the range of different kinds of social network resources that can be called upon. The scores on each of these items were summed and then collapsed into a parsimonious measure, the range of which was 0 to 4. The resultant condensed scale produced a normal distribution with acceptable skewness. The average scale score among respondents was 2.0, indicating a moderate level of social connectedness.

Activity participation was measured as the number of activities a respondent reported having taken part in, at least once a month, in the prior 12-month period. The activities included volunteer work, educational courses, sport or social clubs, religious organization events, political or community events, games involving others, reading, word or number games, vigorous sports or activities, and moderate energy activities (e.g., gardening or taking walks). The total score thus ranged from 0 to 10; the higher the score, the greater the range of activities. The average number of activities reported in this sample of older European adults (mean age = 66.5 years) was 3.5.

Two positive indicators of well-being were considered in this study—the CASP scale for quality of life, which was detailed earlier, and a global measure of subjective life satisfaction. In the latter measure, respondents were asked, "How satisfied are you with your life?" and were allowed to respond on a scale of 0 to 10 in which a score of 0 reflects complete dissatisfaction and a score of 10, complete satisfaction. The average CASP quality of life score among respondents was about 37, out of a total possible score of 48. The average score for life satisfaction was 7.5, out of a possible score of 10.

As in the previous studies described, several background and health factors were controlled in the analysis as well. These included age, gender, marital status, education, financial status, country, chronic conditions, mobility dependence, functional dependence (ADL), and cognitive functioning (memory). Finally, the analysis took into account the interrelationship of activities and social connectedness. An interaction term was entered into the regression analysis to see whether activity and social connectedness interact with each other to alter the respective associations with well-being in later life. This is because the literature suggests that activity seems to include a social network component in itself (Litwin & Shiovitz-Ezra, 2006a).

Figure 4.4 presents a graph of the primary statistical results. As before, the dark bars show the correlation between the independent variables (activity and connectedness) and the two well-being measures, before taking the control variables into account (Model 1). The figure shows that both activity and connectedness were positively correlated with the two well-being indicators, but the effect of activity on the CASP and life satisfaction outcomes was greater than that of social connectedness. The light gray bars in the figure show these same correlations after taking all the control variables into account (Model 2). The graph reveals that the significant associations between both activity and connectedness, on the one hand, and the respective well-being outcomes, on the other hand, remained. However, whereas the effect of activity on well-being dropped after the entry of the control variables, the relative effect of the social connectedness score increased.

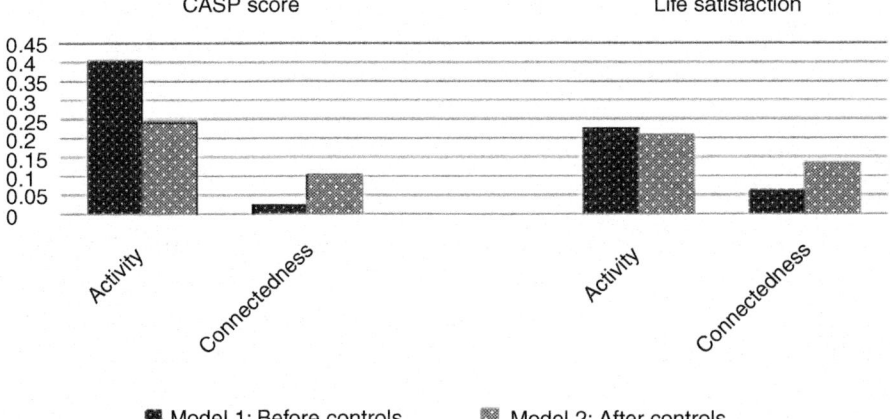

FIGURE 4.4 Activity and social connectedness as correlates of well-being among older Europeans (age 50+): Before and after controlling for country and background characteristics: Beta weights.

Note: Model adjusted for country, age, gender, marital status, education, household income, chronic conditions, symptoms, mobility, dependence, ADL difficulties, and memory.

The addition of interaction terms to the analyses shed further light on this particular finding (not shown in the figure). The coefficient of the interaction term was negative and significant in both cases. This suggests that the combination of the two measures, activity and connectedness, alters the associations with the respective well-being outcomes, CASP and life satisfaction.

Specifically, the negative association of the interaction term means that as the social connectedness scale increased, the positive association of activities on CASP and life satisfaction weakened. Stated differently, the positive effect of activity on both indicators of well-being was greater among those who had no (or minimal) social connectedness. Conversely, for those with a high degree of social connectedness, the number of activities in which they engaged was less important for their state of well-being; it did contribute positively, but to a much lesser degree.

These findings suggest that encouraging older people who are socially isolated to engage in activities may indeed be beneficial for their mental state. This is because such activity might lead to the development of new relationships, which in turn can mitigate the sense of loneliness they may feel. However, an equally important implication of the findings from this study is that it is not necessarily beneficial to push inactive people into activity engagement (something that many well-intending social service professionals tend to do). If the people in question are already socially connected, even if only informally, the introduction of additional formal activities, such as going to a senior center, will probably not add much to their mental state. It might be better, instead, to concentrate efforts and assistance toward facilitating their access to the close informal social ties that they already have.

NETWORK CHANGES AND MENTAL HEALTH

The studies reviewed thus far were all cross-sectional in nature. Therefore, one must be a bit cautious in interpreting their results. While it is most plausible that social networks affect well-being, one cannot rule out the reverse possibility, namely, that well-being is what drives social relations. To reach robust conclusions in this area of inquiry, longitudinal analysis is required. Fortunately, the SHARE data provide this opportunity. The name-generating social network inventory that was introduced in 2011 was readministered in 2015, enabling researchers to examine the effects of baseline social relations and social connectedness on well-being some 4 years later. Such analysis strengthens the possibility to verify causal connections and to establish whether or not social relations are indeed associated with mental health changes.

An initial study of this kind was recently published (Schwartz & Litwin, 2017). The sample included respondents from the 14 SHARE countries that participated in the data collection, both in 2011 and in 2015 (Hungary and the Netherlands did not participate in 2015). The analysis was limited to respondents who were 65 years or older at baseline (2011) and who reported having had at least one meaningful social tie at that time. The participants with full data on the study variables numbered 14,101. Their average age was 73.5 years. They reported 2.8 depressive symptoms, on average, in 2011, and 3.0 symptoms at follow-up in 2015. Their CASP score in 2011 was 36.2 and only 35.8, 4 years later.

In terms of social relations, the average respondent in 2011 named 2.6 persons in his or her network. At the second measurement in 2015, some 1.2 new persons were named, on average, while 1.1 persons who had been previously named in the network were no longer mentioned. Overall, only a bit more than one third of the participants did not "lose" any network members and about the same proportion did not add new members. The figures thus suggest that the majority of respondents did experience some sort of change in their social networks, indicating that social relations are quite dynamic in the latter part of life.

The analysis reported in the article looked at the effects of selected baseline network measures on changes in the respondents' well-being over the 4-year period, as measured by both the number of depressive symptoms (EURO-D) at follow up, and the quality of life scores (CASP), controlling for the baseline scores of both of these measures. As in the previously reviewed studies, here too the analysis controlled for country as well as for the relevant background and health characteristics. Interaction terms were also employed, as will become apparent in the presentation of the key results, which appear in Table 4.1.

As Model 1 in the table shows, the higher the emotional closeness of the network at baseline, the fewer the depressive symptoms and the greater the quality of life reported at follow-up. Greater baseline contact frequency was related to lower CASP scores at follow-up, suggesting perhaps that the frequent contact at baseline was necessitated by problems or greater needs of the respondent, yielding lower quality of life 4 years later. Finally, adding new social ties to the network was associated with better quality of life, but was unrelated to depressive symptoms. Having lost social ties, on the other hand, did not affect either of the two well-being indicators.

Model 2 summarizes the main results in relation to the interaction terms. As may be seen, adding new social relations with high emotional closeness significantly reduced depressive symptoms and improved perceived quality of life. Losing social ties that had high contact frequency, on the other hand, increased depressive symptoms (but did not affect the CASP scores). These findings show that it is not sufficient to make new ties when old ties get lost.

TABLE 4.1 *Social network, network changes, and well-being among older Europeans (age 50+): Beta coefficients*

Variable	Depressive Symptoms	CASP Quality of Life
Model 1		
Baseline emotional closeness	−.03*	.04†
Baseline contact frequency	ns	−.04*
Acquired new social ties	ns	.05‡
Lost previous social ties	ns	ns
Model 2		
New ties × high emotional closeness	−.07‡	.09‡
Lost ties × high emotional closeness	ns	ns
New ties × high contact frequency	ns	ns
Lost ties × high contact frequency	.06†	ns

*$p < .05$, †$p < .01$, ‡$p < .001$.
ns, not significant.

Rather, it is necessary to recruit meaningful new social relations if the goal is to maintain one's mental health in advanced years. Substituting valued lost ties with superficial new ones does not seem to contribute to the well-being of older people.

SUMMARY

This review of recent research findings from Europe underscores the contention that social relations are quite important for mental health in later life. They also point to the complexity of the task of disentangling the effects of the different components of the interpersonal environment on well-being. Despite the conceptual and methodological challenges inherent in this complicated enterprise, the evidence from an increasing number of studies tends to support the declaration that social networks do indeed matter in old age, although "more" is not necessarily better.

Given the ever-growing number and increasing proportion of older people in contemporary societies, and particularly the rising number of those at risk of social isolation in old age, with its many negative implications, much more thought needs to be given as to how to prevent loneliness and how to foster more satisfying interpersonal environments in the latter part of life. It is a daunting, but highly necessary task.

The question as to whether social service professionals can intervene in the social networks of their older clients, and indeed, whether they should, is another topic that requires additional attention. Suffice it to say that the findings of the studies that were reviewed in this chapter clearly confirm that this is a question that cannot be ignored in the near future. New professional roles, knowledge, and skills are required to meet the social needs of the older population and to promote their optimal well-being.

REFERENCES

Berkman, L. F., Glass, T., Brissette, I., & Seeman, T. E. (2000). From social integration to health: Durkheim in the new millennium. *Social Science & Medicine, 51*(6), 843–857. doi:10.1016/S0277-9536(00)00065-4

Börsch-Supan, A., Brandt, M., Hunkler, C., Kneip, T., Korbmacher, J., Malter, F., . . . Zuber, S. (2013). Data resource profile: The Survey of Health, Ageing and Retirement in Europe (SHARE). *International Journal of Epidemiology, 42*(4), 992–1001. doi:10.1093/ije/dyt088

Doubova, S. V., Perez-Cuevas, R., Espinosa-Alarcon, P., & Flores-Hernandez, S. (2010). Social network types and functional dependency in older adults in Mexico. *BMC Public Health, 10*, 104. doi:10.1186/1471-2458-10-104

Fiori, K. L., Antonucci, T. C., & Cortina, K. S. (2006). Social network typologies and mental health among older adults. *Journals of Gerontology, Series B, Psychological Sciences and Social Sciences, 61*(1), P25–P32. doi:10.1093/geronb/61.1.P25

Fiori, K. L., Smith, J., & Antonucci, T. C. (2007). Social network types among older adults: A multidimensional approach. *Journals of Gerontology, Series B, Psychological Sciences and Social Sciences, 62*(6), P322–P330. doi:10.1093/geronb/62.6.P322

Kawachi, I., & Berkman, L. F. (2001). Social ties and mental health. *Journal of Urban Health-Bulletin of the New York Academy of Medicine, 78*(3), 458–467. doi:10.1093/jurban/78.3.458

Krause, N., & Rook, K. S. (2003). Negative interaction in late life: Issues in the stability and generalizability of conflict across relationships. *Journals of Gerontology Series B-Psychological Sciences and Social Sciences, 58*(2), P88–P99. doi:10.1093/geronb/58.2.P88

Litwin, H. (Ed.). (1996). *The social networks of older people: A cross-national analysis*. Westport, CT: Praeger.

Litwin, H. (1998). Social network type and health status in a national sample of elderly Israelis. *Social Science & Medicine, 46*(4–5), 599–609. doi:10.1016/S0277-9536(97)00207-4

Litwin, H. (2001). Social network type and morale in old age. *Gerontologist, 41*(4), 516–524. doi:10.1093/geront/41.4.516

Litwin, H., & Shiovitz-Ezra, S. (2006a). The association between activity and well-being in later-life: What really matters? *Ageing and Society, 26*, 225–242. doi:10.1017/S0144686X05004538

Litwin, H., & Shiovitz-Ezra, S. (2006b). Network type and mortality risk in later life. *Gerontologist, 46*(6), 735–743. doi:10.1093/geront/46.6.735

Litwin, H., & Shiovitz-Ezra, S. (2011). Social network type and subjective well-being in a national sample of older Americans. *Gerontologist, 51*(3), 379–388. doi:10.1093/geront/gnq094

Litwin, H., & Stoeckel, K. J. (2014a). Confidant network types and well-being among older Europeans. *Gerontologist, 54*(5), 762–772. doi: 10.1093/geront/gnt056

Litwin, H., & Stoeckel, K. J. (2014b). Engagement and social capital as elements of active aging: An analysis of older Europeans. *Sociologia e Politiche Sociali, 17*(3), 9–31. doi:10.3280/SP2014-003002

Litwin, H., Stoeckel, K. J., Roll, A., Shiovitz-Ezra, S., & Kotte, M. (2013). Social network measurement in SHARE wave 4. In F. Malter & A. Börsch-Supan (Eds.), *SHARE wave 4: Innovations & methodology* (pp. 18–37). Munich: MEA, Max-Planck-Institute for Social Law and Social Policy.

Litwin, H., Stoeckel, K. J., & Schwartz, E. (2015). Social networks and mental health among older Europeans: Are there age effects? *European Journal of Ageing, 12*(4), 299–309. doi:10.1007/s10433-015-0347-y

Prince, M. J., Reischies, F., Beekman, A. T. F., Fuhrer, R., Jonker, C., Kivela, S. L., . . . Copeland, J. R. M. (1999). Development of the EURO-D scale: A European Union initiative to compare symptoms of depression in 14 European centres. *British Journal of Psychiatry, 174*, 330-338. doi:10.1192/bjp.174.4.330

Rowe, J. W., & Kahn, R. L. (1997). Successful aging. *Gerontologist, 37*(4), 433–440. doi:10.1093/geront/37.4.433

Schwartz, E., & Litwin, H. (2017). Are newly added and lost confidants in later life related to subsequent mental health? *International Psychogeriatrics, 29*(12), 2047–2057. doi:10.1017/S1041610217001338

Wenger, G. C. (1991). A network typology—from theory to practice. *Journal of Aging Studies, 5*(2), 147–162. doi:10.1016/0890-4065(91)90003-B

Wiggins, R. D., Netuveli, G., Hyde, M., Higgs, P., & Blane, D. (2008). The evaluation of a self-enumerated scale of quality of life (CASP-19) in the context of research on ageing: A combination of exploratory and confirmatory approaches. *Social Indicators Research, 89*(1), 61–77. doi:10.1007/s11205-007-9220-5

PART II

Proven Strategies and Programs for
Promoting Social Integration and Health

5

Friend Power—A View From the Front Lines: The Importance of Relationships in the Lives of the Disabled, People With Dementia, and Older Adults

Hope Reiner

Few would disagree that our sense and definition of community is undergoing a revolution. Our culture leads us to focus on what newspapers or news blogs we read, what social media platforms we are part of, and which celebrities we follow. But it does not inspire us to consider how to establish and nurture caring relationships in today's new "communities."

Humans evolved for most of our history in small hunter–gatherer tribes—maybe 15 to 40 people in a group. Caring relationships were easily built into that kind and size of community; we traveled together, cooked and ate together, defended ourselves together, and suffered losses and victories together. Today, we live in a more solitary and impersonal world of text messages, Ubers, passwords, and online shopping. Our way of life today does not easily bring us together or encourage friendships and other caring relationships. This takes not only an emotional toll on our lives but a physical one too (Hyman, 2012).

There is ample evidence that the nature of our relationships has been changing and that people feel more isolated. In the 1980s, 20% of Americans said they were lonely. Now it is 40% (Brooks, 2018). As we grow older, we may lose lifelong friendships we once had through illness and death or loved ones moving away. Likewise, children leave the nest or start their own family, sometimes in other states or countries. Social isolation is often the result of these changes, often bringing with it devastating consequences to physical and emotional well-being (Cacioppo & Patrick, 2008). Former Surgeon General Vivek Murthy summarized his experiences as a doctor in the *Harvard Business Review*: "The most common pathology I saw was not heart disease or diabetes; it was loneliness" (Murthy, 2017).

Fortunately, the science of neuroplasticity (the brain's inherent capacity to be modified) provides evidence of how adults across the life span can harness their brain's neural systems and cognitive functions to build stronger, higher performing brains, enhancing the capacity for friendship. And conversely, research shows that friendship is associated with better cognitive function, although it is important to point out that this does not prove cause and effect (Cook Maher et al., 2017; Zunzunegui, Alvarado, Del Ser, & Otero, 2003).

Cognitive training and physical exercise are gaining momentum as ways to build cognitive resilience and brain reserves throughout life. We know now that decision making, intellect, and psychological well-being do not need to decline with age, nor does the capacity for happiness. Studies show that one of the key indicators of happiness, regardless of age, is the quality of our relationships. Moreover, loving relationships can transform and enrich lives, and loving relationships can best be formed in small groups or one on one.

This is all well and good for those in our society who have genuine and loving connections. But what about those who do not? What about older people living alone without significant relationships, people with disabilities who find themselves isolated, or people without the means to find or pay for companionship? Is there any reason for hope for those currently without loving and understanding people in their lives?

FRIENDSHIP: THE POWER BEHIND SUCCESSFUL AGING

What I call *friend power* is an opening, unlocking, and constructive force. When surrounded by people who see us, understand us, elevate us, and support us, we feel like anything is possible. A sense of community and the feeling of belonging are indispensable elements in the bigger picture of whole body health.

Over the past 30 years, in my work as a Certified Geriatric Care Manager and Dementia Practitioner and the founder of HOPE CARES, I have helped dozens and dozens of people experience deep connection and genuine friendship regardless of their disabilities. Of course, casual friendships or paid professionals such as aides, social workers, case managers, and music therapists can help, but *one* very close friend can do so much more to relieve stress and depression.

Working with people with dementia, having an authentic friendship with one individual, forces us to listen, to slow down. It is a gift to both partners in the friendship. Learning to listen and slow down often positively affects our other relationships. Plus, we often forget that for people with dementia, emotional memory remains strong. Therefore, it is likely that a strong emotional connection can be the basis for a new and fulfilling relationship.

What do genuine friendship and authentic connection provide? Here are just a few of the benefits:

- Increase the sense of belonging and purpose
- Boost happiness and reduce stress
- Improve self-confidence and a sense of self-worth
- Help cope with traumas, serious illness, or death of a loved one
- Encourage us to change or avoid unhealthy lifestyle habits

The work I do, simply, is to offer a long-term caring and trusting friendship. This friendship never disappoints; it is always patient and loving and fun.

Client A was in her early 50s and had social anxiety issues throughout her life. She had never had friends. Her sister heard about my work and thought she would give me a try, never thinking that her sister would be able to connect with others.

Client A and I did a variety of things together. She enjoyed the light-hearted and sincere way I dealt with her. She liked the idea of going to Atlantic City with me when I suggested a two-day adventure there. We also went to the circus, which thrilled her. Other activities followed. We went shopping, saw movies and plays. Slowly, she began reaching out on her own and joined one or two groups. She realized that she had a serious friend in me and was able to feel more confident in her ability to engage with others.

A more challenging situation was Client B, age 63. This client had both borderline personality disorder and dementia and could be very difficult. She had raging encounters with those around her, and her family was at their wits' end.

I can not say it was easy forming a relationship with her. On a trip I took with her, she was abusive and extremely angry. It took time and a great deal of patience, but I remained present for her while most of those in her life retreated in the face of her anger. The fact that I cared so much about her did not go unnoticed. She began to trust me, even exhibiting empathy for a few problems of my own that I shared with her. I chose activities that did not exacerbate her anger issues, and that we mutually enjoyed. We shared our love for animals, movies, theater, art, and opera. We became great friends, always happy to be with each other and always saying goodbye with a hug.

There was never another angry encounter.

Client C was 98 when I began working with her. She came from an aristocratic American family. She had begun to withdraw from life years before, and in her isolation, she developed dementia. By the time I met her, she had full-time aides and a variety of other professionals in her life—geriatric care managers, bill payers, trustees, and occupational therapists. She had occasional visits from members of her church. She received wonderful care which served her well. She maintained her health and was able to get around for short distances with the help of her aide and her walker.

I forged a loving friendship with her and have been seeing her every week for 3 years. She is now 101. What she began to do as a result of our loving and consistent friendship was to speak coherently, laugh and joke, and to even give me advice about my own life!

We read more everyday about evidence-based science, which proves that cognition improves in the right circumstance with the right person. Fortunately, there is growing skepticism about social media and its effects on people's lifestyles and relationships. Still, if we are to support members of the older generation, as they once supported us, there are many challenges ahead. We must understand what people need as they grow older, regardless of our culture or their disability. We need to truly "see" and then engage with them; slow down and show compassion and understanding.

We need to provide genuine caring and authentic friendship, particularly to the most needy—older adults, people with disabilities, and people dealing with dementia in its various forms.

REFERENCES

Brooks, D. (2018, April 17). The blindness of social wealth. *New York Times*, p. A27.

Cacioppo, J., & Patrick, W. (2008). *Loneliness: Human nature and the need for social connections.* New York, NY: W. W. Norton.

Cook Maher, A., Kielb, S., Loyer, E., Connelley, M., Rademaker, A., Mesulam, M. M., . . . Rogalski, E. (2017). Psychological well-being in elderly adults with extraordinary episodic memory. *Plos One, 12*(10), e0186413. doi:10.1371/journal.pone.0186413

Hyman, M. (2012, April 15). How social networks control your health [Blog]. *Huffington Post.* https://www.huffingtonpost.com/dr-mark-hyman/community-health_b_1271880.html

Murthy, V. H. (2017, September 26). Work and the loneliness epidemic. *Harvard Business Review.* https://hbr.org/cover-story/2017/09/work-and-the-loneliness-epidemic

Zunzunegui, M. V., Alvarado, B. E., Del Ser, T., & Otero, A. (2003). Social networks, social integration, and social engagement determine cognitive decline in community-dwelling Spanish older adults. *The Journals of Gerontology. Series B, Psychological Sciences and Social Sciences, 58*(2), S93–S100. doi:10.1093/geronb/58.2.s93

6

Physical Activity for Older Adults: Supporting Social Integration

Marilyn R. Gugliucci, Erica Robertson,
Susan Wehry, and Shirley A. Weaver

Anyone willing to try can exercise.
—UNE COM U-ExCEL Tag Line

INTRODUCTION

The wave of older adults, particularly the increased numbers of our (United States) oldest adults (85+ years), has stimulated changes in social policy, scientific research, and healthcare. These changes have not only focused on reducing the cost of medical care but are personally important to older adults as they have focused on increasing the quality of life. Physical activity for older adults has become a central feature of our culture. For example, there are health promotion strategies fostered within healthcare, town planning for age-friendly communities, and exercise facilities and services in adult living environments.

Physical activity programs intended for older adults call for an understanding of the social, psychological, and physical factors that influence their receptivity and effectiveness in supporting individual well-being. This chapter is organized into three sections, each addressing older adult social integration and physical activity in specific ways that are applicable to health professionals. In Section I, we define key terms, present concepts on aging, and offer evidence to enhance well-being through social integration and physical activity. In Section II, we provide a practical approach to working with older adults through physical activity that includes benefits, guidelines, recommendations, opportunities and barriers to physical activity, and a resource guide to best practices and approaches for older adults.

In Section III, two cases based on individuals the authors have worked with provide physical activity progressions and considerations for social integration. By addressing social integration and physical activity within each section, the intention is to build on the foundational concepts in Section I through to practical approaches in Sections II and III.

SECTION I: SOCIAL INTEGRATION AND PHYSICAL ACTIVITY

The importance of social integration for individual well-being has been recognized since the late 19th century and has relevance across the life span (Berkman, Glass, Brissette, & Seeman, 2000; Mirucka, Bielecka, & Kisielewska, 2016). Research over the last three decades—much of it focused on older adults—has greatly increased our understanding of the ways social systems impact both health and well-being and, to some extent, helped shape public policy. The same can be said for the importance of physical activity for both physical and mental health and well-being.

Imprecise and interchangeable use of terms such as social integration, social network, social cohesion, social engagement, social health, social relationships, and so forth, risks losing the key factors that can improve practice, inform public policy, and stimulate research. As this chapter is focused on social integration and physical activity, the following definitions frame these two key terms.

Social integration incorporates notions of *social cohesion* (the extent of connectedness and solidarity among groups in society) and personal *social connectedness*. Social connectedness at the personal level is centered on the individual, forming personal relations and social supports that are often emotionally based providing support for conflict and stress (Berkman et al., 2000).

Physical activity includes any bodily movement produced by skeletal muscles that results in energy expenditure. Physical activities can be categorized into occupational, sports, conditioning, household, or other activities (World Health Organization, 2018). Terms related to physical activity include exercise, which is a subset of physical activity and physical fitness. However, physical fitness tends to be defined as a set of attributes that are either health- or skill-related and not as encompassing as physical activity (Caspersen, Powell, & Christenson, 1985).

Aging and Old Age

Aging is universal and inevitable, an incontrovertible and generally accepted statement. Old age on the other hand and what it means to *be* old are notions about which there is little agreement, especially among adults of every age. As a practical matter, policy makers and advocacy organizations have opted for operational definitions based on chronological age for social programs such as the Older Americans Act (age 60+), Medicare (age 65+), Social Security (age 62+), and for membership in organizations such as the AARP (age 55+).

The question of what old age means has yielded to the question of what it means to age successfully. Models of successful aging became increasingly popular after Rowe and Kahn made a distinction between "usual" and "successful" aging (Rowe & Kahn, 1987) and told us how to master our own aging fates through diet, exercise, productive activities, attitude, self-control, and choice. Indeed, the embrace of a healthy lifestyle and social connections has been felt to be nearly synonymous with the three pillars of successful aging: the avoidance of disease and disability, the maintenance of cognitive and physical function, and social engagement (Rowe & Kahn, 1997).

A corollary to this movement, active aging, emphasizes the importance of social role participation to create a positive adjustment to old age (Havighurst, 1963; Havighurst & Albrecht, 1953; Havighurst, Neugarten, & Tobin, 1963). According to Havighurst et al., the older person who ages optimally is the person who stays active and who manages to resist the shrinking of his or her social world. He or she maintains the activities of middle age as long as possible, and then finds substitutes for those activities that he or she is forced to relinquish (paraphrased, 1963, p. 419). Since the late 1990s, the concept of active aging has been at the heart of the World Health Organization's policy programs related to aging. It represents "a fundamental transformation in the expectations persons have regarding their old age. It is no longer a matter of reaping what one has sown. Instead, continuing to 'sow' and participate actively is a precondition for living a good life, throughout a person's entire lifetime" (Lamb et al., 2017, p. 5). And as Tornstam reminds us, not all people thrive in social environments; some thrive in and even require solitude (Tornstam, 1997).

We understand *old age* to be a multidimensional (biological, cultural, functional, psychological, and predominantly social) construct, which can have a profound impact on an older adult's sense of self-esteem and self-efficacy; of what is achievable; and of what behaviors are acceptable. We adopt a more inclusive picture of aging well, which is essentially *whatever the older adult defines it to be now and pictures it will be in the future*. When needed, we use the construct of young-old (65–74), old-old (75–84), and oldest-old (85) to underscore the significant longevity of older adults and the significant heterogeneity both between and within these groups (Garfein & Herzog, 1995; Lowsky, Olshansky, Bhattacharya, & Goldman, 2013; Neugarten, 1974[1]).

> Many of us know nonagenarians who are mostly able-bodied, relatively healthy, active decision-makers, resilient, and multifaceted . . . today's elders are helping craft what it means to live into the eighties, nineties, and beyond . . . the oldest old who survived the Great Depression and two World Wars, a cohort commonly referred to as the Greatest Generation, continue to value the American ideal of rugged individualism but recognize they cannot do it alone. (Loe, 2017, p. 220)

What is most critical for providers to bear in mind is the diversity and heterogeneity among the young-old through to the oldest-old. Respecting older adult autonomy means accepting the older adult's vision of what constitutes aging well; best practice means providing strategies that will support that vision. This includes enhancing older adults' ability to preserve quality of life through physical activity in the face of advancing age (Rejeski & Mihalko, 2001).

SECTION II: PRACTICAL APPROACH

Physical Activity and Aging

There is overwhelming evidence that physical activity promotes cognitive and psychological well-being, improves physical function, prevents and manages chronic disease, and reduces risk of falling, all of which is attributed to increasing longevity (American College of Sports Medicine [ACSM], 2014; Chodzko-Zajko, 2014; Chodzko-Zajko, Schwingel, & Park, 2009; Nelson et al., 2007). Conversely, physical inactivity has been proven to exacerbate negative health consequences (ACSM, 2014; Chodzko-Zajko, 2014; Chodzko-Zajko et al. 2009; Nelson et al., 2007). Poorer health associated with sedentary lifestyle leads to more visits to practitioners, more medications, and increased medical care costs (Greaney, Lees, Blissmer, Riebe, & Clark, 2016). Being physically active improves quality of life and helps maintain physical independence; keeping intact the activities of daily living (ADLs) and instrumental activities of daily living (IADLS). Although the defining factors of old age remain a mystery, people are quick to equate physical or functional challenges with being old, no matter what age the person may be. Regardless of chronological age (a birth date signifying

---

[1] It is interesting to note that when Neugarten's seminal work was published, "oldness" had only two subdivisions: the young-old (55–74) and the old-old (75+).

the passing of each year), other aspects of life such as the basic drives—the need for physical comfort, love, and status or purpose—continue essentially unchanged. Habit systems tend to persist with great tenacity, as do characteristic ways of meeting frustrations, personality patterns of dominance or submission, and the individual's whole array of attitudes (Atchley, 1998; 2010). Oftentimes, we hear older adults state they "are the same person they always were." This is precisely the opportunity and challenge dichotomy that must be addressed when working with older adults. Understanding, or at least being aware of, what has shaped the older adult, what persists, and how they choose to move through their own aging processes are important to consider. Awareness of these can help frame how health professionals may work with older adults. The cultural mores that have been established in the United States about aging, much of it based on the disease, decline, and withdrawal model, thrives in our society and affects how older adults proceed, and how we work with them through physical activity.

Considerations and Guidelines for Older Adult Physical Activity

We didn't have gym class or sports when I was a young girl. Phys Ed. consisted of the teacher walking into the classroom, having us stand up and face the windows, open the windows and take a deep breath. That was it!
—*Evelyn Fenderson, 92, Scarborough, ME*

For many, physical activity is not a fundamental component of daily life and that inactivity increases with age. By age 75, about one in three men and one in two women do not engage in physical activity (Resnick & Boltz, 2016). Being physically active tends to take on a different meaning for older adults. Organized athletics were likely not available during the adolescent years of the earlier generational cohorts such as the G.I or Greatest Generation (birth years 1901–1924) and the Silent Generation (1925–1942). Instead, these cohorts played out on the street, often making up games and rules that kept them moving. Terms such as *athletics, physical fitness,* and *exercise* were considered organized activities and tended to follow external rules for engagement.

Instead, those activities that had a purpose in their daily lives (necessity or individual creativity) were the drivers for activity. Regardless of which older adult cohort the provider works with, it may be necessary to reframe what physical activity entails and explain its importance in augmenting physical, mental, and social function.

As the adage goes, "if you don't use it, you lose it." By utilizing the term *physical activity*, we broaden the possibilities of engagement for older

> **TOO OLD TO EXERCISE? STUDIES SAY NO!**
>
> - Together, exercise and lifestyle changes, such as becoming more active and eating healthy food, reduce the risk of diabetes in high-risk older people. In one study, lifestyle changes led to a 71% decrease in diabetes among people age 60 and older.
> - In another study, moderate exercise was effective at reducing stress and sleep problems in older women caring for a family member with dementia.
> - Older people who exercise moderately are able to fall asleep quickly, sleep for longer periods, and get better quality of sleep.
> - Researchers also found that exercise, which can improve balance, reduced falls among older people by 33%.
> - Walking and strength-building exercises by people with knee osteoarthritis help reduce pain and maintain function and quality of life.

Source: National Institute on Aging. (n.d.). Talking with your older patient: Encouraging wellness in older patients. Retrieved from https://www.nia.nih.gov/health/encouraging-wellness-older-patients

adults and provide a variety of ways to have these activities count toward weekly goals for improved health outcomes. Learning the individual's goals, whether medical or personal, his or her general health status, and the individual's understanding of the potential benefits of specific activity is a necessary first step in guiding the older adult's activity program. Before older adults engage in new or more strenuous physical activities, it is wise for them to get approval from their primary care practitioner. Exhibit 6.1 lists physical activities that can help improve aerobic capacity (breathing and endurance) capacity and muscle strength (stability).

Determining the amount of physical activity required for health benefit, while unique to the individual and his or her goals, has been studied. During a study aimed at comparing the well-being outcomes of prescribed exercise (aerobics and strength training) and purposeful physical activity (housework and gardening), Whitehead and Blaxton (2017) revealed that prescribed exercise as well as purposeful physical activity were associated with fostering independent daily well-being benefits. For example, positive effects included improved sleep quality, improved perceived health, and reduced perceived stress, to name a few (Whitehead & Blaxton, 2017). Being physically active through exercise or functional activities can make a difference in how a

EXHIBIT 6.1   Physical Activities

Aerobic Activities	Muscle Strengthening
• Walking • Dancing • Swimming • Water aerobics • Jogging • Aerobic exercise classes • Bicycle riding (stationary or on a path) • Activities such as gardening, raking, and pushing a lawn mower (increases heart rate for 10 minutes or more) • Tennis • Golf (without a cart)	• Exercises using exercise bands, weight machines, hand-held weights • Exercises using one's own body weight (provides resistance to movement) • Yoga exercises • Tai chi exercises • Digging, lifting, and carrying as part of gardening • Carrying groceries • Resistance activities requiring pulling or pushing a weight (vacuuming, raking, etc.)

Source: Adapted from Health.gov. (2018). *Chapter 5: Active older adults*. Retrieved from https://health.gov/paguidelines/guidelines/chapter5.aspx

person adapts to the aging process. Older adults would do well to include some type of physical activity every day regardless of whether it is continuous (such as walking for 30 minutes) or intermittent (such as taking three 10-minute walks). Exhibit 6.2 provides the key physical activity guidelines for adults age 65 and older.

The recommendations for physical activity for healthy adults age 65 years and older provided in Exhibit 6.2 should be considered as a general starting point. In order for an older adult to achieve greater health benefits, the amount of time is either doubled or the intensity of the exercise is increased from moderate to vigorous (Health.gov, 2018). For those who are able to go beyond these recommendations, additional health benefits may be gained. In this case, providers would do well to be knowledgeable about the older adult's health, physical function abilities, and personal drive to be active. However, the individual should know best what his or her ability is and comfort level when being physically active. There are many creative ways to adapt physical activity when physical limitations or conditions are present (see Contraindications and Modifications discussed subsequently). It is important to keep the person's personal safety in mind while encouraging participation and adherence to physical activity. *The bottom line:* doing something is better than doing nothing.

Contraindications and Modifications

Older adults may experience either temporary or ongoing functional issues that could affect the amount, time, and/or type of physical activity

EXHIBIT 6.2 *Key Physical Activity Guidelines for Older Adults*

1. For substantial health benefits, the goal is for older adults to do at least 150 minutes (2 hours and 30 minutes) a week of moderate-intensity, or 75 minutes (1 hour and 15 minutes) a week of vigorous-intensity aerobic physical activity, or an equivalent combination of moderate- and vigorous-intensity aerobic activity.
2. Additional health benefits can be gained by engaging in muscle-strengthening activities that are moderate or high intensity and involve all major muscle groups on two or more days a week.

HOWEVER:

3. Some physical activity is better than none, and those who participate in any amount of physical activity gain some health benefits. All older adults should avoid inactivity.
4. Aerobic activity can be performed in two to three episodes of at least 10 minutes in length on a given day rather than one 20- to 30-minute duration of activity.
5. Knowing one's ability and determining the level of effort for physical activity relative to his or her level of fitness and health contributes to a person's safety.
6. When chronic or other health conditions keep an individual from attaining the goal of 150 minutes of moderate-intensity aerobic activity a week, doing any physical activity within the person's abilities, and as conditions allow, is a good place to begin.
7. A focus on exercises that maintain or improve balance is important if the individual is at risk of falling.

Source: Adapted from Health.gov. (2018). *Chapter 5: Active older adults.* Retrieved from https://health.gov/paguidelines/guidelines/chapter5.aspx

in which they engage. There are some medical conditions that may limit an older adult from engaging in moderate to vigorous physical activity (Panton & Loney, 2018). However, the fact remains that it is more harmful to omit physical activity from a person's life and promote sedentary behaviors. There are times when either an activity or exercise is contraindicated, or when a modification to an exercise or activity is warranted, for the person to safely participate. A *contraindication* is defined as a specific situation in which a particular exercise or activity should not be performed because it may be harmful to the person (ACSM, 2018). For example, deep knee bends, whether weights are used or not, is harmful to the knee joint. As a result, this type of exercise should always be avoided by everyone regardless of age. However, when a person presents with functional limitations, the need to modify or alter the activity may arise. In this scenario, for those who present with chronic knee or back conditions, or are recovering from a joint replacement, aquatic or pool-based physical activity is recommended. Being surrounded by water reduces strain and impact on the joints and has been shown to statistically improve knee and hip flexibility, strength, and aerobic fitness (Wang, Belza, Thompson, Whitney, & Bennett, 2007). Additionally, individuals with osteoporosis may benefit from weight-bearing physical activity. Research with older adults who have arthritis report significantly higher mean values of bone mineral density of the lumbar spine, neck of femur, and distal radial head in groups prescribed weight-bearing exercises than those without weight-bearing exercises (Shanb & Youssef, 2014). This evidence makes a case for older adults with arthritis to participate in weight-bearing activities.

All exercises, whether water based or land based, can be modified for safety when working with older adults. It can be as simple as lengthening the warm-up or reducing the amount of resistance or number of repetitions. One can gradually work up to a level that is challenging enough to gain benefit, but not too stressful on the body. For individuals with mobility and balance problems, an activity or exercise can be modified by increasing points of contact (the surface area of the foot in contact with the floor or hand position on a stable object). Every muscle group of the body can be exercised while seated in a chair. A good instructor will have the ability and knowledge to modify activities to meet the older adult's needs. Knowledge and experience with activity modifications and contraindications when promoting physical activity for older adults is essential.

Physician Approval

There are conditions that may limit a person's ability to attain the recommended guidelines for physical activity including terminal illnesses and severe behavioral problems (Panton & Loney, 2018). Prior to starting physical activity or a planned exercise program, a primary care provider (or physician specialist when appropriate) should be consulted (Panton & Loney, 2018). For some conditions, modifications can be made so the individual may continue some movement and avoid being completely sedentary. Exhibit 6.3 outlines the conditions requiring a primary care provider's approval as a safety measure before physical activity is engaged in.

Barriers to Physical Activity

People of all ages experience obstacles that prevent them from taking part in physical activity. For older adults, these barriers could be quite powerful, based on fear or long-time entrenchment in negative beliefs about activity. A Rhode Island Focus Group study sought to determine what exactly stood in the way of older adults meeting the physical activity recommendations that have been scientifically shown to improve quality of life (Lees, Clark, Nigg, & Newman, 2005). This study identified 12 barriers to exercise and how they were defined by the focus groups. Exhibit 6.4 lists the 12 top barriers to exercise for older adults.

EXHIBIT 6.3 *Conditions Requiring Physician Approval*

Conditions	Modification Considerations NOTE: Physician Approval Is Essential
Any new symptoms that have not been discussed with a doctor	Depends on the symptoms; check with the physician before implementing physical activity
Dizziness or shortness of breath	Depends on the cause; chair activities, including range of motion for those with vertigo or pulmonary disease, may be possible
Chest pain or pressure	Depends; if symptoms are controlled or uncontrolled, check with the physician before implementing physical activity
Heart is skipping, racing, or fluttering, or feels that way	Check with the physician before implementing physical activity
Blood clots	Per physician approval, hand and dexterity activity
Infection with fever and muscle aches	Check with the physician before implementing physical activity
Unplanned weight loss or sudden weight gain	Per physician approval, range of motion, non–weight bearing activities
Foot or ankle sores that will not heal	Upper body activities; check with physician before implementing physical activity
Joint swelling	Depends on the joint; conduct activities that do not involve the affected joint. Physical activity is recommended from arthritis. Pool activities may be best
Eye surgery, laser treatment, or has a detached retina	Non–weight bearing activity, no strenuous activity including finger dexterity and joint range of motion while sitting or lying down
Hernia	Per physician approval, range of motion, non–weight bearing activities
Recent hip, knee, or back surgery	Depends on the type of surgery; conduct activities that do not involve the affected joint/area (i.e., a person with a recent back surgery may be able to perform hand, arm, and shoulder activities and possibly some leg, upper thigh [quadriceps], lower leg [gastrocnemius], and ankle flexibility or strengthening activity)

Source: Adapted from Panton, L., & Loney, B. (2018). *Exercise of older adults* (pp. 8–11). Retrieved from http://file.lacounty.gov/SDSInter/dmh/216745_ExerciseforOlderAdultsHealthCareProviderManual.pdf

A more extensive 7-year study was published in Germany in 2011 in which 1,937 older adults with a median age of 77 (range 72–93) years, of whom 53.3% were female, identified barriers (Moschny, Platen, Klaaßen-Mielke, Trampisch, & Hinrichs, 2011). Of the participants not getting enough exercise, these barriers included poor health, lack of company, lack of interest, lack of opportunities, afraid of falls/injury, lack of transport, and lack of time. As a

EXHIBIT 6.4 *Top Barriers (rank order 1–12)*

Barriers	Definition
1. Inertia	Characterized by passivity, including being too busy, lazy, and bored
2. Fear of falling/safety	Afraid of falling, have fallen, or know of others who have fallen; fear for personal safety
3. Time	Doctor's appointments, volunteer work
4. Negative affect	Characterized by feelings of depression and lack of motivation
5. Physical ailments	Barriers resulting from injury, chronic illness, or poor health
6. Social	Lack of social support or demands of others—friends, relatives
7. Discomfort	Unpleasant sensations associated with exercise, including pain, dizziness, and shortness of breath
8. Weather	Bad weather, heat, or humidity
9. Age	Personal and social perception of age appropriateness
10. Inconvenience	Scheduling, access
11. Perceived capability	The belief that one cannot perform the activity
12. Verbal persuasion	Physician advice, or the advice of others, generally not to exercise

Source: Based on Lees, F. D., Clark, P. G., Nigg, C. R., & Newman, P. (2005). Barriers to exercise behavior among older adults: A focus-group study. *Journal of Aging & Physical Activity, 13*(1), 23–33. doi:10.1123/japa.13.1.23

provider, it is important to determine the barrier or combination of barriers preventing an individual from being physically active. Each barrier has a solution; whether the person accepts it and participates is another matter.

Opportunities That Support Physical Activity

One of the best ways to build a person's confidence is to suggest participating in any physical activity for a few minutes and work up to more time while maintaining comfortable exertion and staying within one's ability. There is no support for the "no pain, no gain" mentality when starting or maintaining physical activity. Eventually, time, level of activity, resistance, and/or number of repetitions can be increased once the body's reaction to physical activity is understood and adjustments are made, if needed. When promoting physical activity, it is imperative that the following are considered: safety, program structure, movement is within the person's comfort level, and social engagement. These components will work to combat many of the barriers that are present. Additionally, health professionals would do well to consider the five factors that are presented in Exhibit 6.5, which provides guidance on how to support anyone who is beginning or wanting to maintain physical activity.

EXHIBIT 6.5 Five Factors

Five Factors to Form New Physical Activity Habits	Guidance for Health Professionals to Support Physical Activity for Older Adults
Enjoyment	• Encourage individuals (who may be patients/clients) to try different types and combinations of physical activity until they find something they enjoy. • Suggest they explore different types of physical activity if they get bored with something. • It is important to note that the type of exercise or physical activity someone prefers is not as important as how much time they regularly spend performing that exercise.
Self-efficacy	• Both self-directed motivation and self-efficacy are important determinants of short-term (6-month) exercise adherence. • To boost self-efficacy, ensure the person seeks support from friends, providers, or a personal trainer, to build his or her knowledge around exercise technique and workout structures. • Provide online resources (see Exhibit 6.6) that are specific to older adults or their condition.
Social support	• Encourage and facilitate social support for those who are engaging in physical activity. • Suggestions include (a) inviting friends and family to join in the new exercise habit; and/or (b) seeking out new social opportunities with people who share an interest in the same activities. • Encourage partner or group workouts or refer them to walking or other active groups in the community. • For those who prefer to be active on their own, ask about how they get social support.
Accountability	• Accountability can be established by working out with a friend or two, or a coach. • Encourage each person to share his or her exercise journey online or with friends/family.
Integration into the daily routine	• Encourage a daily routine that incorporates physical activity. • Suggest creating a schedule of weekly workouts in their calendar to make sure it fits into their day. • Workouts can also be broken up into smaller blocks to better fit into the day.

Source: Adapted from Black-Larcom, A. (2018). *5 Factors that help people stick to a new exercise habit.* Office of Disease Prevention and Health Promotion. Retrieved from https://health.gov/news/blog-bayw/2018/01/5-factors-help-people-stick-new-exercise-habit

There are a number of opportunities to support older adults who are either starting or continuing physical activity. The key for health professionals is that whatever physical activity choice is selected by the individual (choice being the operant word), *interest* in the activity gets them started, *motivation* helps to maintain it, and *safety* is the golden rule.

Physical Activity and Social Integration

The following organizations offer myriad information and evidence-based programs to support physical activity for older adults. Any web-based search engine should work and once on the organization home page do a search on "Physical Activity."

EXHIBIT 6.6 *Resources on Older Adult Physical Activity*

Web-based resources
Note: As website addresses may change, see "Search" terms to find information

NCOA
Description: The NCOA is a respected national leader and trusted partner to help people age 60+ meet the challenges of aging. They partner with nonprofit organizations, government, and business to provide innovative community programs and services, online help, and advocacy.
View: "Healthy Aging" tab
Search: "Physical Activity"

NIA
Description: NIA, one of the 27 institutes and centers of NIH, leads a broad scientific effort to understand the nature of aging and to extend the healthy, active years of life. NIA is the primary federal agency supporting and conducting Alzheimer's disease research.
Search: NIA Go4Life offers free, evidence-based resources for older adults in one convenient place for four types of exercise—endurance, strength, balance, and flexibility!
Search: "Encouraging Wellness in Older Patients"
Information for Practitioners: "Talking With Your Older Patient: Exercise and Physical Activity"

AHA
Description: The AHA is a nonprofit organization in the United States that fosters appropriate cardiac care in an effort to reduce disability and deaths caused by cardiovascular disease and stroke.
Search: "Physical Activity in Older Americans"

ACS
Description: American Cancer Society
Search: "ACS Guidelines for Nutrition and Physical Activity"

Alz.Org®—Alzheimer's Association
Description: Alzheimer's Association advances research to end Alzheimer's and dementia while enhancing care for those living with the disease.
Search: "Stay Physically Active"
Search: "Exercising the Brain"

Health.gov
Description: Health.gov is a portal for health-related resources and news from the U.S. government. Information on prevention topics, dietary and physical activity guidelines, and other health resources are provided.
Search: Physical Activity

(continued)

EXHIBIT 6.6 *Resources on Older Adult Physical Activity (continued)*

University of New England U-ExCEL Balancing Act Program
Description: U-ExCEL is an auxiliary functional fitness program for older adults. Online training in balance through video and written manuals are available for free.
Search: "UNECOM U-ExCEL Balancing Act"

ACS, American Cancer Society; AHA, American Heart Association; NCOA, National Council on Aging; NIA, National Institute on Aging; NIH, National Institute of Health; U-ExCEL, University of New England's Exercise and Conditioning for Easier Living; UNECOM, University of New England College of Osteopathic Medicine.

SECTION III: CASES: RECOMMENDED PROGRESSIONS

Case 1. Beatrice: An 87-Year-Old Widowed Woman Living in a Continuing Care Retirement Community (CCRC) in an Assisted Living Apartment

Beatrice has macular degeneration, vertigo when standing, and is overweight. After undergoing several tests, no causation for vertigo has been discovered. Beatrice currently gets about 75 minutes of physical activity each week (three times per week for 25 minutes) and prefers to exercise in the pool owing to poor vision and balance. Beatrice enjoys interacting with others and desires to build her strength and endurance to rejoin a "sit and fit" land-based exercise class that meets three times per week for 45 minutes (135 minutes per week).

- To increase Beatrice's physical activity output and get her back in a group exercise class, an exercise prescription of aquatic and land-based physical activity is recommended. Beatrice can begin by increasing time in the water to 30 minutes three times per week with specific strength- and aerobic-based exercises. These are provided in large print with pictures and protected in plastic. Two nonconsecutive days per week, Beatrice will work with an instructor doing land-based weight-bearing exercises to build strength and also incorporate balance exercises into her routine. Strength-based exercises can be administered while seated in a chair until she progresses to a standing position, and balance exercises are conducted where support is available.
- Gradually, Beatrice will increase active time in the pool to 150 minutes per week along with 8 to 10 muscle-strengthening exercises that target all major muscle groups two to three times per week on land. Each exercise should be performed for one set with 10 to 15 repetitions in a slow and controlled manner. After 2 weeks Beatrice can then increase the amount of resistance and complete one set of 8 to 12 repetitions until she can build up to 15 repetitions.

Case 2. Robert: A 74-Year-Old Single Male, Living Independently in a Two-Room Apartment He Has Lived in for 15 Years

Robert has terminal lung cancer, atrial fibrillation, chronic obstructive pulmonary disorder (COPD), spinal stenosis, obesity, two knee replacements, one shoulder replacement, arthritis, multiple myeloma (in remission), and sleep apnea. The lung cancer is managed with intravenous immunotherapy treatments every 3 weeks, and the sleep apnea requires the use of a C-Pap machine. He is taking 20 medications to manage his health conditions. It is expected that Robert has approximately 24 to 36 months to live due to the immunotherapy. Robert, although obese throughout his adult life (he was a chef), is in the habit (for many years) of participating in 200 minutes of physical activity 5 days per week (20 minutes on his exercise bike and 20 minutes of stretching). Additionally, once every week he drives 30 minutes to his favorite town and shops at four different locations getting in and out of his car unassisted, although not without struggle, and walks up and down every aisle in each store with the aid of a shopping cart. Robert prefers not to participate in group activities and finds that he now has to take a couple days off from his exercise when he gets his immunotherapy treatments. His favorite pastime is sitting in his recliner watching sports.

- Robert is dedicated to his exercise and stretching routine. He has continued this routine even through his past chemotherapy and radiation treatments, although he had to cut back owing to shortness of breath. He built back up again once treatments ceased. In Robert's case, the COPD is exacerbated by his lung cancer; maintaining aerobic exercise on his bike for 20 minutes 5 days a week helps manage his COPD. This is a motivator for him and aids in maintaining his quality of life. Each of his many physicians acknowledge his dedication to physical activity. It is clear this is his badge of honor.
- Exercise is clearly part of his weekly routine and he pays attention to his own progress and is aware of his own ability. Health professionals are supporting Robert's routine by acknowledging it. He has stated that he will not increase or change his routine; maintaining his routine is his goal. Getting out each week to shop on his own aids his quality of life.

SUMMARY

This chapter is intended to assist health and service providers who work with older adults to (a) introduce the social context in which older adults may or may not be eager to engage in physical activity; and (b) provide the foundation and practical resources that support getting older adults to be physically active. It is essential to be aware of the ever-present disease, decline, and withdrawal model that has been and continues to be associated with aging in our society. Actually, this is the first hurdle that providers and older adults alike need to get past in order to consider physical activity as a path to well-being.

As providers, we consider, and especially want to facilitate, older adults' autonomy, health, well-being, and social connectedness. These may well be the tenets of life satisfaction that reflect the extent to which older adults are able to preserve quality of life through physical activity in the face of advancing age (Rejeski & Mihalko, 2001). Integration, in this chapter, includes both social integration, overall level of involvement with informal and formal social relationships (Umberson & Montez, 2010), and self-integration, a redefining of the self in relationship to others; being more selective in the choice of social and other activities (Tornstam, 1990). Both types of integration, social and self, are important to consider when working with older adults.

Expanding our understanding of, and addressing the many factors associated with, physical activity among older adults is important for promoting and maintaining physical activity within this population (Greaney et al., 2016). The bottom line may well be that older adults are a diverse and heterogeneous group. They will exhibit differences in psychosocial factors based on age, race/ethnicity, income, socioeconomic status, location (urban, suburban, or rural), and presence or type of disability. Additionally, internal factors such as motivation, personality, desire, and coping mechanisms will also affect the degree to which each person engages in physical activity, the type of activity, and how long they will continue it. Our suggestion: Apply person-centered care and do your best to get every older adult you know moving!

REFERENCES

American College of Sports Medicine. (2014). Benefits of regular physical activity and/or exercise. In L. S. Pescatello, R. Arena, D. Riebe, & P. Thompson (Eds), *ACSM's guidelines for exercise testing and prescription*. Baltimore, MD: Lippincott Williams & Wilkins.

American College of Sports Medicine, Riebe, D. (2018). *ACSM's guidelines for exercise testing and prescription* (10th ed.). Philadelphia, PA: Wolters Kluwer.

Atchley, R. C. (1998). Activity adaptations to the development of functional limitations and results for subjective well-being in later adulthood: A qualitative analysis of longitudinal panel data over a 16-year period. *Journal of Aging Studies*, 12(1), 19–38. doi:10.1016/s0890-4065(98)90018-4

Atchley, R. C. (2010). *Spirituality and aging*. Baltimore, MD: The Johns Hopkins University Press.

Berkman, L. F., Glass, T., Brissette, I., & Seeman, T. E. (2000). From social integration to health: Durkheim in the new millennium. *Social Science & Medicine*, 51(6), 843–857. doi:10.1016/S0277-9536(00)00065-4

Black-Larcom, A. (2018). *5 Factors that help people stick to a new exercise habit*. Retrieved from https://health.gov/news/blog-bayw/2018/01/5-factors-help-people-stick-new-exercise-habit

Caspersen, C. J., Powell, K. E., & Christenson, G. M. (1985). Physical activity, exercise, and physical fitness: Definitions and distinctions for health-related research. *Public Health Reports, 100*(2), 126–131. Retrieved from https://www.ncbi.nlm.nih.gov/pmc/articles/PMC1424733

Chodzko-Zajko, W. (Ed.). (2014). *ACSM's exercise for older adults*. Baltimore, MD: Lippincott Williams & Wilkins.

Chodzko-Zajko, W., Schwingel, A., & Park, H. E. (2009). Successful aging: The role of physical activity. *American Journal of Lifestyle Medicine, 3*(1), 20–28. doi:10.1177/1559827608325456

Garfein, A. J., & Herzog, A. R. (1995). Robust aging among the young-old, old-old, and oldest-old. *Journal of Gerontology: Social Sciences, 50B*, S77–S87. doi:10.1093/geronb/50B.2.S77

Greaney, M. L., Lees, F. D., Blissmer, B. J., Riebe, D., & Clark, P. G. (2016). Psychosocial factors associated with physical activity in older adults. *Annual Review of Gerontology & Geriatrics, 36*, 273–291. doi:10.1891/0198-8794.36.273

Havighurst, R. J. (1963). Successful aging. In R. H. Williams, C. Tibbetts, & W. Donahue (Eds.), *Processes of aging: Social and psychological perspectives* (Vol. I, pp. 299–320). New York, NY: Atherton.

Havighurst, R. J., & Albrecht, R. (1953). *Older people*. New York, NY: Longmans Green.

Havighurst, R. J., Neugarten, B. L., & Tobin, S. S. (1963). Disengagement, personality and life satisfaction in the later years. In P. E. Hansen (Ed), *Age with a future* (pp. 419–425). Copenhagen, Denmark: Munksgaard.

Health.gov. (2018). *Chapter 5: Active older adults*. Retrieved from https://health.gov/paguidelines/guidelines/chapter5.aspx

Lamb, S., Taylor, J. S., Robbins-Ruszkowski, J., Corwin, A., Calasanti, T., King, N., . . . Buch, E. (2017). *Successful aging as a contemporary obsession: Global perspectives*. New Brunswick, NJ: Rutgers University Press.

Lees, F. D., Clark, P. G., Nigg, C. R., & Newman, P. (2005). Barriers to exercise behavior among older adults: A focus-group study. *Journal of Aging & Physical Activity, 13*(1), 23–33. doi:10.1123/japa.13.1.23

Loe, M. (2017). Comfortable aging: Lessons for living from eighty-five and beyond. In S. Lamb et al. (Ed.), *Successful aging as a contemporary obsession: Global perspectives* (pp. 218–229). New Brunswick, NJ: Rutgers University Press.

Lowsky, D. J., Olshansky, S. J., Bhattacharya, J., & Goldman, D. (2013). Heterogeneity in healthy aging. *Journal of Gerontology, Series A Biological Sciences/Medical Sciences, 69*(6), 640–649. doi:10.1093/gerona/glt162

Mirucka, B., Bielecka, U., & Kisielewska, M. (2016). Positive orientation, self-esteem, and satisfaction with life in the context of subjective age in older adults. *Personality and Individual Differences, 99*, 206–210. doi:10.1016/j.paid.2016.05.010

Moschny, A., Platen, P., Klaaßen-Mielke, R., Trampisch, U., & Hinrichs, T. (2011). Barriers to physical activity in older adults in Germany: A cross-sectional study. *The International Journal of Behavioral Nutrition and Physical Activity, 8*, 121. doi:10.1186/1479-5868-8-121

National Institute on Aging. (n.d.). *Talking with your older patient: Encouraging wellness in older patients*. Retrieved from https://www.nia.nih.gov/health/encouraging-wellness-older-patients

Nelson, M. E., Rejeski, W. J., Blair, S. N., Duncan, P. W., Judge, J. O., & King, A. C., . . . American Heart Association. (2007). Physical activity and public health in older adults: Recommendation from the American College of Sports Medicine and the American Heart Association. *Circulation, 116*(9), 1094–1105. doi:10.1161/circulationaha.107.185650

Neugarten, B. (1974). Age groups in American society and the rise of the young-old. *The Annals of the American Academy of Political and Social Science, 415*(1), 187–198. doi:10.1177/000271627441500114

Panton, L., & Loney, B. (2018). *Exercise of older adults* (pp. 8-11). Retrieved from http://file.lacounty.gov/SDSInter/dmh/216745_ExerciseforOlderAdultsHealthCareProviderManual.pdf

Rejeski, W. J., & Mihalko, S. L. (2001). Physical activity and quality of life in older adults. *The Journals of Gerontology: Series A, 56*(sSuppl_. 2), 23–35. doi:10.1093/gerona/56.suppl_2.23

Resnick, B., & Boltz, M. (2016). Incorporating function and physical activity across all settings. *Annual Review of Gerontology and Geriatrics, 36*(1), 293–321. doi:10.1891/0198-8794.36.293

Rowe, J. W., & Kahn, R. L. (1987). Human aging: Usual and successful. *Science, 237*(4811), 143–149. doi:10.1126/science.3299702

Rowe, J. W., & Kahn, R. L. (1997). Successful aging. *The Gerontologist, 37*(4), 433–440. doi:10.1093/geront/37.4.433

Shanb, A., & Youssef, E. (2014). The impact of adding weight-bearing exercises versus non-weight bearing programs to the medical treatment of elderly patients with osteoporosis. *Journal of Family and Community Medicine, 21*(3), 175. doi:10.4103/2230-8229.142972

Tornstam, L. (1990). Dimensions of loneliness. *Aging Clinical and Experimental Research, 2*(3), 259–265. doi: 10.1007/BF03323926.

Tornstam, L. (1997). Gerotrancendence in a broad cross-sectional perspective. *Journal of Aging and Identity, 2*(1), 17–36. doi:10.1016/S0890-4065(97)90018-9

Umberson, D., & Montez, J. K. (2010). Social relationships and health: A flashpoint for health policy. *Journal of Health and Social Behavior, 51*(Suppl), S54–S66. doi:10.1177/0022146510383501

Wang, T., Belza, B., Thompson, E. F., Whitney, J., & Bennett, K. (2007). Effects of aquatic exercise on flexibility, strength and aerobic fitness in adults with osteoarthritis of the hip or knee. *Journal of Advanced Nursing, 57*(2), 141–152. doi:10.1111/j.1365-2648.2006.04102.x

Whitehead, B. R., & Blaxton, J. M., (2017). Daily well-being benefits of physical activity in older adults: Does time or type matter? *The Gerontologist, 57*(6), 1062–1071. doi:10.1093/geront/gnw250

World Health Organization. (2018). *Let's be active!* Retrieved from http://www.who.int/topics/physical_activity/en

7

Designing Age Friendly Communities as a Strategy for Enhancing Social Connectedness

Patricia Huffman Oh

INTRODUCTION

Social connectedness—formal participation in activities and groups and informal contacts with friends, neighbors, and other residents—is important for everyone in a community to thrive, but is critical for the health and well-being of older residents (Levasseur, Richard, Gauvin, & Raymond, 2010; Newall, McArthur, & Menec, 2015). Everyday social connections build trust and encourage active involvement in community life (Helliwell & Putnam, 2004). The simple act of leaving the house every day—for whatever reason—is associated with a lower risk of mortality (Jacobs, Hammerman-Rozenberg, & Stessman, 2018). The risk for social isolation increases when physical limitations make it harder for an older person to participate in community activities (Pettigrew, Donovan, Boldy, & Newton, 2014). Ideally, municipalities have accessible physical environments and inclusive social environments that provide residents with what they need to be as active as they want to be (Emlet & Moceri, 2011; Jeste et al., 2016).

An "age-friendly" community promotes active, healthy, socially connected aging through inclusive policies, infrastructure, and services (Alley, Liebig, Pynoos, Benerjee, & Choi, 2007; Scharlach & Lehning, 2013). It is easier for older people to be involved in the community when it has age-friendly features, such as reliable public transportation; safe, welcoming gathering places; and accessible services. However, the benefits are not only for the old. When a community is inclusive, everyone has an easier time enjoying what the community has to offer and interacting with other residents (Rantakokko et al., 2014; Vogt, Kho, & Sia, 2017). For example, a well-designed park with wide paths, benches, and recreational opportunities for a range of interests and abilities encourages active, healthy aging for older residents—and everyone else.

One way that some states, counties, cities, towns, and villages structure a commitment to age-friendly municipal planning is by joining the AARP Network of Age-Friendly Communities (NAFC). In this context, "community" refers to a municipality. Membership does not mean that a community has achieved age-friendly nirvana. It means that the municipality has committed to include older residents in planning in eight aspects of the physical and social environment that contribute to livability. Joining the NAFC is appropriate for communities of all sizes—from the largest urban metropolis to a small rural community. Each municipality in the NAFC is unique; the age-friendly initiative reflects its cultural and socioeconomic diversity, community values, age-friendly assets, and what older residents need and want to fully engage in community life.

Although considerable research has pointed to the importance of social connectedness for the health and well-being of older people (Hogan et al., 2016; Shor & Roelfs, 2015) and to community characteristics that help older people to remain active in their communities (Lui, Everingham, Warburton, Cuthill, & Bartlett, 2009; Menec, Means, Keating, Parkhurst, & Eales, 2011), few studies have explored whether age-friendly communities include increasing social connectedness as a goal, and, if so, the kinds of changes communities implement to encourage older residents to be socially connected (Glicksman, Ring, & Kleben, 2016; Lehning & Greenfield, 2017; Menec et al., 2015; Scharf & Moceri, 2012). This chapter presents original findings from a study the authors did to explore the strategies age-friendly communities employ to encourage people to spend time with others in their community.

BENEFITS OF AGE-FRIENDLY COMMUNITIES

Where a person lives has a profound impact on how he or she ages (Wahl, Iwarsson, & Oswald, 2012). A community is more than the geographic area where someone lives; it is where a person chooses to put down roots and build a life. Most people want to age in their own home (Feldman, Oberlink, Simantov, & Gursen, 2004; AARP, 2018) and, if that is no longer possible, want to find an alternative in their own community (Hillcoat-Nalletamby & Ogg, 2014). Older people want more than to live in the community; they want to continue the patterns of informal and formal social connections that gave them a sense of purpose and belonging in their younger years (Black, Dobbs,

& Young, 2012; Wiles & Jayasinha, 2013). However, that is not always possible. Whether people of all ages and abilities can participate in community life is largely dependent on municipal policies, services, and infrastructure. Easy access to information about local activities and services, meaningful opportunities for civic participation, and accessible public spaces and businesses encourage older residents to remain actively engaged in the community, even if physical or cognitive ability declines (Emlet & Moceri, 2011; Wiersma & Denton, 2013).

Municipalities benefit from the involvement of older residents when barriers to social connections are removed. Adults age 60+ have purchasing power; give their time, talents, and experience for volunteer activities; continue to work and mentor younger employees; start new businesses; and are active in the cultural and civic life of the community. Almost half (47%) of people over 65 who volunteer give more than 100 hours of service each year (United States Department of Labor, Bureau of Labor Statistics, 2016b). People age 65+ are also generous with their charitable giving, donating an average of $1,672 every 12 months (AARP & Oxford Economics, 2016).

The lack of federal or state funding and tight local budgets mean that age-friendly initiatives depend on volunteers, many of whom are older, to ensure that identified changes are implemented and maintained (Buffel et al., 2014). For example, in Wayne, Maine, the age-friendly committee worked with the town to add signals and signage that increased pedestrian safety. Living Well in North Yarmouth, Maine, the town's age-friendly committee hosts an annual kite festival and ice cream social that brings together residents of all ages. Older volunteers in Augusta, Maine, teach young people at the Boys and Girls Club how to sew. Flannel hats, mittens, and other items made by the teenagers are donated to a local warming shelter. These initiatives increase social ties in the community. In fact, age-friendly community development may improve neighborhood cohesion, increase intergenerational ties, and promote health (Finkelstein & Netherland, 2010; Lambrinos, 2013; Neal, DeLaTorre, & Carder, 2014).

Municipal commitment to age-friendly planning may prevent out-migration and attract retiree in-migrants (Gilroy, 2008; Jackson, Illsley, Curry, & Rapaport, 2008; Ryser & Halseth, 2013), which can be a boon for the local economy. Older residents shop, hire contractors, and enjoy eating out or buying a cup of coffee. Humphreys and Kochut (2013) found that for each 1.8 retiree in-migrants to a rural area, one new job was created. People age 55+ are responsible for 41% of consumer spending (United States Department of Labor, Bureau of Labor Statistics, 2016a), launch 25% of all new business start-ups in the United States (U.S. Census Bureau, 2017), and are increasingly likely to seek part- or full-time work after traditional retirement (AARP & Oxford Economics, 2016). Far from a drain on local economies, older people can represent a silver wellspring of economic activity for municipalities.

THE AARP NETWORK OF AGE-FRIENDLY COMMUNITIES

Noting aging population trends internationally, in 2010, the World Health Organization (WHO) launched the Global Network of Age-Friendly Cities and Communities (GNAFCC) to promote social and physical environments that support healthy, active, and engaged aging. WHO describes an age-friendly community as

> a place that enables people of all ages to actively participate in community activities. It is a place that treats everyone with respect, regardless of their age. It is a place that makes it easy to stay connected to those around you and those you love. It is a place that helps people stay healthy and active even at the oldest ages. And it is a place that helps those who can no longer look after themselves to live with dignity and enjoyment. (World Health Organization [WHO], 2007)

Based on research in 33 cities worldwide, WHO identified eight domains of livability—housing, social participation, respect and social inclusion, community support and health services, civic participation and employment, transportation, outdoor spaces and buildings, and communication and information—that affect health and well-being (Plouffe & Kalache, 2011). The eight domains are central to municipal planning using the WHO–GNAFCC framework.

In 2012, AARP partnered with WHO to promote age-friendly work in the United States (Whitman, 2013). AARP developed the NAFC to help communities assess, plan, implement, and evaluate age-friendly changes in the eight domains of livability. More than 200 municipalities in the United States have enrolled. Communities that join the network commit to a 5-year planning cycle. During the first 2 years, the age-friendly team develops a 3-year action plan that builds on community strengths to implement changes. As part of the plan, the team identifies evaluation tools that allow the team to respond to changing circumstances and adjust the plan as needed. Three years after starting implementation, the team evaluates progress in the eight domains and develops an action plan with new goals and action items to continue the ongoing process of age-friendly development. Municipalities that join the AARP NAFC also become members of the WHO GNAFCC and have the benefit of local technical support from AARP and participation in a peer learning network with other communities in both networks (AARP, 2014).

With 65% of households in rural areas, Maine is the most rural state in the United States (U.S. Census Bureau, 2010). Rural communities have their own unique set of challenges. Research in England suggests that older rural dwellers are more likely to experience social isolation (Jivraj, Nazroo, & Barnes, 2012) and that about 9% of older rural dwellers feel isolated from their community (De Koning, Stathi, & Richards, 2017). In a recent article, Len Kaye (2017) argues that rural dwelling older people in the United States are also at greater risk for social isolation than their urban counterparts.

Maine has more communities enrolled in the AARP NAFC than any other state. The median size of a Maine community in the AARP NAFC is 3,895, compared with 43,202 for AARP–NAFC communities nationwide. Three Maine cities in the network—Portland, Bangor, and Biddeford—have populations greater than 20,000; 17—Gilead, Newry, Greenwood, Brooklin, Brooksville, Wayne, Jackman, Sedgwick, Penobscot, Sullivan, Woodstock, Eastport, Castine, Greenville, Surry, Deer Isle, and Hallowell—have fewer than 2,500 residents. Because of their small size, several Maine communities have joined forces to create regional approaches to age-friendly community development. Communities that are part of a regional approach share resources and develop a plan that covers all the cities and towns in the region, but each community retains its own distinct approach to implementation.

AGE-FRIENDLY NETWORK COMMUNITIES AND SOCIAL CONNECTEDNESS

By addressing factors in the eight domains of livability, age-friendly communities remove barriers in the social and physical environment that make it harder for people to be actively involved in the community. When people—even the frailest and most vulnerable—have what they need to thrive, the community is an easier place for everyone to live and to make social connections. The "social participation" domain includes formal and informal interactions with other people in the community. However, each domain affects social connectedness. A recent study showed that giving people age 65+ free bus passes reduced depression and loneliness and increased social connections and civic engagement (Reinhard, Courtin, van Lenthe, & Avendano, 2018). Free accessible transportation options make it easier to join a group of friends at a local coffee shop, volunteer at the local grammar school, or participate in a book club at the library. Not only does the person gain by being able to participate, the community benefits because the individual is able to be present.

Inclusion in community life may be as important for health and well-being as access to medical care, fresh food, affordable home repair, and recreation (Emlet & Moceri, 2011). Time with friends and casual acquaintances, such as the clerk at the grocery store, friendly neighbors, and people interested in the same volunteer opportunity or hobby, is important for self-identity and can make it easier to ask for help in times of trouble (De Koning, Stathi, & Richards, 2017; Rowles & Watkins, 1993). Formal and informal social connections help older people to continue meaningful roles as vital, productive members of the community at a time when other roles (e.g., paid worker, parent) are either lost or change (Burns, Lavoie, & Rose, 2012; Erickson, Call, & Brown, 2012). Older people—whatever their needs—benefit from social connectedness.

To increase social connectedness in age-friendly communities requires developing diverse strategies—some in the domain of social participation and some in domains that facilitate social participation—to encourage older people to be as engaged in community life as they want to be. This study explores whether—and if so, how—communities that have enrolled in the AARP NAFC consider social connectedness when they are planning local changes in the eight domains of livability.

Methods
Age-Friendly Action Plans

The research discussed here focuses on the 206 communities that joined the AARP NAFC prior to February 5, 2018, with special emphasis on the communities in Maine. When a municipality joins the network, it commits to including older adults in the 5-year planning cycle of continuous improvement. Within the first 2 years, the initial action plan is submitted for approval by AARP NAFC and WHO GNAFCC. Approved plans are posted on the AARP Livable Communities website (www.aarp.org/livable-communities) and may be posted on municipal websites. Communities are required to assess livability in all eight domains but are not required to develop goals in each domain. Thus, an approved action plan may not include strategies in each domain of livability. If the community has a plan to address a domain, such as social participation, it is included in the plan.

As of February 5, 2018, 41 action plans covering 51 counties, cities, and towns in the AARP NAFC were approved. An action plan can include more than one jurisdiction if, for example, a county plan covers municipalities that have joined the AARP NAFC in that county or a group of towns works together on a regional approach to age-friendly development. The 38 plans that were reviewed for this research were downloaded from the AARP NAFC website or downloaded from municipal age-friendly websites. Three plans were not available so they were not included in the analysis. Each plan was manually content analyzed to identify the following: (a) whether increasing social connectedness was part of the mission, vision, or goals of the age-friendly effort as included in the plan; (b) whether the social participation domain was included as an area of focus in the plan; and (c) if social participation was not included, if enhancing social connectedness was indirectly addressed in another domain.

Maine

There are 30 age-friendly initiatives in Maine that cover the 47 municipalities enrolled in the AARP NAFC. Two communities—Sullivan and Eliot—joined in January 2018, so they are not included in this discussion. The communities range in size from Maine's largest city—Portland—to Gilead, a rural community with 209 residents. Given the small size of many of the communities, several municipalities have joined forces to work on a regional approach to age-friendly planning. Four regional approaches have developed: (1) Bethel area (Bethel, Newry, Woodstock, Greenwood, and Gilead), (2) Blue Hill Peninsula (Blue Hill, Brooklin, Brooksville, Castine, Penobscot, Sedgwick, Surry, Deer Isle, and Stonington), (3) Piscataquis County (Dover-Foxcroft, Greenville, Dexter, and Milo), and (4) Somerset County (Jackman, Madison, and Skowhegan). Twenty-six initiatives (that include 43 municipalities) have started to implement changes in one or more of the eight domains; 19 initiatives that include 31 communities are working on or have completed action plans. Many communities start implementing changes in the community prior to developing a plan and submitting it for AARP/WHO approval.

To dig deeper into the way an age-friendly planning committee implements a strategy to enhance social connectedness, the 26 Maine initiatives that have started implementing changes (even if they have not completed an action plan) were contacted by email and asked: (a) if creating opportunities to increase social connectedness in the community is a focus for their work, and (b) if it was, how. All the communities responded by phone or email between January 8, 2018, and February 5, 2018. The responses (email or telephone transcriptions) were manually content analyzed to (a) identify whether social connectedness was an area of focus for the community, and (b) if so, the type of strategy employed.

Findings
Age-Friendly Action Plans

The researcher read through the mission, vision, and value statements of the 38 plans included in this study to determine if improving social connectedness was a guiding principle of the age-friendly work. Fifteen plans did not include mission, vision, or value statements. Of the remaining 23 plans, 17 included encouraging social connectedness. There was no single place—mission, vision, or values—where social connectedness was consistently emphasized. About half of the statements focused on increasing social involvement by older adults ($n = 9$) and half emphasized connectedness for all ages ($n = 8$). Des Moines, Iowa, focused on the contributions of people age 50+ in its mission, which reads, in part: ". . . .promote the civic and social inclusion and contribution of the 50+ population in all areas of community life."

The Age-Friendly Pittsburgh plan took an intergenerational approach. The initiative adopted three guiding principles—action, connection, and innovation. Connection aimed to, ". . . strengthen intergenerational relationships to combat social isolation and loneliness, creating spaces that encourage coming together and celebrating initiatives that put relationships first." Regardless of the approach, the statements indicate that enhancing social connectedness is a priority. The six plans that did not include social connectedness either focused on the role of the age-friendly committee or had a very broad goal of making the community age friendly or livable. All six included goals for social participation in their action plans.

Of the 38 plans reviewed, 35 included the social participation domain. Several plans combined social participation with other domains—such as respect and social inclusion, civic participation and employment, transportation, and outdoor spaces. The most common strategies (followed by at least one example from an action plan) were

- *Raising awareness in the community about how to be more inclusive:* Age-Friendly Cleveland, Ohio, planned to develop a guide with tips to help event planners and organizations plan activities and events that are inclusive of all ages and abilities.
- *Increasing intergenerational opportunities:* Colorado Springs, Colorado, planned to create "adult fitness zones" with exercise equipment to draw adults into parks and develop a guide to help businesses and organizations develop intergenerational programming.
- *Coordinating and distributing information:* West Sacramento, California, planned to start a quarterly printed newsletter with highlighted resources, a list of activities and events, and updates about their age-friendly efforts so that people who do not use the Internet will have ready access to the information they need.
- *Expanding current programs:* Age-Friendly Berkshires, a countywide effort in western Massachusetts, planned to partner with local arts and recreational organizations to create and expand opportunities throughout the county.

- *Involving older people in volunteer opportunities:* One of the tactics developed by Age-Friendly Atlanta, Georgia, to combat social isolation was to recruit older veterans to help aspiring new citizens study for their citizenship test.
- *Training in technology:* Auburn Hills, Michigan, planned to partner with a local high school, a university, and private technology companies to expand technology trainings for older residents.
- *Promoting an age-friendly business program:* Age-Friendly Sausalito, California, planned to partner with local businesses to create an age-friendly business program.
- *Making outdoor spaces more accessible:* One of the tactics used to encourage social connectedness in Honolulu, Hawaii, was to start a beach wheelchair program.
- *Increasing awareness of transportation options:* Corte Madera, California, planned to increase awareness of volunteer driver programs and public transit options.

Thirty-five of the 38 plans reviewed included at least one strategy to encourage social connectedness. However, the action plans do not show whether the strategies were implemented.

AARP NAFC Communities in Maine

Twenty-three of the 26 age-friendly initiatives in Maine that were contacted said that fostering social connectedness was an explicit goal. Some had developed multipronged approaches while others identified one or two strategies. The strategies fell into the following six broad categories (with an example after each):

1. *Services and activities as a tool for social connectedness*: Nineteen initiatives described services and activities that increase opportunities for social connections. Age-Friendly Readfield volunteers deliver buckets of sand and conversation during the winter months to residents who are isolated because of mobility impairment. The city of Eastport donated space for a senior center that is open for games and socialization 5 days a week.
2. *Communication*: Fourteen initiatives described communication strategies to reach isolated residents. The age-friendly team in Yarmouth, Maine, works with local organizations to create a wide variety of activities that meet different interests. The group spreads the word in a free quarterly paper newsletter, posts on social media, and distributes paper fliers at the library and town hall. Free rides assure that transportation is not a barrier.
3. *Transportation*: Seven initiatives developed transportation programs to encourage social participation. Bethel Area Age-Friendly Community

Initiative volunteers provide rides to medical appointments, errands, social and recreational activities, and community events.

4. *Creating social opportunities for isolated residents*: Six initiatives described activities designed specifically to increase the social connectedness of isolated residents. In Age-Friendly Saco, the Hampton Inn offers a special rate for older residents to enjoy a "stay-cation" during the winter months. The hotel provides van service to activities and a place for the "stay-cationers" to socialize. Age-Friendly Bowdoinham gives elevated garden beds to isolated residents who use the food pantry and have a mobility impairment. A new social group, "Not Your Mother's Garden Club," is open to everyone but focuses on the elevated gardens.

5. *Outdoor spaces and buildings*: Five initiatives addressed barriers in the physical environment that kept people from engaging in the community. Age-Friendly Bucksport's *Show You Care* campaign encourages public and private buildings to make simple changes, such as an automatic door opener and easier access to parking, for people with a disability, that make the community more welcoming for everyone. Age-Friendly Portland developed an age-friendly business program to encourage businesses to create welcoming spaces, services, and products for the community's aging population.

6. *Intergenerational volunteering*: Four of the age-friendly initiatives described intergenerational volunteer opportunities developed to increase social connectedness. In Cumberland, Greely High School students help older people with outdoor chores and routine home maintenance. On the Blue Hill Peninsula, the age-friendly team is working with high school students on a project to record the oral histories of residents.

While many of the Maine cities and towns enrolled in the NAFC developed strategies to increase the social connectedness of their community, they were also aware that not everyone wants to spend time with other people in the community. The age-friendly initiatives sought to increase opportunities by addressing barriers so that those residents who wanted to become more engaged in community life could do so.

SUMMARY AND LIMITATIONS

This exploratory study suggests that communities in the AARP NAFC plan to increase social connectedness. However, there are several limitations that need to be considered. Although there are many models of age-friendly community development, this study only included communities that are part of the AARP NAFC. The choice was one of convenience; membership in the NAFC requires that communities create a written action plan and those plans are posted to the online list of AARP NAFC member communities. The requirement for a plan framed by the eight domains of livability increased the comparability of the plans. A second, related weakness is that the AARP NAFC is less than 8 years old. The first communities enrolled on April 4, 2012. None of the municipalities has completed an approved evaluation, so there is no way to know if the plans were implemented, and if they were implemented, whether they increased social contacts or social participation. The NAFC communities in Maine described initiatives implemented to increase social connections but had not evaluated the work to find out if the initiatives were successful. A third limitation is that the researcher works with AARP Maine to support NAFC communities. As an engaged advocate, there is a pro–age-friendly bias in the presentation of these results. Although NAFC planning happens at the local level so the ideas shared by Maine communities reflected the community context and what residents need to thrive, it is also possible that the communities could have been motivated to share what they had done to increase social connectedness by a desire for their work to be perceived as "effective" by AARP Maine.

Despite the weaknesses of this exploratory study, it suggests that the AARP NAFC framework effectively encourages municipalities that have joined the NAFC to consider how the age-friendly effort can increase social connectedness. Of the AARP NAFC plans reviewed, 92% included strategies to encourage social participation and 88% of Maine communities developed strategies to increase social connectedness. Many communities used a multipronged approach to create an environment and infrastructure that supports active involvement by older residents. This is an important finding because social connectedness at the local level is a key contributor to the health and well-being of older people. The innovative, multipronged approaches adopted in NAFC communities may increase the social connectedness of older residents and, in turn, enrich community and economic development in communities that join the AARP NAFC.

REFERENCES

AARP. (2014). The AARP Nnetwork of Aage-Ffriendly Ccommunities: An Iintroduction. *AARP Network of Age-Friendly States and Communities*. Retrieved from http://www.aarp.org/livable-communities/network-age-friendly-communities/info-2014/an-introduction.html

AARP. (2018, August). 2018 Home and Community Preferences Survey: A National Survey of adults age 18–plus. Retrieved from www.aarp.org/livablesurvey2018

AARP & Oxford Economics. (2016). *The Llongevity Eeconomy: How Ppeople over 50 are Ddriving Eeconomic and Ssocial Vvalue in the US*. Washington, DC: AARP. Retrieved from https://www.aarp.org/content/dam/aarp/home-and-family/personal-technology/2016/09/2016-Longevity-Economy-AARP.pdf

Alley, D., Liebig, P., Pynoos, J., Banerjee, T., & Choi, I. H. (2007). Creating elder-friendly communities: Preparations for an aging society. *Journal of Gerontological Social Work*, 49(1–2), 1–18. doi:10.1300/j083v49n01_01

Black, K., Dobbs, D., & Young, T. L. (2012). Aging in community: Mobilizing a new paradigm of older adults as a core social resource. *Journal of Applied Gerontology*, 34(2), 219–243. doi:10.1177/0733464812463984

Buffel, T., McGarry, P., Phillipson, C., De Donder, L., Dury, S., De Witte, N., . . . Verté D. (2014). Developing age-friendly cities: Case studies from Brussels and Manchester and implications for policy and practice. *Journal of Aging & Social Policy*, 26(1–2), 52–72. doi:10.1080/08959420.2014.855043

Burns, V. F., Lavoie, J. P., & Rose, D. (2012). Revisiting the role of neighbourhood change in social exclusion and inclusion of older people. *Journal of Aging Research*, (2012), 1482–1487. doi:10.1155/2012/148287

De Koning, J. L., Stathi, A., & Richards, S. (2017). Predictors of loneliness and different types of social isolation of rural-living older adults in the United Kingdom. *Ageing & Society*, 37(10), 2012–2043. doi:10.1017/s0144686x16000696

Emlet, C. A., & Moceri, J. T. (2011). The importance of social connectedness in building age-friendly communities. *Journal of Aging Research*, 2012, 1–9. doi:10.1155/2012/173247

Erickson, L. D., Call, V. R., & Brown, R. B. (2012). SOS—satisfied or stuck, why older rural residents stay put: Aging in place or stuck in place in rural Utah. *Rural Sociology*, 77(3), 408–434. doi:10.1111/j.1549-q831.2012.00084.x

Feldman, P. H., Oberlink, M. R., Simantov, E., & Gursen, M. D. (2004). *A tale of two older Americas: Community opportunities and challenges.* New York, NY: Center for Home Care Policy and Research.

Finkelstein, R., & Netherland, J. (2010). Age-friendly New York City. In D. Vlahov, J. I. Boufford, C. Pearson, & L. Norris (Eds.), *Urban health: Global perspectives* (pp. 91–103). San Francisco, CA: Jossey-Bass.

Gilroy, R. (2008). Places that support human flourishing: lessons from later life. *Planning Theory & Practice*, 9(2), 145–163. doi:10.1080/14649350802041548.

Glicksman, A., Ring, L., & Kleban, M. H. (2016). Defining a framework for age-friendly interventions. *Journal of Housing for the Elderly*, 30(2), 175–184. doi:10.1080/02763893.2017.1309925

Helliwell, J. F., & Putnam, R. D. (2004). The social context of well-being. *Philosophical Transactions of the Royal Society B: Biological Sciences*, 359(1449), 1435–1446. doi:10.1098/rstb.2004.1522

Hillcoat-Nalletamby, S., & Ogg, J. (2014). Moving beyond "ageing in place": Older people's dislikes about their home and neighborhood environments as a motive for wishing to move. *Ageing and Society*, 34(10), 1771–1796. doi:10.1017/SO144686X13000482

Hogan, M. J., Leyden, K. M., Conway, R., Goldberg, A., Walsh, D., & McKenna-Plumley, P. E. (2016). Happiness and health across the lifespan in five major cities: The impact of place and government performance. *Social Science & Medicine*, 162, 168–176. doi:10.1016/j.socscimed.2016.06.030

Humphreys, J. M., & Kochut, B. (2013). *Golden rules: A study commissioned by the One Georgia Rural Policy Center.* Athens, GA: University of Georgia, Terry College of Business, Selig Center for Economic Growth. Retrieved from https://www.terry.uga.edu/media/documents/selig/golden-rules-2013.pdf

Jacobs, J. M., Hammerman-Rozenberg, A., & Stessman, J. (2018). Frequency of leaving the house and mortality from age 70 to 95. *Journal of the American Geriatrics Society*, 66(1), 106–112. doi:10.1111/jgs.15148

Jackson, T., Illsley, B., Curry, J., & Rapaport, E. (2008). Amenity migration and sustainable development in remote resource-based communities: Lessons from northern British Columbia. *International Journal of Society Systems Science, 1*(1), 26–48. doi:10.1504/IJSSS.2008.020044

Jeste, D. V., Blazer, D. G., Buckwalter, K. C., Cassidy, K. L. K., Fishman, L., Gwyther, L. P., . . . Feather, J. (2016). Age-friendly communities initiative: Public health approach to promoting successful aging. *The American Journal of Geriatric Psychiatry, 24*(12), 1158–1170. doi:10.1016/j.jagp.2016.07.021

Jivraj, S., Nazroo, J., & Barnes, M. (2012). Change in social detachment in older age in England. In J. Banks, J. Nazroo, & A. Steptoe (Eds.), *The dynamics of ageing. Evidence from the English longitudinal study of ageing 2002-2010 (Wave 5)*. Retrieved from http://www.ifs.org.uk/ELSA/publicationDetails/id/6367

Kaye, L. W. (2017). Older adults, rural living, and the escalating risk of social isolation. *Public Policy & Aging Report, 27*(4), 139–144. doi:10.1093/ppar/prx029

Lambrinos, J. (2013). Age-friendly living in Guanajuato, Mexico. *Generations, 37*(4), 48–50.

Lehning, A. J., & Greenfield, E. A. (2017). Research on age-friendly community initiatives: Taking stock and moving forward. *Journal of Housing for the Elderly, 31*(2), 178–192. doi:10.1080/02763893.2017.1309937

Levasseur, M., Richard, L., Gauvin, L., & Raymond, E. (2010). Inventory and analysis of definitions of social participation found in the aging literature: pProposed taxonomy of social activities. *Social Science & Medicine., 71*(12), 2141–2149. doi:10.1016/j.socscimed.2010.09.041

Lui, C. W., Everingham, J. A., Warburton, J., Cuthill, M., & Bartlett, H. (2009). What makes a community age-friendly: A review of international literature. *Australasian Journal on Ageing, 28*(3), 116–121. doi:10.1111/j.1741-6612.2009.00355.x

Menec, V. H., Hutton, L., Newall, N., Nowicki, S., Spina, J., & Veselyuk, D. (2015). How "age-friendly" are rural communities and what community characteristics are related to age-friendliness? The case of rural Manitoba, Canada. *Ageing & Society, 35*(1), 203–223. doi:10.1017/s0144686x13000627

Menec, V. H., Means, R., Keating, N., Parkhurst, G., & Eales, J. (2011). Conceptualizing age-friendly communities. *Canadian Journal on Aging, 30*(3), 479–493. doi:10.1017/SO144686X13000627

Neal, M. B., DeLaTorre, A. K., & Carder, P. C. (2014). Age-friendly Portland: A university-city-community partnership. *Journal of Aging & Social Policy, 26*(1–2), 88–101. doi:10.1080/08959420.201.854651

Newall, N., McArthur, J., & Menec, V. (2015). A longitudinal examination of social participation, loneliness, and use of physician and hospital services. *Journal of Aging and Health, 27*(3), 500–518. doi:10.1177/0898264314552420

Pettigrew, S., Donovan, R., Boldy, D., & Newton, R. (2014). Older people's perceived causes of and strategies for dealing with social isolation. *Aging & Mental Health, 18*(7), 914–920. doi:10.1080/13607863.2014.899970

Plouffe, L. A., & Kalache, A. (2011). Making communities age friendly: State and municipal initiatives in Canada and other countries. *Gaceta Sanitaria, 25*(S), 131–137. doi:10.1016/j.gaceta.2011.11.001

Rantakokko, M., Iwarsson, S., Vahaluoto, S., Portegijs, E., Viljanen, A., & Rantanen, T. (2014). Perceived environmental barriers to outdoor mobility and feelings of loneliness among community-dwelling older people. *Journals of Gerontology: Medical Sciences, 69*, 1562–1568. doi:10.1093/gerona/glu069

Reinhard, E., Courtin, E., van Lenthe, F. J., & Avendano, M. (2018). Public transport policy, social engagement and mental health in older age: A quasi-experimental evaluation of free bus passes in England. *Journal of Epidemiology and Community Health, 72*, 361–368. doi:10.1136/jech-2017-210038

Rowles, G. D., & Watkins, J. F. (1993). Elderly migration and development in small communities. *Growth and Change, 24*(4), 509–538. doi:10.1111/j.1468-2257.1993.tb00136.x

Ryser, L. M., & Halseth, G. (2013). So you're thinking about a retirement industry? Economic and community development lessons from resource towns in northern British Columbia. *Community Development, 44*(1), 83–96. doi:10.1080/15575330.2012.680476

Scharf, C. A., & Moceri, J. T. (2012). The importance of social connectedness in building age-friendly communities. *Journal of Aging Research, 2012*, 1–9. doi:10.1155/2012/173247

Scharlach, A., & Lehning, A. (2013). Ageing-friendly communities and social inclusion in the United States of America. *Ageing and Society, 33*, 110–136. doi:10.1017/S0144686X12000578.

Shor, E., & Roelfs, D. J. (2015). Social contact frequency and all-cause mortality: aA meta-analysis and meta-regression. *Social Science & Medicine, 128*, 76–86. doi:10.1016/j.socscimed.2015.01.010

United States Department of Labor, Bureau of Labor Statistics. (2016a, January 04). Annual expenditures by age group, 2013. *TED: The Economics Daily*. Retrieved from https://www.bls.gov/opub/ted/2016/annual-expenditures-by-age-group-2013.htm

United States Department of Labor, Bureau of Labor Statistics. (2016b, February 25). *Volunteering in the United States, 2015*. Retrieved from https://www.bls.gov/news.release/volun.nr0.htm

U.S. Census Bureau. (2010). *Table H2: Urban and Rural*.Table H2: Urban and rural. Retrieved from https://factfinder.census.gov/faces/tableservices/jsf/pages/productview.xhtml?pid=DEC_10_SF1_H2&prodType=table

U.S. Census Bureau. (2017). Statistics for owners of respondent employer firms by owner's age by sector, gender, ethnicity, race, veteran status, and years in business for the U.S., States, and top 50 MSAs: 2015 annual survey of entrepreneurs, Retrieved from https://factfinder.census.gov/faces/tableservices/jsf/pages/productview.xhtml?src=bkmk

Vogt, C. A., Kho, C., & Sia, A. (2017). Urban greening and its role in fostering human well-being. In P. Y. Tan & C. Y. Jim (Eds.), *Greening cities: Forms and functions* (pp. 95–111). Singapore: Springer.

Wahl, H. W., Iwarsson, S., & Oswald, F. (2012). Aging well and the environment: Toward an integrative model and research agenda for the future. *The Gerontologist, 52*(3), 306–316. doi:10.1093/geront/gnr154

Whitman, D. (2013). Age-friendly communities. *AARP International: The Journal*, 14–17. Available from http://www.aarpinternational.org/the-journal/past-editions/aarp-the-journal-2013

Wiersma, E. C., & Denton, A. (2013). From social network to safety net: Dementia-friendly communities in rural northern Ontario. *Dementia, 15*(1), 51–68. doi:10.1177/1471301213516118

Wiles, J. L., & Jayasinha, R. (2013). Care for place: The contributions older people make to their communities. *Journal of Aging Studies, 27*(2), 93–101. doi:10.1016/j.jaging.2012.12.001

World Health Organization. (2007). *Towards an age-friendly world*. Retrieved from http://www.who.int/ageing/age-friendly-world/en

8

Healthy Places and the Social Life of Older Adults

Keith Diaz Moore, Ivis Garcia, and Ja Young Kim

INTRODUCTION

The impact that social life has upon later life has received significant investigation within gerontology for decades (Carstensen, 1993; Cumming & Henry, 1961; Dannefer, 2003; Kahn & Antonucci, 1980). Wong and Waite (2016) suggest that social relationships influence aging well through both main effects and stress buffering. Main effect influences are exemplified by social relations directly encouraging healthier lifestyle choices and providing needed care when one is ill. Stress buffering suggests that emotional, informational, or tangible resources (e.g., food, money) are provided to promote the adaptive capacity of the receiving older individual. In both cases, healthy aging is viewed as not just an attribute of the individual, but of the reciprocal transactions between the older adult and his or her environment.

Often, social gerontology limits the conceptualization of that environment to social relations. As an example, the highly influential concept of the Convoy Model of Social Supports (Kahn & Antonucci, 1980) suggests that supportive others surround individuals and that these relationships may vary regarding variables such as closeness, quality, function, and structure (Antonucci, Ajrouch, & Birditt, 2013). Smith and Ekerdt (2011) extend this concept to the world of material culture by suggesting that possessions support daily life and self-identity, and thereby create a material convoy. Concerning social isolation, it is clear that not only the microenvironment of possessions but both the mesoenvironment of architecture (e.g., home, institutions, workplaces) and the macroenvironment of neighborhood design and settlement patterns play a significant role. In fact, one could assert that as much as individuals have both social and material convoys, they also have environmental convoys that either constrict or facilitate potential social connectedness.

This chapter examines three intentionally designed and planned places that provide the social and physical connectedness necessary to support healthy aging among historically marginalized populations: (a) older adults across the United States living in or with accessory dwelling units (ADUs); (b) Chicago's ethnically and racially diverse older adults who find an affordable third space at Mather's—More Than a Café (MMC); and (c) Latinx immigrants moving to a senior housing mixed-use development from Centro Civico Mexicano in Salt Lake City.

ENVIRONMENTAL CONVOY OF SOCIAL CONNECTEDNESS

In their chapter, "Theories of Social Connectedness and Aging," Wong and Waite (2016, p. 357) state that "environmental conditions (1) shape the ways individuals access resources and experience the social world, and (2) influence individuals' exposure to pollutants that are detrimental to health." Access and exposure are both critical concepts in understanding the environmental convoy.

First, access may be inhibited or facilitated at the proximate, site, neighborhood, and settlement scales. As an example, for individuals aging-in-place in the same dwelling of their child-rearing years, the home itself may prove increasingly difficult to navigate: upper shelves may become out of reach; household maintenance (e.g., cleaning roof gutters) may no longer be routine; and stairs may become difficult if not dangerous. Even if the home is modified to enable optimal functioning, it may well be situated in a neighborhood whose characteristics may thwart further accessibility. These features may include limited sidewalks or no meaningful destinations within a walkable distance. Or if we think even more broadly, it is possible that both the home and the neighborhood provide optimal functionality and yet can be disconnected from the larger fabric of urban life (e.g., no public transit, no access to cultural functions). Access is, therefore, a concept that must consider the ecology of settings: that the accessibility of room–building–neighborhood–settlement are interrelated, as asserted by the Ecological Framework of Place (Diaz Moore, 2014).

Second, exposure implies the lack of protection from a negative external element, such as pollutants or toxins. Recent research in the area of environmental health has found that

1. Poor outdoor air quality leads to long-term damage to respiratory and cardiovascular systems, increased rates of cancer, and premature death (Curtis, Rea, Smith-Willis, Fenyves, & Pan, 2006).

2. Poor water quality is linked to infection as well as chemical poisoning (G. F. Craun, 1979; M. F. Craun, Gunther, Craun, Calderon, & Beach, 2006).
3. Homes and workplaces may have indoor air pollution, house mold or bacteria, or merely have toxins such as volatile organic compounds (VOCs; S. K. Brown, Sim, Abramson, & Gray, 1994).

The area of health disparities research asserts that racial/ethnic minorities and those of low income are more likely to live in neighborhoods with these types of exposures. The Flint, Michigan, water crisis provides a vivid insight as to how macrolevel policy decisions connect with microlevel exposure, in this case from one's own residential faucets. However, one could extend the concept of exposure to other environmental impacts on social connectedness such as environmental incivilities and crowding.

Together, access and exposure are both about the availability of resources, albeit with access implying availability of a positive resource and exposure the converse. Both are attributes of the person–place transaction as certain characteristics of either the person (e.g., cognitive or physical ability, financial capacity) or the place (e.g., physical accessibility, the presence of incivilities) may alter the degree of accessibility (or exposure) assessed.

SOCIAL CONNECTEDNESS AND AGING-FRIENDLY (HEALTHY) PLACES

Emlet and Moceri (2012) connect the concept of social connectedness to the idea of elder or age-friendly communities. According to Scharlach and Lehning (2015, p. 49), "aging-friendly communities enhance person–environment fit (e.g., mobility and environmental accessibility, residential normalcy and stability, and autonomy) to achieve age-related compensatory goals (e.g., promoting safety and security while protecting physical and mental well-being) and enabling goals (e.g., facilitating engagement in meaningful social roles and other opportunities for personal fulfillment)." More specifically, they offer an "integrated model" of what those goals would be, such as

1. *Continuity:* self-construct preservation
2. *Compensation:* behavioral and psychological adaptation to challenges
3. *Control:* preservation of self-efficacy
4. *Connection:* meaningful interpersonal relationships
5. *Contribution:* generativity in public or private spheres
6. *Challenge:* stimulation and growth in multiple domains of functioning

In very recent work, Diaz Moore, Greenfield, and Scharlach (2018, p. 345) define healthy places as "those milieus of people, program and physical settings that facilitate continuity, compensation, control, connection, contribution, and challenge/comfort." By this definition, healthy places would be both "aging-friendly" and promote social connectedness, as asserted by Emlet and Moceri.

DESIGN AND PLANNING RESPONSES TO SOCIAL ISOLATION OF OLDER ADULTS

The issue of social isolation of older adults has predicates in the design choices our society has made over the last 100 years. From conceptualizing aging primarily within a biomedical perspective (and hence the archetype of the nursing home based upon hospital design [Vladeck, 1980]) to separate zoning (which has led to the placement of many nursing homes and assisted livings at the fringes of communities rather than at their core [Kling, 2002]), design responses to our aging demographic have treated them primarily in terms of loss and otherness. Separating older adults and those with chronic conditions from the broader community has tended to physically embody the stigmatization of aging (Charmaz, 1983).

Yet, change has been afoot since the 1980s, with the recognition of trailblazing older adults creating naturally occurring retirement communities (Lysack & Stark, 2016), the emergence of assisted living and memory care facilities in the 1990s (Cohen & Weisman, 1991; Regnier, 1994), the growth in adult day services and Program for All-Inclusive Care for the Elderly (PACE) models in the early 21st century (Diaz Moore, Geboy, & Weisman, 2006), and a variety of grassroots age-friendly community initiatives (AFCIs) launched over the last decade (Diaz Moore et al., 2018). In each case, a richer and more systemic understanding of the aging experience has driven design innovation, often with social isolation as a critical driver of change. Unfortunately, our fragmented approach to care provision for older adults makes navigating access to these valuable alternatives challenging.

This section briefly describes three emergent models of design and planning responses to social isolation that provide critical insights into the next generation of environmental opportunities our society needs to provide those in the third and fourth age (Weiss & Bass, 2001).

Accessory Dwelling Units

ADUs are small houses built on the same lot as a stand-alone single-family home. They typically have their own kitchen, bedroom(s), and bathroom space. Throughout the United States, ADUs are called by many names: accessory apartment, ancillary unit, backyard cottage, *casita* (little house), garden suite, granny flat, in-law unit, and secondary unit, among others. While the concept of an ADU is not new, it has been advocated as a valuable strategy to support aging-in-place by providing economic support to individual homeowners and enhancing social connectedness (Gellen, 1985; Liebig, Koenig, & Pynoos, 2006; Varady, 1990).

The majority of older adults want to "age-in-place"—that is, live in their homes and communities as long as possible (Farber, Shinkle, Lynott, Fox-Grage, & Harrell, 2011). However, current housing arrangements (e.g., single family homes) may not meet the changing needs of a household's life cycle (Howe, 1990). This is likely to be exacerbated by the growing trend of grandparents caring for their grandchildren. Moreover, older adults tend to live on a fixed income and might become unable to maintain an unnecessarily large house in later life (Municipal Research & Services Center of Washington [MRSC], 1995). With this in mind, we can look at ADUs in two ways: older adults as either ADU owners or ADU renters. First, the young-old, typically the "empty nesters," are more likely to add ADUs (Chapman & Howe, 2001). In the case of Portland, Oregon, 46% of ADU owners are 55 years and older. Of special importance, a higher proportion of ADU owners in the 55- to 64-year-old and 65- to 74-year-old age groups, respectively, form about 29% and 17% of ADU owners, versus 21% and 11% of all Portland homeowners (M. J. Brown & Palmeri, 2014). In the San Francisco Bay Area, although there seem to be no critical demographic differences between homeowners with ADUs and those without ADUs, the former are slightly older, moderately lower income, and somewhat more racially/ethnically diverse (Wegmann & Chapple, 2012).

In general, the age distribution of ADU renters and all renters are similar in shape. Studies found no significant difference between the two groups in terms of median age; however, it is interesting to note that the distribution of ADU renters is binomial with a high concentration in young tenants under age 30 and those over age 65 (Chapman & Howe, 2001).

ADUs and Social Connectedness

The key difference between ADUs and other housing developments seems to be the empowerment of homeowners with choice and control. Each homeowner is the decision maker of creating ADUs in the first place and then manages the renter relationship as life circumstance demands. Although developers and investors do not care much about to whom they rent their housing units, homeowners of ADUs choose the renters carefully because they are finding people who will reside on the same lot in very close proximity. Thus, the relationships between ADU owners and renters need to be based on trust. This explains why a significant portion of ADUs are occupied by homeowners' families and friends.

ADUs allow individuals and families opportunities to live close to one another, facilitating compensation. About 80% of caregiving is provided by one's family, and the physical proximity an ADU provides may benefit the caregiving relationship (Koebel, Beamish, & Danielsen, 2003; Liebig et al., 2006). Considering the unpredictability of caregiving needs for aging parents, Chapman and Howe (2001) argue that adding an ADU allows evolution in its use over time to best fit family needs. Besides caregiving aspects, multigenerational families strengthen family ties, and can reduce the parenting burdens of child care on the adult children comprising the middle generation (Liebig et al., 2006; Uhlenberg, 2000).

A diversity of housing types can create "life cycle communities" which are good places for people of all ages to live (Chapman & Howe, 2001; Freshley, 1995). Whether living with family members or significant others, ADUs enable social connection by maintaining older adults in their lifelong communities (Antoninetti, 2008; Koebel et al., 2003; Liebig et al., 2006). ADUs stimulate social connectedness by increasing the interactions among generations and learning the value of service to each other.

ADUs: Keys to Success

Despite the growing attention on ADUs and their potential to provide social connectedness (Cobb & Dvorak, 2000), there are obstacles to building ADUs in many jurisdictions in the United States. These include concerns over traffic and/or parking, increased density, and concerns over possible negative impact on property values. Many of these concerns can be overcome; however, it is crucial that the neighborhood residents form a consensus on ADU development with shared goals. While some communities would benefit from ADUs as an aging-in-place strategy enhancing social connectedness and social sustainability, others might view ADUs as a way of providing affordable housing and mitigating the housing crisis. In addition, ADUs, as a source of additional income to aging homeowners, would enable some communities to revitalize with young working professionals and students. Each aspiration could inform action within neighborhoods prepared for innovation. The development of model ordinances, demonstration programs, and the like within such leading-edge neighborhoods will prove essential in the diffusion of this housing approach to enable aging-in-place.

Mather (More Than a) Cafés

In 2000, Mather Lifeways, a Chicago-area–based not-for-profit foundation focused on issues of older adults, launched its first Mather Café, which has now evolved into Mather's—More Than a Café. Described as a hybrid between a neighborhood café and a senior center (Rosenbaum, Sweeney, & Windhorst, 2009), MMCs offer customers typical café options (e.g., breakfast, lunch, snacks) but also a range of daily activities such as yoga, art classes, blood pressure screenings, and the like. In other words, it is a café with enhanced sociability through active programming for its patrons. More recently, MMCs now offer extended wellness options to older adults through both "telephone topics," or scheduled conference calls on a range of topics, and lifestyle tips sent to patrons through email, Facebook, or Twitter.

Currently, Mather Lifeways operates three MMCs in the Chicago metropolitan area, all located in lower income to middle-income neighborhoods with a significant aging population (Windhorst, Hollinger-Smith, & Sassen, 2010). The demographics of one neighborhood, Chatham, are 98% Black, 99.4% non-White with a median household income of $35,300/year (statisticalatlas.com). Each MMC offers a tailored café menu, in this case offering items such as "loaded grits with toast," and chicken and waffles. All MMCs offer a bottomless cup of coffee for less than a dollar, and the Chatham café offers a cup of soup for "the price of the temperature" during winter, reflecting its philanthropic orientation. Similarly, its programming offers both common as well as customized offerings. Programming includes computer classes (such as "Getting Started With Facebook"), cooking, exercise, and other informational classes (matherlifeways.com). The MMC organizes not only daylong cultural trips (e.g., Chicago Symphony Orchestra) but also multiple day trips (e.g., travel to Branson, MO). Each MMC has cultural programming, and in February, for instance, the Chatham MMC focuses on Black History Month.

MMC and Social Connectedness

MMCs' basic assumptions are twofold: that older adults prefer to reside in their current homes for as long as possible and that over 80% believe it is the place they will always live (Farber et al., 2011); and that as such, easy and "normalized" access to engagement opportunities in neighborhoods will prove essential (Windhorst et al., 2010). Of the goals for age-friendly communities, MMCs prioritize both continuity and connection.

Regarding continuity, MMCs may well facilitate older adults to age-in-place longer in the residence of their choice. In so doing, the rituals of daily life can be extended in a predictable and familiar environment. MMCs promote belonging through creating a "hybrid third place"; one that looks and feels like a typical café, but offering enhanced programming more familiar to a senior center. These programs are then merely available choices, furthering a sense of control for those participating by making participating entirely optional. A sense of belonging within this hybridized third place allows Mather Lifeways to provide an easier means of access to the otherwise fragmented realm of care for older adults. This is then likely to result in earlier intervention and better health and quality-of-life outcomes over time. Current research on MMCs suggests that visits are strongly associated with increased satisfaction, wellness, and quality-of-life scores (Windhorst et al., 2010), and that one third of attendees find restoration of directed attention (Rosenbaum et al., 2009)—a particularly important consideration for older adults experiencing mild cognitive impairment (Diaz Moore, 2007; Kolanowski et al., 2012).

Maintaining meaningful social relationships is what is meant by the term *connection*. MMCs through providing a third place—defined as places that "host the regular, voluntary, informal, and happily anticipated gatherings of individuals beyond the realms of home and work" (Oldenburg, 1989, p. 16)—affords individuals a sense of belonging to a community. These third places are typified by the neighborhood bar or café, parks, libraries, or, depending on the neighborhood, barber shops and manicure parlors. Oldenburg (1989) identifies the hallmarks of third places as free (no entrance fee or ticket); food and drink; proximate for walking; involves regular attendees; welcoming and comfortable; and both familiar faces and new faces should be found there. As a café where one can attend regularly, MMCs may provide older adults ways to achieve homeostasis in their social networks rather than the decline associated with inevitable death, illness, and relocation of family and friends. As a hybrid third place offering activity programming, neighborhood-residing older adults may engage in activities that provide not only cognitive stimulation but social stimulation as well.

MMC: Keys to Success

Rosenbaum et al. (2009) offer several insights regarding the success of the MMC concept. First is the need to have enough regular attendees who utilize nine activities or more offered by the MMC. Those most likely to become regulars are those who are already more socially integrated, those who participate in more activities and typically do so with a group of friends. Rosenbaum and colleagues suggest that organizations consider developing an ambassador program with the specific purpose of encouraging participation among hard-to-reach groups, such as widowers. Windhorst et al. (2010) identify that the MMC concept is highly adaptable and may inform quasi-Mather Cafés in organizations such as continuing care retirement communities and senior centers. One innovative adaptation is the Millcreek Community Center in Millcreek, Utah. Inspired by the MMC program, this building is an impressive hybridization of the community library, recreation center, and senior center—a union of classic third places all under one roof. In doing so, it integrates, rather than segregates, services for older adults, and reciprocally the growing aging population of the town serves as the place's core constituency. This hybrid community center's "common house" is Café Evergreen serving typical diner fare. Members of the senior center get a significantly discounted price.

Latinx Housing

Centro Civico Mexicano (CCM) is the oldest Hispanic organization in Utah; the nonprofit was founded in 1939 by immigrants from Mexico who came to work in the railroads and mines during World War I (McKellar, 2016). The organization started as a way for immigrant families and individuals to celebrate their culture, traditions, and heritage, as well as promote the overall well-being of the Latinx community. The current mission of CCM is to serve low- to moderate-income individuals in the Salt Lake Valley by providing "educational, cultural, social, and athletic activities" as well as housing (Riddle, 2017b).

A few years ago, CCM recognized the need to develop affordable housing geared toward older adults. Leadership from CCM approached former Salt Lake County Mayor and developer Peter Corroon—who specializes in assisting small nonprofits with little housing development experience—to envision, finance, complete, and sustain affordable housing plans. Together, they planned a six-story, 61-unit senior apartment building and cultural center near Salt Lake City's Depot District in a vacant lot in an area that has been declared blighted (Smart, 2016). A total of 44 units will be affordable at 50% of the area median income (AMI), and 18 units will be market rate (Riddle, 2017a).

Latinx Housing and Social Connectedness

The mixed-income and mixed-use project will include a number of spaces where older adults can be socially connected including a clubhouse with a kitchen, dining area, and an interior courtyard plaza (Gellner, 2017). Most of the facilities in the cultural center (e.g., a multipurpose theater, an art gallery, an exercise room, an open-air teaching/soccer facility, a computer room, game area, classrooms for life-skills classes, and a day-care center) are open to CCM members of all ages (Gellner, 2017). It is expected that many older adults who have interacted with CCM through earlier years of life will choose to move to CCM's senior housing.

The decision of making CCM senior housing a permanent home, as opposed to a third space, offers older adults control and continuity by allowing them to enjoy the relationships they have built over the years, as well as maintaining the interests that brought them there in the first place—being their love for soccer or cultural activities. In addition, CCM encourages lifelong learning by offering classes and challenging older adults to learn new things and acquire new interests. CCM is mostly driven by volunteers, suggesting that older adults could contribute their experience and share their interests with the general Mexican community.

CCM hired Bernando Flores, an architect from Mexico, to incorporate culturally relevant features such as a Mexican-style interior courtyard plaza with seating space, shade trees, outdoor eating areas, and public art (Flores, 2017). This element provides a level of comfort and safety for older adults while at the same time providing them with a space to interact with their neighbors in a familiar setting and with familiar faces.

In addition, the project includes a semipublic midblock walkway, open to the public, that goes through the center of CCM property (Gellner, 2017). This walkway (with its street lighting) is a key strategy to encourage walkability between the senior housing and the cultural center, as well as the broader neighborhood. Sidewalks in front of CCM's retail space are entirely public, and glass has been incorporated at ground level to facilitate pedestrian interest and interaction (Gellner, 2017). Moreover, the plan development is classified "transit-oriented development"—only two blocks from the light rail system named TRAX (Gellner, 2017). It is also located less than one-third of a mile from a public park and a shopping mall (Gellner, 2017).

Latinx Housing: Keys to Success

As demonstrated earlier, three levels of social connection could be exemplified in the design of the CCM plan development: a semiprivate plaza, a semipublic midblock walkway, and public sidewalks to destinations. All of these features are about creating a space that is socially and physically connected, welcoming, and safe for older adults while offering them control or the choice to engage in various activities. Walkable and mixed-use environments are not foreign to older adults from Latin America, who in their countries walked, took transit, and spent time in public plazas. The CCM development is considered "new urbanist," intended to encourage a mix of residential, commercial, and social uses within an urban neighborhood atmosphere. In a way, this project might be considered "Latinx new urbanism" providing

Latinx older adults with a familiar non-suburban environment that satisfies their cultural preferences (Mendez, 2005).

All of these mixed-use elements contribute to livability. The concept of livability outlines best practices for urban residential development for older adults including (a) safety and security; (b) choice and convenience; and (c) relationship to the street and neighborhood (Gellner, 2017). The CCM development has been successful in creating a rich and vibrant urban environment for Latinx older adults while celebrating their way of life, heritage, and helping them to compensate in the context of the potential functional decline in later life. In this way, the project offers continuity for older adults who might transition from visiting CCM to living in the housing-cultural complex. Moreover, they could participate as cocreators of CCM by volunteering their time and contributing to their community. Overall, CCM likely maximizes the well-being of older adults by facilitating continuity, compensation, control, connection, contribution, and challenge/comfort.

SUMMARY

For decades, gerontologists have concentrated on investigating the unique requirements of older adults when it comes to social life. A number of studies have determined that when older adults are surrounded by supportive others, they make healthier lifestyle choices, feel less stressed, are more secure, and can improve their adaptive capacity to the changes they might be experiencing related to aging. But most of these studies tend to overlook the importance of the environment. With that in mind, in this chapter, we have argued that the social life of older adults is largely influenced not only by their social environment but also the physical environment, or what we here discussed as the "environmental convoy." As architects and planners, we have chosen to explore how design innovation in both programming and the built environment—rooms, buildings, neighborhoods, and settlements—might impact connectedness, both social and physical.

Older adults prefer to live in their own home in their own neighborhood rather than in retirement communities. Thus, ADUs allow older adults to build a home in their backyard while family members or renters live in the main unit—adding both extra income and social contact. Older adults could also move into an ADU built by their relatives or significant others, instead of moving to a private institution, keeping their social connections with family and friends. In this way, older adults are able to maintain social connectedness while having their space independence by aging-in-place. ADUs can be a relatively flexible option during someone's life cycle—they could be rented for extra income, receive family and friends when needed, and so on. Because they are located alongside single family homes, they can also contribute to the diversity of a neighborhood in terms of both age and kinds of households.

Quality of life for the growing older-adult population depends on their ability to stay in place and live in neighborhoods where third spaces (not home or work) can allow them to remain socially connected through active programming. The MMC was developed with forward thinking on how to leverage the critical role of "third places" to social connectedness in neighborhoods for the purposes of creating a softer transition toward accessing care that promotes independence. MMCs facilitate meaningful, personal, and communal engagement of older adults that is culturally and socioeconomically relevant and increases their overall well-being.

Similarly, the CCM case study shows that many communities have begun to create and plan developments that support the unique needs of older adults and take into account the affordability of housing. CCM does not offer just housing; it is a mixed-use development, showing the importance of proximity to various resources, such as stores, transportation, and other services that are vital to promoting livability and for older adults to maintain an active role in their community. The project is also developed by Latinx for Latinx, and it celebrates the history of this community in Salt Lake City by incorporating elements of the Mexican sociocultural landscape, architecture, and built environment.

By analyzing these three approaches that can combat the social isolation likely experienced by marginalized populations of older adults, we look into the future and the promise of architecture and urban design. To meet the demands of a growing aging population, architecture and urban design need to become more empathetic to the powerful role the environment plays in social connectedness. Not only social convoys but environmental convoys at different scales play a crucial role in providing access as well as supporting and sustaining many older adults' quality of life. The aging experience is not homogeneous nor is the aging population; therefore, diverse approaches to furthering social connectedness through design and planning innovation should only increase in prevalence. The creative use of places, from programming to their spatial organization, make it possible for older adults to realize their well-being while enjoying a life firmly connected to the people and the places they love and that foster their self-identity.

REFERENCES

Antoninetti, M. (2008). The difficult history of ancillary units: The obstacles and potential opportunities to increase the heterogeneity of neighborhoods and the flexibility of households in the United States. *Journal of Housing for the Elderly, 22*(4), 348–375. doi:10.1080/02763890802458320

Antonucci, T. C., Ajrouch, K. J., & Birditt, K. S. (2013). The convoy model: Explaining social relations from a multidisciplinary perspective. *The Gerontologist, 54*(1), 82–92. doi:10.1093/geront/gnt118

Brown, M. J., & Palmeri, J. (2014). *Accessory dwelling units in Portland, Oregon: Evaluation and interpretation of a survey of ADU owners*. Portland, OR: Department of Environmental Quality.

Brown, S. K., Sim, M. R., Abramson, M. J., & Gray, C. N. (1994). Concentrations of volatile organic compounds in indoor air–A review. *Indoor Air, 4*(2), 123–134. doi:10.1111/j.1600-0668.1994.t01-2-00007.x

Carstensen, L. L. (1993). Motivation for social contact across the life span: A theory of socioemotional selectivity. *Nebraska Symposium on Motivation, 40*, 209–254.

Chapman, N. J., & Howe, D. A. (2001). Accessory apartments: Are they a realistic alternative for ageing in place? *Housing Studies, 16*(5), 637–650. doi:10.1080/02673030120080099

Charmaz, K. (1983). Loss of self: A fundamental form of suffering in the chronically ill. *Sociology of Health & Illness, 5*(2), 168–195. doi:10.1111/1467-9566.ep10491512

Cobb, R. L., & Dvorak, S. (2000). *Accessory Ddwelling Uunits: Model Sstate Aact and Llocal Oordinance*. Public Policy Institute of the AARP. Retrieved from https://assets.aarp.org/rgcenter/consume/d17158_dwell.pdf

Cohen, U., & Weisman, G. D. (1991). *Holding on to home: Designing environments for people with dementia*. Baltimore, MD: Johns Hopkins University Press.

Craun, G. F. (1979). Waterborne disease—A status report emphasizing outbreaks in ground-water systems. *Ground Water, 17*(2), 183–191. doi:10.1111/j.1745-6584.1979.tb03300.x

Craun, M. F., Gunther, F., Craun, R., Calderon, L., & Beach, M. J. (2006). Waterborne outbreaks reported in the United States. *Journal of Water and Health, 4*(S2), 19–30. doi:10.2166/wh.2006.016

Cumming, E., & Henry, W. E. (1961). *Growing old, the process of disengagement*. New York, NY: Basic Books.

Curtis, L., Rea, W., Smith-Willis, P., Fenyves, E., & Pan, Y. (2006). Adverse health effects of outdoor air pollutants. *Environment International, 32*(6), 815–830. doi:10.1016/j.envint.2006.03.012

Dannefer, D. (2003). Cumulative advantage/disadvantage and the life course: Cross-fertilizing age and social science theory. *The Journals of Gerontology Series B: Psychological Sciences and Social Sciences, 58*(6), S327–S337. doi:10.1093/geronb/58.6.S327

Diaz Moore, K. (2007). Restorative dementia gardens: Exploring how design may ameliorate attention fatigue. *Journal of Housing for the Elderly, 21*(1–2), 73–88. doi:10.1300/J081v21n01_05

Diaz Moore, K. (2014). An ecological framework of place: Situating environmental gerontology within a life course perspective. *The International Journal of Aging and Human Development, 79*(3), 183–209. doi:10.2190/AG.79.3.a

Diaz Moore, K., Geboy, L., & Weisman, G. (2006). *Designing a better day: Guidelines for adult and dementia day services centers*. Baltimore, MD: Johns Hopkins University Press.

Diaz Moore, K., Greenfield, E., & Scharlach, A. (2018). Healthy aging and its implications for public health: Healthy communities. In W. A. Satariano & M. Maus (Eds.), *Aging, place, and health*. Burlington, MA: Jones & Bartlett.

Emlet, C. A., & Moceri, J. T. (2012). The importance of social connectedness in building age-friendly communities. *Journal of Aging Research, 2012*, 1–9. doi:10.1155/2012/173247

Farber, N., Shinkle, D., Lynott, J., Fox-Grage, W., & Harrell, R. (2011). *Aging in place: A state survey of livability policies and practices*. Retrieved from https://trid.trb.org/view/1128168

Flores, B. (2017, August 23). "PLNSUB2017-00370 & PLNPCM2017-00525–Centro Civico Senior Housing–Planned Development & Conditional Building and Site Design Review." Planning Commission, Salt Lake City, UT: Planning Division.

Freshley, H. (1995). Planning in an aging society: Examples from the Twin Cities, In American Association of Retired Persons (Ed.), *Expanding housing choices for older people: Conference papers and recommendations*. Washington, DC: American Association of Retired Persons.

Gellen, M. (1985). *Accessory apartments in single-family housing*. New Brunswick, NJ: Center for Urban Policy Research.

Gellner, D. (2017, August 23). "PLNSUB2017-00370 & PLNPCM2017-00525–Centro Civico Senior Housing–Planned Development & Conditional Building and Site Design Review." Planning Commission. Salt Lake City, UT: Planning Division.

Howe, D. A. (1990). The flexible house designing for changing needs. *Journal of the American Planning Association*, 56(1), 69–77. doi:10.1080/01944369008975746

Kahn, R. L., & Antonucci, T. C. (1980). Convoys over the life course: Attachment, roles, and social support. In P.B. Baites & O. G. Brim, Jr. (Eds.), *Life-Span Development and Behavior* (Vol. 3, pp. 253–267). New York: Academic Press.

Kling, M. (2002). Zoned out: Assisted-living facilities and zoning. *Elder Law Journal*, 10, 187. Retrieved from http://publish.illinois.edu/elderlawjournal/files/2015/02/Kling.pdf

Koebel, C. T., Beamish, J., & Danielsen, K. A. (2003). *Evaluation of the HUD Elder Cottage Housing Opportunity (ECHO) program*. Virginia Polytechnic Institute and State University. Retrieved from http://digitalscholarship.unlv.edu/sea_fac_articles/351

Kolanowski, A. M., Fick, D. M., Yevchak, A. M., Hill, N. L., Mulhall, P. M., & McDowell, J. A. (2012). Pay attention! The critical importance of assessing attention in older adults with dementia. *Journal of Gerontological Nursing*, 38(11), 23–27. doi:10.3928/00989134-20121003-05

Liebig, P. S., Koenig, T., & Pynoos, J. (2006). Zoning, accessory dwelling units, and family caregiving: Issues, trends, and recommendations. *Journal of Aging & Social Policy*, 18(3–4), 155–172. doi:10.1300/j031v18n03_11

Lysack, C., & Stark, S. (2016). Naturally occurring retirement communities. In S.K. Whitbourne (Ed.), *The Encyclopedia of Adulthood and Aging*. Hoboken, NJ: Wiley. doi:10.1002/9781118521373.wbeaa001

McKellar, K. (2016). Centro Civico Mexicano wins $400K in grants for cleanup, renovations. Retrieved from https://www.ksl.com/?sid=42393600

Mendez, M. (2005). Latino new urbanism: Building on cultural preferences. *Opolis*, 1(1), 33–48. Retrieved from https://escholarship.org/uc/item/0mz4k5pb.pdf

Municipal Research & Services Center of Washington. (1995). *Accessory Ddwelling Uunits: Iissues and Ooptions*. Retrieved from http://mrsc.org/getmedia/54c058a5-4d57-4192-a214-15f2fa5ac123/Accessory-Dwelling-Units.pdf.aspx?ext=.pdf

Oldenburg, R. (1989). *The great good place: Café, coffee shops, community centers, beauty parlors, general stores, bars, hangouts, and how they get you through the day*. New York, NY: House.

Regnier, V. (1994). *Assisted living housing for the elderly: Design innovations from the United States and Europe*. New York, NY: Van Nostrand Reinhold.

Riddle, I. (2017a, July 31). Commission wants more life from Centro Civico proposal. *Building Salt Lake*. Retrieved from https://www.buildingsaltlake.com/commission-wants-life-centro-civico-proposal

Riddle, I. (2017b, July 11). Council considers housing loan for Centro Civico. *Building Salt Lake*. Retrieved from https://www.buildingsaltlake.com/council-considers-housing-loan-centro-civico

Rosenbaum, M. S., Sweeney, J. C., & Windhorst, C. (2009). The restorative qualities of an activity-based, third place café for seniors: Restoration, social support, and place attachment at Mather's--More Than a Café. *Seniors Housing & Care Journal, 17*(1), 39–54.

Scharlach, A., & Lehning, A. (2015). *Creating aging-friendly communities*. Oxford, UK: Oxford University Press.

Smart, C. (2016). Centro Civico Mexicano and Latino community to get a big, new home. *The Salt Lake Tribune*. Retrieved from http://archive.sltrib.com/article.php?id=4649663&itype=CMSID

Smith, G. V., & Ekerdt, D. J. (2011). Confronting the material convoy in later life. *Sociological Inquiry, 81*(3), 377–391. doi:10.1111/j.1475-682X.2011.00378.x

Uhlenberg, P. (2000). Introduction: Why study age integration? *The Gerontologist, 40*(3), 261–266. doi:10.1093/geront/40.3.261

Varady, D. P. (1990). Which elderly home owners are interested in accessory apartment conversion and home-sharing. *Journal of Housing for the Elderly, 6*(1), 87–100. doi:10.1300/J081V06N01_06

Vladeck, B. C. (1980). *Unloving care: The nursing home tragedy*. New York, NY: Basic Books.

Wegmann, J., & Chapple, K. (2012). Understanding the market for secondary units in the east bay. Berkeley: Institute of Urban and Regional Development, University of California, Berkeley. Retrieved from http://escholarship.org/uc/item/9932417c.pdf

Weiss, R. & Bass, S., (Eds.). (2001). *Challenges of the Third Age: Meaning and purpose in later life*. OXford, UK: Oxford University Press.

Windhorst, C., Hollinger-Smith, L., & Sassen, B. (2010). The café plus concept: A different model for different times. *Generations, 34*(1), 91–93.

Wong, J., & Waite, L. (2016). Theories of social connectedness and aging. In V. Bengston & R. Setterson, Jr. (Eds.), *Handbook of theories of aging* (3rd ed., 349–364). New York, NY: Springer Publishing.

9

Volunteering as a Strategy for Combatting Social Isolation

Jennifer A. Crittenden

INTRODUCTION

Socially isolated older adults often lack opportunities to establish the social connections that support positive health and well-being. Volunteering, either formal or informal, is one strategy to prevent and even address social isolation among older adults.

Volunteering is a common activity among older adults with as many as 11 million people over the age of 65 volunteering each year in the United States, amounting to nearly a quarter of the overall older adult population. The amount of time and effort spent through such endeavors is considerable. In fact, adults age 65 and older provide close to 2 billion hours of volunteer service to their local communities each year totaling over $45 billion of economic value annually (Corporation for National and Community Service, 2016).

Depending on the type of volunteer work completed and the circumstances surrounding the activity, volunteering can be considered either formal or informal. The former is defined as volunteering that is facilitated by a third party, often a nonprofit or civic organization, and the latter form of volunteering constituting time, effort, and assistance provided to others in the community through informal social networks. Informal volunteering is often excluded from official counts of volunteer efforts. When including both formal and informal volunteering in the accounting of volunteer time, as many as 75% of adults age 50 and older volunteer. However, overall participation in formal volunteering is declining, while informal volunteering is increasing slightly among adults age 50 and older (Williams, 2016).

In addition to the different types of volunteering, there are important variations in volunteer participation between different gender and ethnic groups. Generally speaking, women are more likely to participate in volunteer activities compared to men, and when doing so, also tend to commit more time and effort to volunteering than men (Manning, 2010; Williams, 2016). In reviewing statistics about volunteer participation rates, it is important to note that there are key groups of individuals who are often excluded from these data. For example, people with disabilities, older adults from lower socioeconomic backgrounds, individuals who lack social connections, and older adults of color may not be counted. To some extent this lack of visibility within formal volunteering may be due to institutional barriers that keep older adults from participating in formal volunteer work, such as lack of stipends or flexible scheduling (Morrow-Howell, Hong, & Tang, 2009). Furthermore, informal volunteering by older adults of color is particularly common but often not recognized. They may give their time and talent to their communities without a formal organization facilitating such efforts, or even without personal recognition that helping neighbors and friends in need is considered volunteering (Martinez, Crooks, Kim, & Tanner, 2011). It is for this reason that older adults of color are often excluded from established counts of the volunteer ranks. This "invisible" informal volunteering is often connected with a religious community such as a church or synagogue group, making such organizations key stakeholders in efforts to help older adults remain active and engaged in their communities.

The act of volunteering, particularly for older adults, is well researched and has been found to be associated with many positive health and well-being outcomes, including improved physical and mental health, increased physical activity and socialization, the development of personal resilience against stress, gains in knowledge and skills, and reduced mortality risk (Barron et al., 2009; Corporation for National and Community Service, 2012; Konrath, Fuhrel-Forbis, Lou, & Brown, 2012; Morrow-Howell et al., 2009; Warburton & Onyx, 2003). Research has traditionally focused on formal volunteering over informal volunteering; however, it is important to note that both have been associated with positive outcomes for older adults. In addition to these benefits, volunteering can also provide a much deeper sense of purpose and meaning for older adults. Kopera-Frye and Massey (2014) found that older adult volunteers attribute their volunteer work to positive emotional well-being and a personal sense of reward or feeling "blessed" as a result of giving back to their community. For individuals with disabilities in particular, volunteering serves to create and reinforce a positive sense of self and provide an avenue to increase a sense of control in their lives

(Balandin, Llewellyn, Dew, Ballin, & Schneider, 2006). Among its numerous benefits, volunteering is a strategy to combat loneliness and isolation among older adults, especially when such volunteering affords the opportunity to meet new people and increase social interactions (Pettigrew & Roberts, 2008; Smith, 2012; Williams, 2016).

When it comes to formal volunteering, many older adults experience barriers to civic engagement. A study by Martinez et al. (2011) found that African American older adults often face personal and institutional barriers to engaging in volunteerism. Personal barriers include health challenges and personal and familial commitments. Institutional barriers that discourage African Americans from participating in volunteer work include a lack of monetary reimbursement for travel and volunteer-related expenses, and a lack of flexible scheduling that would allow them to pursue personal interests and commitments along with their volunteer obligations. Breaking down the barriers to engagement for these older adults is critical, especially for those older adults who may lack their own personal pathways and connections for volunteering.

Even older adults who reside in nursing homes, those most at risk for social isolation owing to physical or cognitive declines, are able to participate in voluntary pursuits when provided with creative opportunities to do so. Research suggests that as many as a quarter of nursing home residents participate in some form of formal or informal volunteering. Such volunteering can be facilitated by outside organizations such as churches, nonprofits, or civic organizations, or these efforts can be organized from within the nursing home setting. When carried out on-site, volunteering within a nursing home environment can include activities such as visiting other sick residents, tending to a facility/community garden, creating scrapbooks for families and friends, or assisting with facility administrative tasks (Leedahl, Sellon, & Gallopyn, 2017). Even those older adults who have significant health challenges and are at the highest risk for isolation can reap the rewards of volunteering if creative solutions and pathways are offered to such residents.

IMPORTANCE OF VOLUNTEERING: A VIGNETTE

The following vignette illustrating the personal significance of volunteer work is based on the experience of a volunteer participating in a Retired and Senior Volunteer Program (RSVP).[1]

---

[1] Names and some personal circumstances have been changed.

Margaret and her husband are a retired couple living a relatively quiet life at home in a suburban community with their dog, Pete. Prior to retirement, Margaret had worked as a professional staff member at a local college. One day while she was reading the paper, Margaret saw an advertisement from a local nonprofit looking for an older adult volunteer leader for a senior fitness class facilitated by the local RSVP. Up until this point, Margaret and her husband maintained only a few local connections outside their family, and Margaret was interested in reconnecting with others as she settled into her retirement. Recently, Margaret had experienced some health challenges and found herself, as a result, becoming more and more isolated. Despite this, Margaret was keenly interested in volunteering for this fitness group opportunity. After joining the class as a volunteer leader, Margaret experienced gains in both her health and social life. The exercise was giving her newfound strength and the social connections were giving her a sense of purpose and something to look forward to a few times a week. After a short while, Margaret quickly gained the confidence needed to be an inspiring coleader for the exercise group, and the experience brought her new friendships beyond the few that she had maintained prior to her volunteer work. Reflecting on her work, Margaret had this to say about her experience:

> If it were not for being a volunteer, I would be sitting on my couch with a "woe is me" attitude. After all these years in this town, I still only know three or four people. This [volunteer program] has enabled me to meet new people. . . . Thirty plus years at my job kept me in my extrovert mode, and I interacted with so many people. Some were just acquaintances and others became friends. But it seems like once you retire and you're no longer part of that "inner circle," you get forgotten rather quickly. Thanks for letting me be a part of this great program—it's making me whole again and has given me purpose.

Margaret's story clearly illustrates the benefits of volunteering. First, volunteering assists older adults in maintaining social connections and continuity in their lives. According to continuity theory, the pursuit of healthy aging is built on the concept of continuity over the life course as we seek to maintain a sense of continuity with life roles and functions over time (Atchley, 1989). Applied to Margaret's particular situation, we see that her previous employment provided her with the opportunity to interact with others, or what she refers to as her "extrovert mode." Continuity theory suggests that her newfound role as a volunteer has allowed Margaret to once again be in a position of interacting with others, an adaptive strategy when faced with dwindling social connections in retirement.

Second, Margaret's volunteering brought her not only continuity with her prior work roles but also gave her a sense of purpose. Research has historically linked volunteering to the experience of a strong sense of purpose among older adults. This sense of purpose provides a clear reward for the time and effort provided by volunteer endeavors. For older adults like Margaret, volunteering can help to moderate the negative effects of role identity loss and role changes over time, protecting a sense of purpose that may otherwise be lost without volunteering or some other productive activity (Greenfield & Marks, 2004).

As she relates her story, Margaret discusses how retirement put her at risk of experiencing social isolation when she says, "You get forgotten rather quickly." For individuals who place a great deal of importance on their role as a worker, retirement becomes an important transition, one that can either reduce or exacerbate feelings of depression and loneliness. Those individuals who either rely on the workplace for a significant portion of their social interaction or who use work to stave off loneliness are at risk of experiencing negative mental health during this transition time (Segel-Karpas, Ayalon, & Lachman, 2018). For Margaret, the use of volunteering allowed her to successfully transition during a time when she faced the loss of her work role and social connections provided by that role.

As she describes her engagement with the RSVP program, Margaret suggests that without her volunteer work she would be "sitting on my couch" indicating that her volunteer work is a major motivating force for her to leave her home. This too has been supported by existing research that has demonstrated that volunteer work, even when not directly physical in nature, helps older adults to maintain physical activity levels and positive physical health outcomes (Barron et al., 2009; Kopera-Frye & Massey, 2014). Volunteering gives older adults a reason to leave the house and remain active in the community as an alternative to TV viewing or time that would otherwise be spent in sedentary and solitary pursuits. Such work provides a ready-made outlet for engagement in the retirement years.

PATHWAYS TO VOLUNTEERING

National Service

There are a variety of pathways that can lead an older adult into formal and informal volunteer service. This section discusses some existing pathways and opportunities for engagement that can be either accessed locally or replicated through new program efforts.

First, there are existing federal programs designed to connect individuals with volunteer service that are not specifically aimed at older volunteers but engage volunteers from a wide range of ages and backgrounds. The most well known of these include AmeriCorps and the Peace Corps. While traditionally marketed to a younger volunteer set, older adults are increasingly engaging with these programs as a way to contribute to local programs and see other parts of the world.

There are two programs under AmeriCorps that engage adults over the age of 18 in national service. These are the AmeriCorps State and National Program and the AmeriCorps Volunteers in Service to America (VISTA) program. Both programs engage adults who have a range of experience in the target issue areas. The State and National Program deploys volunteers through local and statewide organizations to address a variety of issues of local importance, such as disaster relief, land preservation, and supporting military families. The VISTA program focuses on capacity building within nonprofits and community organizations rather than the provision of direct service. While no experience is necessary, the VISTA program may be a good fit for a retired professional or someone with a background in administrative work. A VISTA assignment can provide job skills training, an opportunity for those older adults looking to stay current or refresh their skills. AmeriCorps volunteer assignments also provide tangible benefits such as a living allowance, healthcare benefits, and an education award (Corporation for National and Community Service, n.d.). Thanks to recent changes in national service programming realized through the Edward M. Kennedy Serve America Act of 2009, the education tuition award earned under a National Service Program is transferrable to a grandchild. This policy change was enacted to encourage more older adults to participate in national service opportunities (Corporation for National and Community Service, 2009).

The Peace Corps, often thought of as the mainstay of postcollege worldly experience, continues to welcome individuals age 50+ into its ranks. Peace Corps assignments take individuals to other countries to complete service in areas of agriculture, environmental issues, economic and community development, education, and youth development. The Peace Corps offers training and support to assist its members in successfully completing their assignments, including medical support and training specific to the assignment and country (Peace Corps, n.d.). Recently, Alice Carter, at the time the oldest Peace Corps volunteer, was interviewed by National Public Radio (2016). In this interview, she discussed her assignment in Morocco and reflected on being an older volunteer, living and working in a foreign country well into her 80s. Interestingly, Alice noted that the Peace Corps helped to expand her social network: Alice notes that her experience with Peace Corps helped her to combat social isolation by making new friends, both from among the

Peace Corps volunteers that were in Morocco with her and among local community members (National Public Radio, 2016).

Aside from AmeriCorps and Peace Corps, there are several federal programs that have been established to create pathways to volunteerism specifically for older adults. The Senior Corps programs, a collection of older adult volunteer programs, are facilitated by the Corporation for National and Community Service and reach out into communities nationwide through local program sites. These programs include the Retired and Senior Volunteer Program, Foster Grandparents Program, and Senior Companion Program. All three programs, while offering different volunteer assignments and focal areas, exclusively recruit and engage adults age 55 and older in volunteer service.

The RSVP engages over 300,000 older adults from across the country in a wide range of volunteer activities from literacy volunteering, disaster services, providing healthy living and healthy aging supports in the community, environmental volunteerism, and supporting veterans and their families. Currently billed as the largest older adult volunteer network in the country, RSVP allows volunteers the flexibility to commit as much or as little volunteer time to their local volunteer work as they see fit. While training and supplemental volunteer insurance is provided, this is not a stipended program (Corporation for National and Community Service, 2013b). Given the breadth of this program and the issue areas addressed, older adults are more likely to find a local assignment that fits their personal volunteer interests.

Foster Grandparents (FG) is a stipended volunteer program that connects older adult volunteers with youth to support their educational, behavioral, and job skills needs. The FG program engages 30,000 older adults in this work and reaches over 280,000 youth in the process. Volunteers carry out their work in various youth settings including schools, day cares, and after-school program sites (Corporation for National and Community Service, 2013a). The FG program model is an easily accessible model of volunteering as it does not require that volunteers have a specialized skill set or a significant amount of formal education to participate in youth mentorship activities. In fact, 21% of older adults serving in the FG program have not completed a high school diploma program. It is also a model that has successfully engaged communities of color in service provision as nearly 41% of FGs are African American (Tan et al., 2016).

Like FG, the Senior Companion program is a stipended program that addresses one of the main institutional barriers to volunteer participation: the personal cost involved in participating in volunteer work. As stipended volunteers, low-income older adults (senior companions) conduct friendly visits, provide socialization, assist with errands and appointments, and provide other supports to older adult clients, allowing them to remain in their homes and communities while they age (Corporation for National and Community Service, 2013c).

Research further supports the personal benefits and social connections derived from participating in programs like Senior Companions and FG. A recent longitudinal study followed older adult volunteers in both of these programs to assess the benefits of participation for volunteers. The results indicate that volunteers in these programs experience an increase in health and well-being outcomes over time as well as a decrease in loneliness, social isolation, and depressive symptoms. A majority of older volunteers (67%) who began the study reporting that they "often" lacked companionship experienced improvements in their social connections over time (Corporation for National and Community Service, 2017). A study conducted by Butler (2006) found that over 40% of senior companions interviewed noted companionship as a key benefit of their volunteer work, and over a quarter of those interviewed noted that their volunteer work provided them with an opportunity to remain active and avoid stagnation in their lives.

Other Volunteer Models

The Senior Companion program model is one example of a volunteer program model that focuses on facilitating friendships between a friendly visitor (volunteer) and an older adult. In some cases, such programs pair two older adults who are at risk of social isolation together for mutual benefit. In other instances, the recipient of the intervention is an at-risk older adult, and the volunteer may be of any age and background. Through these volunteer programs, friendly visits and socialization take place on a regular basis. Such initiatives are likely to combat isolation not just for the recipient but for the volunteer as well. Pennington and Knight (2008) studied one such program in Australia and found that volunteers are often drawn to such opportunities out of their own desire for social connection. Such arrangements often begin as structured volunteer opportunities and soon blossom into friendships between the volunteer and recipient. This was also the case for the Visible Voices program, a program that brought together socially isolated older adults with volunteers to complete expressive arts projects. Through the work of this program, both volunteers and program recipients experienced positive growth in creativity and expression as well as social connectedness and friendship (MacLeod, Skinner, Wilkinson, & Reid, 2016).

Unique programs designed to harness the time and energy of older adults continue to crop up around the country. One such program, Retirees in

Services to the Environment (RISE), was developed by faculty at Cornell University. This program engages older adults in environmental volunteering first through a series of trainings designed to build environmental knowledge and capacity, and then deployment of that knowledge through individualized community-based environmental projects. This program is designed to "level the playing field" for older adults with an interest in environmental issues but who may lack the experience or formal training to affect environmental change locally. Approximately 69% of RISE program participants consist of first-time environmental volunteers, indicating that this model is successful in attracting older adults with an interest in environmental volunteering but who may lack formal training or background in such work. First-time volunteers were also found to benefit the most from the RISE program, with such individuals demonstrating significant increases in measures of social connection and generativity as compared with their peers who had more environmental volunteering experience (Pillemer et al., 2017).

Experience Corps, facilitated by the AARP foundation, engages over 2,000 older adults nationwide in local schools where they support elementary literacy skills among children through in-class activities. This program is available in many major cities (currently 20 participating cities) and volunteers spend up to 15 hours per week working within school settings to support literacy, reaching over 30,000 students each year. These children benefit not only from the opportunity to socialize with older adults, but the program itself has been found to increase their literacy skills and engagement in school, and decrease behavioral disruptions in the classroom (AARP, n.d.). Experience Corps research has underscored not only the impact of the program on children and schools served but also on the older adults themselves who demonstrate health-related improvements over time in connection with their Experience Corps volunteer work. Experience Corps participation has been linked to an increase in memory and cognitive function (Carlson et al., 2008). Additional findings have linked Experience Corps participation to a decrease in television viewing and an increase in physical mobility over time, helping participants become less sedentary and more social as a result of participating in Experience Corps activities (Barron et al., 2009).

Another innovative approach to volunteering that is gaining traction within communities is citizen science. Citizen science initiatives pair volunteerism and science in a way that a lay person can participate in, and even shape, research that is conducted locally. One well-known citizen science project is the Christmas Bird Count facilitated by the Audubon Society, one of the longest running citizen science initiatives in the United States. The

Christmas Bird Count entails working within an established bird count geographical area and within an established group of volunteers who travel a given route to count and document the presence of birds over a given period of time. Individuals without birding experience are paired with an experienced birder for the count (Audubon Society, n.d.). Citizen science projects, like the bird count, are increasingly drawing on the use of technology to communicate with and gather data from volunteers. The use of technology allows such initiatives to not only expand their reach and engagement, but it gives older adults an opportunity to participate in volunteer work from greater distances from the lead organization. Citizen science seeks to give community members an active role in scientific endeavors without regard for formal science education. In fact, the most successful citizen science efforts are geared toward those without a science background. This strategy, like RISE, offers the opportunity to marry learning and volunteering. This is a particularly effective approach to engagement as research indicates that coupling learning and volunteering can be a powerful pathway to self-improvement and the establishment of social relationships (Chen, 2016).

PRACTITIONER STRATEGIES FOR ENCOURAGING VOLUNTEERISM

Volunteer opportunities available to older adults hinge on pathways and connections that assist individuals with finding such opportunities. Clinical practitioners should consider the following strategies for encouraging older adult volunteering.

Make "the Ask"

While Margaret was lucky enough to see the RSVP advertisement in her local paper, finding and connecting with volunteers and volunteer opportunities remains a challenge for both nonprofits and older adults alike. One of the most important predictors of volunteering is being asked to do so by a friend, family member, or another trusted individual (Sellon, 2014). Based on research by AARP (Williams, 2016), as many as 77% of current volunteers felt that being asked to participate in volunteering was an important factor behind their current volunteer work. Individuals who are isolated are not likely to be asked to volunteer, which further entrenches their isolation. Practitioners who work with individuals who are currently experiencing or are at risk of isolation must be ready to make "the ask" and connect older adults with volunteer opportunities, whether that ask is delivered in-person or through other means, such as newspaper announcements, flyers, or mailers.

For those who run programs that engage older adult volunteers, making the ask entails either directly reaching out to older adults or asking existing volunteers to help your program connect with individuals in the community who may be at risk of isolation. This invitation to volunteering should include key information such as the nature of the volunteer work, why the work is important to a given cause, time requirements, skill or experience requirements, and so forth. If an older adult is new to volunteering or seems uncertain, offer an opportunity for a trial run. Allow him or her to sit in or shadow a volunteer activity. This may help to ease the transition for those new to volunteering.

Connect With Formal Programs and Leverage Informal Networks

Formal volunteer programs, like those listed earlier, provide a ready-made option for connecting socially isolated individuals with volunteer service. Such programs are likely to have the volunteer management infrastructure necessary to recruit, deploy, and retain older adult volunteers. National service programs provide a uniform volunteer program experience that is available throughout the country for older adults to connect with and are more likely to be accessible than other volunteer opportunities. However, local programs may provide more meaning to older adults who feel a connection to their communities and the issues that are most relevant and timely to those contexts.

Research indicates that there is an interplay between formal and informal volunteering such that those who participate in one are likely to participate in the other. Likewise, participating in both church and secular organizations may help individuals to transition from informal to formal volunteering (Lee & Brudney, 2012). Such connections make informal networks an invaluable source of potential volunteers and volunteer opportunities alike. Approaching existing groups and organizations within the community or assisting older adults in connecting with such groups holds the potential to establish an additional pathway into volunteer service for older adults. This pathway, when paved with friendly faces and established relationships, can help open the door to additional volunteer opportunities that can further support an older adult's health and well-being. Assessing existing informal networks is an important first step to connecting an older adult with volunteer opportunities.

Focus on Strengths

Sellon, Chapin, and Leedahl (2016) present a strengths-based framework to engage nursing home residents in volunteer work, which could be applied to other settings as well. The tenets of this approach are based on a commitment to inclusivity and the recognition that even for individuals who have significant health challenges, there are opportunities for engagement. These tenets include first identifying that older adults possess strengths that can be applied to volunteer work, avoiding assumptions about a person's ability to engage in volunteer work, and using these strengths as a starting point for developing engagement opportunities. For example, asking an older adult to list his or her interests and skills that are particularly important to him or her would help to identify engagement opportunities for that individual. For those individuals who may need accommodations, collaborating with another professional with expertise in accessibility, technology, and occupational therapy can help to identify ways to make volunteering accessible and enjoyable. A strengths-based approach is driven first by the older adult and his or her needs and interests, rather than volunteer program needs.

Remove Institutional Barriers to Engagement

Participation in formal volunteering can be positively or negatively impacted by the institutional structures, policies, and procedures in place for engaging older adult volunteers. Through these mechanisms, organizations communicate their priorities to current and potential volunteers. Sellon (2014) conducted a review of the older adult volunteer literature and through that work identified organizational best practices that are associated with older adult recruitment and retention. Factors that help to encourage older adult volunteer recruitment include offering volunteer role flexibility that allows volunteers to attend to other personal obligations, and stipends to offset the personal costs of volunteering. Organizational factors that encourage retention of volunteers once they are on board include training and support from staff and volunteer recognition. Two additional factors were found to impact both recruitment and retention: offering volunteer opportunities that create a sense of meaningfulness for volunteers, helping them feel that the work they are doing is important to an overall cause, along with providing the opportunity for social interaction as a component of the volunteer experience. Identifying volunteer opportunities that fit with these criteria will ensure not only a good fit between volunteers and their volunteer work, but will also ensure that an older adult volunteer is likely to continue to benefit from this work over time.

SUMMARY

Volunteering is a productive aging activity that has been associated with numerous physical and mental health benefits for older adults. Older adults who are isolated or at risk of isolation may lack the opportunity to engage with volunteer activities, and as such practitioners should identify and connect such individuals with both formal and informal volunteer opportunities. There are numerous pathways to volunteering of which several examples have been given including programs that pair older adults with other older adults, youth in their communities, or community members in other countries. Volunteer pathways can be made accessible through the provision of training and support as well as creative configuration of opportunities. Formal programs and informal social networks offer a starting point to help an older adult to connect with and benefit from volunteer work and the socialization that grows from such work. Volunteer programs are most effective when institutional barriers such as scheduling, stipend support, staff supports, and volunteer recognition are provided.

REFERENCES

AARP. (n.d.). Experience Corps. *Experience Corps*. Retrieved from https://www.aarp.org/experience-corps

Atchley, R. C. (1989). A continuity theory of normal aging. *The Gerontologist, 29*(2), 183. doi:10.1093/geront/29.2.183

Audubon Society. (n.d.). Christmas bird count. Retrieved from http://www.audubon.org/conservation/science/christmas-bird-count

Balandin, S., Llewellyn, G., Dew, A., Ballin, L., & Schneider, J. (2006). Older disabled workers' perceptions of volunteering. *Disability & Society, 21*(7), 677–692. doi:10.1080/09687590600995139

Barron, J. S., Tan, E. J., Yu, Q., Song, M., McGill, S., & Fried, L. P. (2009). Potential for intensive volunteering to promote the health of older adults in fair health. *Journal of Urban Health: Bulletin of the New York Academy of Medicine, 86*(4), 641–653. doi:10.1007/s11524-009-9353-8

Butler, S. S. (2006). Evaluating the Senior Companion Program. *Journal of Gerontological Social Work, 47*(1), 45–70. doi:10.1300/J083v47n01_05

Carlson, M. C., Saczynski, J. S., Rebok, G. W., Seeman, T., Glass, T. A., McGill, S., . . . Fried, L. P. (2008). Exploring the effects of an "everyday" activity program on executive function and memory in older adults: Experience Corps. *The Gerontologist, 48*(6), 793–801. doi:10.1093/geront/48.6.793

Chen, L. (2016). Benefits and dynamics of learning gained through volunteering: A qualitative exploration guided by seniors' self-defined successful aging. *Educational Gerontology, 42*(3), 220–230. doi:10.1080/03601277.2015.1108150

Corporation for National and Community Service. (n.d.). AmeriCorps. Retrieved from https://www.nationalservice.gov/programs/americorps/join-americorps

Corporation for National and Community Service. (2009). The Edward M. Kennedy Serve America Act summary. Retrieved from https://www.nationalservice.gov/sites/default/files/documents/09_0421_serveact_summary.pdf

Corporation for National and Community Service. (2012). *The health benefits of volunteering for older Americans: A review of recent research*. Retrieved from http://www.nationalservice.gov/pdf/healthbenefits_factsheet.pdf

Corporation for National and Community Service. (2013a). *Foster Grandparents: Share today, shape tomorrow* [brochure]. Retrieved from https://www.nationalservice.gov/sites/default/files/upload/F_Grandparents_1024.pdf

Corporation for National and Community Service. (2013b). *RSVP: Leading with experience* [brochure]. Retrieved from https://www.nationalservice.gov/sites/default/files/upload/RSVP_4panel_1024.pdf

Corporation for National and Community Service. (2013c). *Senior Companions: Make independence a reality* [brochure]. Retrieved from https://www.nationalservice.gov/sites/default/files/upload/S_Companion_1024.pdf

Corporation for National and Community Service. (2016). Volunteering and civic life in America: Demographics. Retrieved from https://www.nationalservice.gov/vcla/demographic/older-adults-age-65

Corporation for National and Community Service. (2017). Senior Corps and health benefits issue brief. Retrieved from https://www.nationalservice.gov

Greenfield, E. A., & Marks, N. F. (2004). Formal volunteering as a protective factor for older adults' psychological well-being. *The Gerontologist, 59*(5), S258–S264. doi:10.1093/geronb/59.5.s258

Konrath, S., Fuhrel-Forbis, A., Lou, A., & Brown, S. (2012). Motives for volunteering are associated with mortality risk in older adults. *Health Psychology, 31*(1), 87–96. doi:10.1037/a0025226

Kopera-Frye, K., & Massey, R. (2014). The meaning of volunteerism to older adult RSVP volunteers. In M. Augustin, E. Bachman, K. P. R. Bartels, J. Benenson, V. Beynon, . . . T. A. Bryer (Eds.), *National service and volunteerism: Achieving impact in our communities* (pp. 31–44). Blue Ridge Summit, PA: Lexington Books.

Lee, Y., & Brudney, J. L. (2012). Participation in formal and informal volunteering: Implications for volunteer recruitment. *Nonprofit Management and Leadership, 23*(2), 159–180. doi:10.1002/nml.21060

Leedahl, S. N., Sellon, A. M., & Gallopyn, N. (2017). Factors predicting civic engagement among older adult nursing home residents. *Activities, Adaptation & Aging, 41*(3), 197. doi:10.1080/01924788.2017.1310581

MacLeod, A., Skinner, M. W., Wilkinson, F., & Reid, H. (2016). Connecting socially isolated older rural adults with older volunteers through expressive arts. *Canadian Journal on Aging, 35*(1), 14–27. doi:10.1017/s071498081500063x

Manning, L. K. (2010). Gender and religious differences associated with volunteering in later life. *Journal of Women & Aging, 22*(2), 125–135. doi:10.1080/08952841003719224

Martinez, I. L., Crooks, D., Kim, K. S., & Tanner, E. (2011). Invisible civic engagement among older adults: Valuing the contributions of informal volunteering. *Journal of Cross-Cultural Gerontology, 26*(1), 23–37. doi:10.1007/s10823-011-9137-y

Morrow-Howell, N., Hong, S., & Tang, F. (2009). Who benefits from volunteering? Variations in perceived benefits. *The Gerontologist, 49*(1), 91–102. doi:10.1093/geront/gnp007

National Public Radio. (2016). Peace Corps volunteer values staying active in old age. Retrieved from https://www.npr.org/2016/02/13/466592640/peace-corps-volunteer-values-staying-active-in-old-age

Peace Corps. (n.d.). Home page. Retrieved from http://www.peacecorps.gov
Pennington, J., & Knight, T. (2008). Staying connected: The lived experiences of volunteers and older adults. *Ageing International, 32*(4), 298–311. doi:10.1007/s12126-008-9020-5
Pettigrew, S., & Roberts, M. (2008). Addressing loneliness in later life. *Aging & Mental Health, 12*(3), 302–309. doi:10.1080/13607860802121084
Pillemer, K., Wells, N. M., Meador, R. H., Schultz, L., Henderson, C. R., & Cope, M. T. (2017). Engaging older adults in environmental volunteerism: The retirees in service to the environment program. *The Gerontologist, 57*(2), 367. doi:10.1093/geront/gnv693
Segel-Karpas, D., Ayalon, L., & Lachman, M. E. (2018). Loneliness and depressive symptoms: The moderating role of the transition into retirement. *Aging & Mental Health, 22*(1), 135–136. doi:10.1080/13607863.2016.1226770/13607863.2016.1226770
Sellon, A. M. (2014). Recruiting and retaining older adults in volunteer programs: Best practices and next steps. *Ageing International, 39*(4), 421–437. doi:10.1007/s12126-014-9208-9
Sellon, A. M., Chapin, R. K., & Leedahl, S. N. (2016). Engaging nursing home residents in formal volunteer activities: A focus on strengths. *Ageing International, 42*(1), 93–114. doi:10.1007/s12126-016-9252-8
Smith, J. M. (2012). Toward a better understanding of loneliness in community-dwelling older adults. *Journal of Psychology, 146*(3), 293–311. doi: 10.1080/00223980.2011.602132
Tan, E. J., Georges, A., Gabbard, S. M., Pratt, D. J., Nerino, A., Roberts, A. S., . . . Hyde, M. (2016). The 2013–2014 Senior Corps study: Foster Grandparents and Senior Companions. *Public Policy & Aging Report, 26*(3), 88–95. doi:10.1093/ppar/prw016
Warburton, J., & Onyx, J. (2003). Volunteering and health among older people: A review. *Australian Journal on Ageing, 22*(2), 65–69. doi:10.1111/j.1741-6612.2003.tb00468.x
Williams, A. (2016). Connecting, serving, and giving: Civic engagement among mid-life and older adults. Retrieved from https://www.aarp.org/research/topics/life/info-2016/connecting-serving-giving-civic-engagement.html

10

Using Technology to Advance Social Health

Hiroko H. Dodge

INTRODUCTION

Although the World Wide Web was developed less than 40 years ago, our societies, cultures, and way of life have been heavily impacted by this new information system. Many are now facing information overload through email, Facebook, Twitter, YouTube, and other social media. If we want to, we can surf the Internet and spend all day reading news and articles, posting comments, sharing pictures, and receiving comments from other people around the globe. In this chapter, social media is defined broadly by including any human interactions through the Internet such as email, group networking sites, and any commercial Internet network sites (e.g., dating sites), not limiting to big social media sites (e.g., YouTube, Facebook, Snapchat, Instagram, Twitter). According to the Pew Internet and American Life Project, 65% of American adults used social media in 2005. This number has increased rapidly over the last 10 years and the trend includes seniors. In 2005, 2% of seniors (age 65 and older) used social media compared with 35% more recently (Perrin, 2015). Digital social networking is essentially limitless, but it requires an Internet connection, a device, and the ability to use the technology.

The questions to be addressed in this chapter include the following: (a) To what extent do older adults take advantage of the Internet and social media for their social interactions? (b) Is it possible to reduce the epidemic of social

---

This work is supported by R01AG051628, R01AG056102, R01AG033581, P30AG008017, and P30AG053760 from the National Institute of Health. I would like to thank Ms. Nora Mattek for her editing and proofreading.

isolation through these technologies? The chapter is organized as follows: First, I will review some facts about how older adults are adopting new technologies and the barriers that prevent their adoption. Second, I will introduce new research areas which utilize modern technologies and have implications for combating the modern-day social isolation epidemic. Finally, I will discuss some cautions and research areas that need to be addressed before advocating digital socialization among older adults.

Before moving on, I would like to share some interesting discussion exchanges among members of the Gerontological Society of America (GSA) posted in its open forum a few months ago. A retired professor emeritus posted the following question in the GSA open forum.

> I live in a CCRC (Continuing Care Retirement Community) where the community is very lively, stimulating, and we feel like a large family. Recently we are going through two periods of quarantine due to first, the flu, and secondly, a gastrointestinal infection. That has meant about three weeks without activities, van trips, and cautions against "congregating." My husband and I are healthy and can go out and about, but others are more limited. I would be interested in any research on what can be done to keep communication going during this kind of period. We have an email group with more than 60 members but there are many who are not on email. Does anyone have any experience with this?

In response to her post, a PhD student who has worked in care communities for 20 years responded by supporting the importance of keeping communities active when "quarantines" occur. She asked whether some technological system could be provided that would allow the opportunity to stay connected via computers (with a screen in each unit) and offering interactive games and conversation. The professor responded:

> Thanks so much for your reply to my question. We are now nearing the end of the second week of quarantine for norovirus. At the end of January there was one week of quarantine for the flu. So, people are really missing the sense of community they enjoyed before. I think they were probably effective in limiting the infection. About 16 people (out of 300) had the norovirus but I felt it would be good to know specifically what healthy, uninfected people could reasonably do. We do have a not very good system called TouchTown which has a channel that most residents can access on their TV. At our suggestion, the exercise director did put some videos on there and people enjoyed doing exercises, knowing that others were doing them in their apartments. The activities director

said she couldn't put on some of her videos, including Great Courses, because of technological limits to TouchTown. I think technology could be used more effectively. I was also wondering about more low-tech interactive activities, like art or book clubs. The email list was great for giving people the feel of a virtual community, but we do have a significant number of people who don't do email.

The previous comment was responded to by another GSA member as follows:

If residents have Internet access (or Internet-capable TVs), there's a site called TogetherTube that allows a group of people to watch the same YouTube video together at the same time. This might be good for exercise videos, documentaries, concerts, old movies, whatever, and would allow quarantined residents to share experiences with others. It has a built-in chat feature, too. Togethertube.com

These communications were posted under the thread title "Keeping socialization going during a quarantine in senior housing." I wanted to share this exchange because it elicits vivid images of lives in senior housing when such a quarantine strikes. Also, it provides important insights surrounding technology and seniors including that many do not use email and that the technology implemented in senior housing may not be optimal even though some devices are available. Even if useful technology is available (e.g., a built-in chat feature in YouTube), it may take time before the seniors find out about it. Therefore, it is likely to require initiations and training by the senior housing management teams before it will be translated into the daily lives of the seniors.

I. TECHNOLOGY ADAPTABILITY AND BARRIERS: FACTS

According to a 2014 Pew Research Center study, many older adults (those age 65 years and older) remain largely unattached from online and mobile life: 41% of seniors do not use the Internet at all, 53% do not have broadband access at home, and 23% do not use cell phones. Internet usage drops sharply as age increases. Among those age 80 years and older, only 21% have broadband at home. Looking at the existing data, Internet usage does not seem to have alleviated social isolation thus far. In fact, the data suggest that lack of Internet access could further widen the gap between older adults with abundant opportunities for social interaction and engagement and those with fewer opportunities. In the text that follows, I summarize potential factors thath may widen the gap in social interactions among seniors.

First, broadband accessibility and Internet use depend highly on income and educational levels (Yu, Ellison, McCammon, & Langa, 2016). Second, many seniors have physical conditions or health issues that make using these tools a challenge. Pew Research estimates that about 39% of older adults have physical conditions or health issues that prevent them from fully participating in many common daily activities and these seniors are significantly less likely than healthy seniors to go online (49% vs. 66%), to have broadband at home (38% vs. 53%), and to have a smartphone (13% vs. 22%). Since those with physical limitations are more likely to be at risk of being home bound, this further contributes to the gap in social interaction opportunities. Third, there is a positive correlation between social media usage and socialization with others (i.e., those with high socialization tend to use social media sites more), according to the Pew Research. This correlation persists even after controlling for demographic factors such as age, income, or geographic area of residence. Fourth, older adults who do not use digital technologies are also less likely to believe that they are at a disadvantage by not using them: Only 35% of older non-Internet users agree with the assessment that they are missing out on important information. On the other hand, over 79% of older adults who use the Internet agree with the statement that "people without Internet access are at a real disadvantage because of all the information they might be missing." And 94% agree with the statement that "the Internet makes it much easier to find information today than in the past." In conclusion, there seems to be a spiral effect such that older adults with larger social networks may expand their network further using social media, while those who lack these social ties are less exposed to the opportunity of digital social media. As our society is more and more centered around Internet, those who do not have access to this information technology are being left behind; not only in terms of social network opportunities, but also a fundamental way of life such as getting essential information including community services and health resources. In the next section, I would like to introduce some new research efforts relevant to combating social isolation epidemics.

II. POTENTIAL CONTRIBUTIONS OF TECHNOLOGY FOR COMBATING SOCIAL ISOLATION EPIDEMICS: NEW AREAS OF RESEARCH

Identifying Seniors With Social Isolation and Loneliness Objectively in Communities

Those socially isolated rarely ask for help to alleviate their isolation. Furthermore, assessing loneliness in older adults is challenging owing to negative desirability biases associated with being lonely. Therefore, a priority is to develop more objective techniques to assess social isolation and loneliness in older adults so that preventive efforts may provide interventions before negative consequences accrue. Monitoring in-home daily activities continuously could identify subtle changes in behaviors that might indicate early onset of diseases but are likely to be missed if people are only assessed infrequently or at the time of emergency hospital visits. On the forefront of efforts to develop and apply more objective ecologically valid metrics of social isolation through home-based passive sensing and mobile health technologies is research led by the team at the Oregon Center for Aging and Technology (ORCATECH; www.orcatech.org), which was established over 10 years ago at Oregon Health & Science University at Portland, OR (Kaye et al., 2011; Lyons et al., 2015). The center has been providing evidence that continuously monitored in-home activities such as walking speed (Dodge, Mattek, Austin, Hayes, & Kaye, 2012; Kaye et al., 2012), sleep quality and duration (T. L. Hayes, Riley, Mattek, Pavel, & Kaye, 2014; Seelye et al., 2015), driving patterns (Seelye et al., 2017), and computer usage (Kaye et al., 2014) could aid in identifying early signs of developing dementia, long before more obvious clinical symptoms emerge. This research has been focusing on detecting early dementia and related neurodegenerative disease, and extending the approach of capturing frequent objective activity measures to identifying not only structural aspects of the social network (infrequent social interactions), but also psychological outcomes of social isolation (loneliness or depression) (Petersen, Austin, Kaye, Pavel, & Hayes, 2014; Petersen, Austin, Mattek, & Kaye, 2015; Thielke et al., 2014). For example, by combining multiple metrics of in-home behaviors (gait speed, computer use, time out of home, phone use), algorithms have been identified that predict loneliness (Austin et al., 2016). Monitoring daily behavioral patterns and their changes over time at home have a major advantage compared with the traditional infrequent and brief assessment conducted at clinic visits, since the signals detected allow one to examine intraindividual changes as opposed to only applying normative group data (e.g., group means and median, etc.) to identify individual specific "deviations" or signals. The use of intraindividual changes over time enhances signal-to-noise ratios, providing more powerful metrics for the identification of the early onset of diseases (Dodge, Zhu, Mattek, Austin, et al., 2015). Findings suggest that involvement in this unobtrusive in-home monitoring approach is well accepted, and older adults are, in general, willing to share information from monitoring systems with family members and clinicians (Boise et al., 2013). Recently, the monitoring platform has been further refined through an National Institutes of Healh–Veterans Administration (NIH-VA) supported initiative to make it readily deployable to a larger number of households across the larger research community and to include diverse populations (low income, rural, ethnic minorities [www.carthome.org]). Wearable mobile technology (mHealth) could also potentially contribute to the early identification of social isolation in the future, although to our knowledge, none of the current interventions using mHealth are specifically aimed to alleviate social isolation or loneliness (Rathbone & Prescott, 2018).

Randomized Controlled Trials (RCTs) Targeting Socially Isolated Seniors to Enhance Their Social Interactions

Can we enhance social interactions through Internet use and improve the psychological well-being and cognitive function of socially isolated older adults? Our team, I-CONECT (Internet-Based Conversational Engagement Clinical Trials, www.i-conect.org), is conducting a series of RCTs that aims to examine whether digital social interactions, specifically video chat with interviewers, can improve cognitive functions and psychological well-being among socially isolated seniors. In our previous proof of concept study, which was completed in 2014 (Dodge, Zhu, Mattek, Bowman, et al., 2015) (Clinicaltrials.gov registration number NCT01571427), the experimental group received daily (five times per week) 30-minute conversations with interviewers while the control group received only once per week check-in calls. Despite a short duration of 6 weeks, we found improved cognitive functions in the domains of language-based executive function and semantic memory among the experimental group compared with the control group (Dodge, Zhu, Mattek, Bowman, et al., 2015). This pilot study was not limited to those with social isolation. Building on these promising results and foundation work, our team is currently conducting a follow-up study, specifically targeting social isolated seniors age 75 and older (Clinicaltrials.gov registration number NCT02871921). The participants are recruited mainly from the local Meals on Wheels programs. Although the primary outcomes of this RCT are cognitive functions (i.e., preintervention and postintervention changes in domain-specific cognitive functions), we are also examining whether change in psychological well-being, such as mood and loneliness, mediates or moderates the effect of social interaction on cognition and, if so, to what extent. In this project, social isolation is operationally defined using Lubben's Social Isolation Score, 6 items version (LSNS-6; Lubben et al., 2006) of 12 or lower. The study has a duration of 12 months of intervention with two "doses" of conversational engagement or "chatting" (4 days per week for 6 months and 2 days per week for 6 months). These projects are the first series of prevention trials examining the effects of social interactions on cognitive reserve, targeting the socially isolated seniors who are less likely to volunteer for research despite their high risk of cognitive impairment. Besides recruiting from an underserved population, unique features of this project include the use of preintervention and postintervention changes in brain structures and integrities assessed by volumetric and resting state functional MRI to clarify the underlying mechanisms of efficacies. Exploratory outcomes include objective assessment of instrumental activities of daily living using an electronic pillbox that collects time-stamped data when the box is opened (i.e., to monitor medication adherence) and changes in speech characteristics over time. These exploratory outcomes are introduced based on the promising results from the previous trial. For example, using the transcribed conversations between interviewers and participants recorded during the video chats, the team found that speech characteristics could distinguish early mild cognitive impairment from those with normal cognition (Asgari, Kaye, & Dodge, 2017; Dodge et al., 2015). Data on personality is also being collected as a potential effect modifier. The results of the RCT will be available in the year 2023. Lancet Commissions (Livingston et al., 2017) recently estimated that 2% of people with dementia occurs because of social isolation among seniors. A comparative figure of population attributable risk (PAR) of diabetes was estimated to be only 1%. That is, the impact of social isolation on dementia is higher than that of diabetes among seniors. The results of this RCT may answer questions initiated by epidemiological studies such as, "What are the effects of social interactions on brain integrity, psychological well-being, and loneliness?" and "What are the mediation effects of improved psychological well-being on the association between cognitive functions and social interactions?" If this RCT confirms promising results, we plan to deliver the approach identified in this trial to a larger community, scalable to a national level, for example, by introducing video chat with seniors as a part of college gerontology program curriculums.

Development of User-Friendly Multifunctional Devices

In addition to identifying social isolation at the earliest stage and providing social interactions through the Internet (e.g., video chats) as discussed earlier, another area of technology-intensive research is the development of user-friendly devices that can be deployed to a large number of seniors cost effectively. A significant majority of older adults need assistance when using new digital devices. According to the Pew Research study, just 18% would feel comfortable learning to use a new technology device such as a smartphone or tablet on their own, while 77% indicate they would need someone to help walk them through the process. Among seniors who go online but do not currently use social networking sites such as Facebook or Twitter, 56% would need assistance if they wanted to use these sites to connect with friends or family members. Recently Czaja and colleagues (Czaja, Boot, Charness, Rogers, & Sharit, 2017) reported their trial results evaluating the impact of a specially designed computer system, PRISM (Personal Reminder Information and Social Management), for social isolation, loneliness, and well-being. The PRISM device contains various easy-to-use senior-focused features including Internet access with vetted links, an annotated resource guide, a dynamic classroom feature, a calendar, a photo feature, email access, games, and online help. In the 12-month trial, the experimental group was compared to a control condition that included a binder containing content that paralleled the PRISM system in a nonelectronic form (e.g., paper resource guides, paper calendar). They found that at 6 months, those who received PRISM reported significantly decreased loneliness and increased perceived social support and well-being as compared with those who received the binder. Although the difference between the experimental and the control groups was not significant at the 12-month assessment, this study showed that user-friendly devices like PRISM are well accepted among seniors. The study also provided evidence that by making this type of user-friendly device available to larger and more diverse populations through cost reductions via a public–private partnership, we might be able to reduce social isolation among seniors and enhance their psychological well-being.

The Efforts to Narrow the Digital Gap: National Efforts

There have been some national movements to narrow the digital gap. For example, ConnectHomeUSA (formerly ConnectHome Nation) is an organization that started in 2012 to bridge the digital divide for Housing and Urban Development (HUD)-assisted housing residents in the United States in collaboration with the national nonprofit EveryoneOn. It provides free or low-cost broadband access, devices, and digital literacy training by creating a platform for community leaders, local governments, nonprofit organizations, and private industry to join together and produce locally tailored solutions for narrowing the digital divide. Originally, the aim of ConnectHomeUSA was to provide educational tools for school-age children in HUD-assisted housing, but the platform has been extended to assist seniors. For example, in 2017, the Jewish Healthcare Foundation in Pittsburgh, PA, launched Virtual Senior Academy (virtualsenioracademy.org), which is a free interactive platform that offers virtual classes through video conferences. It brings seniors together without leaving their homes. They recruit Virtual Senior Academy facilitators of all ages and lead classes. The project is largely run by volunteers. Although the senior participation rate is increasing rapidly, those without Internet or a computer have no way to join. The foundation is currently working with ConnectHomeUSA to alleviate this barrier to access by bringing Internet connections and providing devices to senior high rises in the area. More information is available at the ConnetHomeUSA website.

III. DIGITAL SOCIAL NETWORK USAGE AND PSYCHOLOGICAL WELL-BEING: SOME CAUTIONS

So far, my discussion was centered on enhancing Internet usage among seniors to alleviate social isolations. In this section, I would like to provide some cautions for doing so. Recent studies on Internet social network site use and psychological well-being among seniors provided some positive results. For example, using the 2012 Health and Retirement Study (HRS), Yu, McCammon, Ellison, and Langa (2015) showed that among those age 50 and older, Internet social network site use is positively associated with social well-being outcomes, including perceived support from friends and feelings of connectedness, and perceived support from children. Other cross-sectional studies also showed that the frequency of going online (Cotten, Anderson, & McCullough, 2013) was associated with decreased loneliness scores. One Australian study reported that greater use of the Internet as a communication tool was associated with a lower level of social loneliness, but greater use of the Internet to find new people was associated with a higher level of emotional loneliness (Sum, Mathews, Hughes, & Campbell, 2008). These studies tend to have a smaller sample size with a wide age range (e.g., including lower age bound of 50) or are limited to cross-sectional analyses and to those who are already Internet users. Studies with a more inclusive sample, assessments of long-term effects, and age-stratified analyses (e.g., younger old vs. oldest old) are warranted. Among studies with younger participants, recent meta-analyses showed that social network usage does not necessarily lead to improved psychological well-being and psychological connectedness (Verduyn, Ybarra, Résibois, Jonides, & Kross, 2017). The study found that especially passive usage (e.g., monitoring of other people's posts without engaging in direct exchanges with others such as scrolling through news feeds or looking at other users' profiles, pictures, and status updates) of social network sites has a negative impact on subjective well-being, possibly because it provokes social comparisons and envy, while active usage of social network sites predicts subjective well-being by creating social capital and stimulating feelings of social connectedness. Older adults use social media less actively than young adults (i.e., they are likely to be more passive users) (M. Hayes, van Stolk-Cooke, & Muench, 2015). Few investigators have examined granular usage patterns and psychological well-being among seniors. More research is needed before prescribing Internet and social media use among seniors.

Another area that should not be ignored is potential benefits of nondigital in-person interactions. It is well documented that nonsexual physical contact such as hugging and handholding has stress-buffering effects and may improve perceived feelings of social support. For example, Cohen, Janicki-Deverts, Turner, and Doyle (2015) examined whether global perceptions of social support and the actual receipt of physical touch or hugging during daily life attenuated the association of an interpersonal stressor (social conflict) with subsequent risk for infection, cold signs, and clinical disease in response to an experimentally administered cold virus. The authors found people who receive more hugs are more protected from infection and illness-related symptoms. A number of laboratory studies also show that touch from a trusted individual buffers the effects of stress. The well-known handholding study by Coan showed that married women were subjected to the threat of electric shock to a lesser extent while holding their husband's hand, in comparison with holding a stranger's hand. Furthermore, the extent of the threat reduction was associated with the quality of the relationship with their husband (Coan, Schaefer, & Davidson, 2006). Encouraging seniors to stay connected without leaving their house through enhanced digital social engagement may be beneficial to their well-being. However, relying on this platform heavily could leave out some important aspects of social interactions that exist only in traditional human-to-human encounters. Advocating digital media usage without confirming its possible negative effects or "side effects" has risks.

Finally, cybercrime has increased dramatically over the years. Seniors, especially those with impaired cognitive abilities or those socially isolated without anyone to consult with, are particularly vulnerable to becoming a victim of identity theft or Internet fraud by opening spam mail, catching computer viruses, or being lured by illegitimate advertisement sites. Older adults have a diverse range of cognitive ability as well as large variation in their computer proficiency. Identifying specific pathways through which seniors are more likely to be victimized and developing effective prevention against cybercrimes is urgently needed. Enhancement of social media access has to be accompanied by educational opportunities against cybercrimes.

SUMMARY

In this chapter, I summarized the current state of Internet and social media usage among seniors and discussed the digital divide among older adults which may further expand the gap in social interaction opportunities. Then three new research initiatives were discussed that use modern technology intensively and have implications for social isolation epidemics. Finally, some cautions were raised in advocating social media use among seniors. Recent technological advancement is unprecedented. I am optimistic that these technologies can alleviate social isolation epidemics as long as we do not blindly facilitate the use of these technologies among seniors.

REFERENCES

Rathbone, A. L., & Prescott, J. (2018). The use of mobile apps and SMS messaging as physical and mental health interventions: Systematic review. *Journal of Medical Internet Research, 19*(8), e295. doi:10.2196/jmir.7740

Asgari, M., Kaye, J., & Dodge, H. (2017). Predicting mild cognitive impairment from spontaneous spoken utterances. *Alzheimers Dement (N Y), 3*(2), 219–228. doi:10.1016/j.trci.2017.01.006

Austin, J., Dodge, H. H., Riley, T., Jacobs, P. G., Thielke, S., & Kaye, J. (2016). A smart-home system to unobtrusively and continuously assess loneliness in older adults. *IEEE Journal of Translational Engineering in Health and Medicine, 4*, 2800311. doi:10.1109/JTEHM.2016.2579638

Boise, L., Wild, K., Mattek, N., Ruhl, M., Dodge, H. H., & Kaye, J. (2013). Willingness of older adults to share data and privacy concerns after exposure to unobtrusive in-home monitoring. *Gerontechnology, 11*(3), 428–435. doi:10.4017/gt.2013.11.3.001.00

Coan, J. A., Schaefer, H. S., & Davidson, R. J. (2006). Lending a hand: Social regulation of the neural response to threat. *Psychological Science, 17*(12), 1032–1039. doi:10.1111/j.1467-9280.2006.01832.x

Cohen, S., Janicki-Deverts, D., Turner, R. B., & Doyle, W. J. (2015). Does hugging provide stress-buffering social support? A study of susceptibility to upper respiratory infection and illness. *Psychological Science, 26*(2), 135–147. doi:10.1177/0956797614559284

Cotten, S. R., Anderson, W. A., & McCullough, B. M. (2013). Impact of Internet use on loneliness and contact with others among older adults: Cross-sectional analysis. *Journal of Medical Internet Research, 15*(2), e39. doi:10.2196/jmir.2306

Czaja, S. J., Boot, W. R., Charness, N., Rogers, W. A., & Sharit, J. (2017). Improving social support for older adults through technology: Findings from the PRISM randomized controlled trial. *Gerontologist, 58*(3), 467–477. doi:10.1093/geront/gnw249

Dodge, H. H., Mattek, N. C., Austin, D., Hayes, T. L., & Kaye, J. A. (2012). In-home walking speeds and variability trajectories associated with mild cognitive impairment. *Neurology, 78*(24), 1946–1952. doi:10.1212/WNL.0b013e318259e1de

Dodge, H. H., Mattek, N., Gregor, M., Bowman, M., Seelye, A., Ybarra, O., . . . Kaye, J. A. (2015). Social Markers of mild cognitive impairment: Proportion of word counts in free conversational speech. *Current Alzheimer Research, 12*(6), 513–519. doi:10.2174/1567205012666150530201917

Dodge, H. H., Zhu, J., Mattek, N. C., Austin, D., Kornfeld, J., & Kaye, J. A. (2015). Use of high-frequency in-home monitoring data may reduce sample sizes needed in clinical trials. *PLoS One, 10*(9), e0138095. doi:10.1371/journal.pone.0138095

Dodge, H. H., Zhu, J., Mattek, N., Bowman, M., Ybarra, O., Wild, K., & Kaye, J. A. (2015). Web-enabled conversational interactions as a means to improve cognitive functions: Results of a 6-week randomized controlled trial. *Alzheimers Dement (N Y), 1*(1), 1–12. doi:10.1016/j.trci.2015.01.001

Hayes, M., van Stolk-Cooke, K., & Muench, F. (2015). Understanding Facebook use and the psychological affects of use across generations. *Computers in Human Behavior, 49*, 507–511. doi.org/10.1016/j.chb.2015.03.040

Hayes, T. L., Riley, T., Mattek, N., Pavel, M., & Kaye, J. A. (2014). Sleep habits in mild cognitive impairment. *Alzheimer Disease and Associated Disorders, 28*(2), 145–150. doi:10.1097/WAD.0000000000000010

Kaye, J., Mattek, N., Dodge, H., Buracchio, T., Austin, D., Hagler, S., . . . Hayes, T. (2012). One walk a year to 1000 within a year: Continuous in-home unobtrusive gait assessment of older adults. *Gait Posture, 35*(2), 197–202. doi:10.1016/j.gaitpost.2011.09.006

Kaye, J., Mattek, N., Dodge, H. H., Campbell, I., Hayes, T., Austin, D., . . . Pavel, M. (2014). Unobtrusive measurement of daily computer use to detect mild cognitive impairment. *Alzheimers & Dementia, 10*(1), 10–17. doi:10.1016/j.jalz.2013.01.011

Kaye, J. A., Maxwell, S. A., Mattek, N., Hayes, T. L., Dodge, H., Pavel, M., . . . Zitzelberger, T. A. (2011). Intelligent systems for assessing aging changes: Home-based, unobtrusive, and continuous assessment of aging. *Journals of Gerontology. Series B, Psychological Sciences and Social Sciences, 66 Suppl 1*, i180–i190. doi:10.1093/geronb/gbq095

Livingston, G., Sommerlad, A., Orgeta, V., Costafreda, S. G., Huntley, J., Ames, D., . . . Mukadam, N. (2017). Dementia prevention, intervention, and care. *Lancet, 390*(10113), 2673–2734. doi:10.1016/S0140-6736(17)31363-6

Lubben, J., Blozik, E., Gillmann, G., Iliffe, S., von Renteln Kruse, W., Beck, J. C., & Stuck, A. E. (2006). Performance of an abbreviated version of the Lubben Social Network Scale among three European community-dwelling older adult populations. *Gerontologist, 46*(4), 503–513. doi:10.1093/geront/46.4.503

Lyons, B. E., Austin, D., Seelye, A., Petersen, J., Yeargers, J., Riley, T., . . . Kaye, J. A. (2015). Pervasive computing technologies to continuously assess Alzheimer's disease progression and intervention efficacy. *Frontiers in Aging Neuroscience, 7*, 102. doi:10.3389/fnagi.2015.00102

Perrin, A. (2015). Social Nnetworking Uusage: 2005–2015. Retrieved from http://www.pewinternet.org/2015/10/08/social-networking-usage-2005-2015

Petersen, J., Austin, D., Kaye, J. A., Pavel, M., & Hayes, T. L. (2014). Unobtrusive in-home detection of time spent out-of-home with applications to loneliness and physical activity. *IEEE Journal of Biomedical and Health Informatics, 18*(5), 1590–1596. doi:10.1109/JBHI.2013.2294276

Petersen, J., Austin, D., Mattek, N., & Kaye, J. (2015). Time out-of-home and cognitive, physical, and emotional wellbeing of older adults: A longitudinal mixed effects model. *PLoS One, 10*(10), e0139643. doi:10.1371/journal.pone.0139643

Seelye, A., Mattek, N., Howieson, D., Riley, T., Wild, K., & Kaye, J. (2015). The impact of sleep on neuropsychological performance in cognitively intact older adults using a novel in-home sensor-based sleep assessment approach. *Journal of Clinical Neuropsychology, 29*(1), 53–66. doi:10.1080/13854046.2015.1005139

Seelye, A., Mattek, N., Sharma, N., Witter, P., Brenner, A., Wild, K., . . . Kaye, J. (2017). Passive assessment of routine driving with unobtrusive sensors: A new approach for identifying and monitoring functional level in normal aging and mild cognitive impairment. *Journal of Alzheimers Disease, 59*(4), 1427–1437. doi:10.3233/JAD-170116

Sum, S., Mathews, R. M., Hughes, I., & Campbell, A. (2008). Internet use and loneliness in older adults. *Cyberpsychology and Behavior, 11*(2), 208–211. doi:10.1089/cpb.2007.0010

Thielke, S. M., Mattek, N. C., Hayes, T. L., Dodge, H. H., Quinones, A. R., Austin, D., . . . Kaye, J. A. (2014). Associations between observed in-home behaviors and self-reported low mood in community-dwelling older adults. *Journal of the American Geriatrics Society, 62*(4), 685–689. doi:10.1111/jgs.12744

Verduyn, P., Ybarra, O., Résibois, M., Jonides, J., & Kross, E. (2017). Do social network sites enhance or undermine subjective well-being? A critical review. *Social Issues and Policy Review, 11*(1), 274–302. doi:10.1111/sipr.12033

Yu, R. P., Ellison, N. B., McCammon, R. J., & Langa, K. M. (2016). Mapping the two levels of digital divide: Internet access and social network site adoption among older adults in the USA. *Information, Communication & Society, 19*(10), 1445–1464. doi:10.1080/1369118X.2015.1109695

Yu, R. P., McCammon, R., Ellison, N., & Langa, K. (2015). The relationships that matter: Social network site use and social wellbeing among older adults in the United States of America. *Ageing and Society, 36*(9), 1826–1852. doi:10.1017/S0144686X15000677

11

Spirituality and Religion in the Lives of Elders

Kenneth J. Doka

INTRODUCTION

The study of religion and spirituality has been somewhat neglected in gerontology. This is unfortunate as both spirituality and religion offer significant connections for elders in their social lives as well as a transcendental connection that facilitates later life development. In this chapter, we explore the roles that spirituality and religion play in the lives of older persons as well as assess the ongoing challenges and opportunities that religious institutions face in an aging society.

Before that, it is necessary to define *religion* and *spirituality*. A New Zealand study, for example, involving both patients and providers found divergent definitions. Some simply equated religion and spirituality. A second group saw spirituality in the nonphysical and extraordinary dimensions of life, while a third group defined it in more humanistic and existential terms (Egan et al., 2011). A Consensus Conference funded by the Archstone Foundation brought together scholars and practitioners from a broad range of fields and disciplines in 2009. The agreed-upon definition emerging from the Consensus Conference was, "Spirituality is the aspect of humanity that refers to the ways that individuals seek and express meaning and purpose and the way they experience their connectedness to the moment, to self, to others, to nature, and to the significant or sacred" (Puchalski et al., 2009, p. 887). The International Workgroup on Death, Dying and Bereavement defined spirituality as "concerned with the transcendental, inspirational, and existential way to live one's life" (International Work Group on Death, Dying and Bereavement, 1990, p. 75). Miller's definition is more poetic:

Spirituality relates to our souls. It involves the deep inner essence of who we are. It is an openness to the possibility that the soul within each of us is somehow related to the Soul of all that is. Spirituality is what happens to us that is so memorable that we cannot forget it, and yet we find it hard to talk about because words fail to describe it. Spirituality is the act of looking for meaning in the very deepest sense; and looking for it in a way that is most authentically ours. (Miller, 1994)

To Miller, spirituality is inherently individual, personal, and eclectic. Religion, however, is more collective. Religion is a belief shared within a group of people. Miller again offers a lyrical perspective: "Now religion works in a very different way. While spirituality is very personal, religion is more communal. In fact, if you take the word back to its origins, 'religion means that which binds together,' 'that which ties things into a package.'" Religion has to do with collecting and consolidating and unifying. Religion says, "'Here are special words that are meant to be passed on. Take them to heart.'" Religion says, "'Here is a set of beliefs that form a coherent whole. Take them as your own.'" Religion says, "'Here are people for you to revere and historical events for you to recall. Remember them.'" Religion says, "'Here is a way for you to act when you come together as a group, and here's a way to behave when you're apart'" (1994).

Thus, while spirituality is very personal, a person's spirituality may very well be shaped by an individual's religious beliefs. Yet, because of the individual nature of spirituality, religious affiliation is not likely to be the sole determinant of spiritual beliefs. Often, developmental outlooks, personal experiences, and cultural perspectives will join with religious beliefs in shaping an individual's spirituality.

THEORETICAL PERSPECTIVES ON THE ROLES OF SPIRITUALITY IN THE LIVES OF ELDERS

Case I

Frank generally attended synagogue—at least when work did not interfere; but now that he has retired, he has become far more active—serving as treasurer on the temple's board. A former comptroller, he enjoys working with numbers and takes pleasure in creating more efficient accounting systems for the temple. He enjoys the sense of helping as well as the recognition his position affords.

Case 2

Yolanda too enjoys her role at a local Pentecostal church. Yolanda has been a long-time member of the congregation. She takes pride in sitting in the same pew she did when her grandmother and mom "dragged" her to church. She feels a sense of satisfaction for them to know that she sits there with her daughter and grandchild. Always active in the church, Yolanda now serves as a "visitor"—visiting shut-ins. While she hopes she can always attend, she takes comfort from knowing that even if she is shut-in, she too will have the companionship of her minister as well as congregational visitors.

As the field of gerontology developed, varied theoretical approaches have addressed issues related to the roles of spirituality and religion in the social lives of elders. Perhaps the first significant theoretical perspective to do so was *disengagement theory* (Cumming & Henry, 1961). Cumming and Henry's disengagement theory challenged what they believed was the prevalent perspective that they labeled *activity theory*—later more formally developed by Havighurst (1963). Activity theory emphasized that older adults had the same social needs as young adults. However, modern society tended to minimize the social roles and opportunities for older adults by social institutions as retirement. Healthy aging then involved finding new activities and opportunities for interaction. In addition, one of the roles of gerontologists and advocates for the aging individuals was to press for more options for involvement and activity as individuals aged.

Disengagement theory challenged those assumptions. Disengagement theory posited that individual withdrawal was a natural and normal aspect of the aging process. As energy began to lag, Cumming and Henry suggested that elders began to withdraw from activities and become more self-reflective as they prepared for eventual death. It seems that disengagement might have a dual approach in regard to spirituality and religion; that is, as older individuals withdraw from the social worlds of their faith communities, spirituality—the search for meaning—may even become more significant.

Others such as Streib and Schneider (1971) have suggested modifications to disengagement theory that emphasized differential disengagement. This meant that as individuals withdraw from some activities, such as retiring from their work roles, other roles, such as those related to family or faith, may have increased salience. Frank, for example, may represent such a pattern. As he disengages from other roles, such as retiring as a corporate comptroller, he takes on a similar role in his synagogue. While a volunteer role, he still takes a small part of the time and expertise of his former job and offers a bit of status.

Disengagement theory, in its challenge to the conventional wisdom of the day, had significant heuristic importance. It created both a significant body of research on the social lives of elders as well as alternate theoretical stances.

One of these approaches was *continuity theory* (Atchley, 2000). Continuity theory emphasized that older persons aged as they lived. In other words, as they continued to mature into adulthood, they developed coping skills that allowed them to adapt to the changing environment experienced as they aged. Hence, if religiously related activities, spiritual coping strategies, and spirituality were important earlier in their lives, it would remain so now. Yolanda certainly represents continuity theory. Always active in her church, she remains continuous in her commitment to her congregation. Yet, Frank's experience can also be viewed as illustrative of continuity theory. As one activity—a work role—recedes, Frank maintains a sense of continuity by using his skills in a related area. His commitment to his synagogue and faith has always been a constant in his life.

Developmental perspectives on aging, such as Erikson's (1963), offer another alternative. Developmental theory stresses that at varied stages of life, critical issues arise that must be effectively settled, enabling an individual to successfully continue to the next developmental stage. As individuals age, they begin to review their life, assessing their achievements and challenges against their life goals. Those who find worth in their lives reach a state of *ego integrity* while those who perceive that they wasted their lives fall into what Erikson called *ego despair*. To Erikson, the ego quality that emerges from the successful resolution of the process is wisdom. Spirituality is a critical aspect of this developmental process as it arouses concerns such as life goals, forgiveness, purpose, and meaning. Moreover, to Erikson, these issues are best resolved in dialog with others. Again, both Frank and Yolanda demonstrate such developmental perspectives. Most developmental theorists acknowledge that as people age, they do have to readjust their social space and find new ways to meet basic psychological needs. Yolanda and Frank have both found that their involvement in their faith communities allows them to do so while offering a sense of connection and purpose that contributes to ego integrity.

However, Frank and Yolanda do not illustrate one prevalent myth of spirituality and aging that might arise out of a developmental perspective—that older persons inevitably become more spiritually oriented and return to their faith communities. The older adults who populate pews and seats within their places of worship were likely sitting there—like Frank and Yolanda—throughout their lives. There is, in fact, little evidence to support the belief that persons become more religious as they age (Moody, 2000).

These perspectives offer divergent notions on the importance of social activity in the lives of elders. Yet together, they emphasize both the continuity of religious behaviors and the importance of spirituality, however defined, in later life. Furthermore, they stress the importance of connection, whether with others or the transcendental. That becomes the focus of the remainder of the chapter as we explore these connections—both to the human and the divine—in the lives of elders.

THE HUMAN CONNECTION

Both Frank and Yolanda illustrate another aspect of the role of spirituality and religious/faith communities in the social lives of older persons. As other opportunities for involvement diminish, faith and philosophical communities can offer opportunities for social interaction as well as significant social roles that can offer meaning to an older person's sense of meaning and purpose.

A number of years ago, I completed a study of Lutheran churches within the New York Metropolitan region (Doka, 1986). The study indicated the multifaceted roles that these churches had in the lives of older members. Many clergy emphasized that they strove to integrate older members within the larger congregation. And, in fact, many older persons held leadership roles within the church. Yet, in this study, such roles were often held by the younger-old—those between 65 and 74 years old—and that the older persons were, in general, underrepresented in leadership roles—a finding consistent with Moberg (1955) over a quarter century earlier.

The churches also reported that elderly members were involved in numerous church activities, some age segregated such as "senior clubs" or others that were age integrated such as a "men's club" or "women's club." Interestingly, some were self-segregated—developing a reputation for appealing to certain age groups. One pastor noted, "We have two women's organizations—the Mary and Martha Society and the Ladies Guild. One meets during the day, the other in the evening. They were originally designed as being for homemakers and working women. Now older women are steered by their peers to the Ladies Guild while younger women are encouraged to join Mary and Martha."

Many faith communities also sponsor events that can facilitate the integration of older persons—joining them with both age peers as well as wider opportunities to interact with members of other age cohorts. For example, some faith communities offered Foster Grandparent programs. In some cases, this was limited to older persons assisting in day care or educational programs such as reading stories to children or assisting in other ways. In other cases, the role demands were far more extensive. Older persons became a part of an intergenerational network with families where the older "grandparent" generation was either missing or distant. In the 1970s, for example, one synagogue found this to be an incredible gift to Holocaust survivors—creating a sense of intergenerational families to those where family ties had been decimated by that genocide.

Most faith communities held regular social events such as dinners, movies, shows, trips, and fundraisers. These events too provided older members with opportunities for diversion, entertainment, interaction, and, of course, involvement in the planning and implementation of the activity.

Churches also reported much mutual support. There were often active programs to visit shut-ins (those too infirm to attend church in person) both by clergy and designated visitors. Relationships formed within the church also offered socialization to older members. The churches encouraged families to consider inviting older members who were alone during the holidays. Clergy were a source both of counseling and referral to community agencies. In fact, many engaged speakers from these agencies to inform members about such services. Some congregations sponsored other activities that appealed to older members. A number, for example, offered widows-to-widows programs or other grief groups. A few held "Longest Night" services on the winter solstice that sought to comfort and confront grief as experienced during the holidays. Most provided transportation to and from church to assist older members who wished to attend but lacked ready transport.

Yet there were also areas that caused concern. Most of the churches that had high percentages of older persons were themselves older structures, often in the urban center. Few were readily handicap accessible. While many clergy acknowledged the very physical barriers that precluded participation, especially by those with limited mobility, most of these congregations had limited means and were unable to undertake the costs of renovation.

Finally, churches often sent mixed messages to older members—often bemoaning the fact that their congregation was aging. Such rhetoric devalues the very same aging members that sustain the congregation.

THE MINISTRY OF PRESENCE

Beyond the opportunities for socialization and the assumption of social roles, faith communities can offer a caring presence. By that, I mean that older persons may take comfort even in knowing, even if there are physical constraints on the ability to fully participate, that they are in a caring community.

For example, Ann has numerous disabilities that inhibit her from attending worship services at a church where she has been a long-time member. While her pastor visits her monthly and offers the sacrament of communion—an important ritual within her faith—and she sees other visitors from the church somewhat regularly, Ann takes great comfort from the fact that she is on the congregational prayer list. That means that at every worship service, congregants pray for her health along with the health and other needs of other members on that list. Ann takes comfort in the fact that she is remembered by her congregation regularly as well as the occasional visits of clergy and other members. Moreover, she finds comfort in the consistent calls from other congregants—some old friends who are themselves "shut-in." Finally, Ann is confident that should an emergency arise, there are multiple people she could call to arrange for any necessary assistance.

In summation, faith communities can offer extensive opportunities that can enrich the lives of older members. While these can involve varied activities and social roles, they too can assure that even the most isolated members of the community retain a sense of connection.

THE TRANSCENDENTAL CONNECTION

Spirituality leads to another type of connection as well—a transcendental connection that spans space and time. One aspect of this is connection to a Higher Power, whether it is defined as a deity or deities or as some sort of overarching idea. As individuals in later life review their lives and prepare unconsciously or consciously for death (see Butler, 1963), the transcendental connection can assist in many ways.

One is that it can facilitate the grieving process as one inevitably faces the losses associated with later life. Neimeyer (2004) asserts that one of the critical aspects of the grieving process is the reconstruction of meaning. In other words, a significant loss challenges the assumptive world, throwing into doubt whatever the individuals believed about self or the world. In the reconstruction of meaning then, spirituality can play a key role.

Creating a meaningful context for loss ("meaning making") has a number of distinct components. One aspect of meaning making is *assigning blame*. Here, individuals find it important to assess who is reasonable for the death or other significant loss. For example, in an early study, Doka and Schwarz (1979) found that assigning was a critical aspect of the way that lifeguard staffs responded to drowning. To restore the "sentimental order"—that is, returning to a sense of normalcy—lifeguards had to assign blame as a way of accounting for the death. In some cases, the drowning was blamed on the weather or conditions, the victim, those family and friends deemed to have responsibility to and for the victim, or a particular guard.

For Rabbi Kushner (1981) and C. S. Lewis (1963), assigning blame was a spiritual struggle as both grappled with how a benevolent God could allow a person they deeply loved to die such a cruel and premature death. In the end, both resolved their struggle in different ways. To Kushner, blame ultimately was placed on the genetic laws of nature in place since creation. Lewis's conclusion was different. He ultimately decided that assigning blame was not important and he could accept the mystery of why. While both their struggles ended in different places, both experienced significant spiritual growth—reaffirming a stronger faith.

In other cases, individuals may blame themselves for the death or loss. Yet here, too, spirituality can play a significant role as individuals struggle with guilt. Their philosophy of life, and their spiritual beliefs, practices, and rituals, may play a significant role in how they cope with such guilt. For example, in one case, a mother whose adolescent son had died of a drug overdose felt an incredible sense of guilt over his death. A child of the 1960s, she believed that her casual attitude toward his early use of marijuana was the beginning of her son's decline, ultimately leading to the use of other drugs. Ultimately, she returned to the Roman Catholic faith of her own childhood, finding solace in the Catholic Rite of Confession and Absolution.

Another aspect of meaning making is the *reconstruction of identity*. Here, a loss may challenge an individual's sense of self. How do someone redefine himself or herself after a significant loss? Is one still a father after the death of one's only child? Again, spiritual or philosophical beliefs can be helpful here as such perspectives often reaffirm the worth and value of person irrespective of role.

Two of the most important components on meaning making are the *reconstruction of the assumptive world* and *transcendental reconstruction*. The reconstruction of the assumptive world is the attempt to find a renewed sense of order, control, justice, and meaning in the world that is now damaged by the experienced loss. Transcendental reconstruction refers to reformulating one's belief that the world or God is generally benevolent. Both processes are inherently spiritual as one struggles with how an individual's belief system or philosophical framework speaks to the reality of the loss. This is the essence of C. S. Lewis's (1963) and Kushner's (1981) books as they try to make sense of their losses. It is the center of the Old Testament book of *Job* as Job confronts the fairness and reasons why a good and just man experiences devastating loss. It is evident in even the earliest extant written pieces such as the *Gilgamesh Epic* that recounts Gilgamesh's spiritual quest to find meaning in the death of a close friend.

In addition to meaning making, the second critical role of a transcendental connection is helping individuals maintain a sense of continuing bonds—with those who are now deceased—and to believe that they too will retain a connection to their progeny. The concept of *continuing bonds* was a corrective to the prior perspective that as persons were grieving they slowly detached emotional energy from the deceased and reinvested it into new relationships. Newer understandings of grief now recognize that individuals always retain bonds with prior attachments (Klass, Silverman, & Nickman, 1996).

These bonds may be retained and reinforced in a variety of ways. Obviously, memory is a major way continuing bonds are retained. The important attachments in life are always remembered—whether they are other human relationships, animals, or even beloved objects such as a bike or toy. Individuals even remember the negative attachments such as the schoolyard bully or the nasty neighbor. These memories can be readily evoked as well as spontaneously emerge. And it is these memories that can, even years later, create surges of grief as one recalls the absence of important individuals at some significant point in life.

A second bond is that individuals who are significant in one's life leave an imprint upon an individual's own biography. For example, even one's place in the family will affect a person's identity. As individuals develop, their lives are influenced by those around them in both positive and negative ways. Others bestow legacies and liabilities that influence every aspect of life from mannerisms to habits to beliefs and values.

Individuals also maintain continuing bonds through their own spiritual beliefs or philosophy. These may vary from faith in a distinct and individual existence in an afterlife, reincarnation, and reconnection in a future life, some form of transcendental connection, to simply existing in memories. In fact, many faith systems have distinct rituals such as *Kaddish* (specifically the Mourner's *Kaddish*), the veneration of ancestors in traditional Chinese traditions, memorial masses, or All Saints services. Whatever these beliefs or perspectives may be, they still allow, through spirituality, an ongoing connection that allows older mourners a continuing bond with the deceased as well as a reaffirmation that they too will be remembered.

The transcendental connection also can facilitate life review—an essential spiritual process where one reviews one's life in order to reaffirm that one's life had meaning. Both Erikson (1963) and Butler (1963) believed that to be *the* major developmental task of later life. Spiritual beliefs—a connection to the transcendental—can facilitate that process both by offering a wider sense framework for meaning making, such as interpreting one's life as a spiritual journey, or part of a larger plan, as well as allowing a sense of forgiveness for any failures.

Finally, the transcendental connection can ultimately affirm a sense of self-integrity and self-esteem. Most philosophical and faith systems emphasize that each individual is unique and of value. These beliefs assert that whether human existence is the crowning creation of a creator or an evolutionary process, human life has inherent worth.

SUMMARY

Spirituality can have a large role in assisting the older person. It offers ongoing social roles and opportunities for interaction with both age peers and others at different points in the life cycle. Spiritual beliefs provide a framework for meaning making and creating continuing bonds. In doing so, spiritual beliefs, practices, and rituals can link the lives of elders to connections from the past, present, and future—connections that span both time and space.

REFERENCES

Atchley, R. (2000). *Social forces in aging: An introduction to social gerontology* (9th ed.). Belmont, CA: Wadsworth

Butler, R. (1963). Life review: An interpretation of reminiscence in the aged. *Psychiatry: Interpersonal and Biological Perspectives, 26*, 65–76. doi:10.1080/00332747.1963.11023339

Cumming, E., & Henry, W. (1961). *Growing old*. New York, NY: Basic Books.

Doka, K. J. (1986). The church and the elderly: The impact of changing age strata on congregations. *International Journal of Aging and Human Development, 22*, 291–300. doi:10.2190/W9D2-5KCD-GG4K-FMTJ

Doka, K. J., & Schwarz, E. (1979). Assigning blame: The restoration of the sentimental order following an accidental death. *Omega: The Journal of Death and Dying, 9*, 287–292. doi:10.2190/GWU6-98P4-A2GM-YNK7

Egan, R., MacLeod, R., Jaye, C., McGee, R., Baxter, J., & Herbison, P. (2011). What is spirituality? Evidence from a New Zealand hospice study. *Mortality, 16*, 307–324. doi:10.1080/13576275.2011.613267

Erikson, E. (1963). *Childhood and society*, New York, NY: MacMillan.

Havighurst, R. (1963). Successful aging. In R. Williams, C. Tibbitts, & W. Donahue (Eds.), *Processes of aging: Social and psychological perspectives* (pp. 299–320). New York, NY: Altherton.

International Work Group on Death, Dying and Bereavement. (1990). Assumptions and principles of spiritual care. *Death Studies, 14*, 75–81. doi:10.1080/07481189008252346

Klass, D., Silverman, P., & Nickman, S. (Eds.). (1996). *Continuing bonds: New understandings of grief*. Washington, DC: Taylor & Francis.

Kushner, H. S. (1981). *When bad things happen to good people*. New York, NY: Anchor Books.

Lewis, C. S. (1963). *A grief observed*. New York, NY: Bantam Books.

Miller, J. (1994, November 5). *The transforming power of spirituality*. Presentation at the Transformative Grief conference, Burnsville, NC.

Moberg, D. (1955). The Christian religion and personal adjustment in old age. *American Sociological Review, 18*, 87–90. doi:10.2307/2087855

Moody, H. R. (2000). *Aging: Concepts and controversies* (3rd ed.). Thousand Oaks, CA: Sage.

Neimeyer, R. (2004). *Meaning reconstruction and the experience of loss.* Washington, DC: The American Psychological Association.

Puchalski, C., Ferrell, B., Virani, R., Otis-Green, S., Baird, P., Bull, J., . . . Sulmasy, D. (2009). Improving the quality of care as a dimension of palliative care: The report of the Consensus Conference. *Journal of Palliative Medicine, 12,* 885–904. doi:10.1089/jpm.2009.0142

Streib, G., & Schneider, C. (1971). *Retirement in American society.* Ithaca, NY: Cornell University Press.

12

Involving Our Pets in Relationship Building—Pets and Elder Well-Being

Aubrey H. Fine and Erika Friedmann

INTRODUCTION

Morning begins with a soft whimper which, if not acknowledged, is followed by a wet paw still damp from the morning dew from the backyard. "It's time to get up human! Time to feed me and walk me. The snooze alarm is set. I'll be back in 15 minutes to make sure you're up." In the summer it's easy to jump out of bed and get dressed and start the day, but in winter it's so tempting just to stay snuggled down in my warm bed, and so I can expect in 15 minutes or so Daisy'll be back, this time a little less patient and more willing to smack me with a paw to get me out of bed. I have no idea how this routine developed; I just know I woke up one day aware of it and appreciative for it as well. Old age doesn't come with any directions, and as we ease into it, we may become much more sedentary than we used to be. I'm sure if it weren't for my companion, Daisy, I'd lay in bed until midday, if my wife would let me, but because of her, I'm usually up around 6 a.m. and no later than 7 a.m.

Once up, it's breakfast and meds for her and then breakfast and meds for my wife and myself, followed by a short break and then off for a morning walk. Daisy is a beagle, and likes to follow her nose, so I give her free rein and we're out the door to explore the world around us and visit with whomever we encounter. The truth is Daisy has helped make the neighborhood and environment around me more familiar and in many ways helped me ease into retirement. We are known for blocks around and many times as we walk those who know us honk the car horns at us as they head for work. Daisy has helped me make friends and stay active. When she was much younger, we would walk for hours, but as she has gotten older, our walks together have become shorter, but I still walk without her after our initial morning walk. The activity that I experienced with her has become part of my daily schedule, and although she can't go as far as she used to, it hasn't stopped me. I need the activity because now it's part of my daily routine, and it will continue for me as long as I can totter out the door, but it's a routine that I would never have developed on my own. The truth is, without Daisy, I would have never started walking as much as I do, and I would have never met the many neighbors I have. I fear I would have been content just watching television, reading quietly, and doing occasional "honey-does" until I became seriously overweight and died of a coronary.

I don't think we fully understand the value of animals in our lives. If Daisy had been a cat, would she have gotten me out of bed in the morning to feed her and walk her, or would she have just curled up beside me and made it a bit more comfortable in my warm bed? Thank goodness Daisy is a dog. She completes me; she gives me purpose and responsibility. Without her, I would have little motivation to get up and get the day in gear. I help her, and she helps me. I guess that's what makes her "man's best friend."

Rudy and I have been friends for many years now. He is a month short of his 85th birthday, and it is hard to imagine Rudy without his beloved Daisy. Rudy and Daisy met for the first time in 2003. Daisy was actually his mother's dog, but after spending time with her for a few weeks, she became quite connected to Rudy. In fact, when he left Florida, his mother called Rudy to tell him how much Daisy missed her friend. When his mother passed away later that year, Rudy felt the need to adopt her. They have been inseparable ever since.

Daisy has become a vital ingredient in Rudy's daily life. She makes his life more interesting and keeps him busy and on his toes. Rudy, like many seniors, seems to benefit from his interactions with companion animals. Today's assumption that animals are good for our well-being is seemingly very accurate. Science seems to be catching up to what many of us have known for decades: animals are good for one's welfare (psychologically, socially, emotionally, and physically).

This chapter provides an overview in regard to the importance of animals in our lives; more specifically, it will address how animals help support individuals in their later years. It is amazing to appreciate that the warm heart, cold nose, and wagging tail of a four-legged creature would make such an impact. Attention is also given to considerations for people who may want to adopt pets in their later years as well.

PETS AND OLDER FAMILY MEMBERS

We have witnessed an increase in life span over the last several decades. Many of the elderly people continue of have rich fulfilled lives while others face numerous challenges to staying socially engaged. Some of the risk factors for isolation include being widowed or divorced, health-related issues affecting mobility, poverty, and reduced opportunities for social contact. Furthermore, Needell and Mehta-Naik (2016) point out that depression is also prominent in many elderly persons. Research seems to point out that depression has significant and serious medical outcomes as well as financial challenges for older adults.

It is evident that younger seniors may have been accustomed to having companion animals in their lives in their middle years. Surveys suggest that as people age, many want to live with pets (Fine, 2014). Furthermore, evidence points out the numerous benefits that can be derived from these relationships. Baun and Johnson (2010) and Johnson and Bibbo (2015) stress that increasing longevity results in eventual loss of spousal companionship and diminished interactions with extended family members who have busy lives of their own. Although animals do not replace family and friends, human–animal interactions can lessen loneliness as well as reduce numerous negative health behaviors (Baun & Johnson, 2010; Johnson & Bibbo, 2015). Researchers find that seniors who are pet owners seem to live in the "here and now," rather than reminiscing about their yesterdays (Raina, Waltner-Toews, Bonnett, Woodward, & Abernathy, 1999). Having a companion animal allows seniors the chance to be a giver rather than be a receiver of support. For some, it gives them a purpose to wake up in the morning, and to cook, to go on a walk, and/or to shop. It is not uncommon for all of us to walk with our companion animals and to do other things with them that enhances and even enriches our daily lives. This engagement enriches the relationship and enhances our bond.

WHY WE LOVE ANIMALS

Over the years, pet ownership has grown in America. According to the American Pet Products Association (APPA; 2017) National Pet Owner Survey, 68% of households own a pet; that equates to about 84.6 million homes. In fact, in 1988 when the first survey was conducted by APPA, only 56% of U.S. households owned a pet; therefore, we see a modest growth of about 12% in close to 30 years. Tables 12.1 and 12.2 provide a breakdown of the various dimensions of pet ownership in the United States for 2017 to 2018. Table 12.1 identifies that dogs are in approximately 60.2 million U.S. households, while cats are in 47.1 million households in the United States. Table 12.2 clarifies the

TABLE 12.1 *Breakdown of pet ownership in the United States according to the 2017–2018 APPA National Pet Owners Survey*

Type of Animal	Number of U.S. Households That Own a Pet (millions)
Bird	7.9
Cat	47.1
Dog	60.2
Horse	2.6
Freshwater fish	12.5
Saltwater fish	2.5
Reptile	4.6
Small animals	6.7

Souorce: From American Pet Products Association. (2017). Industry statistics and trends. Retrieved from https://www.americanpetproducts.org/pressindustrytrends.asp

actual breakdown of the total number of pets in the United States. Although cats are in fewer homes in the United States, there are more cats than dogs. There are 89.7 million dogs in our homes while there are 94.2 million cats. Other species of animals are clearly identified in Table 12.2 as well.

In fact, our pets become so much a part of our daily lives that we often endow them with human characteristics. We talk to them like people and we attribute to them such human qualities as reason, intention, cognition, emotion, and perception. Most devoted animal owners will swear to "the fact" that their pets know far more than they are letting on! Pets can also facilitate our social relationships. For example, we often connect with neighbors who have pets that we connect to. Animals are easier to talk to than people, or they act as a bridge into an introduction.

TABLE 12.2 *Breakdown of pet ownership in the United States according to the 2017–2018 APPA National Pet Owners Survey*

Type of Animal	Total Number of Pets Owned in the United States (millions)
Bird	20.3
Cat	94.2
Dog	89.7
Horse	7.6
Freshwater fish	139.3
Saltwater fish	18.8
Reptile	9.4
Small animal	14.0

Souorce: From American Pet Products Association. (2017). Industry statistics and trends. Retrieved from https://www.americanpetproducts.org/pressindustrytrends.asp

WHAT IS THE HUMAN–ANIMAL BOND?

The most respected definition of the human animal bond was developed by the American Veterinarian Medical Association and highlights the mutual benefits of the relationship and its impact on the physical and emotional well-being of both parties. Readers are encouraged to go to the AVMA site for further clarification (www.avma.org/KB/Resources/human-animal-bond/Pages/Human-Animal-Bond-AVMA.aspx). In many ways, the phrase *human–animal bond* (HAB) captures the spirit of the infant–parent bond (Fine, 2014). The first "official" use of the term *human–animal bond* appeared in the *Proceedings of the Meeting of Group for the Study of Human–Companion Animal Bond* in Dundee, Scotland (Fine & Beck, 2015). In essence, healthy relationships with pets and their owners involve a complex psychological and physiological interaction that appears to have a profound influence both on human and animal health and behavior.

Fine (2014) elaborates on some of the factors within the definition of the human–animal bond. The first factor pertains to behaviors elicited by the pet that appear humanlike. This anthropomorphic position suggests some people view animals' characteristics as having human qualities. According to James Serpell (1996), anthropomorphism is the attribution of human mental states to nonhuman animals. He suggests that this trait is almost unavoidable, considering that many pet owners name their companion animals with human names and even celebrate their birthdays. Serpell (1996) points out that "our willingness to anthropomorphize was critical to the domestication of wild animals and forming bonds with them. . . . We were particularly drawn to those species that seemed responsive to our Dr. Dolittle overtures." Research suggests animals with more infantile features are more likely to be adopted than animals with more adult features. Just as there is something cute in a baby or child's face that melts our hearts, there is something in an animal's "cuteness" that attracts us.

The animal's dependence on humans is the second critical factor. Many individuals recognize their responsibility to their pets and how much their pets depend on them. Legally, animals are considered property, but when one interviews people, most view their pets more humanely and consider them companions (Fine, 2014).

PHYSIOLOGICAL AND PSYCHOLOGICAL BENEFITS OF HUMAN–ANIMAL INTERACTIONS

The first research evidence that pet ownership was associated with health outcomes was the study by Friedmann et al. in 1980 (Friedmann, Katcher,

Lynch, & Thomas, 1980) of psychosocial predictors of 1-year survival of patients with coronary heart disease. Including pet ownership in a study of contributors to cardiovascular health was a timely application of the biopsychosocial model to the contribution of psychosocial factors to people's health. The biopsychosocial model provided the basis for exploration of the mechanisms for these benefits and can be applied to health in aging. Health is conceptualized as ranging from minimum to maximum in a continuous dynamic process that requires ongoing adaptation to challenges. The biopsychosocial model emphasizes the interactive nature of the biological, psychological, and social realms (Lindau, Laumann, Levinson, & Waite, 2003). Disruptions or enhancements in any realm impact the others and together they comprise health. From this perspective, psychological and social factors either promote health by moderating or promote disease by enhancing pathological processes. Pet ownership and human–animal interaction are conceptualized as a component of the social realm of the model that impacts other aspects of social function as well as biological and psychological function. Activities with animals can moderate or mediate the impact of these challenges on the biological, psychological, and social components of health. Cardiovascular disease was among the first physical health outcomes with recognized psychosocial etiology. Contributions of stress, anxiety, depression, and loneliness to poor cardiovascular health were recognized long before their influences on other chronic, nonpsychosomatic diseases (Haynes, Feinleib, & Kannel, 1980; Ruberman, Weinblatt, Goldberg, & Chaudhary, 1984).

Subsequent studies of the contributions of pet ownership to survival of older adults generally indicate that pets, especially dogs, are associated with cardiovascular health including survival (Gillum & Obisesan, 2010) and lower incidence of cardiac disease (Chowdhury, Nelson, Jennings, Wing, & Reid, 2017; Gillum & Obisesan, 2010; Mubanga et al., 2017). Of course, the differences may be due to characteristics of pet owners, rather than the effects of pet ownership as suggested by findings that if many demographic and health status indicators are included in the models, the beneficial contributions of pet ownership disappear in some analyses (Gillum & Obisesan, 2010; Ogechi et al., 2016).

The association of pet ownership with improved cardiovascular outcomes led to questions about the possible mechanisms for this benefit. The socializing property of human–animal interaction derived from the clinical beliefs of earlier eras was included as one aspect of the potential benefits. Benefits derived from human–animal interactions included decreased stress and anxiety, decreased loneliness and depression, and increased physical function by providing an impetus for exercise. Researchers began investigating these mechanisms using a variety of strategies ranging from qualitative interviews to observational and experimental traditions.

Stress and Anxiety

The presence of a companion animal makes people feel less stressed and anxious. Some people view having animals in their homes as a source of security (Fine, 2014). This may be even more significant to the elderly who may view their companions as protectors.

Experimental research in populations ranging from children, through college students, to adults provided evidence that human–animal interaction reduces stress, as indicated by decreased blood pressure and heart rate; moderated stress responses to challenges, as indicated by changes in blood pressure and heart rate; and reduced anxiety (Friedmann, Son, & Saleem, 2015). More recently, studies using other stress biomarkers such as cortisol, immunoglobulin A, alpha amylase, and skin conductance confirm the physiologic effects of human–animal interactions on people (Beetz, Julius, Turner, & Kotrschal, 2012; Krause-Parello, 2008, 2012). While it is clear that the presence of a companion animal reduces stress, it is not clear from these studies whether physical contact with the animal is necessary for stress reduction (Friedmann, Son, & Salem, 2015). In the only randomized clinical trial of the contribution of pet ownership to stress, Allen, Shykoff, and Izzo (2001) found that stress responses were reduced in hypertensive individuals who obtained pet dogs or cats compared with those who did not obtain pets. Both groups were receiving anti-hypertensive medications. In many situations, individuals cannot own pets, so it is important to understand the potential health-promoting contribution of human interaction with companion animals who are not their own.

Evidence from several studies also supports that human–animal interaction is sufficient to reduce stress responses. Further attitudes about animals are related to the magnitude of the reduction in stress; in a study of college students, those who had more positive attitudes toward dogs had lower stress responses with a friendly dog present than those who had less positive attitudes (Friedmann, Locker, & Lockwood, 1993). One major question is whether the support from human–animal interaction is complementary or a substitute for support from other people. From the cardiovascular data, it appears that both types of support can contribute, and therefore are valuable. Both the 1980 study of pet ownership and survival of individuals with coronary heart disease and a subsequent study by the same researchers showed that the contribution of pet ownership to survival in patients with heart disease was independent of the effect of support from other people. Both types of support were associated with decreased mortality (Friedmann & Thomas, 1995; Friedmann et al., 1980). Furthermore, the presence of a friendly animal reduced stress responses more than the presence of other supportive friends or a spouse (Allen, Blascovich, & Mendes, 2002). None of the physiological studies were conducted in healthy older adults. While findings may generalize to an older population, additional research may be required to confirm them.

Loneliness and Depression

Considerable evidence supports the position that pet ownership or interaction with animals decreases social isolation and loneliness, and facilitates social interaction. Historically, animals were used as therapeutic agents in clinical settings prior to quantitative assessment of their value to promote specific health outcomes. In fact, beginning in the late 18th century, animal companionship was valued for socialization of children and individuals with mental illness (Serpell, 2015).

Pet owners perceive pets as an important source of social support. A vast majority of pet owners indicate that pets are members of their families. Pets' importance is demonstrated by their place in attachment hierarchies. University students are more attached to their pets than to their siblings, but less attached to pets than to romantic partners, parents, and close friends (Meehan, Massavelli, & Pachana, 2017). The relative importance of pets in the attachment hierarchy likely increases as people age and parents and close friends die. People may seek out animal companionship when they are lonely or feeling bad about their social situation. Even thinking about cats or dogs provided relief from social rejection (Brown, Hengy, & McConnell, 2016).

A recent systematic literature review suggested that loneliness may be reduced by interaction with service dogs or other animals; however, the evidence of causation is weak. Further, the amount of time spent with the animals necessary for this effect is not evident (Gilbey & Tani, 2015). A large population-based survey, not included in the review, found a 36% reduction in loneliness in older adult cat owners compared with nonowners (Stanley, Conwell, Bowen, & Van Orden, 2014). Fine (2014) points out that elderly individuals, especially those who are socially isolated, turn to a pet for a sympathetic ear. Among older women, pet owners were more likely to report higher levels of happiness than nonowners (Ory & Goldberg, 1983).

Ample evidence supports the notion that the presence of an animal encourages social interaction. Perhaps one of the greatest benefits that animals provide elderly persons is their role in acting as *social capital*. Lang and Hornburg (1998) define social capital as the glue that holds society together.

Pets function as one source of social capital; they enhance communication and solidarity among people and act as lubricants for social interaction in the community (Wood, 2011; Wood, Giles-Corti, & Bulsara, 2005; Wood, Shardlow, & Willis, 2009). Additionally, pet owners perceived greater friendliness and more amiable environments in their communities (Arkow, 2015).

When a young adult added a dog to accompany her during her typical daily activity, the presence of a dog catalyzed social interactions, especially with strangers (McNicholas & Collis, 2000). Increased social interaction occurs even when an individual with the pet looks scruffy or ill kempt. While in this study the "pet owner" was a young adult; the larger effect with strangers suggests increased value for socially isolated older adults. In a study of young adults in a work environment, participants exhibited more prosocial behavior in work groups when a dog was present than without a dog present. People also were perceived as more trustworthy when the dog was present (Colarelli, McDonald, Christensen, & Honts, 2017).

Much of the research on the contribution of human–animal interactions to social interaction in older adults is derived from studies of animal-assisted interventions (AAIs) for individuals with cognitive impairment who reside in long-term care facilities. Overall, AAIs improved both the quantity and the quality of social interaction in these populations (Bernabei et al., 2013). Use of a robot pet dog or seal also increased social interaction compared with a visit by a person, but lacked the impetus for sustained interactions when compared with pet visits (Kramer, Friedmann, & Bernstein, 2009; Thodberg et al., 2016).

Depression is a major problem among socially isolated older adults; the antidepressant impact of human–animal interaction can help break a spiral cycle of increasing depression and poorer health as individuals age. Several studies with older adults demonstrate that human–animal interaction leads to decreases in depression among psychiatric patients, individuals with disabilities, or individuals who live in assisted living facilities (Friedmann, Galik, et al., 2015; Moretti et al., 2011; Olsen et al., 2016; Souter & Miller, 2007). The health benefits of pet ownership may be more important for some individuals than others. For example, pet ownership tended to be associated with survival in community living individuals who had experienced a heart attack, who had more symptoms of depression, but not in those who had fewer symptoms (Friedmann, Thomas, & Son, 2011).

As one would expect, not all older adults benefit equally from pet ownership or interacting with a companion animal. Pet attachment support mediated the relationship between loneliness and poor health in older community living women (Krause-Parello, 2008). The relationship between loneliness and poor health decreased when pet attachment increased. In contrast, social support did not influence the magnitude of the relationship. These findings imply the possibility of a major impact on health and psychological function for individuals who own pets. Pets or human–animal interaction will not be beneficial for everyone, only for individuals who like and are attached to them.

Physical Activity

Pets, especially dogs, motivate owners to exercise, both because they require walking and because they provide companionship during walks. In a qualitative study of dog walking by individuals with chronic health conditions, most of whom were older adults, social isolation and connections were themes affected by dog walking (Smith, Treharne, & Tumilty, 2017). Large cross-sectional national surveys indicate that dog owners exercise more than owners of other pets or pet nonowners (Anderson, Reid, & Jennings, 1992; Bauman, Russell, Furber, & Dobson, 2000; Dembicki & Anderson, 1996; Mullersdorf, Granstrom, Sahlqvist, & Tillgren, 2010; Oka & Shibata, 2009; Sirard, Patnode, Hearst, & Laska, 2011). Dog walking is related to meeting national recommendations for moderate to vigorous physical activity (Coleman et al., 2008). Not all dog owners walk their dogs; in one U.S. national survey, among dog owners who reported walking for pet care, 59% took two or more walks per day and 80% took at least one 10-minute walk a day (Ham & Epping, 2006). Walking speed decreases with age, and decreases may precede recognition of mobility-related difficulty (Simonsick et al., 2008). In data from the Health Aging and Body Composition (ABC) study, the 36% of 71- to 82-year-olds who walked their dogs at least three times per day had faster gait speed than nonowners or dog owners who did not walk their dogs regularly. In longitudinal analysis, dog walkers showed similar declines in gait speed but still maintained higher speeds than dog nonwalkers (Thorpe et al., 2006). Walking a dog has a purpose and thus can increase adherence with a walking exercise program (Friedmann, Son, & Salem, 2015). The findings that dogs promote physical activity combined with the social facilitation occurring when individuals are accompanied by a dog have particular importance for individuals with chronic health conditions who may be more socially isolated than their healthy contemporaries.

The health benefits of human–animal interaction may be most important for individuals who live alone, are socially isolated, and have limited access to other sources of social support. The Centers for Disease Control and Prevention's (CDC's) website recognizes increased social interaction and reduced loneliness as well as reduction in heart disease risk factors and providing an impetus to exercise as health benefits of human–animal interaction (Centers for Disease Control and Prevention, 2014). The cardiovascular studies that established the relationship of pet ownership supported the independent contributions of human–animal interaction and human–human interaction as sources of social support that promote health. The studies also suggest separate roles of pet attachment support and human social support in the relationship of loneliness to health. The CDC confirms the widespread understanding that pet ownership contributes to social and physiological aspects of cardiovascular health, including reducing blood pressure (a biological component of health that is related to stress—a psychological component of health), decreasing loneliness and increasing socialization (social components of health), and promoting exercise (www.cdc.gov/healthypets/health-benefits/index.html).

UNDERSTANDING THE HUMAN–ANIMAL BOND

But why do people naturally gravitate to foster meaningful relationships with animals? Theoretically, there are three accepted theories. The first hypothesis suggests that animals serve as *social supports*. In essence, it is believed that animals provide comfort and strength through difficult times. In regard to persons with disabilities, they may rely on these animals as an outlet for their feelings during stressful circumstances (Fine & Eisen, 2016; Melson, 2001; Strand, 2004). The pets may also physically calm down their owners by reducing blood pressure and heart rate and decreasing the levels of stress hormones such as cortisol (Handlin et al., 2011). Beetz, Uvnas-Moberg, et al. (2012) and Wohlfarth, Mutschler, Beetz, Kreuser, and Korsten-Reck (2013) hypothesized that the interaction with animals by playing, petting, or being around them impacted several hormonal agents including decreasing cortisol (destressing) as well as increasing serotonin, oxytocin, and dopamine. Ironically, what has been sensationalized over the years as being a magical relationship is now being better understood scientifically and neurobiologically.

Of course, strong relationships with animals may also exist because of our innate attachment needs. Attachment theory was developed by Bowlby (1969) to describe parent–child relationships and humans' desire to protect. Zilcha-Mano, Mikuliner, and Shaver (2012) suggest that there is evidence that humans also view their companion animals in a similar fashion. Barba (1995) described owners' relationship with their pets as parallel to the parent–child relationship. Pets depend on humans for care and protection (Fine, 2014). This caretaking role may provide persons with disabilities opportunities to be caregivers rather than receivers. Further, there is also biological evidence that the neurotransmitter oxytocin is prevalent not only in parent–child relationships (highlighting familial love) but also between owners and their pets (Odendall & Meintjes, 2003). Additionally, research by Carlisle (2014) indicated an increase in social behavior among children, suggesting that children also seem to show strong levels of attachment to their animals.

E. O. Wilson and Stephen R. Kellert developed a theory called "biophilia," which suggested that humans evolved to bond with other forms of life as a means of survival (Kellert, 1997; Wilson, 1984). As can be seen, each of these orientations provides a different glimpse to why we have this unique relationship with animals.

HOW TO SELECT A PET

It is critical to recognize that when one recommends a pet for an older adult, certain things need to be considered. Baun and Johnson (2010) urge that the primary consideration needs to be the safety and health of the individual. For some people, companionship may be best served by having a dog or a cat, while in other cases having a caged animal, such as a bird, for company may be just as valuable. Fine (2015) developed the Lifestyle Attributes for Pet Selection (LAPS) scale, which analyzes several elements that should be considered when integrating an animal into one's life. Table 12.3 identifies some of the key variables.

SUMMARY

When one considers the prospects of aging, considerations of variables that could be found to help individuals age more gracefully are paramount to appreciate. Within this chapter, attention has been given to understand the value of pets in the lives of the elderly. Over the course of the last few decades, more prominent attention has been given to understand the mechanisms and the rationale for animal companionship. The authors believe that pet companionship is a viable consideration for many older individuals, especially if there is an affinity toward animals. It is cautioned that relationships with animals should not be viewed unrealistically as a panacea for change, but rather as a healthy alternative in making a difference in the lives of many. As George Graham Vest elegantly stated in a speech he gave to the U.S. Senate in 1884, "The one absolutely unselfish friend that man can have in this selfish world, the one that never deserts him, the one that never proves ungrateful or treacherous, is his dog. When all other friends desert, he remains." It is the authors' hope that the readers will consider this position and recognize that the impact of our relationships are more than just "puppy love."

TABLE 12.3 *Considerations for Pet Selection*

A. **Knowing the species you select: Understanding the behavior and health needs of the animal you want.**
B. **Recognizing two critical variables: Activity level and size of animal.** Smaller and less active animals seem to relate well with people who were not very active individuals.
C. **Lifestyle.** People also need to think about how they live their life, rather than only considering a specific species/breed of animal. An animal may contribute to a lifestyle, but probably will not change it tremendously.
D. **Lifestyle questions to consider:** One needs to take stock of his or her lifestyle and try to find a companion animal who seems to fit best that individual's activity level, home, and yard size. Additional considerations include if the individual prefers an independent and/or slightly aloof animal. The following list contains several other questions and answers that you may want to consider:
   1. **Do we want a puppy or a dog, a kitten or a cat, or a small caged animal?** This is an important question that needs examination. For example, if you get a puppy, you need to spend a lot of time shaping and training the behaviors and developing the relationship. A cute puppy will grow up quickly. An older dog comes with many benefits. What you see is often what you get. Older dogs often tend to not have the chewing issues or the problems that very young puppies pose. Also, it is important to keep in mind that a 1-year-old dog is still a juvenile and was a puppy just a short time ago. Sometimes older dogs or cats are a great addition. They require less time and they can be less active.
   2. **Do you have the time?**
   3. **Do you have the finances?** Not just for the acquisition, but also for the continued care throughout a lifetime, which may include veterinary support during illness.
   4. **Possible changes in your life.**
   5. **Do you have the space?**
   6. **Health-related concerns: Does anyone have allergies?**
   7. **Are you prepared to invest time and resources into training on how to coexist with a pet?**
   8. **Living arrangements: Do you have the landlord's permission?**
   9. **What will you do if you go on vacation?**
   10. **Is this going to be a safe pet? How big will it get? How long will this pet live? Could it be dangerous?**

REFERENCES

Allen, K., Blascovich, J., & Mendes, W. B. (2002). Cardiovascular reactivity and the presence of pets, friends, and spouses: The truth about cats and dogs. *Psychosomatic Medicine, 64*, 727–739. doi:10.1097/00006842-200209000-00005

Allen, K., Shykoff, B. E., & Izzo, J. L. (2001). Pet ownership, but not ACE inhibitor therapy, blunts home blood pressure responses to mental stress. *Hypertension, 38*, 815–820.

American Pet Products Association. (2017). Pet industry market size & ownership statistics. Retrieved from https://www.americanpetproducts.org/press_industrytrends.asp

Anderson, W. P., Reid, C. M., & Jennings, G. L. (1992). Pet ownership and risk factors for cardiovascular disease. *The Medical Journal of Australia, 157*, 298–301.

Arkow, P. (2015). Animal therapy on the community level: The impact of pets on social capital. In A. Fine (Ed.), *Handbook on animal-assisted therapy: Theoretical foundations and guidelines for practice* (4th ed., pp. 43–52). San Diego, CA: Elsevier.

Barba, B. E. (1995) A critical review of research on human/companion animal relationship: 1988 through 1993. *Anthrozoös, 8*(1), 9–20. doi:10.2752/089279395787156509

Bauman, A. E., Russell, S. J., Furber, S. E., & Dobson, A. J. (2000). The epidemiology of dog walking: An unmet need for human and canine health. *The Medical Journal of Australia, 175*, 632–634.

Baun, M., & Johnson, R. (2010). Human/Animal interaction and successful aging. In A. Fine (Ed.), *Handbook on animal-assisted therapy: Theoretical foundations and guidelines for practice* (3rd ed., pp., 283–301). San Diego, CA: Elsevier.

Beetz, A., Julius, H., Turner, D., & Kotrschal, K. (2012). Effects of social support by a dog on stress modulation in male children with insecure attachment. *Frontiers in Psychology, 3*, 352. doi:10.3389/fpsyg.2012.00352.

Beetz, A., Uvnas-Moberg, K., Julius, H., & Kotrschal, K. (2012). Psychosocial and psychophysiological effects of human-animal interactions: The possible role of oxytocin. *Frontiers in Psychology. 3*, 1–15. doi:10.3389/fpsyg.2012.00234

Bernabei, V., De Ronchi, D., La Ferla, T., Moretti, F., Tonelli, L., Ferrari, B., . . . Atti, A. R. (2013). Animal-assisted interventions for elderly patients affected by dementia or psychiatric disorders: aA review. *Journal of Psychiatric Research, 47*, 762–773. doi:10.1016/j.jpsychires.2012.12.014

Bowlby, J. (1969). Disruption of affectional bonds and its effects on behavior. *Canada's Mental Health Supplement, 69*, 1–17

Brown, C. M., Hengy, S. M., & McConnell, A. R. (2016). Thinking about cats or dogs provides relief from social rejection. *Anthrozoös, 29*, 47–58. doi:10.1080/20414005.2015.1067958

Carlisle, G. K. (2014). The social skills and attachment to dogs of children with autism spectrum disorder. *Journal of Autism and Developmental Disorders, 45*(5), 1137–1145. doi:10.1007/s10803-014-2267-7

Centers for Disease Control and Prevention. (2014). Healthy pets healthy people. Retrieved from https://www.cdc.gov/healthypets/health-benefits/index.html

Chowdhury, E. K., Nelson, M. R., Jennings, G. L., Wing, L. M., & Reid, C. M. (2017). Pet ownership and survival in the elderly hypertensive population. *Journal of Hypertension, 35*, 769–775. doi:10.1097/hjh.0000000000001214

Colarelli, S. M., McDonald, A. M., Christensen, M. S., & Honts, C. (2017). A companion dog increases prosocial behavior in work groups. *Anthrozoös, 30*, 77–89. doi:10.1080/08927936.2017.1270595

Coleman, K. J., Rosenberg, D. E., Conway, T. L., Sallis, J. F., Saelens, B. E., Frank, L. D., & Cain, K. (2008). Physical activity, weight status, and neighborhood characteristics of dog walkers. *Preventive Medicine, 47*, 309–312. doi:10.1016/j.ypmed.2008.05.007

Dembicki, D., & Anderson, J. (1996). Pet ownership may be a factor in improved health of the elderly. *Journal of Nutrition for the Elderly, 15*, 15–31. doi:10.1300/J052v15n03_02

Fine, A. H. (2014). *Our faithful companions: Exploring the essence of our kinship with animals.* Crawford, CO: Alpine Publications.

Fine, A. H. (2015). *Handbook on animal-assisted therapy: Theoretical foundations and guidelines for practice* (4th ed.). San Diego, CA: Elsevier.

Fine, A. H., & Beck, A. (2015). Understanding our kinship with animals: Input for healthcare professionals interested in the human/animal bond. In A. H. Fine (Ed.), *Handbook on animal-assisted therapy: Theoretical foundations for guidelines and practice* (3rd ed., pp. 3–15). San Diego, CA: Elsevier.

Fine, A. H., & Eisen, C. J. (2016). *Afternoon with puppy: Inspirations from a therapist and his animals* (2nd ed.). West Lafayette, IN: Purdue University Press.

Friedmann, E., Galik, E., Thomas, S. A., Hall, P. S., Chung, S. Y., & McCune, S. (2015). Evaluation of a pet-assisted living intervention for improving functional status in assisted living residents with mild to moderate cognitive impairment: A pilot study. *American Journal of Alzheimer's Disease & Other Dementias, 30,* 276–289. doi:10.1177/1533317514545477

Friedmann, E., Katcher, A. H., Lynch, J. J., & Thomas, S. A. (1980). Animal companions and one-year survival of patients after discharge from a coronary care unit. *Public Health Reports, 95,* 307–312.

Friedmann, E., Locker, B. Z., & Lockwood, R. (1993). Perception of animals and cardiovascular responses during verbalization with an animal present. *Anthrozoos, 6,* 115–134. doi:10.2752/089279393787002303

Friedmann, E., Son, H., & Saleem, M. (2015). The animal-human bond: Health and wellness. In A. H. Fine (Ed.), *Handbook of animal assisted therapy* (4th ed., pp. 73–90). New York, NY: Academic Press.

Friedmann, E., & Thomas, S. A. (1995). Pet ownership, social support, and one-year survival after acute myocardial infarction in the Cardiac Arrhythmia Suppression Trial (CAST). *The American Journal of Cardiology, 76,* 1213–1217. doi:10.1016/s0002-9149(99)80 343-9

Friedmann, E., Thomas, S. A., & Son, H. (2011). Pets, depression and long term survival in community living patients following myocardial infarction. *Anthrozoos, 24,* 273–285. doi:10.2752/175303711X13045914865268

Gilbey, A., & Tani, K. (2015). Companion animals and loneliness: A systematic review of quantitative studies. *Anthrozoos, 28,* 181–197. doi:10.1080/08927936.2015.11435396

Gillum, R. F., & Obisesan, T. O. (2010). Living with companion animals, physical activity and mortality in a U.S. national cohort. *International Journal of Environmental Research and Public Health, 7,* 2452–2459. doi:10.3390/ijerph7062452

Ham, S. A., & Epping, J. (2006). Dog walking and physical activity in the United States. *Preventing Chronic Disease, 3,* A47.

Handlin, L., Eva Hydbring-Sandberg, E., Nilsson, A., Ejdebäck, M., Jansson, J., & Uvnäs-Moberg, K. (2011). Short-term interaction between dogs and their owners: Effects on oxytocin, cortisol, insulin and heart rate-An exploratory study. *Anthrozoös, 24*(3), 301–315. doi:10.2752/175303711X13045914865385

Haynes, S., Feinleib, M., & Kannel, W. B. (1980). The relationship of psychosocial factors to coronary heart disease in the Framingham Study. III. Eight-year incidence of coronary heart disease. *American Journal of Epidemiology, 111,* 37–58. doi:10.1093/oxfordjournals.aje.a112873

Johnson, R., & Bibbo, J. (2015). Human-animal interaction in the aging boom. In A. Fine (Ed.), *Handbook on animal-assisted therapy: Theoretical foundations and guidelines for practice* (4th ed., pp. 249–261). San Diego, CA: Elsevier.

Kellert, S. (1997). *From kinship to mastery: Biophilia in human evolution and development.* Washington, DC: Island Press.

Kramer, S. C., Friedmann, E., & Bernstein, P. L. (2009). Comparison of the effect of human interaction, animal-assisted therapy, and AIBO-assisted therapy on long-term care residents with dementia. *Anthrozoos, 22,* 43–57. doi:10.2752/175303708X390464

Krause-Parello, C. A. (2008). The mediating effect of pet attachment support between loneliness and general health in older females living in the community. *Journal of Community Health Nursing, 25,* 1–14. doi:10.1080/07370010701836286

Krause-Parello, C. A. (2012). Pet ownership and older women: The relationships among loneliness, pet attachment support, human social support, and depressed mood. *Geriatric Nursing, 33,* 194–203. doi:10.1016/j.gerinurse.2011.12.005

Lang, R., & Hornburg, S. (1998). What is social capital and why is it important to public policy? *Housing Policy Debate, 9*(1), 1–16. doi:10.1080/10511482.1998.9521284

Lindau, S. T., Laumann, E. O., Levinson, W., & Waite, L. J. (2003). Synthesis of scientific disciplines in pursuit of health: The interactive biopsychosocial model. *Perspectives in Biology and Medicine, 46,* S74. doi:10.1353/pbm.2003.0055

McNicholas, J., & Collis, G. M. (2000). Dogs as catalysts for social interactions: Robustness of the effect. *British Journal of Psychology, 91,* 61–70. doi:10.1348/000712600161673

Meehan, M., Massavelli, B., & Pachana, N. (2017). Using attachment theory and social support theory to examine and measure pets as sources of social support and attachment figures. *Anthrozoos, 30,* 273–289. doi:10.1080/08927936.2017.1311050

Melson, G. F. (2001). Child development and the human-companion animal bond. *American Behavioral Scientist, 47,* 31–39. doi:10.1177/0002764203255210

Moretti, F., De Ronchi, D., Bernabei, V., Marchetti, L., Ferrari, B., Forlani, C., . . . Atti, A. R. (2011). Pet therapy in elderly patients with mental illness. *Psychogeriatrics, 11,* 125–129. doi:10.1111/j.1479-8301.2010.00329.x

Mubanga, M., Byberg, L., Nowak, C., Egenvall, A., Magnusson, P. K., Ingelsson, E., & Fall, T. (2017). Dog ownership and the risk of cardiovascular disease and death—A nationwide cohort study. *Scientific Reports, 7,* 15821. doi:10.1038/s41598-017-16118-6

Mullersdorf, M., Granstrom, F., Sahlqvist, L., & Tillgren, P. (2010). Aspects of health, physical/leisure activities, work and socio-demographic data associated with pet ownership in Sweden. *Scandinavian Journal of Public Health, 38*(1), 53–63. doi:10.1177/1403494809344358

Needell, N. J., & Mehta-Naik, N. (2016). Is pet ownership helpful in reducing the risk and severity of geriatric depression? *Geriatrics, 1,* 24. doi:10.3390/geriatrics1040024

Odendall, J. S., & Meintjes, R. A. (2003). Neurophysiological correlates of affiliative behavior between humans and dogs. *The Veterinary Journal, 165*(3), 296–301. doi:10.1016/S1090-0233(02)00237-X

Ogechi, I., Snook, K., Davis, B. M., Hansen, A. R., Liu, F., & Zhang, J. (2016). Pet ownership and the risk of dying from cardiovascular disease among adults without major chronic medical conditions. *High Blood Pressure & Cardiovascular Prevention, 23,* 245–253. doi:10.1007/s40292-016-0156-1

Oka, K., & Shibata, A. (2009). Dog ownership and health-related physical activity among Japanese adults. *Journal of Physical Activity & Health, 6,* 412. doi:10.1123/jpah.6.4.412

Olsen, C., Pedersen, I., Bergland, A., Enders-Slegers, M.-J., Patil, G., & Ihlebaek, C. (2016). Effect of animal-assisted interventions on depression, agitation and quality of life in nursing home residents suffering from cognitive impairment or dementia: A cluster randomized controlled trial. *International Journal of Geriatric Psychiatry, 31,* 1312–1321. doi:10.1002/gps.4436

Ory, M. G., & Goldberg, E. L. (1983). Pet possession and well-being in elderly women. *Research on Aging, 5,* 389–409. doi:10.1177/0164027583005003007

Raina, P., Waltner-Toews, D., Bonnett, B., Woodward, C., & Abernathy, T. (1999). Influence of companion animals on the physical and psychological health of older people: An analysis of a one-year longitudinal study. *Journal of the American Geriatric Society, 47,* 323–329. doi:10.1111/j.1532-5415.1999.tb02996.x

Ruberman, W., Weinblatt, E., Goldberg, J. D., & Chaudhary, B. S. (1984). Psychosocial influences on mortality after myocardial infarction. *New England Journal of Medicine, 311,* 552–559. doi:10.1056/NEJM198408303110902

Serpell, J. (1996). *In the company of animals: A study of human-animal relationships*. Cambridge, UK: Cambridge University Press.
Serpell, J. (2015). Animal assisted interventions in historical perspective. In A. H. Fine (Ed.), *Handbook of animal assisted therapy* (4th ed., pp. 11–20). New York, NY: Academic Press.
Simonsick, E. M., Newman, A. B., Visser, M., Goodpaster, B., Kritchevsky, S. B., Rubin, S., . . . Harris, T. B. (2008). Mobility limitation in self-described well-functioning older adults: Importance of endurance walk testing. *The Journals of Gerontology Series A: Biological Sciences and Medical Sciences, 63*, 841–847. doi:10.1093/gerona/63.8.841
Sirard, J. R., Patnode, C. D., Hearst, M. O., & Laska, M. N. (2011). Dog ownership and adolescent physical activity. *American Journal of Preventive Medicine, 40*, 334–337. doi:10.1016/j.amepre.2010.11.007
Smith, C. M., Treharne, G. J., & Tumilty, S. (2017). "All those ingredients of the walk": The therapeutic spaces of dog-walking for people with long-term health conditions. *Anthrozoos, 30*, 327–340. doi:10.1080/08927936.2017.1311063
Souter, M. A., & Miller, M. D. (2007). Do animal-assisted activities effectively treat depression? A meta-analysis. *Anthrozoos, 20*, 167–180. doi:10.2752/175303707X207954
Stanley, I. H., Conwell, Y., Bowen, C., & Van Orden, K. A. (2014). Pet ownership may attenuate loneliness among older adult primary care patients who live alone. *Aging & Mental Health, 18*, 394–399. doi:10.1080/13607863.2013.837147
Strand, E. B. (2004). Interparental conflict and youth maladjustment: The buffering effect of pets. *Stress, Trauma, and Crisis: An International Journal, 7*(3), 151–168. doi:10.1080/15434610490500071
Thodberg, K., Sorensen, L. U., Videbech, P. B., Poulsen, P. H., Houbak, B., Damgaard, V., . . . Christensen, J. W. (2016). Behavioral responses of nursing home residents to visits from a person with a dog, a robot seal or a toy cat. *Anthrozoos, 29*, 107–121. doi:10.1080/08927936.2015.1089011
Thorpe, R. J., Jr., Simonsick, E. M., Brach, J. S., Ayonayon, H., Satterfield, S., Harris, T. B., . . . Health, Aging and Body Composition Study. (2006). Dog ownership, walking behavior, and maintained mobility in late life. *Journal of the American Geriatrics Society, 54*, 1419–1424. doi:10.1111/j.1532-5415.2006.00856.x
Wilson, E. O. (1984). *Biophilia*. Cambridge, MA: Harvard University Press.
Wohlfarth, R., Mutschler, B., Beetz, A., Kreuser, F., & Korsten-Reck, U. (2013). Dogs motivate obese children for physical activity: Key elements of a motivational theory of animal-assisted interventions. *Frontiers in Psychology, 4*, 796. doi:10.3389/fpsyg.2013.00796
Wood, L. (2011). Community benefits of human-animal interactions. . .the ripple effect. In P. McCardle, S. McCune, J. A. Griffin, L. Esposito, & L. S. Freund (Eds.), *Animals in our lives: Human–animal interaction in family, community, & therapeutic settings* (pp. 23–42). Baltimore, MD: Paul H. Brookes Publishing.
Wood, L., Giles-Corti, B., & Bulsara, M. (2005). The pet connection: Pets as a conduit for social capital? *Social Science & Medicine, 61*, 1159–1173. doi:10.1016/j.socscimed.2005.01.017
Wood, L., Shardlow, T., & Willis, S. (2009). *Living well together: How companion animals can help strengthen social fabric*. Pert, Australia: Petcare Information & Advisory Service Pty Ltd and the Centre for the Built Environment and Health, School of Population Health, at the University of Western Australia.
Zilcha-Mano, S., Mikuliner, M., & Shaver, P. R. (2012). Pets as safe havens and secure bases: The moderating of pet attachment orientation. *Journal of Research in Personality, 46*(5), 571–580. doi:10.1016/j.jrp.2012.06.005

PART III
Special Challenges Influencing Social Connectedness in Later Life

13

Social Networks and Social Isolation Among LGBT Older Adults

Sandra S. Butler

INTRODUCTION AND POPULATION DESCRIPTION

It is only recently that the experiences of older lesbian, gay, bisexual, and transgender (LGBT) adults have come into the public eye. This population has been largely invisible both in mainstream society and in the youth-oriented gay communities. Two national trends—one demographic and one cultural—have served to change that situation (Services and Advocacy for Gay, Lesbian, Bisexual and Transgender Elders [SAGE], 2014). As our society ages, so do members of the LGBT community, and increasing numbers have led to greater awareness of some of the challenges faced by these individuals. Simultaneously, there has been a cultural shift toward greater acceptance and increasing civil rights for LGBT individuals, making it far more likely for them to live openly and more visibly than in the past.

In discussing LGBT older adults, it is critical to keep in mind what a diverse group of people this represents. There are significant differences among the populations making up the LGBT acronym (see Box 13.1 for definitions) in terms of race and ethnicity, socioeconomic status, family structure, and geography. Unfortunately, this heterogeneity among LGBT older adults has often been ignored owing to the scarcity of data and the "effort to crack the wall of invisibility that has surrounded LGBT aging" generally (Adams, 2016, p. 94).

According to estimates by the Aging with Pride: National Health, Aging and Sexuality/Gender Study (NHAS)—the largest national study to date on the health and well-being of LGBT older adults—2.4% of adults age 50 and

> **BOX 13.1 DEFINITIONS OF TERMS**
>
> **Lesbian** refers to women who are physically and/or emotionally attracted to women.
> **Gay** generally refers to men who are physically and/or emotionally attracted to men. It can sometimes be used as an umbrella term to include lesbians.
> **Bisexual** refers to people who are physically and/or emotionally attracted to both genders.
> **Transgender** refers to people whose gender identity and/or expression does not align with the sex they were assigned at birth (Fredriksen-Goldsen, 2016).

older in the United States self-identify as LGBT (Fredriksen-Goldsen & Kim, 2017). Approximately 2.7 million adults age 50 and older and 1.1 million age 65 and older self-identified as LGBT in 2014; this is expected to more than double by 2060, with over 5 million adults age 50 and older self-identifying as LGBT (Fredriksen-Goldsen & Kim, 2017). Studies indicate that many more people than those who self-identify as LGBT engage in same-sex behavior and/or are attracted to members of the same sex. Including such individuals would expand the estimate of LGBT older adults in 2060 to 20 million (Fredriksen-Goldsen & Kim, 2017).

Similar to all populations of older adults is the issue of age: We often talk of young-old and old-old, for example. Among older LGBT individuals, there is an important cohort effect related to the historical and social context of their lives. Those who came of age in the 1940s and the 1950s lived with overt discrimination and often feared for their safety should their private lives be discovered. Members of the baby boom generation, on the other hand, were still relatively young at the time of the Civil Rights movement and its aftermath, shaping a different life experience (Fredriksen-Goldsen et al., 2011). All LGBT older adults have faced stigma owing to their sexual orientation or gender identity, a phenomenon that affects how they carry out their social lives.

HISTORICAL CONTEXT

Today's LGBT adults, age 65 and older, lived their formative years prior to the gay liberation of the 1970s. Although homophobia, heterosexism, and transphobia still exist today, they were far more pervasive when current older adults were in their adolescence and young adulthood. Many older LGBT individuals lived their early years before the Stonewall rebellion of 1969, often considered the watershed event initiating gay civil rights. The New York City Stonewall Inn was a gay bar frequently raided by police in the 1960s when being gay was considered a crime. During one such raid in the summer of 1969, patrons fought back (Butler, 2004). The resulting 3 days of rioting marked the start of active resistance to antigay violence.

The current cohort of LGBT older adults grew up at a time when gay sex was considered illegal. Sodomy statutes existed throughout the country until the 1960s and 1970s when some states repealed their laws. As recently as 1986, the Supreme Court upheld Georgia's sodomy law in *Bowers v. Hardwick*. This decision served to remind LGBT individuals that society considered them criminals, underscoring the necessity to conceal much of whom they were (American Civil Liberties Union [ACLU], n.d.). Not until 2003 did the Supreme Court overturn this decision in *Lawrence v. Texas*, finally striking down the sodomy laws that still existed in 14 states at the time. During this era, LGBT individuals were not only considered criminals, but also deviant, classified as child molesters, voyeurs, exhibitionists, and people who committed antisocial and destructive crimes in the first two editions of the *Diagnostic and Statistical Manual of Mental Disorders* (*DSM*), published by the American Psychiatric Association in 1952 and 1968. It was not until 1973 that homosexuality was removed from the list of *DSM* disorders (Butler, 2004).

Given this historical landscape, the current cohort of LGBT older adults has learned to conceal their identities and to be distrustful of healthcare providers. Some have internalized the stigma that has surrounded them for years. On one hand, these natural coping mechanisms have had an impact on the health and well-being of older LGBT adults, including their susceptibility to social isolation. On the other hand, they have had to be resilient to survive the challenges of living in a hostile society, and rich communities have formed to support one another.

HEALTH WELL-BEING, AND RISKS OF SOCIAL ISOLATION FOR LGBT OLDER ADULTS

Early research on sexual minorities began in the second half of the 20th century. Studies tended to be conducted with small convenience samples, but despite methodological weaknesses, they began to counter myths that old gay men and lesbians were unhappy and lonely (Fredriksen-Goldsen, Kim, Shiu, Goldsen, & Emlet, 2015). These early studies demonstrated that older gay men and lesbians had thriving community and family lives, and even had some advantages over the general aging population with regard to social connectedness. Some authors submitted that as LGBT older adults had spent their entire lives facing discrimination and stigma, the challenges of aging were perceived as less difficult than for their non-LGBT peers. In other words, a developed "crisis competence" helped LGBT individuals to adjust to old age (Butler, 2004; Fredriksen-Goldsen, 2016; Fredriksen-Goldsen et al., 2015).

Two recent national studies—the ongoing longitudinal NHAS study, based on a sample of 2,450 LGBT adults age 50 and older (Fredriksen-Goldsen & Kim, 2017), and the earlier cross-sectional Caring and Aging with Pride (CAP) study, based on a sample of 2,560 LGBT adults age 50 to 95 (Fredriksen-Goldsent et al., 2011)—provide us with a more nuanced profile of the health and well-being of this population than was previously available. In the CAP study, the researchers compared the national sample with state-level, population-based data on older non-LGBT individuals in the state of Washington; some health disparities surfaced. Lesbian, gay, and bisexual older adults had higher rates of disability and mental distress than heterosexual adults of a similar age. They were also more likely to smoke and engage in excessive drinking than their non-LGBT counterparts. Gay and bisexual men were more likely to be in poor physical health than heterosexual men, and lesbians and bisexual women were more likely to be obese and at higher risk for cardiovascular disease than heterosexual women (Fredriksen-Goldsen et al., 2011). Within the LGBT sample, transgender older adults experienced higher rates of disability, stress, and poor mental and physical health than the non-transgender study participants (Fredriksen-Goldsen, Hoy-Ellis, Goldsen, Emlet, & Hooyman, 2014).

These health disparities may arise in part owing to the historical context of victimization and discrimination. Among the 2,560 study participants in the CAP study, 82% had been victimized at least once in their lifetime owing to their sexual orientation or gender identity, and 64% had been victimized three or more times (Fredriksen-Goldsen et al., 2011). Transgender older adults experienced the highest rates of victimization (Fredriksen-Goldsen, Hoy-Ellis, et al., 2014). Negative messages about LGBT people that were prevalent at the time that older LGBT adults were growing up are often internalized. The CAP study revealed that victimization and internalized stigma are associated with poorer health, depressive symptoms, and greater disability (Emlet, 2016). Transgender older adults in the study reported higher rates of internalized stigma and lifetime victimization, and were more likely to conceal their gender identity than non-transgender study participants (Fredriksen-Goldsen, Cook-Daniels, et al., 2014). Furthermore, bisexual men and women reported higher levels of sexual identity concealment than lesbians and gay men (Fredriksen-Goldsen et al., 2012). A 2013 Pew Research Center survey found that only 18% of bisexual individuals age 45 and older disclosed their sexual orientation to the most important people in their life. This high rate of identity secrecy may well contribute to the high level of depression that has been documented among older bisexual adults (MAP & SAGE, 2017).

Social isolation can happen at any age, but becomes increasingly likely for older adults as partners and friends die; they are no longer connected to the social networks of employment, or physical or cognitive disabilities constrain their ability to drive or travel. Like their non-LGBT counterparts, older LGBT adults also face these circumstances, but they are compounded by the fact that LGBT older adults are twice as likely to live alone and four times less likely to have children as their non-LGBT peers (Espinoza, 2011). Living alone puts one at higher risk of loneliness and social isolation (Kim & Fredriksen-Goldsen, 2016). Population-based studies indicate that while about one-fifth of older heterosexual adults live alone, about half of older gay and bisexual men do and about one-quarter of lesbian and bisexual women do (Kim & Fredriksen-Goldsen, 2016). A Harris Poll found 32% of LGBT older adults were very or extremely concerned about being alone or growing old alone, as compared to 19% of non-LGBT older adults (as cited in SAGE, 2014).

FAMILIES OF CHOICE, SOCIAL SUPPORTS, AND SOCIAL NETWORKS

Owing to the unaccepting historical context within which LGBT older adults grew up, many faced hostility from their families when they disclosed their sexual orientation or gender identity. Frequently this led to becoming estranged from their families of origin, leading them to create "families of choice." Such families of choice include partners, ex-partners, friends, neighbors, and/or coworkers (Orel & Coon, 2016). Not only was family rejection widespread, but also the thought of raising children with a partner of the same gender was rarely considered. As a result, older LGBT adults are less likely to have children, grandchildren, siblings, or married spouses than non-LGBT elders. This lack of legal family ties can be problematic in two ways (MAP & SAGE, 2017). First, families of choice are often made up of friends about the same age, peers who may be facing their own health challenges and thus less able to provide needed support (Fredriksen-Goldsen, 2016). Moreover, the AIDS/HIV crisis of the 1980s affected this generation of older

LGBT profoundly, with many gay men losing partners and friends to the disease, resulting in thinner social networks and less social support. The second issue facing LGBT elders is that their friend networks generally do not have legal recognition to make medical decisions, share health insurance, or take time off work to provide care (MAP & SAGE, 2017).

Social support is generally defined as the "emotional, practical, financial, and social guidance from a network of friends, family, co-workers, among others" (Masini & Barrett, 2008, p. 93). Substantial evidence indicates that the presence of social support eases some of the stresses of the aging process, and is related to better physical, psychological, and emotional health (Masini & Barrett, 2008). The CAP study of 2,560 LGBT adults age 50 to 75 revealed significant proportions of this population lack social support: 33% reported that they did not have someone to help with daily chores if they were sick and 29% said they did not have someone to love and make them feel wanted (Fredriksen-Goldsen et al., 2011). Nearly three in five of the study participants (59%) reported lacking companionship, and over half said they felt isolated (53%) and/or left out (53%). Levels of loneliness were measured on a scale from 1 to 3, with 3 representing more loneliness. Levels differed among the five populations, but all were above the midpoint. For lesbians, the average level was 1.6; for bisexual women, 1.8; for gay men, 1.7; for bisexual men, 2.0; and for transgender study participants, 2.0 (Fredriksen-Goldsen et al., 2011). A 2014 Harris Poll had similar findings: nearly twice as many LGBT older adults (30%) as compared to non-LGBT older adults (16%) were very or extremely concerned about not having someone to take care of them as they age; and LGBT older adults were more concerned that they would be lonely in old age than their non-LGBT counterparts (32% vs. 19%; SAGE, 2014).

Based on a national sample of 220 lesbian, gay, and bisexual adults age 50 and older, Masini and Barrett (2008) provide evidence that this population possesses complex social networks, fairly evenly distributed among partners, friends, and family members. The type of support received from each group varied: close friends and partners were more likely to provide emotional, practical, and socializing support than family members. Moreover, social support from friends was predictive of higher quality of life and lower depression, anxiety, and internalized homophobia, while support from family members was not. So, while friends and family members were equally distributed in the social networks, their impact differed in terms of study participants' well-being, further supporting the importance of networks that extend beyond traditional family boundaries for LGB older adults (Masini & Barrett, 2008).

Caregiving represents intensified social support that occurs when an older adult needs assistance with activities of daily living (such as bathing or transferring) or instrumental activities of daily living (such as shopping or cooking). Similar to their non-LGBT counterparts, care provided by a partner is the most common type of caregiving. But because LGBT older adults generally have few family supports, such as children, they are more likely than heterosexual older adults to rely on their friends when they need help (Shiu, Muraco, & Fredriksen-Goldsen, 2016). One national study found LGBT older adults were more likely to provide care to a friend than heterosexual older adults (Metlife Mature Market Institute, 2010), reflecting a historical behavior that developed during the AIDS/HIV epidemic in the 1980s and 1990s (Shiu et al., 2016).

Social networks, similar to social support, have been shown to be related to increased health and well-being (Kim, Fredriksen-Goldsen, Bryan, & Muraco, 2017). Social networks can be seen as social capital in which both size and diversity are important (Erosheva, Kim, Emlet, & Fredriksen-Goldsen, 2015). Among older adults in the general population, determinants of larger social networks include being married, having children, and access to senior centers and neighbors (Erosheva et al., 2015). The determinants for LGBT older adults are likely different and impacted by the issue of identity disclosure. While disclosing one's identity may help older LGBT adults build relationships in the LGBT community, concealment has served as a protective factor against discrimination and victimization (Erosheva et al., 2015; Kim et al., 2017).

Two-fifths of LGBT adults, age 45 to 75, in a 2014 Harris Poll said their social networks were growing smaller over time (SAGE, 2014). Among those polled, African Americans were far more likely than their White or Latino counterparts to say people from their religious institutions were part of their support system (26% vs. 8% and 8%; SAGE, 2014). The CAP study revealed that social network size for LGBT older adults was positively related to being female, transgender, and/or employed; having higher income, a partner, and/or a child; identity disclosure to a neighbor; and participation in programs and services for LGBT older adults and/or religious activities. Network diversity was associated with younger age, being female and/or transgender, participation in religious activities, disclosure to a friend, and service use (Erosheva et al., 2015). While transgender older adults had larger and more diverse social networks, previous research has indicated they have limited social support (Witten, 2017).

Exploring the diversity of social networks among LGBT older adults, Kim and colleagues analyzed data from the first wave (2017) of the longitudinal

NHAS study. They found five social network types with varying degrees of access to social support. The five types were diverse, diverse/no children, immediate family–focused, friend-centered/restricted, and fully restricted. Three of these network types have been found among older adults in general (diverse, immediate family–focused, and fully restricted), while the other two appear to be unique to the older LGBT population, and were the most common in this sample (Kim et al., 2017). Those LGBT older adults in this study with the least diverse and most restricted social networks reported poorer mental health and more difficulty with activities of daily living (Kim et al., 2017). Ultimately, although differences exist in the level of social support and the size and composition of social networks in the LGBT older adult population, the large majority of study participants in the CAP study (90%) felt good about belonging to their communities. Protections against social isolation should build on this resiliency and community identity (Emlet, 2016).

DISCLOSURE MANAGEMENT AND ACCESS TO SERVICES

That older LGBT adults are cautious about disclosure is understandable. They make decisions on a daily basis as to whether it is safe to come out about their sexual orientation or gender identity. The process of disclosure management requires ongoing vigilance and can be fatiguing, as one must weigh the potential negative consequences—physical, financial, legal, emotional, or social—against the potential psychological or social benefits (Orel, 2017). Such disclosure management also applies to accessing social and healthcare services. Fredriksen-Goldsen et al. (2011) found that 13% of the study participants in the CAP study had been denied or received inferior healthcare because of their sexual orientation or gender identity; this was true for 40% of the transgender study participants. Older LGBT adults are also wary of and hesitant to access mainstream social service programs (MAP & SAGE, 2017). Their fears are well founded. Surveys of aging service providers have underscored the general lack of sensitivity or readiness to meet the needs of this population (Hughes, Harold, & Boyer, 2011; Knochel, Quam, & Croghan, 2011). A national study of Area Agencies on Aging revealed that few provided LGBT services or outreach (Knochel, Croghan, Moone, & Quam, 2012). A plethora of examples exist of older LGBT adults facing discrimination or ostracism in assisted living and nursing facilities (MAP & SAGE, 2010).

To compound this potential ostracism, LGBT older adults frequently face ageism in the broader LGBT community, which tends to be very youth oriented (Hoy-Ellis, Altor, Kerr, & Milford, 2016; MAP & SAGE, 2010). This focus on youth appears to be stronger in gay male communities than among lesbians (MAP & SAGE, 2010). Only recently have LGBT advocates and organizations become more welcoming to older adults and begun to intentionally confront the existing ageism (MAP & SAGE, 2010). This work has led to some promising programs that serve to increase opportunities for social connections for LGBT older adults and decrease the risks of social isolation.

RECOMMENDATIONS AND BEST PRACTICES

Like all older adults, LGBT individuals need social connections to thrive as they age. Because a large proportion of LGBT older adults live alone and rely on support networks made up primarily of peers that condense over time, social isolation is a concern for this population. In some parts of the country—generally the more urban regions with established gay communities—programs specifically for LGBT older individuals have been created. These programs are sparse and need to be better funded and replicated to reach all parts of the country (SAGE, 2014). The LGBT Movement Advancement Project (MAP)—an organization focused on full social and political equality for LGBT people—and Services and Advocacy for Lesbian, Gay, Bisexual and Transgender Elders (SAGE)—the oldest and largest organization serving LGBT older adults—provide very specific recommendations for increasing funding for and provision of LGBT elder programs. These recommendations include encouraging the Administration on Aging to identify LGBT elders as vulnerable. Such a designation could help increase funding for LGBT elder programs, services to LGBT older adults in mainstream aging programs, cultural competency training of service providers in the field of aging, organizational nondiscrimination policies, and data collection to better understand the specific needs of LGBT older adults (MAP & SAGE, 2010).

In the meantime, programs do exist to meet the social needs of LGBT elders. Some have grown out of established LGBT organizations and others out of mainstream aging organizations. An example of the latter illustrates not only the great need, but also what one compassionate and committed individual can do to address gaps in services. Moore (2002) describes becoming aware of the fact that lesbian and gay caregivers to people with Alzheimer's disease were not being well served by existing caregiver support groups in a rural area in the southeast region of the United States. The assumption by existing services and practitioners that caregivers were all in heterosexual relationships left gay and lesbian caregivers in the awkward position of having to conceal their sexual orientations. When that author contacted the regional Alzheimer's Association to suggest providing services for lesbian and gay caregivers, he was informed "the chapter was reluctant to expand its programs to this population group because of concerns about professional appearance, propriety, and fund-raising" (Moore, 2002, p. 27). Given the lack of receptivity from the mainstream organization and the rural nature of the region, the author created a six-session psychoeducational telephone support group for gay and lesbian caregivers. All participants participated in all sessions, contacted one another between sessions, and maintained contact after the group terminated (Moore, 2002). One member's comment indicates just how important such a group can be for an LGBT elder: "'For me, my life partner was my social world, my primary source of emotional support. My immediate family disowned [me] and closed the curtain to my existence. Here in the group I feel I have found family'" (Moore, 2002, p. 37).

In the years that have passed since this 2002 example of a mainstream aging organization refusing to accommodate the specific needs of LGBT old adults, there have been welcomed changes in some communities. Hoy-Ellis et al. (2016) write of a promising collaborative in Houston between an LGBT center and a federally qualified healthcare center, to provide mental health services to LGBT older adults. The Seniors Preparing for Rainbow Years (SPRY) was created to address the documented social isolation, depression, and resistance to and distrust of traditional services among LGBT elders in the area. The SPRY program focuses on peer support and began with men's and women's groups led by lay peer counselors. This evolved to a congregate meal drop-in center 3 days a week funded by a local Area Agency on Aging, as well as monthly social events including movies, field trips, potluck dinners, and wellness activities. In addition, the program utilizes trained LGBT older adults as outreach workers to actively engage isolated members of their community by linking them with social and civic groups (Hoy-Ellis et al., 2016).

Fenway Health in Boston hosts the LGBT Aging Project, which provides training about LGBT older adults to mainstream service providers. In its 20 years of operation, the project has seen pockets of LGBT programming emerge throughout the state, but a closer look indicated a lack of diversity in the populations participating in these programs (Linscott & Krinsky, 2016). The LGBT Aging Project convened a group of stakeholders from Boston's communities of color to explore ways of meeting the needs of LGBT elders of color. The stakeholders group decided to start by targeting the old African American LGBT population and planned an event they knew would be appealing—an honoring of the community's history—taking place on a Sunday afternoon after church services. More than 100 people attended the

"Flashback Sunday: Honoring the Legacy of LGBT Elders of Color"; this initial success led the group to fundraise for ongoing programming, including the opening of a congregate meal site in a local church that was targeted toward LGBT elders of color (Linscott & Krinsky, 2016).

New York City is the home to SAGE and a number of fairly well-developed programs for LGBT older adults. SAGE operates five senior centers across the city including its most recently opened in the ethnically and racially diverse borough of the Bronx. In order to be sensitive to the needs and desires of a diverse community, SAGE Center Bronx holds monthly planning sessions with Center participants to determine which programs are of interest and which are irrelevant. As not all participants enjoy the same types of programs, the Center attempts to offer a wide array to cater to as many participants as possible (Thurston, 2016). Also initiated in New York City—in Brooklyn in 1995—GRIOT Circle is an advocacy and service organization committed to the well-being of LGBT older adults of color. Griot is a West African word for story teller, which was adapted to the acronym for Gay Reunion in Our Times (GRIOT; Kim, Acey, Guess, Jen, & Fredriksen-Goldsen, 2016). One of its first initiatives—the Buddy-2-Buddy Program—continues to this day and has a focus on reducing social isolation through pairing older adults to provide mutual support and companionship. The organization's ongoing mission is to address both racism and homophobia and to develop awareness that the barriers to service for LGBT older adults of color may be different from those of heterosexual and White aging communities. Current programming addresses the identified needs of social support, health promotion, and economic security (Kim et al., 2016).

The state of Maine, with its largely White population, provides a contrast to New York City, both culturally and owing to its low population density. In 2013, through the establishment of SAGE Maine, the state became a part of SAGENet, which currently includes 30 regional or urban-based affiliates across the country (Services and Advocacy for Gay, Lesbian, Bisexual and Transgender Elders [SAGE], n.d.b). SAGE Maine has the daunting task of meeting the needs of LGBT older adults across a very large, and sparsely populated, geographic region. This has been done with regular drop-in center times in the major—though relatively small—cities in the state, regularly scheduled social meals in a number of locations, wellness programs, and planned outings in the beautiful natural surroundings. To accommodate those who live hundreds of miles from any of these events, virtual drop-in social groups also occur monthly, one for LGBT older adults in general, and one for transgender older adults (SAGE Maine, n.d.). These events have served to bring otherwise isolated individuals together and to foster lasting connections. For example, one lesbian couple, who had attended some of the monthly meals and drop-in center gatherings in the city of Bangor, reported that before joining SAGE Maine activities, they had never had any other lesbian friends owing to a lifetime of concealing their sexual orientations and partnership status and not living in an urban center with an openly gay community (personal communication Leah Kravette, social work intern, SAGE Maine, January 17, 2018).

Clearly, progress is being made toward increasing socialization opportunities for LGBT older adults and breaking down barriers that prevent them from accessing health and social services. In 2010, the U.S. Department of Health and Human Services provided funding to SAGE to create a National Resource Center on LGBT Aging. This Center is available to aging providers, LGBT organizations, and LGBT older adults who are interested in receiving educational resources, technical assistance, or cultural competence training (Services and Advocacy for Gay, Lesbian, Bisexual and Transgender Elders [SAGE], n.d.a), assuring this positive trend can continue.

SUMMARY

Many of today's LGBT older adults grew up in a time of intense homophobia and transphobia, when homosexual behavior was both criminalized and seen as a disease. The risk of social isolation for current LGBT older adults is likely increased as they are more than twice as likely to live along and four times less likely to have children than their non-LGBT peers. And although many may have rich social networks, recent national research has shown that a majority of LGBT older adults lack companionship or feel isolated and/or left out. Similar to older adults in general, strong social networks—which are often made up of "families of choice" for LGBT older adults—are related to improved health and mental health outcomes. Despite increased social acceptance in recent years, a life time of discrimination, stigma and fear has its consequences, including a tendency to conceal one's true identity and a distrust of health care professionals. Many LGBT older adults are wary of and hesitant to access mainstream social and health programs believing they will not be accepted for who they are, a belief that is often based on previous experiences of discrimination. Fortunately progress is being made both within mainstream social and health services organizations and with increased development of specialized programs for LGBT older adults. The National Resource Center on LGBT Aging is available for those interested in making their services more accessible and welcoming to this population.

REFERENCES

Adams, M. (2016). An intersectional approach to services and care for LGBT elders. *Generations*, *40*(2), 94–100.

American Civil Liberties Union. (n.d.). *History of sodomy laws and the strategy that led to today's decision*. Retrieved from https://www.aclu.org/other/history-sodomy-laws-and-strategy-led-todays-decision

Butler, S. S. (2004). Gay, lesbian, bisexual and transgender (LGBT) elders: The challenges and resilience of this marginalized group. *Journal of Human Behavior in the Social Environment*, *9*(4), 25–44. doi:10.1300/J137v09n04_02

Emlet, C. A. (2016). Social, economic, and health disparities among LGBT older adults. *Generations*, *40*(2), 16–21.

Erosheva, E. A., Kim, H-J., Emlet, C., & Fredriksen-Goldsen, K. I. (2015). Social networks of lesbian, gay, bisexual and transgender older adults. *Research on Aging*, *38*(1), 98–123. doi:10.1177/0164027515581859

Espinoza, R. (2011). The Divers Elders Coalition and LGBT aging: Connecting communities, issues, and resources in a historic moment. *Public Policy & Aging Report*, *21*(3), 8–12. doi:10.1093/ppar/21.3.8

Fredriksen-Goldsen, K. I. (2016). The future of LGBT+ Aging: A blueprint for action in services, policies, and research. *Generations*, *40*(2), 6–15.

Fredriksen-Goldsen, K. I., Cook-Daniels, L., Kim, H-J., Erosheva, E. A., Emlet, C. A., Hoy-Ellis, C. P., . . . Muraco, A. (2014). Physical and mental health of transgender older adults: An at-risk and underserved population. *The Gerontologist*, *54*(3), 488–500. doi:10.1093/geront/gnt021

Fredriksen-Goldsen, K. I., Emlet, C. A., Kim, H-J, Muiraco, A., Erosheva, E. A., Goldsen, J., & Hoy-Ellis, C. P. (2012). The physical and mental health of lesbian, gay and bisexual (LGB) older adults: The role of key health indicators and risk and protective factors. *The Gerontologist*, *53*(4), 664–675. doi:10.1093/geront/gns123

Fredriksen-Goldsen, K. I., Hoy-Ellis, C. P., Goldsen, J., Emlet, C. A., & Hooyman, N. K. (2014). Creating a vision for the future: Key competencies and strategies for culturally competent practice with lesbian, gay, bisexual, and transgender (LGBT) older adults in the health and human services. *Journal of Gerontological Social Work*, *57*(2–4), 80–107. doi:10.1080/01634372.2014.890690

Fredriksen-Goldsen, K. I., & Kim, H-J. (2017). The science of conducting research with LGBT older adults-An introduction to Aging with Pride: National Health, Aging and Sexuality/Gender Study (NHAS). *The Gerontologist*, *57*(S1), S1–S14. doi:10.1093/geront/gnw212

Fredriksen-Goldsen, K. I., Kim, H-J., Emlet, C. A., Muraco, A., Erosheva, E. A., Hoy-Ellis, C. P., . . . Petry, H. (2011). *The aging and health report: Disparities and resilience among lesbian, gay, bisexual and transgender older adults*. Seattle, WA: Institute for Multigenerational Health. Retrieved from http://age-pride.org/wordpress/published-articles

Fredriksen-Goldsen, K. I., Kim, H-J., Shiu, C., Goldsen, J., & Emlet, C. A. (2015). Successful aging among LGBT older adults: Physical and mental health-related quality of life by age group. *The Gerontologist*, *55*(1), 154–168. doi:10.1093/geront/gnu081

Hoy-Ellis, C. P., Ator, M., Kerr, C., & Milford, J. (2016). Innovative approaches address aging and mental health needs in LGBTQ communities. *Generations*, *40*(2), 56–62.

Hughes, A. K., Harold, R. D., & Boyer, J. M. (2011). Awareness of LGBT aging issues among aging services network providers. *Journal of Gerontological Social Work*, *54*, 659–677. doi:10.1080/01634372.2011.585392

Kim, H-J., Acey, K., Guess, A., Jen, S., & Fredriksen-Goldsen, K. I. (2016). A collaboration for health and wellness: GRIOT Circle and Caring and Aging with Pride. *Generations, 40*(2), 49–55.

Kim, H-J., & Fredriksen-Goldsen, K. I. (2016). Living arrangements and loneliness among lesbian, gay, and bisexual older adults. *The Gerontologist, 56*(3), 548–558. doi:10.1093/geront/gnu083

Kim, H-J., Fredriksen-Goldsen, K. I., Bryan, A. E. B., & Muraco, A. (2017). Social network types and mental health among LGBT older adults. *The Gerontologist, 57*(S1), S84–S94. doi:10.1093/geront/gnw169

Knochel, K. A., Croghan, C. F., Moone, R. P., & Quam, J. K. (2012). Training, geography, and provision of aging services to lesbian, gay, bisexual, and transgender older adults. *Journal of Gerontological Social Work, 55*, 426–443. doi:10.1080/01634372.2012.665158

Knochel, K. A., Quam, J. K., & Croghan, C. F. (2011). Are old lesbian and gay people well served? Understanding the perceptions, preparation, and experiences of aging services providers. *Journal of Applied Gerontology, 30*, 370–389. doi:10.1177/0733464810369809

Linscott, B., & Krinsky, L. (2016). Engaging underserved populations: Outreach to LGBT elders of color. *Generations, 40*(2), 34–37.

Masini, B. E., & Barrett, H. A. (2008). Social support as a predictor of psychological and physical well-being and lifestyle in lesbian, gay, and bisexual adults aged 50 and over. *Journal of Gay & Lesbian Social Services, 20* (1–2), 91–110. doi:10.1080/10538720802179013

Metlife Mature Market Institute. (2010). *Still out, still aging: The MetLife study of lesbian, gay, bisexual, and transgender baby boomers.* Retrieved from https://www.giaging.org/resources/still-out-still-aging-the-metlife-study-of-lesbian-gay-bisexual-and-transge

Moore, W. R. (2002). Lesbian and gay elders: Connecting care providers through a telephone support group. *Journal of Gay & Lesbian Social Services, 14*(3), 23–41. doi:10.1300/j041v14n03_02

Movement Advancement Project & Services and Advocacy for Gay, Lesbian, Bisexual and Transgender Elders. (2010). *Improving the lives of LGBT older adults.* Retrieved from http://www.lgbtmap.org/policy-and-issue-analysis/improving-the-lives-of-lgbt-older-adults

Movement Advancement Project & Services and Advocacy for Gay, Lesbian, Bisexual and Transgender Elders. (2017). *Understanding issues facing LGBT older adults.* Retrieved from http://www.lgbtmap.org/understanding-issues-facing-lgbt-older-adults

Orel, N. A. (2017). Families and support systems of LGBT elders. In K. M. Hash & A. R. Rogers (Eds.), *Annual review of gerontology and geriatrics: Contemporary issues and future directions in lesbian, gay, bisexual and transgender aging* (vol. 37; pp. 89–109). New York, NY: Springer Publishing.

Orel, N. A., & Coon, D. W. (2016). The challenges of change: How can we meet the care needs of the ever-evolving LGBT family? *Generations, 40*(2), 41–45.

SAGE Maine. (n.d.) Community. Retrieved from http://www.sagemaine.org/community

Services and Advocacy for Gay, Lesbian, Bisexual and Transgender Elders. (2014). *Out & visible: The experiences and attitudes of lesbian, gay, bisexual and transgender older adults, ages 45-75.* Retrieved from https://www.sageusa.org/files/LGBT_OAMarketResearch_Rpt.pdf

Services and Advocacy for Gay, Lesbian, Bisexual and Transgender Elders. (n.d.a). National Resource Center on LGBT Aging. Retrieved from https://www.lgbtagingcenter.org

Services and Advocacy for Gay, Lesbian, Bisexual and Transgender Elders. (n.d.b). *SAGENet.* Retrieved from https://www.sageusa.org/what-we-do/sagenet-national-affiliates

Shiu, C., Muraco, A., & Fredriksen-Goldsen, K. I. (2016). Invisible care: Friend and partner care among older lesbian, gay, bisexual and transgender (LGBT) adults. *Journal of the Society for Social Work and Research, 7*(3), 527–546. doi:10.1086/687325

Thurston, C. (2016). The intersectional approach in action: SAGE Center Bronx. *Generations, 40*(2), 101–102.

Witten, T. M. (2017). Health and well-being of transgender elders. In K. M. Hash & A. R. Rogers (Eds.), *Annual review of gerontology and geriatrics: Contemporary issues and future directions in lesbian, gay, bisexual and transgender aging* (vol. 37; pp. 27–41). New York, NY: Springer Publishing.

14

Family and Intergenerational Relationships

Donna M. Butts and Kristin Bodiford

INTRODUCTION

Hal, a retired minister who moved to a senior-only gated community in his late 70s, was restless. He said he'd always worked openly. He thought about the kids and families who lived on the other side of his fence. He was White; they were not. Hal knew his young neighbors were the future and he wanted to help invest in them. He organized his neighbors, opened the gates, and walked outside to begin what grew to be the Gaithersburg Beloved Community Initiative, a multifaceted intergenerational program. Hal said "By building the relationships we are dealing with the racial divide. Amazing things have happened. We all hunger for this relationship."

The United States is experiencing a demographic transformation unlike any we have experienced before with a projected 76% growth in the number of people over the age of 65 between 2012 and 2030, and an 8% growth in children and youth between ages 0 and 17 (Administration on Aging, 2013; ChildStats.gov, n.d.).

At the same time, there is a shift in our racial and ethnic diversity. Today, more than half of Americans under the age of 5 are people of color compared with less than one in five Americans over age 65 (Generations United, 2016b). Unlike other countries, our young population will continue to grow for decades to come. They will replenish the workforce and, with proper investments, continue to propel our economy and country forward. These are the children that motivated Hal to enroll his neighbors and reach outside their gated community to support young people on the other side.

These changes are impacting our communities, families, and other intergenerational relationships. As people live longer, our families are elongating with three, four, or even five generations living at the same time. Family structures have also changed and become more varied including single head of households, same-sex marriages, and multigenerational families in which over one-third are grandparents and other relatives raising children.

Our demographic diversity—in both age and race—is a great asset. Yet, how families and communities fully capitalize on these new assets is still evolving. We spend most of our days interacting with people of the same generation; yet, the solutions to challenges we face at all levels of society are those that value and engage the strength of each generation.

In this chapter, we explore how intergenerational connections can benefit communities and families. We do this by weaving stories, research, and conversations to better understand the value of strengthening intergenerational relationships and families as a path to increasing social connections and improving health and well-being for all ages and for society as a whole. Innovative programs and case studies focused on intergenerational relationships within and outside of the family context offer practice tips and strategies that can be adapted and adopted for professional and personal growth.

COURAGEOUS CONVERSATIONS

In the 1930s, Lee Harvey's family had to leave their native Germany as Hitler's rise to power put Jewish people in peril. In Hungary in the 1940s, because young Maria Roberts' Presbyterian family had Jewish ancestors, the farm that had provided their livelihood was seized and they, too, had to leave their native country. Here in the United States, Yuka Fujikura's Japanese American family was relocated to an internment camp in the 1940s as a result of President Roosevelt's Executive Order. In the 1960s, Annie Rhoades found herself caught in the desegregation of Montgomery County Public Schools when she was placed in a new school where the principal made it very clear that she did not want a "colored teacher." And in the early 1980s, Alice Wong's teenaged daughter came out as a lesbian and Alice, fearing for her daughter's safety, became involved in lesbian, gay, bisexual, and transgender (LGBT) advocacy.

Lee, Maria, Yuka, and Alice are Asbury Methodist Village residents. Annie lives in nearby Derwood. All five women were the victims of

(continued)

prejudices that uprooted their lives and the lives of their families. Several suffered fractured friendships and endured having nasty epitaphs hurled at them. What do these five women, who are now in their 70s, 80s, and 90s, have in common with today's teenagers who were not even alive in these bygone eras? Unfortunately, prejudices are still alive in today's world. The teen years can be traumatic enough, but more so if you live with the possibility of being forced to leave the United States or have to endure bullying and prejudice.

Nouf Bazaz, who counsels Muslim teenagers as a part of the International Cultural Council Crossroads Program, spoke to the Beloved Community Initiative Council about a spike in bullying that has occurred in the current political climate. Nouf shared, "Students feel very alone, and they feel targeted." She pointed out that about one in five of their Muslim students has been harassed or bullied for being a Muslim and about one in ten reports receiving unfair treatment from a teacher or school administrator.

Nouf developed an idea to have seniors who had survived trying times speak with teenagers who were living through similar experiences today. In each of these conversations, people present their stories. Discussion questions are then presented, and the circle methodology is employed as the students grapple with their own experiences. One Muslim student said she felt isolated and that "this is just happening to me, this is just happening to Muslims. All those other people are lucky. But when I heard those other people's stories I thought to myself that it's not just Muslims, it's other cultures, too, that have been discriminated against." She recalled Yuka's (the survivor of the Japanese Internment Camp) advice: "Don't be bitter in life. You'll go through a lot of things. People will try to break you. But you have to be positive and you have to move on with a smile on your face."

REACHING ACROSS GENERATIONS

Around the United States, intergenerational friendships are the exception rather than the rule: for the most part, age segregation prevails. Babies and toddlers are in child-only care centers while children and youth spend their days at school, mostly among peers born the same year that they were. Young and middle-aged adults cluster at work. And elders gather for clubs, classes, and meals that often expressly bar the young. Millions of college students and elders live in age-restricted housing, and most American neighborhoods skew young or old (Generations United & Eisner Foundation, 2017).

It is not enough to say that communities that are good to grow old in are also good to grow up in. Just because a curb that is cut for accessibility is good for a wheelchair and a stroller does not mean their occupants will ever cross paths and get to know each other. Intentional intergenerational engagement needs to become the norm. There is magic when you mix experience, wisdom, and different perspectives that come from intergenerational relationships. Bridging generations improves individual lives, family ties, and communities. It also reduces each generation's sense of social isolation, improves health and well-being, and provides purpose for people of all ages.

If intergenerational practices are embraced, there is an increase in human capital asset that can have tremendous value to our communities. The older adult side of the equation alone is staggering. Today 108 million people are over the age of 50. On average, they watch 47 hours of television each week. A volunteer hour is currently valued at a little over $23. If 2% of the people over the age of 50 gave up 2% of their TV-watching time to do volunteer work, it would generate more than $2.5 billion in new human capital at work in communities across the country (Generations United, 2016a).

Most communities are multigenerational in their make-up, meaning they have members of all generations. But most are not intentional in their efforts to bridge the generations. An intergenerational community is one where individuals of all ages are an integral and valued part of the setting. This perspective is reflected in the families, structures, services, and policies that people of all ages encounter in the community as well as in day-to-day interactions and relationships. Partnerships between local government, older adult living facilities, schools, colleges and universities, multiservice organizations, businesses, cultural and community organizations, and community members of all ages are essential for intergenerational communities. An intergenerational community builds on the positive resources that each generation has to offer to each other and those around them, and advances policies and practices that both acknowledge and promote the better, more efficient results you get when you mix ages.

INTERGENERATIONAL PROGRAMS

The kids are the most empathetic, patient, and accepting of children who look different than they do or have a disability.
—Elementary school teacher remarking about the differences in children who transition from intergenerational child care to public school.

Intergenerational programs, policies, and practices increase cooperation, interaction, and exchange between people of different generations, allowing the sharing of their talents and resources, and supporting each other in relationships that benefit both the individuals and their community. These types of programs enjoy strong support. A recent national survey conducted for Generations United found that 77% of respondents wished there were more opportunities in their community for people from different age groups to meet and get to know one another (Generations United, 2016a).

Programs that build bridges between generations can trace their early roots to the Foster Grandparent program started by the federal government in the 1960s as one of the War on Poverty programs. A small stipend and an annual health examination were used as rewards for low-income older adults to volunteer and work with babies and children. They were individuals often living alone shut in their homes with little contact with the outside world. The goal was to connect this otherwise unconnected generation to others while providing supports and a purpose.

Intergenerational programs have grown in number and variety since the 1960s. They typically fall into four direction-based categories: young serving old, old serving young, young and old serving together, and intergenerational shared sites. Recording oral histories, teaching mobile phone use, and delivering meals to home-bound seniors are all examples of young serving old. Older adults serve younger generations when they tutor, mentor, or pass on history and culture. Younger and older teams can serve together when they assess needs in their neighborhoods and recommend solutions, work to cultivate intergenerational community gardens, or produce music or theater together. Intergenerational shared sites can be adult and child day care offered under one roof, a school and a senior center built together, or providing summer meals for low-income children in the dining room of a continuing care retirement community.

Interest in intergenerational programs has increased with a shift in emphasis from the program to the relationship itself. Whether a person is a biological or social grandparent, aunt, uncle, mentor, or friend, their connection to other generations matters.

DEVELOPING INTERGENERATIONAL RELATIONSHIPS

Hal Garman lives in a retirement community that is a rural oasis in an urban setting outside of Washington, D.C. Just down the street, Gaithersburg High School reflects the rapid demographic diversification that places Gaithersburg, MD, as one of America's most diverse cities. Alicia

DeLashmutt, from Our Home—Inclusive Community Collaborative (www.inclusivecommunitycollaborative.org), recognizes that kind of space where different places meet, like the rural oasis and the urban space, as an area of rich opportunity for a thriving social ecosystem. Alicia grew up on a farm in Iowa. She remembers it was often the space between the farmland and the surrounding area that was the healthiest. In fact, this kind of biodiversity is essential for ecosystem productivity and function and improving the system's resilience in the face of change. Hal was inspired to nurture this space in between and started an initiative called Gaithersburg Beloved Community Initiative, named after Martin Luther King's call for social justice and equality and the ultimate goal of integration or intergroup and interpersonal living. The Beloved Community Initiative fosters relationships and provides learning opportunities for children living in the communities surrounding Asbury Methodist Village. Volunteers get together weekly to mentor students from Gaithersburg Elementary School. Cathy Whitehouse of The Intergenerational Schools in Cleveland, OH (www.intergenerationalschools.org), shares that ongoing relationships are critical to building stronger intergenerational relationships. The Intergenerational Schools provides a global model on how to connect, create, and guide a multigenerational community of lifelong learners and spirited citizens. Cathy recommends creating a place and opportunity for people to come together on a regular basis. Schools provide a captive audience for developing relationships, but often schools do not tend to be open to the community at large. At The Intergenerational Schools, they make it explicit that they are welcoming community members to be part of the life of the school and create regular opportunities for interaction.

Derenda Schubert from Bridge Meadows in Oregon (www.bridgemeadows.org) also reinforces the importance of community. Bridge Meadows is an intentional intergenerational living community—where youth formerly in foster care, their adoptive parents, and elders find a true home built with love and a shared vision of a better tomorrow. When Bridge Meadows opened a new location, neighbors were welcoming and offered to help. "How can we volunteer?" they asked. Derenda responded, "Be a neighbor!" (D. Schubert, personal communication, February 2, 2018). It is the relationship of reciprocity that helps shift the dynamic of helping into one of a lifelong relationship and journey. At Bridge Meadows, they are intentional from how they design how the buildings allow for connection to the surroundings to how they create opportunities for experiences within and outside of Bridge Meadows that promotes integration and connection with the larger community. Alicia also lives in Portland, OR, and is working to build an intentional community, where people of different ages, abilities, and incomes come together based on shared interests, strengths, and values and are living in proximity to each other, bumping into one another in the course of everyday life. This everyday immersion encourages comfort and compassion and knowing the individual as a unique person, versus knowing him or her as "other" and different.

If we think of social integration as a goal, we might ask ourselves how we can help people experience a broad range and increased frequency of social connections. In a meta-analysis by Holt-Lunstad, Smith, and Layton (2010), social integration is defined as participating in a broad range of social relationships and active engagement in a variety of social activities or relationships. Social integration, among a variety of demographic and health variables, was found to be the strongest predictor of reduced mortality rates. A variety of relationships is crucial to a healthy, thriving society. When we see differences between us as a resource, we create a generative space for creativity, new connections, and meaning. Social integration can be enhanced by creating new cultures of inclusion, of being exposed to difference in order to learn how to appreciate difference, and shifting cultures to inclusion and lessen social isolation. It is important to do this at every age, to create a new culture in our society. There are practices that organizations and communities can embrace that help to create this new culture.

Emlet and Moceri (2011) studied the importance of social connectedness in building age-friendly communities through a community forum process using World Café conversations in Tacoma, WA, to explore what it means to be socially connected, how the city could help with life transitions, and what people have to offer their community. Their research reinforced the critical importance of social connectedness, participation, and integration and echoed Derenda's urging to focus on reciprocity, in which giving and receiving were equally important elements of relationships.

Hal also recognized this importance of really knowing each other in a relationship of reciprocity when he started the program with Nouf Bazaz to bridge differences called "Courageous Conversations," in which a diverse group of residents from Asbury Methodist Village share personal stories of discrimination with high school students in the surrounding community. Issues addressed included internment, ethnic and cultural integration, the Holocaust, LGBT issues, and many others. Efforts like these that strengthen intergenerational relationships render ourselves visible to one another as having shared humanity as opposed to the stereotypes we might hold. As Jacqueline Novogratz (2010) shared in her Ted Talk, "Inspiring a Life of Immersion," "What we really yearn for as human beings is to be visible to each other."

"Stories are how we think. They are how we make meaning of life. . . . how we understand our place in the world, create identities, and define and teach social values." (Pamela Rutledge, 2011)

PROGRAM EXAMPLE: ORAL HISTORY PROJECT

Oral history is a method of gathering and preserving historical information through interviews. It is also a wonderful tool for learning more about different points in history or social issues. Oral history interviews and conversations can occur among family members or groups of older and younger people not related to each other. In fact, oral history is a great intergenerational activity for schools and community elders. Sharing stories through oral history is also fun, but preparation is needed to make sure it is successful. There are a number of online resources on oral history. Visit www.oralhistory.org, www.historymatters.gmu.edu, and www.readingrockets.org/article/oral-history for more information. Oral History tips:

- Make sure to take time to prepare, plan questions in advance, and respect the schedules and privacy of older adults.
- Write down questions that you want to ask. Make sure they cannot be answered by a simple "yes" or "no." Some suggested questions are included here.
- If possible, record your sessions. If you can't, write down each answer before going on to the next question. It is often helpful to work with a partner. One person can write down the answers so the interviewer can be planning the next question. Write down all the answers, even the ones you might already know.
- Try to ask brief questions that don't have too many parts.
- Listen to the answers and ask follow-up questions requesting more details. You may need to ask interviewees to describe how something or someone looked or how they felt.
- Help the older adults feel comfortable talking about the past.
- Periods of silence are good. It allows people to collect their thoughts and add more details. Let the older people know how happy you are to learn their stories.

(continued)

- Maintain eye contact. Facial expressions are good indicators of interest and are very important in keeping a conversation going.
- Older children and youth should take notes and, following the interview, write down the stories they learned from their older partners.
- Younger children can draw pictures or make collages illustrating the stories they heard.
- Young people can tap into their creativity by composing poems, songs, or skits based on their conversations with older adults.
- The whole community can get involved by performing the song, skit, or play that portrays the older adults' stories.

RESOURCE: INTERGENERATIONAL PROGRAMMING IN SENIOR HOUSING

Generations United and LeadingAge conducted a study with support from the Retirement Research Foundation to learn more about intergenerational programming in senior housing (Henkin, Patterson, Stone, & Butts, 2017). One motivation that they discovered was a desire to dispel fears and ageist beliefs. "Many providers indicated that they initially implemented intergenerational programs out of a desire to dispel fears of aging and older adults among young people. Several providers, who had observed the tendency for different age groups to avoid each other, also saw intergenerational programming as a way for older adults to gain a greater understanding of the children and young adults in their communities" (p. 7). In this study, they found in programs that engaged youth a greater understanding of issues faced by older adults, while older adults reported feeling less isolated. Both youth and older adults reported increased self-esteem and feelings of worth, increased trust across ages, and increased sense of community.

MULTIGENERATIONAL FAMILIES AND GRANDFAMILIES

Today, people are so disconnected that they feel they are blades of grass, but when they know who their grandparents and great-grandparents were, they become trees, they have roots, they can no longer be mowed down.
—Maya Angelou, January 30, 2003, *The Oprah Winfrey*

The U.S. Census Bureau defines *multigenerational families* as those consisting of more than two generations living under the same roof. Many researchers also include households with a grandparent and at least one other generation. In 19th century America, older adults living with their grown children and grandchildren was commonplace. However, in the 20th century, this type of multigenerational family structure declined with the advent of Social Security and lessening importance of agricultural and occupational inheritance (Ruggles, 2003). Recent years have seen a change. Multigenerational households have rapidly increased with one in six people in the United States currently living in a multigenerational household. There are several factors that appear to contribute to the increase in multigenerational households:

- *Elongating life span:* People are living longer, up to 20 years longer than previous generations. The impact of those years is felt throughout life and not simply tacked on to the end. As a result, younger adults are experiencing what some consider a slower start. People are marrying and establishing their own homes later with more unmarried 20-somethings continuing or returning to live with their parents, by choice or economic necessity. Unlike previous generations who could not wait to leave home, today's younger people and parents are more likely to report they enjoy each other's company.
- *Immigration:* Latin Americans and Asians have immigrated to the United States in large numbers and are more likely to live in multigenerational families. New immigrants have often banded together to pool resources and help extended family members. The largest number of multigenerational households can be found in Hawaii where housing costs are high and living under one roof is a cultural norm.
- *Availability of kin:* There are more people able to offer their parents a place to live in their old age while also providing a home to their own children. This living arrangement can help alleviate the stress of distance caregiving and provide a deeper sense of roots for children as they learn about their family history and traditions.
- *Health and disability issues:* Increasing numbers of people of all ages suffer from chronic conditions and disabilities. They may move in with family members to gain access to caregivers for themselves and/or their children.
- *Economic conditions:* During the Great Recession that started in 2008, many people struggled with job loss or other forms of reduced income.

Many faced the need to retrain for jobs in demand. Sharing household expenses across generations make them more manageable. As the economy strengthened, the number of multigenerational households did not decline, but in fact increased. The families may have come together out of need, but they stayed together by choice. A 2011 survey of multigenerational families found 82% agreed that their multigenerational household arrangement enhanced bonds or relationships among family members. However, 78% also agreed that the arrangement can also contribute to stress among family members. Still, 75% agreed that living under one roof made it easier to provide for the care needs of other family members (Generations United, 2011a).

TIPS FOR MAKING MULTIGENERATIONAL HOUSEHOLDS WORK

Talk about and make decisions in advance when planning to live together, including the following:

- Discuss what is expected of everyone with regard to household finances (who will buy groceries or pay the electric bill) and saving for the future.
- Discuss the length of stay. Make sure everyone has the same expectations about whether the arrangement will be temporary or permanent. Be prepared to renegotiate if the situation changes.
- Establish boundaries that respect privacy, individual needs, parenting, roles, and the hours people keep.
- Ensure open communication via regular family meetings or even family counseling.
- Allow all family members to have separate and shared spaces, or identify family- together-times and alone times.
- Never make assumptions. Accept that people are individuals. Early birds and night owls are most likely not going to change their habits.
- Be sure everyone understands the agreements. Revisit and adjust them when needed. (Generations United, 2011b)

GRANDFAMILIES, GRANDPARENTS, AND OTHER RELATIVES RAISING CHILDREN OR KINSHIP CARE

> I was finally an empty nester and bought a condo with white carpet and displayed all my crystal figures. Then the knock on the door came at 2 a.m. My two- and three-year-old grandchildren were handed off to me. The crystal went back in boxes and the carpet didn't last too long. My dreams went on the backburner. Still I never would have dreamed of not taking my grandkids in—they are family.
>
> —Kansas City Grandmother

Grandfamilies, or kinship families, are families in which children reside with and are being raised by grandparents, other extended family members, and adults with whom they have a close familylike relationship, such as godparents and close family friends. About 7.8 million children across the country live in grandfamilies with more than 2.6 million of these children living without the child's parent(s) in the home (Annie E. Casey Foundation KIDS COUNT Data Center, 2018; Lofquist, Lugaila, O'Connell, & Feliz, 2012).

Grandfamilies are diverse and come together for a variety of reasons—including job loss, out-of-state employment, military deployment, divorce, deportation, illness, death, substance abuse, incarceration, or mental illness. Grandfamilies live in every area in the country, and represent all income levels, races, and ethnicities.

One in four children who live with their grandparents are poor and almost half of the children raised solely by their grandmothers live in poverty compared with one in five children living with their parents (Ellis & Simmons, 2014). Grandfamilies are found within and outside the child welfare system. For every child being raised by a relative in the foster care system, 23 children are being raised by relatives outside of the system with no parent present in the home (The Annie E. Casey Foundation KIDS COUNT Data Center, 2014). By conservative estimates, these relatives who keep families together and 20 children out of foster care save taxpayers more than $4 billion each year.[1]

Grandparents or other relatives often take on the care of children with little or no chance to plan in advance. Consequently, they typically face

---

[1] Generations United calculated this figure based on the following two data sources: Annie E. Casey Foundation Kids Count Data Center. 2014–2016 Current Population Survey, Annual Social and Economic Supplement (CPS ASEC). Annie E. Casey Foundation Kids Count Data Center. Child Trends analysis of data from Adoption and Foster Care Analysis and Reporting System (AFCARS) made available through the National Data Archive on Child Abuse and Neglect (NDACAN).

unique challenges. Many caregivers lack a legal relationship to the children and cannot access educational enrollment, school services, or healthcare on their behalf. Others may have a legal relationship, but taking on sudden caregiving responsibilities often means they do not have suitable housing. Caregivers are also often in their prime retirement savings years and rather than save for their retirement, they find themselves providing for their grandchildren. Almost 20% of all kinship caregivers are retired and may not have the finances to take on the many extra expenses of raising children. They are also more than twice as likely to face the threat of hunger than older adults who do not live with their grandchildren (Ziliak & Gundersen, 2014). When compared with grandparents who are not living with their grandchildren, grandparent caregivers are more likely to be living in poverty, more likely to be working at least part time, and more likely to be disabled (Ellis & Simmons, 2014).

CASE EXAMPLE

Lynn is raising her grandson and is a kinship services director in Olympia, WA. Kinship Care programs link grandparents and other relative caregivers to support groups and provide education and increased access to resources in the community. She reminds us that kinship caregivers don't have months or years to plan on adding a child to their family and may not have resources on hand to get a bigger car or home and may need a little help. She hears of grandparents that don't get their heart medicines because they have to buy shoes for a grandson. She asks us to understand that families are doing the best they can and often need to have a little extra help.

Despite these challenges, research confirms that children thrive in the care of their relatives. Compared with children in nonrelative care, they have more stability, are more likely to maintain connections with brothers and sisters, preserve their cultural heritage and community bonds, and report feeling loved (Kids Are Waiting: Fix Foster Care Now & Generations United, 2007). Caregivers also report experiencing benefits, such as having an increased sense of purpose in life, and birth parents may value that their children remain connected to family and friends.

CASE EXAMPLE

Bob remembers a turning point for him as he was beginning to raise his 13-year-old niece. He felt overwhelmed and decided to go to a support group. He walked into the room, sat down, and listened to all the stories shared by aunts, uncles, and grandparents. At that moment, he realized he was not alone. It didn't matter the different issues that people were facing—simply being able to talk, understand, and support each other was transformational—it changed him. He also realized everyone had loss. His sister had loss, his niece had loss, and he felt he needed to be the strong one. But in the support group, it didn't matter; he could just be what he needed to be.

Becoming a "grandfamily" does not come with a manual. Peer support is essential. Looking back and sharing what he learned, Bob urges people to get help sooner, to not wait until they feel overloaded to seek out support. People often do not search out support in fear that it shows that they "cannot handle it." Bob's hope is that we can address this stigma and that people will seek out support and ask for help. Lynn echoes Bob's experience, that support groups are really important, not only to get to know other people doing the same thing and to feel safe to express frustrations and joys, but also to be able to spend time away. Lynn faces a particular challenge because her husband recently passed away, so she feels an acute sense of isolation in raising her grandson. She shares that activities that are aimed at multigenerational or skipped generation families are important opportunities for grandparents and older relatives to enjoy being with their kids while also having the support of others.

Both Bob and Lynn invite us to advocate for reducing the stigma surrounding relatives raising children. Lynn asks us to "drop the judgment." Grandfamilies hear, "An apple does not fall far from the tree. If you raised an adult child with dysfunction what makes you think you can do better?" She likes to remind people that she has other adult children: a police officer, a school teacher, and a licensed social worker. And yes, she has another child with mental illness. She asks people to look at what relative caregivers are trying to do for children and not put roadblocks in their way.

GRANDFAMILIES SUPPORTING HEALING FROM ADVERSITY AND TRAUMA

> Growing up with a childhood full of trauma and abuse, there were very few moments where I felt safe and very few people with whom I felt protected. Being put into my uncle's care was the best decision that could have ever been made for me. It wasn't an easy road by any means, but I have no doubt in that it completely saved my life. Kindra, raised by her uncle
>
> —CA

One particular issue faced by an increasing number of grandfamilies is children's exposure to significant adversity or trauma. In 2014, more than a third of all children who were removed from their homes because of parental alcohol and drug use were placed with relatives (Generations United, 2016c). Experts say the opioid epidemic contributes to this trend (Stambaugh et al., 2013). In addition, more than half of children involved with the child welfare system have experienced at least four adverse childhood experiences (ACEs), leaving them 12 times more likely to have negative health outcomes than the general child population. The Adverse Childhood Experiences Study[2] examined the link between childhood trauma and lifelong health and found a strong correlation between trauma, an increased risk in behaviors such as smoking, alcohol and drug use, obesity, and sexual risk behavior, and lifelong health.

ACE measures include:

- Emotional, physical, and sexual abuse
- Growing up in a seriously dysfunctional household including:
  - Witnessing domestic violence;
  - Alcohol and other substance abuse in the home;
  - Mentally ill or suicidal household members;
  - Parental separation or divorce; or
  - Imprisoned household members.

THE STATE OF GRANDFAMILIES IN AMERICA, 2017

As the number of children in foster care increases, the child welfare system is increasingly relying on grandparents and other relatives to raise the children. Yet, grandparents and other relatives are less likely than nonrelated foster parents to receive supports and services, including those provided by professionals trained in helping children who have experienced trauma.

Fortunately, children with multiple ACEs are not destined to adopt risky behaviors that result in negative health effects. Grandfamilies protect against trauma and promote resilience. Research shows that

---

[2] The ACEs study is an ongoing collaboration between Kaiser Permanente and the U.S. Centers for Disease Control and Prevention (CDC). In this description, the phrase "general child population" refers to thousands of adult members of Kaiser Permanente who responded to a retrospective survey. For more information on the Adverse Childhood Experiences Study see https://www.cdc.gov/violenceprevention/acestudy

a series of protective factors can mitigate the impact of ACEs and promote resiliency (McConnico, 2017). These factors include positive child–caregiver relationships, stable living environments, and relationships with extended family members. Most important among them is a positive, supportive relationship with a loving adult. Research shows that a positive relationship with even just one caring adult helps children buffer the effects of their stress response systems (McConnico, 2017). With caring adults, these children learn how to cope with stress and develop healthy stress response systems over time.

Children being raised in foster care by relatives have better health outcomes, more stability, and a greater sense of belonging compared with children in foster care with nonrelatives (Figure 14.1). When children cannot remain with their parents, placing them with grandparents and other relatives reduces future trauma and mitigates the impact of past trauma. The stability, supportive relationships and extended family network that grandfamilies provide to children align with research-based protective factors that promote resiliency and healing.

Policy makers and practitioners must promote approaches that prioritize placing children with relatives when they cannot stay with their birth parents, provide trauma-informed training and mental health services to the children and caregivers, and connect the family to comprehensive community-based supports such as legal and financial help, respite, and health care.

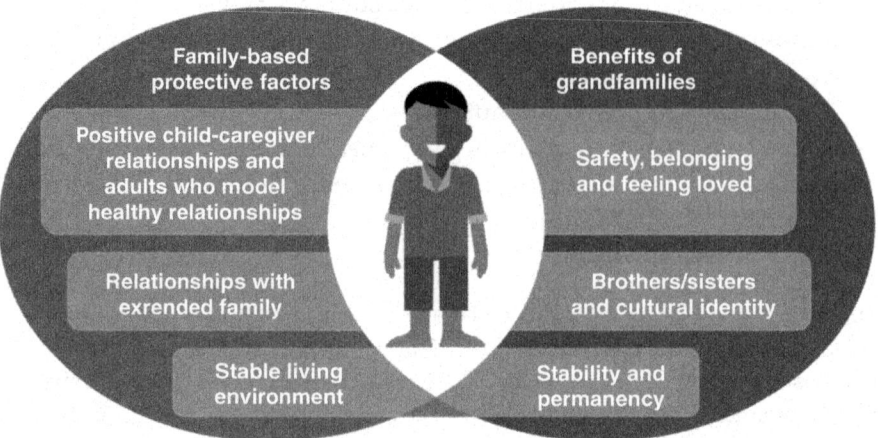

FIGURE 14.1 Raising awareness through elevating voices of grandfamilies.

Generations United, in partnership with National Indian Child Welfare Association (NICWA) and A Second Chance, Inc., launched a 3-year initiative, GrAND Voices: Elevating and Strengthening African American and Native American Grandfamilies. The initiative recruits and prepares family caregivers to join Generations United's GrAND Voices network, a proven group of family caregiver advocates who educate, represent, and testify on behalf of grandparents and other relatives raising children. The GrAND Voices project engages grandfamily caregivers in raising awareness with federal and state policy makers and tribal leaders. It also elevates visibility of grandfamilies in the press as well as highlights the valuable role and need for supportive services for grandfamilies.

The GrAND Voices initiative includes community-based projects to improve local supports and services for grandfamilies. It will culminate with the creation of toolkits and other resources for organizations serving Native American and African American grandfamilies, and the release of an action agenda to promote evidence-based practices for serving the families.

PRACTICE TIPS TO SUPPORT GRANDFAMILIES

- Support groups provide a sense of community and help caregivers know they are not the only ones parenting a new generation. They can also be a key source of accurate information and referral and provide timeout for the children and their caregivers.
- Respite services can go a long way toward helping relatives take a break from the children in their care. Respite takes many forms, including a mentor who takes the child away for outings, in home support, or weekend retreats.
- Baby showers help to provide clothing, diapers, and equipment needed for a new relative caregiver.
- Kinship Navigator programs are a one-stop information source for grandfamilies trying to navigate new systems and access available supports and services.

CASE EXAMPLE

For 7 years, Anntesha and her sister were in foster care placements with her grandparents. Their grandfather eventually lost his eye sight, and that challenge, coupled with no financial support or mental health services for the sisters, meant Anntesha's grandparents couldn't raise them anymore. At age 16, Anntesha and her younger sister returned to nonrelated foster care and eventually aged out. During those years, Anntesha ran away several times and spent a lot of time homeless, while her sister had her own separate challenges.

As an adult, Anntesha's sister struggled with opioids, substance abuse, and homelessness. She had four young children who needed help. When contacted by the child welfare agency, Anntesha stepped forward to raise the young children. After about 18 months in Anntesha's care, the children eventually reunified with their father. He found a job in Alaska, and they moved with him there.

Anntesha's experiences both as a child raised by kin and as a kinship caregiver herself make her uniquely qualified to work at Foster Kinship, a nonprofit advocacy organization in Las Vegas that helps families like hers. Anntesha now trains and supports kinship foster parents. She believes when children cannot be with their parents, they should be with family.

RAISING GRAND VOICES AT THE GRANDRALLY 2017

"We are united in a common thread of love and devotion to our families."

—2017 GrandRally Participant

More than 600 grandparents, relative caregivers, and advocates descended on Washington, D.C., from 27 states and the District of Columbia, coming from as far away as Hawaii to attend the 2017 GrandRally. Another 700 took part in virtual rallies around the country where participants phoned their legislators to raise awareness about the importance of supports and services for grandfamilies.

Michelle Singletary, emcee for the rally, wrote a moving column: "Mother's Day is a tough time for me. Every year it reminds me that my own mother wasn't there. I went to live with my grandmother when I was four. It has taken me most of my adult life to reconcile being abandoned. But amid that pain was the safety of my grandmother, Big Mama."

On the day of the rally, attendees made at least 49 visits to members of Congress from at least 18 states to share their stories and advocate for policies needed to help them successfully raise the children in their care.

(continued)

"Legislators are being educated by grandparents like you and me; grandparents are not silenced by stigma anymore. I am thankful for events like the GrandRally that highlight the value of grandfamilies, the impact we have on our grandchildren, and the positive results of that impact in our communities."– Sherry Griffin, 2017 GrandRally

Reflecting on her first rally in 2011, Adrian Charnick said, "It saved my life. I found out I wasn't alone and I went home and started organizing."

SUMMARY

Gaithersburg Beloved Community Initiative. Inclusive Community Collaborative. The Intergenerational Schools. Bridge Meadows. GrAND Voices. These intergenerational program names evoke empathy, compassion, strength, and resilience. Whether focused on the family or larger community of neighbors, each expresses a desire to increase connectedness while valuing people at all ages and stages of life. It is this kind of vision and passion that strengthens relationships between individuals and between individuals and their community. As our society ages, intergenerational opportunities can awaken the wisdom and strengths of younger and older people. Our families and communities are richer and stronger as a result.

RESOURCES

Youth-Led Intergenerational Projects
  www.gu.org/resources/youth-led-intergenerational-toolkit
Creating an Age-Advantaged Community Toolkit
  www.gu.org/resources/creating-an-age-advantaged-community
Valuing Vaccinations Across Generations Intergenerational Discussion Guide
  www.gu.org/resources/valuing-vaccinations-across-generations
State of Grandfamilies 2017 In Loving Arms: The Protective Role of Grandparents and Other Relatives in Raising Children Exposed to Trauma
  www.gu.org/resources/the-state-of-grandfamilies-in-america-2017

REFERENCES

Administration on Aging. (2013). *A profile of older Americans: 2012*. Retrieved from https://www.acl.gov/sites/default/files/Aging%20and%20Disability%20in%20America/2012profile.pdf

Annie E. Casey Foundation KIDS COUNT Data Center. (2014). 2011-2013 Current Population Survey Annual Social and Economic Supplement (CPS ASEC). Retrieved from https://datacenter.kidscount.org/data/tables/6243-children-in-foster-care?loc=1&loct=2#detailed/2/2-53/false/870,573,869,36,868,867,133,38,35,18/any/12987

Annie E. Casey Foundation KIDS COUNT Data Center. (2018). Children in kinship care. Retrieved from https://datacenter.kidscount.org/data/tables/7172-children-in-kinship-care?loc=1&loct=1#detailed/1/any/false/1652,1564,1491,1443,1218/any/14207,14208

ChildStats.gov. (n.d.). America's children: Key national indicators of well-being. Retrieved from http://www.childstats.gov/americaschildren/demo.asp

Ellis, R. R., & Simmons, T. (2014). Coresident grandparents and their grandchildren: 2012. Retrieved from https://www.census.gov/content/dam/Census/library/publications/2014/demo/p20-576.pdf

Emlet, C., & Moceri, J. (2011). The importance of social connectedness in building age-friendly communities. Retrieved from https://www.hindawi.com/journals/jar/2012/173247

Generations United. (2011a). Family matters: Multigenerational families in a volatile economy. Retrieved from https://www.gu.org/resources/family-matters-multigenerational-families-in-a-volatile-economy

Generations United. (2011b). Multigenerational household information. Retrieved from https://www.gu.org/explore-our-topics/multigenerational-households

Generations United. (2016a). Creating an age-advantaged community: A toolkit for building intergenerational communities that recognize, engage, and support all ages. Retrieved from https://www.gu.org/resources/creating-an-age-advantaged-community

Generations United. (2016b). Out of many, one: Uniting the changing faces of America. *Public Policy & Aging Report, 26*(3), 99–105. doi:10.1093/ppar/prw017

Generations United. (2016c). The state of grandfamilies in America: 2016. Retrieved from https://www.gu.org/resources/the-state-of-grandfamilies-in-america-2016

Generations United & Eisner Foundation. (2017). I need you, you need me. Retrieved from https://www.gu.org/resources/i-need-you-you-need-me-the-young-the-old-and-what-we-can-achieve-together

Henkin, N., Patterson, T., Stone, R., & Butts, D. (2017). Intergenerational programming in senior housing: from promise to practice. Retrieved from https://www.gu.org/resources/intergenerational-programming-in-senior-housing-from-promise-to-practice

Holt-Lunstad, J., Smith, T. B., & Layton, J. B. (2010). Social relationships and mortality risk: A meta-analytic review. Retrieved from http://journals.plos.org/plosmedicine/article?id=10.1371%2Fjournal.pmed.1000316

Kids Are Waiting: Fix Foster Care Now, & Generations United. (2007). Time for reform: Support relatives in providing foster care and permanent families for children. Retrieved from http://www.pewtrusts.org/~/media/legacy/uploadedfiles/wwwpewtrustsorg/reports/foster_care_reform/supportingrelativespdf.pdf

Lofquist, D., Lugaila, T., O'Connell, M., & Feliz, S. (2012). Households and families: 2010. Retrieved from http://www.census.gov/prod/cen2010/briefs/c2010br-14.pdf

McConnico, N. (2017). Little listeners: Protecting young children by reducing community violence. [PowerPoint presentation]. More information about this briefing can be found here. Retrieved from http://dearcolleague.us/2017/07/lunch-briefing-little-listeners-protecting-young-children-by-reducing-community-violence

Novogratz, J. (2010). Inspiring a life of immersion. Retrieved from https://www.ted.com/talks/jacqueline_novogratz_inspiring_a_life_of_immersion

Our big American family with Billy Crystal and Dr. Maya Angelou [Interview by O. Winfrey]. (2003). In *Our big American family with Billy Crystal and Dr. Maya Angelou: 01/30/2003*. The Oprah Winfrey Show.

Ruggles, S. (2003), Multigenerational families in nineteenth century America. *Continuity and Change, 18*(2), 139–165. doi:10.1017/s0268416003004466

Rutledge, P. (2011). The psychological power of storytelling. Retrieved from https://www.psychologytoday.com/us/blog/positively-media/201101/the-psychological-power-storytelling

Stambaugh, L. F., Ringeisen, H., Casanueva, C. C., Tueller, S., Smith, K. E., & Dolan, M. (2013). Adverse childhood experiences in NSCAW. OPRE Report #2013-26, Washington, DC: Office of Planning, Research and Evaluation, Administration for Children and Families, U.S. Department of Health and Human Services. Retrieved from http://www.acf.hhs.gov/programs/opre/abuse_neglect/nscaw

Ziliak, J. P., & Gundersen, C. (2014). The state of senior hunger in America 2012: An annual report. Retrieved from http://nfesh.org/wp-content/uploads/state-of-senior-hunger-2012-full-report.pdf

15

Rethinking Love, Intimacy, and Sexual Relationships in the Later Years

Nicholas Velotta and Pepper Schwartz

INTRODUCTION

The Western practice of pairing off with one's soulmate—someone who meets the intimate as well as sexual, emotional, and self-actualizing needs of his or her partner, as opposed to marrying for social class or security to someone arranged through familial or community networks—became the primary route to marriage in the mid-20th century (Coontz, 2006). Along with this reevaluation of intimate relationships, women's increasing participation in the workforce and more lenient divorce laws enabled men and women to more easily part ways because they felt unfulfilled in their marriage (rather than because of the extreme circumstances like spousal abuse or infidelity, which courts had previously required to legalize divorces). Americans went from marriages that literally lasted "until death do you part" to marriages that lasted as long as both parties remained emotionally and sexually fulfilled. Today's Baby Boomers were in the vanguard of these social movements and liberalized laws, most of which proliferated during Boomer youth and young adulthood. As such, their cohort continued with high rates of marriage but experienced unprecedented rates of divorce. Even today, so-called "gray divorces" have continued on an incline, doubling in the United States since 1990 (Stepler, 2017a). Boomers also got married at later ages than their parents and the number of single-person households increased substantially within their generation (Coontz, 2006). Consequently, we have the largest population of older adults in history who often find themselves single in later life, whether by divorce, bereavement, difficulty finding a compatible partner, or simply by choice.

This is not to say that Boomers care less about finding an intimate or sexual mate than their precursors. Remaining romantically and sexually active has actually garnered more importance in the Baby Boomer cohort than in past generations (Schwartz, Diefendorf, & McGlynn-Wright, 2014). For many older men and women, sex, intimacy, and romance continue to be core relationship values and goals, the same as they were in their young adulthood 40-plus years ago. This is not surprising; in general, higher levels of sexual satisfaction are associated with greater relationship satisfaction, love, commitment, and relationship stability (Sprecher, 2002). However, less is known in terms of how sexual activity affects the relationships that single people form later in life.

While the data on older people are spare, there are indications that single people fare reasonably well in later life. Although the research shows many health and emotional advantages to being partnered (Harvard Men's Health Watch, 2010), being single post-50 does not necessarily create a less satisfactory old age. Many older men and women prefer going solo later in life over living with a romantic partner, friends, or even with family. Yet, it is important to remember that for most older men and women, single and married alike, sexual longevity and romantic connection remain essential components to their life satisfaction. In this chapter, we explore what major factors contribute to and detract from older adults' ability to sustain sexual and romantic satisfaction well into the last half of their lives. We pay particular attention to the ways in which being single can both inhibit and be a positive part of this new stage of love, sexuality, and intimacy for older adults.

SECTION I: THE DEMOGRAPHICS OF INTIMACY POST-50

Sexual Longevity

Clearly, when discussing the behaviors of an entire generation of people, there are many sociological factors to be considered. For one thing, the post-50 population is increasingly more liberal about sexuality than we have seen in past generations. Whereas 73% of older adults believed that there was too much emphasis on sex in our culture in 1999, 65% of older adults held this belief by 2009 (Fisher et al., 2010). And according to an AARP survey, 42% of adults over age 45 believe that sexual activity is important to the overall quality of one's life, with younger age brackets being even more supportive of this pro-sex sentiment (Fisher et al., 2010). Such findings gainsay the validity of common cultural prejudices that regularly minimize the value of sex and intimacy for men and women out of their youth. In fact, appreciation of sex later in the life cycle is not just a value, it is a reality for a substantial number of older men and women. The 2009 AARP Survey of Midlife and Older Adults found that almost one-third of older adults have sexual intercourse at least once a week, and 40% of older adults have intercourse about once a month (Fisher et al., 2010). Surprisingly, frequency of intercourse goes up even more for single older adults who are dating than those with spouses. Nearly half of single daters reported sex at least once a week—significantly more than married couples. However, the same survey found that sexual frequency was the most important predictor in determining sexual satisfaction for *all* older adults. Just over 50% of married older adults reported that they are still sexually satisfied in their marriage and those that were unmarried but partnered reported higher sexual satisfaction ratings than their married counterparts. So, although we see clear incentives to being married later in life (chiefly in long-term health and longevity benefits), the data also supports the claims made by many older men and women who remain single but continue to speak of thriving sex lives.

Single older women, however, are less sexually successful. Not only are older women less likely to remain sexually active when they are without a partner, they are less likely to *find* a partner in the first place. This is due to multiple sociodemographic factors, including the fact that there is a major population disparity between older men and older women (with three women per every one man at age 65 and older). This lopsided ratio creates a large pool of single older women without older male partners (Klinenberg, 2012). Additionally, after the loss of a spouse (through death or divorce), women are less likely to remarry than their older male counterparts (Livingston, 2014). Demographic realities are intensified by the fact that older men prefer to mate with women younger than their own age (England & McClintock, 2009). Thus, heterosexual women, if not married, may have quite a hard time finding an intimate or sexual partner later in life.

In addition, although singles who continue to date have higher sexual frequencies than married adults later in life, older women are less likely to be dating someone than older men (Fisher et al., 2010). Thus, older women's less active sexual life is the result of their values (they are less likely to want random casual sex) and a lack of opportunity (i.e., having a harder time finding viable marriage or dating partners). Some will find these trends concerning for older women; however, based on what data we currently have, the lack of sexual activity later in life may not be distressing to a large number of these women. Whereas 85% of older men surveyed by AARP totally agreed that sex is important to one's overall quality of life, that percentage drops down to 61% for older women (Fisher et al., 2010). In the same survey, researchers found that only about 8% of women reported thinking about sex once or more a day (compared to 45% of men), and even self-stimulation is significantly higher for males than females over age 50. This is not to say that sex is not desired by older women who find themselves without it, but perhaps it has less impact on their overall happiness and quality of life when measured against other factors, such as social support systems, familial connections, physical health, and autonomy over living conditions.

As we have mentioned, men, whether partnered or single, are more likely to make sex a priority at all stages of the life cycle. In fact, men's higher levels of sexual activity, even at older ages, has some negative as well as positive effects. For example, widowers are at an increased risk of acquiring sexually transmitted diseases within the first year of their spouse's passing, a trend that is the opposite of what has been observed in widows (Ball, 2010). Of course, bereavement brings an assortment of negative physical and mental health outcomes for the singled spouse, but it appears that the importance of remaining sexually active is a constant for older men even following the loss of their intimate partner. This is also the case for men who experience gray divorce. Men are especially likely to remarry compared to women (Livingston, 2014); desire for sexual access may be part of the motivation for remarriage, and (when unsatisfied) it may be grounds for separation. In one large-scale survey, two times as many men reported sex as the main cause for relationship stress than did women (Northrup, Schwartz, & Witte, 2012). With such emphasis on sexual longevity, both when married and single, older men continue to seek sexual activity regardless of relationship status.

What about gay men and lesbians? Given the importance that men in general place on sexual longevity, it is not surprising that two men, that is gay men, have very high sexual frequencies compared to any other demographic (Lyons, Pitts, & Grierson, 2013). It is also the case that gay men practice a wide variety of sexual behaviors (Rosenberger et al., 2011). Unfortunately, gay men are more likely to be single later in life than their heterosexual male counterparts (Lyons et al., 2013). Still, because gay men have a more positive attitude about casual sex with friends and acquaintances (Rosenberger et al., 2011), their sexual frequency is not as impeded as their heterosexual counterparts when they are single.

We cannot speak as directly to lesbian sexual longevity because there is a paucity of research on older lesbians. Having said this, some research suggests that, in general, lesbian couples have less frequent sex than gay male or heterosexual couples (Blumstein & Schwartz, 1983). Blair and Pukall (2014) replicated this finding more recently; however, their results indicated that lesbians make love for a longer period of time within a given sexual event than heterosexual or gay male couples. The authors suggest that this increased duration of sexual contact may produce greater emotional or sexual satisfaction and thus counterbalance the lower frequency of sexual encounters that lesbian couples experience. These data, however, are based on younger partnered lesbians because we have not been able to find current statistics on the sexual behaviors of single, older lesbians. This means we are unable to test stereotypes of low lesbian libido or low sexual frequency in lesbian dating behaviors. Low sexual frequencies in lesbian older couples were found in a 1983 study (Blumstein & Schwartz, 1983), but we lack more recent studies that might reflect how changes in women's sexual freedoms, experience, and values have affected older women's sexual profile in recent years. Without those studies, we have little to refute so-called "lesbian bed death," a phrase used to describe a supposed cessation of all sexual activity by older lesbians or lesbians in long-term relationships (Wikipedia, 2018).

Another stereotype that is difficult to reverse is the belief that the quality of one's sex life is diminished with age—that passionate, satisfying sex is only for the young. However, here we do have the data to contest that assumption. A recent study on the sexual quality of life (SQoL) of older adults found that when considering the many domains of sexual satisfaction (e.g., the number of sexual partners, thought and effort put into sex, frequency of sexual encounters), older age is associated with *increased* SQoL (Forbes, Eaton, & Krueger, 2017). Additionally, the quality of sex had a much larger effect on SQoL than did frequency—something that is likely enhanced by the acquisition of skills over one's lifetime that help counter overall declines in sexual functioning.

Relationship Satisfaction

Baby Boomers were trailblazers in setting higher emotional and sexual expectations for their relationships and even casual sexual encounters. A full 87% of Baby Boomers had married at least once by the time they were 46 years old (U.S. Department of Labor, Bureau of Labor Statistics, 2013). But with heightened expectations for marital satisfaction and marital standards also came the increased chance of those expectations not being met, and in marriages where they were not met dissolution increasingly took place. Approximately half of Boomer marriages ended in divorce. And while most age groups' divorce rates have stabilized or reduced in recent years, men and women over age 50 continue to have relatively high frequencies of divorce (Stepler, 2017a). Why are Boomers continuing to get divorced at such high rates? Pew researchers suggest one reason is likely the higher prevalence of second and higher marriages within the post-50 cohort (Stepler, 2017a). Remarriages tend to be less stable and more likely to end in divorce than first marriages; the divorce rate for men and women over age 50 in remarriages is double the rate found in adults over age 50 in first marriages (Stepler, 2017a). Thus, researchers suggest that the high divorce rates that plagued Boomers in their young adulthood may be influencing their marital instability now in late adulthood.

Fortunately, the Pew data also found that the longer adults over age 50 have been married, the less likely they are to divorce (Stepler, 2017a). And this may largely be dependent on how satisfied the woman is in her marriage. A 2004 AARP survey on divorce after midlife found that women are more likely to initiate late-life divorces than men are (Montenegro, 2004)—data that fit well with the narrative of Boomer women gaining socioeconomic independence and being more willing to leave marriages that are not fulfilling, even if they have spent 20 or even 40 years with their spouse. Indeed, about one-third of the divorces that occurred in the post-50 age bracket during 2015 were couples that had been married for 30 years or more (Stepler, 2017a).

For married couples who eschew divorce, sustaining marital satisfaction is certainly important. However, many factors play into the satisfactions of any pairing, especially when it spans over multiple transitions and stages of the life cycle. This makes it rather complicated for researchers to understand how those who have remained married over many years may or may not be better off than if they had divorced or stayed single. Even still, longitudinal studies of marriage generally focus on newlyweds, younger couples, and/or do not focus on marriages spanning over 20 years or more. Therefore, although we have indicators that marital satisfaction declines over time (with the sharpest decline occurring in the first few years of marriage) (Kurdek, 1999), such data may not fully capture the marital trends of older couples or spouses that have been married 20-plus years.

Assessing how durability and satisfaction operate over time is also complicated by the fact that marriage is no longer the only socially acceptable form of partnership later in life. By far, the most popular alternative to marriage for older adults is cohabitation. Since 2007, there has been a 75% increase in the number of Americans 50-and-up who are currently cohabitating (Stepler, 2017b). Although cohabitation is often used as a stepping stone toward marriage by younger adults, cohabitation is becoming an alternative to marriage for older adults seeking to avoid the legal and economic ramifications of a marriage or a divorce. As cohabitation becomes more of a marriage facsimile, we hypothesize that many of the long-term individual benefits, satisfaction levels, and the increased relationship stability associated with married older adults will carry over to older cohabiters. Some research suggests this is already happening (see Brown & Kawamura, 2010; Musick & Bumpass, 2012).

Another form of partnership that is gaining ground in the older U.S. population is couples living apart together (or LATs). This type of relationship includes committed intimate partners who have no intention of ever combining households. Unfortunately, there is a paucity in empirical research on LATs in the United States. However, in his 2012 book *Going Solo*, sociologist Eric Klinenberg provides a sociological narrative largely based on in-depth interviews of older couples who decide moving in together is not for them. Older people who partake in LATs have a multitude of reasons for doing so, but one central theme seems to be a desire for autonomy. Many LAT couples derive satisfaction from having complete control over their respective living spaces and decline to move in with their partner although cohabitation offers obvious economic efficiencies. We do not, however, know how this affects their sexual and emotional intimacy.

BARRIERS TO SEXUAL INTIMACY POST-50

As we have seen, the organization and practice of intimacy later in life can vary greatly. An older couple may be 40 years into a marriage or just starting one; lesbians can marry their long-time partner now or they may prefer to stick to cohabitating; gay men may remain single and continue to have a thriving sex life or try out an LAT relationship. There are many options and what we hope is already apparent from this chapter is that traditional Western notions of sexuality, romance, and intimacy after one's youth lag behind the current landscape of attitudes and behaviors men and women over age 50 express in their daily lives. Still, there are many older traditionalists who want exactly the format their parents had or do not feel comfortable searching for passionate or romantic alliances at older ages. It is not only the demographic challenges that many (especially women) face that may hinder sexual experience and sexual satisfaction after middle age. Thus far, we have concentrated on the demographic traits of the post-50 population that affect sexual and romantic longevity; however, in this section we turn our attention toward some of the psychosocial variables that can impact sex after 50 (such as societal stigma and personal communication styles between partners) as well as some of the more inevitable obstacles to sex older men and women experience (such as poor physical health). We also look at how institutional practices such as the current state of long-term care (LTC) facilities often have policies that inhibit their residents' ability to be sexually active.

Social Stigma and Body Image

American media representations of sexiness have broadened to encompass older ages in recent years, and encouraging bromides like "50 is the new 30" are certainly influencing how much of our society conceptualizes aging in the 21st century. At last, movies and television programs are featuring older actors and actresses like Jane Fonda, Diane Keaton, Meryl Streep, and Tom Selleck in roles that portray them as sexually attractive. This is no minor change considering that just a few decades ago many older actors were largely cast in grandmotherly or grandfatherly roles, and those who did enact sexually suggestive material were often portrayed as perverted or licentious. "Sex columns" in AARP and dating sites specifically for older people help normalize the existence of sexually active and desirable older men and women. Recognition for older people's sexual desires is clearly gaining ground. However, there is some evidence that the long history of stigma toward seniors' sexual activities still bothers many older men and women.

For women, the sexual stigma often comes in the form of judgments about their physical attractiveness. Some research suggests that for many older women, beauty and youth are tightly linked (Hurd, 2000). Certainly, there are women who see their physical signs of aging less as a denigration of their beauty and more of a badge of honor, but for others the internalization of ageist beauty norms is clearly a threat to one's body image later in life. Common phrases like "she has aged well" and "aging gracefully" suggest that there is a specific way women are expected to look as they age and those who miss this arbitrary mark have failed some unclear standard. It is difficult to imagine that widespread criticism of older female bodies has no effect on most women's body image. And research does show that body shame is associated with lower sexual arousal and less sexual pleasure for women (Sanchez & Kiefer, 2007).

But subcultural differences show that body shame is not uniformly experienced. Lesbian women seem to fare better in terms of body image. They have less body dissatisfaction and actually prefer higher body mass indexes than their heterosexual counterparts (Alvy, 2013; Swami & Tovee, 2006). And although findings on lesbians' partner age preference have been mixed, some research finds that lesbians tend to seek partners a bit older than themselves (Silverthorne & Quinsey, 2000) or at least have more tolerance for dating within different age ranges (Conway, Noë, Stulp, & Pullet, 2015), likely making ageist notions of attractiveness less impactful on their ability to partner and stay sexually satisfied post-50.

Exacting beauty standards have not been applied as stringently to men. This may be changing, however. Older males are reporting lower levels of body satisfaction than previous generations (Sanchez & Kiefer, 2007), and with increasing media attention on more muscular and lean male physiques, it is not unlikely that as upcoming generations age we will see further increases in body dissatisfaction among older men.

Gay men may have the harshest of beauty standards. Not only do older gay males prefer younger male partners (Conway et al., 2015), but gay men tend to perceive their age more negatively than people of other sexual orientations. The theory of gay men's *accelerated aging* holds that at any given age, gay men perceive themselves as older than their heterosexual male equivalents (Schope, 2005). Such a dramatic perception of old age paired with a propensity to see young men as far more attractive than older potential partners (or even middle-aged potential partners) makes many older gay men doubt their sexual attractiveness. This is not to say that gay men past age 40 will have no sexual opportunities, but it does indicate that severe pressure is put on gay men to look as youthful as possible at any given age—something that obviously gets exponentially harder with age. Yes, gay men may have additional sexual opportunities since casual sex is not stigmatized, but accelerated aging theory presents a challenging picture for gay men trying to find intimate partners after age 50.

Communication

Communication enhances sexual opportunity and sexual satisfaction. Older couples who can discuss sexual topics, needs, and fantasies, and engage in sexually playful dialogue (even through text messages) are more likely to have a high sexual satisfaction and higher frequencies of intercourse (Gillespie, 2016). Unfortunately, many older men and especially older women do not feel comfortable discussing sexual issues with their partner. This is not a minor problem. In long-term couples, the quality of couples' intimate communication is a significant factor in the longevity of and changes in both their sexual satisfaction and relationship satisfaction (Byers, 2005). And if couples cannot engage in dialogue about how to better satisfy one another (perhaps mentioning the need for lubrication, using a vibrator, or changing positions for additional comfort), sex can become laborious, painful, or boring over many years. Couples who avoid such habituation by including more variety in their sexual lives are in fact the most sexually satisfied (Gillespie, 2016).

Physical Health

Most men and women will face physical challenges that impact their sexual lives. Reduced mobility and reduced sexual functioning (e.g., erectile dysfunction, low vaginal lubrication, reduced sensitivity) will definitely put limitations on behaviors and possibly reduce sexual satisfaction. Fortunately, sexual medicine and/or therapeutic interventions can fix or ameliorate many of these problems. For example, erectile dysfunction which affects about 30% of men over age 45 (Fisher et al., 2010) can generally be treated with an oral medication like sildenafil (e.g., Viagra®) or tadalafil (e.g., Cialis®). Other conditions, such as the effects of heart, blood pressure, depression, and diabetes medications, are presently less easily remedied.

What has been made clear from research on aging is that being in good health and avoiding high stress are major factors in remaining sexually active after age 50. Of those older adults who say that their sex lives are worse now than they were 10 years ago, the top causes include "worse personal health, more stress, and worse health of one's partner" (Fisher et al., 2010, p. 3). Common conditions found in older demographics like high blood pressure, cardiovascular disease, depression, enlarged prostates (in men), diabetes, and arthritis have been found to reduce sexual desire and/or cause sexual dysfunctions (Camacho & Reyes-Ortiz, 2005; Delamater & Sill, 2005). And while some of these ailments can be relieved with lifestyle changes (such as increasing one's daily exercise or lowering the amount of cholesterol in one's diet), many conditions require medication to treat. A range of pharmaceuticals meant to alleviate conditions like those listed earlier can also interfere with sexual functioning for older adults (Delamater & Sill, 2005). Older patients' sex lives may suffer if they do not have a health provider who takes their sexual function into account when either prescribing or reviewing medications.

Long-Term Care

One would hope that in old age, men's and women's right to be sexual would be supported by caretaking institutions. Unfortunately, research is finding that many LTC facilities do not have a patient's sexual rights policy and, worse, have restrictive policies and negative attitudes regarding residents' sexual behavior. It is rare that facilities provide double beds in residents' rooms and the layout of nursing homes often minimizes privacy, thus making intimate connection between people living there quite difficult (Bouman, Arcelus, & Benbow, 2007; Frankowski & Clark, 2009). The restrictiveness seen in some LTC facilities is even worse for older lesbian, gay, bisexual, transgender, and queer (LGBTQ) residents who can face pushback from care staff when expressing their sexual orientation and needs (Hinrichs & Vacha-Haase, 2010).

It is a reality that many older residents in LTC facilities desire romance and passion just like their peers outside of care communities. But even when there is some permission for sexual behavior, residents in caretaking institutions are often so worried about the disapproval they may face from family members or staff that even if privacy is possible, the road to romance is fraught with hesitation and embarrassment. If there is no privacy, sexual interaction can be almost impossible. For a more in-depth discussion of the specific deficits seen in the current LTC system as well as practical solutions to some of these problems, see our forthcoming article "The Changing Nature of Intimate and Sexual Relationships in Later Life" in the *Journal of Aging Life Care* (Schwartz & Velotta, 2018).

Finally, before moving on from how late-life care policies impact residents' sexual agencies, there is another potential barrier to sexual relations in the LTC setting that needs to be mentioned, and that is mutual consent. Given the high prevalence of cognitive impairment and dementia in LTC, concern over a person's ability to consent to intimate relationships and sexual contact is a legitimate and challenging issue. This may also involve consent from a spouse who is not living in the facility when her or his husband or wife in LTC no longer recognizes her or him and seeks physical contact with someone who is living in the same facility. People with dementia can crave physical intimacy and can find comfort in holding hands, hugging, "spooning" in bed, and even sexual contact with another resident in the facility. Balancing the potential for undue influence and coercion of vulnerable people—that is, behaviors that are hurtful to a living spouse and other family members—against the potential comfort these relationships may bring to the persons with dementia in LTC is challenging, to say the least. Developing institutional guidelines and policies that navigate individual rights, recognition of human need, and protection from abuse and harm is a delicate matter.

ISOLATED VERSUS SINGLE: A COMPLICATED RELATIONSHIP

So how much does being single after the fifth decade of one's life matter when it comes to intimate and sexual fulfillment? The data we have indicate that the answer to this question varies widely based on both gender and sexual orientation. Gay men, for instance, seem to be fairly well off remaining single post-50 with more allowances for casual sex (Rosenberger et al., 2011), higher rates of consensual open relationships (likely enabling a wider pool of sexual possibilities even within the context of committed relationships), and satisfying social support networks that tend to grow with age (Lyons et al., 2013). It is a strong possibility that single older gay men can remain sexually active and sustain meaningful social connections as well. One downside to being single and gay, however, may be the quality of sex; gay men age 60 and older are less likely to achieve orgasm when having sex with someone who is not their committed intimate partner (Rosenberger et al., 2011).

Heterosexual men, on the other hand, show a strong preference for remaining partnered later in life. And when they are single, heterosexual men tend to be more socially isolated, which is often attributed to the observation that men tend to get their emotional and social needs fulfilled by their female partner and they are less adept at making and maintaining relationships of any type (Klinenberg, 2012; Vandervoort, 2000). Though heterosexual men, like homosexual men, place a high premium on sexual longevity, heterosexual men may not be satisfied with their sex lives unless they are partnered—and indeed, may suffer other deprivations if they are single for a long time. A survey of 127,545 American men published by Harvard University found that compared with married men, single men face increased risk for many major diseases and tend to die at a younger age (Harvard Men's Health Watch, 2010). Being partnered is definitely a benefit to many men's (and women's) overall health. However, we stress that it is unlikely that marital status alone creates such benefits. People with better health may also be more likely to be partnered, and of course unsatisfactory and stressful marriages may actually degrade one's overall health, not boost it. We should also add that women do not experience as dramatic health benefits as men do from marriage (Wanic & Kulik, 2011).

Since older women tend to place sexual satisfaction lower in their felt needs, many older heterosexual women live fulfilled lives without a sexual partner. Women create intimacy in a number of other ways, including the creation of large social networks and better relationship skills compared to heterosexual men (Klinenberg, 2012). In *Going Solo*, Klinenberg interviewed many older women who, though uninterested in finding a new romantic relationship, were extremely active in their communities and formed many friendships in multiple social groups. These women were notably cautious about romantic relationships at this stage of the life cycle, particularly if they were worried about being someone's caretaker (Klinenberg, 2012). Overall, the association of isolation and being single is less likely for single heterosexual women than single heterosexual men.

Less is known about how intimacy is impacted when older lesbians do not have a romantic partner. However, older lesbians tend to have well-established social support networks and may benefit from even larger networks when they live with a partner who can offer her own social network (Grossman, D'Augelli, & Hershberger, 2000). Having a large group of supportive friends may provide enough emotional connectedness for lesbians later in life; older lesbians tend to emphasize the companionate needs their relationships fill and downplay their sexual needs (Averett, Yoon, & Jenkins, 2012).

DISCUSSION

The reader will note that we have frequently referred to *sexual longevity*. This is because human beings have the ability to feel sexual desire, remain sexually active, and be sexually satisfied throughout the entire life cycle, including well into the last quartile of life. The lived experiences of individuals, however, varies greatly from person to person. So, it is incumbent on healthcare practitioners who serve older clients to make sexual functioning a point of discussion during routine visits and check-ups, and to make no assumptions about sexual needs and desires on the basis of age. This can be uncomfortable for some health and service personnel, but—as is apparent throughout this chapter—sexuality is an important aspect of many older adults' overall health and life satisfaction. We would hope that medical practitioners in particular would treat sexual functioning as a serious topic and be respectful to their patients' individual needs and, if uncomfortable with suggesting treatment for sexual dysfunctions, be ready to provide referrals to a specialist. Further, we suggest that professionals employed by caretaking institutions create a sexual health policy if there is no such policy in place (or if the current policy does not respect clients' sexual rights). A sexual health and rights policy would need to be a written code that would inform clients, their families, and staff about protections for privacy and sexual conduct that would optimize residents' sexual happiness while living under the institution's care. For a practical and real-life tested model of what a "sexual expression policy" could look like, we suggest studying the Hebrew Home of Riverdale's policy, which is deferential to the sexual needs of its residents (even hosting happy hours, senior proms, and creating a dating service for residents) (Hu, 2016). All policies need to explicitly state how welcome and supportive the institution is regarding LGBTQ clients. Institutional policies should be transparent for both the residents and any family or friends that have been designated as the overseers of a given residents' care.

SUMMARY

Leading a satisfying sex life well into one's later years is not only feasible but currently being done by a great number of older men and women. This is true not only for the married; as we have seen, many older single and unmarried adults continue to make romance and intimacy active components of their lives. Being single and isolated is certainly a concern for some older adults (particularly heterosexual men), but single status should not be conflated with isolation. Rather, we emphasize that being single in the later years need not be sexless, and while it is an impediment to a frequent sex life, other forms of creating intimacy among friends and community exist. While not every older person wants or needs a sexual life, still it does behoove us to accurately inform and support those couples or individuals who aspire to long-term sexual longevity and sexual satisfaction and who may need professional help or advice along the way.

REFERENCES

Alvy, L. M. (2013). Do lesbian women have a better body image? Comparisons with heterosexual women and model of lesbian-specific factors. *Body Image, 10*(4), 524–534. doi:10.1016/j.bodyim.2013.06.002

Averett, P., Yoon, I., & Jenkins, C. (2012). Older lesbian sexuality: Identity, sexual behavior, and the impact of aging. *Journal of Sex Research, 49*(5), 495–507. doi:10.1080/00224499.2011.582543

Ball, H. (2010). Death of a spouse may be associated with increased STD diagnosis among older men. *Perspectives on Sexual & Reproductive Health, 42*(1), 64. doi:10.1363/4206410_1

Blair, K. L., & Pukall, C. F. (2014). Can less be more?: Comparing duration vs. frequency of sexual encounters in same-sex and mixed-sex relationships. *The Canadian Journal of Human Sexuality, 23*(2), 123–136. doi:10.3138/cjhs.2393

Blumstein, P., & Schwartz, P. (1983). *American couples: Money, work and sex* (1st ed.). New York, NY: William Morrow.

Bouman, W. P., Arcelus, J., & Benbow, S. M. (2007). Nottingham study of sexuality and ageing (NoSSA II). Attitudes of care staff regarding sexuality and residents: A study in residential and nursing homes. *Sexual and Relationship Therapy, 22*(1), 45–61. doi:10.1080/14681990600637630

Brown, S. L., & Kawamura, S. (2010). Relationship quality among cohabitors and marrieds in older adulthood. *Social Science Research, 39*(5), 777–786. doi:10.1016/j.ssresearch.2010.04.010

Byers, S. (2005). Relationship satisfaction and sexual satisfaction: A longitudinal study of individuals in long-term relationships. *The Journal of Sex Research, 42*(2), 113–118. doi:10.1080/00224490509552264

Camacho, M. E., & Reyes-Ortiz, C. A. (2005). Sexual dysfunction in the elderly: Age or disease? *International Journal of Impotence Research, 17*(S1), S52–S56. doi:10.1038/sj.ijir.3901429

Conway, J. R., Noë, N., Stulp, G., & Pullet, T. V. (2015). Finding your soulmate: Homosexual and heterosexual age preferences in online dating. *Personal Relationships, 22*(4), 666–678. doi:10.1111/pere.12102

Coontz, S. (2006). *Marriage, a history: How love conquered marriage.* New York, NY: Penguin Books.

Delamater, J., & Sill, M. (2005). Sexual desire in later life. *Journal of Sex Research, 42*(2), 138–149. doi:10.1080/00224490509552267

England, P., & McClintock, E. (2009). The gendered double standard of aging in US marriage markets. *Population and Development Review, 35*(4), 797–816. doi:10.1111/j.1728-4457.2009.00309.x

Fisher, L., Anderson, G., Chapagain, M., Montegnegro, X., Smoot, J., & Takalkar, A. (2010). *Sex, romance, and relationships: AARP survey of midlife and older adults.* Retrieved from http://www.aarp.org/research/topics/life/info-2014/srr_09.html

Forbes, M. K., Eaton, N. R., & Krueger, R. F. (2017). Sexual quality of life and aging: A prospective study of a nationally representative sample. *The Journal of Sex Research, 54*(2), 137–148. doi:10.1080/00224499.2016.1233315

Frankowski, A., & Clark, L. (2009). Sexuality and intimacy in assisted living: Residents' perspectives and experiences. *Sexuality Research and Social Policy Journal of NSRC, 6*(4), 25–37. doi:10.1525/srsp.2009.6.4.25

Gillespie, B. J. (2016). Correlates of sex frequency and sexual satisfaction among partnered older adults. *Journal of Sex & Marital Therapy, 43*, 1–21. doi:10.1080/0092623X.2016.1176608

Grossman, A. H., D'Augelli, A. R., & Hershberger, S. L. (2000). Social support networks of lesbian, gay, and bisexual adults 60 years of age and older. *The Journals of Gerontology: Series B, 55*(3), P171–P179. doi:10.1093/geronb/55.3.P171

Harvard Men's Health Watch. (2010). Marriage and men's health. Retrieved from https://www.health.harvard.edu/newsletter_article/marriage-and-mens-health

Hinrichs, K. L. M., & Vacha-Haase, T. (2010). Staff perceptions of same-gender sexual contacts in long-term care facilities. *Journal of Homosexuality, 57*(6), 776–789. doi:10.1080/00918369.2010.485877

Hu, W. (2016, July 12). Too old for sex? Not at this nursing home. *The New York Times*. Retrieved from https://www.nytimes.com/2016/07/13/nyregion/too-old-for-sex-not-at-this-nursing-home.html

Hurd, L. C. (2000). Older women's body image and embodied experience: An exploration. *Journal of Women & Aging, 12*(3–4), 77–97.

Klinenberg, E. (2012). *Going solo: The extraordinary rise and surprising appeal of living alone.* New York, NY: Penguin Books.

Kurdek, L. A. (1999). The nature and predictors of the trajectory of change in marital quality for husbands and wives over the first 10 years of marriage. *Developmental Psychology, 35*(5), 1283–1296. doi:10.1037/0012-1649.35.5.1283

Livingston, G. (2014). Four-in-ten couples are saying "I do," again. Retrieved from http://www.pewsocialtrends.org/2014/11/14/four-in-ten-couples-are-saying-i-do-again

Lyons, A., Pitts, M., & Grierson, J. (2013). Growing old as a gay man: Psychological well-being of a sexual minority. *Research on Aging, 35*(3), 275–295. doi:10.1177/0164027512445055

Montenegro, X. P. (2004). The divorce experience: A study of divorce at midlife and beyond. Retrieved from https://assets.aarp.org/rgcenter/general/divorce.pdf

Musick, K., & Bumpass, L. (2012). Reexamining the case for marriage: Union formation and changes in well-being. *Journal of Marriage and Family, 74*(1), 1–18. doi:10.1111/j.1741-3737.2011.00873.x

Northrup, C., Schwartz, P., & Witte, J. (2012). *The normal bar: The surprising secrets of happy couples and what they reveal about creating a new normal in your relationship.* New York, NY: Harmony Books.

Rosenberger, J. G., Reece, M., Schick, V., Herbenick, D., Novak, D. S., Van Der Pol, B., & Fortenberry, J. D. (2011). Sexual behaviors and situational characteristics of most recent male-partnered sexual event among gay and bisexually identified men in the United States. *The Journal of Sexual Medicine, 8*(11), 3040–3050. doi:10.1111/j.1743-6109.2011.02438.x

Sanchez, D., & Kiefer, A. (2007). Body concerns in and out of the bedroom: Implications for sexual pleasure and problems. *Archives of Sexual Behavior, 36*(6), 808–820. doi:10.1007/s10508-007-9205-0

Schope, R. (2005). Who's afraid of growing old? *Journal of Gerontological Social Work, 45*(4), 23–39. doi:10.1300/J083v45n04_03

Schwartz, P., Diefendorf, S., & McGlynn-Wright, A. (2014). Sexuality in aging. *APA Handbook of Sexuality and Psychology, 1*, 523–551. doi:10.1037/14193-017

Schwartz, P., & Velotta, N. (2018). The changing nature of intimate and sexual relationships in later life. *The Journal of Aging Life Care, 28*(1), 9–16. Retrieved from https://www.aginglifecarejournal.org/the-changing-nature-of-intimate-and-sexual-relationships-in-later-life

Silverthorne, Z., & Quinsey, V. (2000). Sexual partner age preferences of homosexual and heterosexual men and women. *Archives of Sexual Behavior, 29*(1), 67–76. doi:10.1023/A:1001886521449

Sprecher, S. (2002). Sexual satisfaction in premarital relationships: Associations with satisfaction, love, commitment, and stability. *The Journal of Sex Research, 39*(3), 190–196. doi:10.1080/00224490209552141

Stepler, R. (2017a). Led by Baby Boomers, divorce rates climb for America's 50+ population. *Pew Research Center*. Retrieved from http://www.pewresearch.org/fact-tank/2017/03/09/led-by-baby-boomers-divorce-rates-climb-for-americas-50-population

Stepler, R. (2017b). *Number of U.S. adults cohabiting with a partner continues to rise, especially among those 50 and older.*Number of U.S. adults cohabiting with a partner continues to rise, especially among those 50 and older. Retrieved from http://www.pewresearch.org/fact-tank/2017/04/06/number-of-u-s-adults-cohabiting-with-a-partner-continues-to-rise-especially-among-those-50-and-older

Swami, V., & Tovee, M. J. (2006). The influence of body mass index on the physical attractiveness preferences of feminist and nonfeminist heterosexual women and lesbians. *Psychology of Women Quarterly, 30*(3), 252–257. doi:10.1111/j.1471-6402.2006.00293.x

U.S. Department of Labor, Bureau of Labor Statistics. (2013). Marriage and divorce rates among baby boomers vary by educational attainment. *The Economics Daily*. Retrieved from https://www.bls.gov/opub/ted/2013/ted_20131108.htm

Vandervoort, D. (2000). Social isolation and gender. *Current Psychology, 19*(3), 229–236. doi:10.1007/s12144-000-1017-5

Wanic, R., & Kulik, J. (2011). Toward an understanding of gender differences in the impact of marital conflict and health. *Sex Roles, 65*(5-6), 297–312. doi:10.1007/s11199-011-9968-6

Wikipedia. (2018, January 20). Lesbian bed death. Retrieved from https://en.wikipedia.org/wiki/Lesbian_bed_death

16

The Gendered Nature of Later Life Relationships

Edward H. Thompson, Jr. and Kate de Medeiros

INTRODUCTION

Distinguishing later life (customarily age 65–79) from late life (age 80+) is crucial when discussing the gendered nature of personal relationships and the probability of social isolation. First, the two life phases predictably differ in people's risk of isolation. Before late life, most people have networks of same age-group friends and chosen family members that are a source of enjoyment, socializing, and other high-quality interaction (Pinquart & Sörensen, 2000). Most aging men and women maintain their privacy, independence, and exchanges of support; they either continue working or develop post-employment lifestyles that involve emotionally rich activities and a strong sense of purpose (B. Cornwell, Laumann, & Schumm, 2008; National Council on Aging, 2015; Vespa, Lewis, & Kreider, 2013). By late life, however, fewer old men or women remain partnered and many also have begun to outlive friends and family. They are at greater risk of social and emotional isolation.

Second, most discussions of the gendered nature of relationships only call attention to the distinctive ways men's relational lives differ from women's. As often noted, in both later and late life, many more aging men in postmodern societies remain married until their death—less than one-eighth of old men age 65 and older in 2015 were widowers, which is one-third the proportion of widows (Mather, Jacobsen, & Pollard, 2015). Among men age 85 and over, around 50% still reported being married compared to only 16% of women in the same age group (Federal Interagency Forum on Aging-Related Statistics, 2016)). What old men's lesser chance of being widowed, or living alone and frail, can mean in relational terms is that they have a greater

235

chance of being cared for by their spouse when their health declines and lesser chance of institutionalization; women comprised around two-thirds of nursing home residents from 2011 to 2015 (Center for Medicare Medicaid Services [CMS], 2015) and women are America's primary family caregivers. The demographic realities of men's and women's life spans and the age differences between husbands and wives (i.e., men marrying younger women) clearly impact the nature of later- and late-life relationships.

What remains less clear is the variability among aging men's and among aging women's later-life relationships. A body of research is now examining how men's later-life masculinities and aging women's femininities reflect their embodied experiences (*cf.*, Hammond & Mattis, 2005; Thompson, 2018). The intersectionality of social positions notably structure people's relational lives. The plural nouns–men, women–brilliantly acknowledge the variation in people's social and cultural capital and how the gender practices fashioned within cultures, social classes, sexualities, religious faiths, age cohorts or generations, and ethnic ancestries affect later-life relationships.

Class, Ancestry, Generation, or Rural/Urban Residency

To better understand the gendered nature of later-life relationships, we must acknowledge the (dis)similarities among aging men, or among women. Consider three examples. First, for aging men in the United States who are of European or Asian ancestry, nearly three-quarters are living with their spouse; two-thirds of Hispanic (of any race) old men live with their spouse; and about half of old non-Hispanic Black men live within a couple relationship (Federal Interagency Forum on Aging-Related Statistics, 2016). Second, take the case of the later-life relationship options among White and African American men from the "Silent" generation, who were born prior to the Great Depression and as young adults lived through World War II and blatant racial segregation. Strongly connected to their employment discrimination, more of these aging African American men are less likely to have ever married than White or Mexican American men, and when they married they married later and are less likely to stay married (Dixon, 2009). They are, however, likely to have formed cohabitating or living apart together (LAT) relationships as an alternative to marrying, long before cohabitation or LAT relations became nationally normative (Teachman, Tedrow, & Crowder, 2000). We also note that for some African American men, military participation during World War II, the Korean conflict, and the Vietnam War led to opportunities within the armed services while civilian opportunities lagged.

For some, careers in service brought opportunities for family support that might not have been possible.

Third, although the cumulative toll is largest for those living in poverty, the cumulative disadvantage experienced by the never-married and divorced old African American men, whether currently cohabitating or LAT, is recorded in the men's narratives of suffering, greater reliance of fictive kin and extended family, likelihood of living alone, and risk of social isolation (Black, Groce, & Harmond, 2011; Chatters, Taylor, Lincoln, & Schroepher, 2002; Johnson, 1999).

What we want to underscore is how any demographic-based sketch can show the ways later life and later-life relationships are influenced by many social things. They are uniformly affected by the legacy of social inequalities. Life chances, opportunities (e.g., employment, education), and expectations (e.g., marriage, caregiving) among people of common ancestries differ by birth cohort. In 2018, a 65-year-old African American man born in the post–World War II Baby Boom generation would have had different opportunities for healthcare, education, and employment and expectations for his later-life relationships than an 80-year-old African American man born in 1938. These generational differences would also have differed by geographic location given the "Jim Crow" laws that supported racial segregation in the southern United States. Gendered later-life relationships are therefore not just the product of chronological age and gender, but rather the complex social contexts which shaped one's aging process.

The Case of Aging Women

Too often overlooked is how most old men, regardless of ancestry or class, benefit from institutionalized forms of patriarchal privilege (*cf.*, Pinquart & Sörensen, 2001) and how their identity as men is reinforced and maintained by marriage or partnership (Arber, Davidson, & Ginn, 2003). Take the case of how the social norms that men marry women younger than themselves and women typically provide familial care combine to mean that most old men do not go without care in later life. The heteronormative patriarch family system positions most men in later life to have unpaid, informal care more readily available than women, whether it is his daily meal preparation or help with personal care associated with functional decline such as bathing or dressing.

Aging women are more disadvantaged in terms of their later-life relationships, chiefly as a result of the gendered practices within their families, communities, and the paid workplace. Their disadvantage is experienced in terms of being cast as care providers, fewer and more restrictive opportunities for paid work at lower salaries than men, greater financial risk of living solo, and, as we address later, the risk of being neglected and victimized by members of their family. The good news is that women have gained much ground with regard to access to financial resources, making living alone in late life less of a financial burden (albeit still a burden for many) than in the past. In addition, in the last half century, the proportion of older women who are married (or partnered) longer has increased steadily and the proportion of widowed and women living alone has noticeably declined. These slow shifts are mostly due to men's rising life expectancy. Also, as a result of cultural shifts in people's beliefs and practices, the proportion of aging women who free themselves from their difficult marriage by divorce has markedly increased (Mather et al., 2015), and should these women choose to recouple, they may develop a more voluntary arrangement, such as deciding to cohabitate or creating an LAT relationship. E. Y. Cornwell and Waite (2009) find that aging women experience less social disconnectedness and perceived isolation than older men. Older women are also more likely to have relations not connected to or monopolized by their spouse or partner (B. Cornwell, 2011).

The not-good news is that a sizeable gender gap in aging men's and women's relationship status remains, and this legacy perpetuates personal challenges, especially among less-privileged women. We must recognize that in 2015, fewer than one-half of women age 65 and older were married or partnered compared with nearly three-quarters of aging men; and, more than one-quarter of women age 65 to 74 and almost half age 75+ lived alone (Mather et al., 2015). The disadvantages of aging women living solo have been prudently detailed by others—they typically have lower levels of income, are more likely to live in poverty, lack daily companionship, and lack another person to provide care if they are injured or become ill (*cf.*, Calasanti & Slevin, 2001).

In the remainder of the chapter, we delve into and address several aspects of the gendered nature of later-life relationships: the character and quality of social ties, intergenerational relations and caring for a partner in later life, and couple's sexual intimacy. We much more frequently discuss aging and old men's later-life relationships, which have been less often scrutinized.

Gendered Social Ties

Men and women develop and maintain different social relationships. Research has shown that social structural positions (such as indicated by gender) influence the form and content of relationships. For example, unlike what men report, women routinely indicate on measures assessing relational content doing more emotion work (Erickson, 2005; Kulik, 2002) and as a result more intimate social ties, such as having a confidante and socializing with friends (Umberson, Chen, House, Hopkins, & Slaten, 1996). Women also report more positive interactional exchanges with friends and adult children than men, and more negative exchanges with their partners than men (Stafford, McMunn, Zaninotto, & Nazroo, 2011).

Despite differences in the form and content of men's and women's later-life relationships, the research is somewhat equivocal when it comes to the affect of their relationships. Basically, research has not overturned Umberson et al.'s (1996, p. 885) much earlier analysis of a representative sample of older adults, where they concluded that "gender does not appear to make women more sensitive than men to their relationships." On average, aging men and women more similarly than differently feel the closeness and intimacies of long-term marriages, comparably experience identity affirmation within friendships, and similarly derive pleasure from their relations with adult children and grandchildren. This, of course, applies to married heteronormative couples and says little about others.

Men's and women's later-life relationships are predictably fewer in number, more personal, and less rooted in either instrumental or work-related interests than people maintained as younger adults. The reduction in network size as we age is, to a degree, due to lost relationships with siblings and close friends who move or are no longer alive. However, there is a predictable downsizing of social contacts that parallels the beginning of later life. Sociologically, aging men and women adjust their social capital, which becomes based on their smaller postemployment community of friends and family and fewer of the peripheral, instrumental relations they used to maintain. They let go of the outer circle of acquaintances and intensify their socializing with long-term friends, siblings, and chosen family members who provide companionship and enjoyment.

According to Carstensen's (1992, 2006) socioemotional selectivity theory, aging men and women appreciate that time eventually runs out, and as they age their motivational priorities shift toward affectively rich relations. Complementing their preference for rich interactions, the desire to affiliate with less familiar people decreases. The following case illustrates a man weighing the benefits of downsizing: a 67-year-old man talked about his later-life preferences for intimacies with friends, "I think we're a lot more inclined to go to a friend's house for dinner or have them over to our house for dinner rather than going out somewhere. Also . . . I value closer, less hectic encounters" (Wright, 2015, p. 71). Of course, expectations about "coupled" status and the tendency for couples to socially engage with other couples can mask the challenges that noncoupled people might face when socializing. Retirement communities can emphasize difference in "coupled" and noncoupled individuals whereby four-seated tables, especially when reservations are required, can lead single people to feel excluded.

Despite the many commonalities in later life in men's and women's social connections and more intimate, smaller networks, gender differences are more commonly imagined and suggested. Research examining the gendered nature of social ties in later life has relied heavily on a "sex difference perspective" and how it reinforces the common belief that men have some friendly relations, women have friends; or that women's social ties are interpersonal, face to face whereas men's are instrumentally side by side. For example, when she interpreted widowers' narratives about their social ties, van den Hoonaard (2009, 2010) surmised that most of the widowers "either would not or could not" involve themselves in relationships that build close friendships. To support her interpretation, she noted the widowers neither invited people to their home nor often reached out. Instead, they preferred to "bump into" acquaintances and neighbors in local coffee cafes or while shopping. While this observation may describe how men appear to socialize, it ignores the potential of a socially prescribed subtext that may govern what men perceive as appropriate avenues for socialization. In other words, performing masculine ideals of self-sufficiency may be what is observed rather than these men's actual preferences for social engagement.

The quest to identify gender differences may therefore heavily influence researchers' ability to accurately understand social phenomena (Epstein, 1998). van den Hoonaard's "would not or could not" interpretation seems to support the fiction that women connect whereas men participate. What the "would not or could not" interpretation misses is how aging men adapt to being unpartnered more slowly (Stroebe, Stroebe, & Schut, 2001). Riggs (1997) heard from the widowers she interviewed that over time the men not only maintained some friendships but also instigated new ones. Their success in sustaining emotionally rich friendships, replacing lost friends, and making new friends was more common than not. Similarly, when Balaswamy, Richardson, and Price (2004) compared widowers in earlier and later phases of being widowed (before and after 500 days), they found that, with time, widowers reintegrate socially. The researchers argued that other researchers finding widowers' lesser social engagement may be a function of cross-sectional research designs that underrepresent men later in the bereavement process, where the men are more ready to socialize.

When old men's narratives are no longer filtered by a lens comparing his practices vis-à-vis hers, the decisions of men to scale back on friends and friendly relations in later life could be their purposeful decision to redesign their network to fit their postemployment lifestyles (Blieszner & Roberto, 2004, 2012; Carstensen, 2006). For example, often the widowers van den Hoonaard (2010) interviewed made clear that their wives had been their intermediaries with family and friend relations. Take the case of "Keith" who found widowerhood freeing: "It's a lonely life at times, but I'm enjoying my independence, too. You know, I can come and go as I please" (van den Hoonaard, 2009, p. 745). Some widowers in the same study also conveyed their recognition that their prior social world had revolved around couples and a shared friendship network. Being single again permitted a slow evaporation of some friendly relations, especially if they felt being a "third wheel" or "fifth wheel" was uncomfortable for them and/or their former couple friends.

Samuel, a divorced 69-year-old African American who lived in a military retirement community, found that being around others (predominantly men) who shared a common experience of military service helped with social interactions. He mentioned, "You meet a lot of nice people around here and you meet a lot of down people and you meet a lot of sour people. But you take the good with bad and live with it." While he did not describe the other men he socialized with as "friends," he did speak about how much he enjoyed being able to play cards with others. He added, however, that being away from his grandchildren led him to seek treatment for depression due to loneliness. He also acknowledged that he accepted being older and wanted his children to get on with their own lives rather than worry about him. He said,

> I told him [his son], I don't want to see you down here every weekend. Don't come down here bothering me. [laughs] But he still comes, you know. He always calls me—and says, 'Dad, I'm coming down today.' And I say, 'Yeah, O.K'. I just miss the grandchildren mostly. I don't see them as much anymore unless I go up there. But you get used to it.

In contrast to older men's later-life relationships, women's caregiving expectations may lead to a similar (albeit for different reasons) misunderstanding of their later-life relationships. Most aging women encounter feelings of social isolation whenever their husbands' needs require significant care work. For example, "Carol," a widow in her early 80s who now lives alone, explained the challenges of having been a caregiver for her husband who had Alzheimer's disease. She said,

> . . . Now, my husband and I used to go there [a local restaurant] for lunch a lot when he retired to disability. And I knew all those people, I

just didn't want to see anyone. I didn't want anybody asking me, "how is [Bob]?" They never say "how are you?", you know, and you're the one that's hurting.... Everywhere you go, "how's Bob?", "how's Bob?". When somebody dies, you know, you get all your friends and everyone sympathizes with you and they bring food and flowers, but when something like that [Alzheimer's disease] happens, and it's worse than death.

Carol eventually found it necessary to place her husband in a care facility, a decision she felt very guilty about since it ran counter to her deeply embedded value that caregiving was her responsibility. Many other women we spoke to in various research settings had similar views although they recognized that it was often not possible to express these views to others since they felt it was culturally frowned upon for them to question or complain about being a care provider. There is, of course, a rich literature on the challenges of providing care to include depression and feelings of isolation (Neri et al., 2012).

In sum, relationships in later life are gendered in terms of their form and content. There is also a gendered pace in reorganizing the configuration of social networks, especially for men who remain employed and/or experience the ending of their marriage, whether by a wife's death or by divorce. We presented more examples of aging men's and women's social ties and experiences in hopes of drawing greater attention to the gendered nature of their relationships.

Intergenerational Relations

Later-life relationships routinely include adult (step)children and (step) grandchildren, and, in the absence of children, nieces, nephews, or other family. It is also important to note that increasing percentages of men and women do not have children (biological or through other ties) and we caution against pronatalist assumptions about later life. However, for the sake of this chapter, we do emphasize that intergenerational relations—whatever those may encompass—are most certainly gendered; the grandparent–grandchild relationship is the most common intergenerational relationship. Intergenerational ties are stronger along matrilineal lines, and these relationships are also more often voluntary, close, and gratifying than needed and empty or abusive, but this range exists. For the majority of men, their social world slowly becomes more family centric in later life—concentrated on their couple relationship, if they have one, and extending out to selected family connections, especially in terms of grandfathering. For the majority of women born prior to the Baby Boomer generation, their social world was structured to be more family centric than employment centric, and as much as context allows they are the more active grandparent. Baby Boomers have transformed every life stage they have faced (Hanks, 2001), and Boomer grandmothers have Facebook accounts that integrate their workplace friends alongside grandchildren.

Until recently, the *average* age a woman became a grandmother in the United States was in her early 50s, and men become grandfathers when a couple of years older. However, grandparenthood depends on adult children beginning their families, and demographic profiles show, on average, women are now having their first child later in their lives than prior generations. The age of becoming a grandfather has risen to men's early 60s. Still, given the longer lives and better health of men and women now than in previous generations, the odds are some men and women will become a great-grandparent (*cf.*, Rosenbloom, 2006). And, some of these relationships will transition from intergenerational ties into personally and existentially meaningful intergenerational friends (Kemp, 2005).

Grandchildren are the most familiar young people in aging adults' lives. Yet face-to-face interaction with the grandchild seen most often, even by maternal grandmothers, is, on average, about once a month (Dunifon & Bajracharya, 2012; Reitzes & Mutran, 2004), although Skype conversations can now provide added contact. The frequency of contact is governed by the relational bridge—that is, the quality of relations between the grandparent(s) and the parent(s) of the grandchildren (Barnett, Scaramella, Neppl, Ontai, & Conger, 2010; Mueller & Elder, 2003). Historically, with men doing lesser emotion work in building and maintaining grandparental relations, their own relations are often more contributory, activity based, and "stiffer."

Aging also challenges relational quality. By the time grandchildren enter adolescence, they become deeply invested in peer relations, and commonalities of interests are challenged (Silverstein & Marenco, 2001). This is especially so for many grandfathers who embodied traditional masculinities and femininities. These grandfathers' lives may remain employment centric for years, because there were cultural norms defining grandmothers as the prime kin keepers. Research shows grandmothers are in fact more "present" in grandchildren's lives. Grandfathers are normally received as the "accompanying" grandparent (Leeson, 2016), and they remain more peripheral (*cf.*, Buchanan & Rotkirch, 2016; Bullock, 2005). The evidence is that aging men and women do not equally participate in grandparent–grandchild relationships. One man, Ken, in Roberto, Allen, and Blieszner's (2001) study sums this situation well:

My relationship with the grandchildren gradually took up less and less of my time even though I was retired by then. [Soon, they] began having their own friends and doing their own thing.... We spent more time with them, going places together and that sort of thing. But as they got older, particularly since [wife] died, for some reason, maybe because I am going with somebody.... (p. 417)

Ken's diminishing experiences with being a grandfather is more typical than not, particularly if he had been divorced or widowed and even more so had he repartnered.

There are exceptions: Roberto et al. (2001, p. 419) report how Quent, a long-haul truck driver, spent little time with his family and ended up divorced and marginalized from his children; however, when he gave up the trucker lifestyle and remarried, he had an opportunity to become a step-grandfather and took pride in being called "Grandpa."

Perhaps because of their lengthened life span and earlier retirement, recent studies suggest grandfathers are "coming out of the shadows," defining and developing relationships with their grandchildren independently of grandmothers (Mann, 2007; Mann & Leeson 2010). Based on a study of grandfathers in the Netherlands, Leeson (2016) summarizes, "the large majority of the interviewed grandfathers—where conditions allow it—have an independent relationship with their grandchildren, [as well as] a relationship together with the grandmothers" (p. 76). Grandfathers often initially underestimated how attached they would be to their grandchildren. Many of the grandfathers' narratives have backward-looking musing where they had not spent enough quality time with their own children because of their work/career commitments, and now as older men they aim to make up for this with (step)grandchildren (Leeson, 2016, p. 74). Grandfathering can be a humbling awakening to old and new masculinities, as Alex notes:

I was brought up in the years, like a lot of older men, where you didn't show affection, you didn't show hurt, you didn't show pain, you didn't show anything: you were the stalwart of the family and such. And I think the grandchildren seem to undermine all that and bring you down to your knees, and then realize that you're just a human person after all, and you're no different to the next bloke, and all the things you were shown were necessarily that time in my . . . upbringing, was wrong. (Stgeorge & Fletcher, 2014, p. 366)

The wide diversity in types of grandfathering relations across individuals, communities, and historical time are structured by the men's ethnic ancestry, class, embodied masculinities, marital histories, and likelihood of coresidence. Take the example of long-term married African American men compared to old African American men who divorced, often early within their marriages. Most continuously married grandfathers have positive histories with their adult children and likely encounter fewer gatekeeping barriers to being involved with their grandchildren. The divorced men, whether repartnered or not, commonly have reserved, if not strained, or no relations at all with their adult children (*cf.*, Davidson, Daly, & Arber, 2003). Inside "blended" families, divorced and repartnered old men and women have to continuously renegotiate family boundaries. It is their adult (step)children and the (step)grandchildren who control this renegotiation. In these "blended" families, the men may be welcomed replacement grandfathers for some (step)grandchildren and marginalized by some (step)grandchildren. Grandmothers have stronger ties and are less likely to be pushed away.

When intergenerational relations shift from voluntary to necessary, and old men and women become dependent on their adult children and grandchildren for care and daily survival, an unwelcomed window may open for the abuse of a parent or grandparent. Psychological and verbal abuse are more prevalent than physical. According to Roberto (2016), nearly one in ten older adults in the United States experiences abuse, exploitation, or neglect annually by family members, and the prevalence may be as great as one in seven. Kosberg (2014) points out that nongendered explanations for older adults' neglect and abuse still prevail. However, the evidence shows neglect, exploitation, and abuse are not ungendered. The incidence is reported to differentially occur for old men and women, and occur for different reasons. She is frail and vulnerable and at times perceived as draining as a result of her care needs; he is now weak and more likely repaid for his domineering or has his money stolen. Neglect and abuse are more prevalent when the grandparent lives with her or his adult children and grandchildren, especially when the older person is the custodial parent (Kosberg & MacNeil, 2003). Since it is grandmothers who are more often living with the custodial parent, it is old women's intergenerational relationships that increase their risk and warrant greater scrutiny. A cultural lens also reveals that ethnic ancestry affects old men's and women's perception of abuse. For example, face-to-face interviews with African Americans, Korean American immigrants, and White old adults revealed that the White elders had significantly higher tolerance for verbal abuse than either African American or Korean American elders (Lee, Lee, & Eaton, 2012). Even though the abusive aspect of intergeneration relations is far less common than warm, positive relations, the dark side has been too disregarded. While we are not suggesting that abuse is a normative experience, we are suggesting that it is a topic that has gained little attention, especially in the literature on grandparenting.

Sexual Intimacy

The gender nature of sexuality in later-life relationships hinges more on the masculinities that aging men practice. Old couple's sexual practices are gendered less by the hegemonic model of penetrative sex and more by closeness and intimacy. In fact, there may well be a greater range of sexual practices among old couples than younger age cohorts. The latter are actively involved in work and family matters and may have less recreational time for extended foreplay, cuddling, and other noncoital sex, or the lived experience of needing to renegotiate satisfying sexual practices with their partner following the slow onset of erectile difficulty. Most aging couples remain sexually active partly because sexual desire continues throughout their later years, whether gay or heterosexual (Kontula & Haavio-Mannila, 2009; Wierzalis, Barret, Pope, & Rankins, 2006), and partly because old men embody mature masculinities (Wentzell, 2013) or aging masculinities (Jackson, 2016; Thompson, 2018) that prioritize "we" over "me" intimacy over coital sex.

National survey-based studies of later-life sexuality have identified a variety of background social forces that shape aging individuals' sexual expression such as religion, generation, and marital status. In every study, being coupled (whether through marriage, cohabitation, or LAT) is the critical determinant of engaging in nonsolo sexual activity. As self-evident as it may seem, those aging adults without a later-life relationship lack opportunity for anything other than solo sex (i.e., masturbation) and are also twice as likely to lack interest in sex (Lindau et al., 2007: Table 4).

The most influential predictor of sexual activity among couples seems to be his physical health, followed by the quality of their relationship. In spite of bothersome health problems, couples' sexual activity does not decrease substantially with increasing age (*cf.*, Lindau et al., 2007). Sexual practices can be maintained until very late in life. In a qualitative study of 17 midlife and later-life U.S. couples in long-term marriages, where the spouses were interviewed separately, sex meant vaginal intercourse (Lodge & Umberson, 2012) and 13 of the 17 couples were sexually active. Narrating past lives, participants reported a decline in the frequency of sex, and most attributed the decline to his bodily aging and health complications, not hers. At the same time, the researchers note men's (and women's) narratives "belied the assumption that a decline in frequency . . . necessitates as decline in quality" (Lodge & Umberson, 2012, p. 434). As one man, "Matthew (age 69) said, '[Sex] has gotten better and less frequent.' His wife, Pat (age 68), agreed" (Lodge & Umberson, 2012, p. 434).

Sarah Murray and her research team's (2017) exploratory study examined what elicited or inhibited sexual desire among middle-aged men (average age 43 years old) in relationships (average duration 13 years). Murray and her colleagues note that although men "did not explicitly use the term *relational* or *intimacy*, the way they talked about their experiences implied that what was desired (or missing) was the perception that sexual encounters were mutual and cocreated" (Murray, Milhausen, Graham, & Kuczynski, 2017, p. 326, italics original). Intimate communication was reported by the majority of the men as important to sexual desire and intimacy. Cody, age 65, commented:

> So for me sex is communication. It's not just physical intercourse. It's communicating while you're having the intercourse, and fun, and talking about 'What can I do?' And I think once you start asking the other partner what they want, it embellishes the relationship. And it gives the partner the feeling of acceptance and love and belonging. . . , (Murray et al., 2017, p. 325)

Also noted was the way men deviated from their past and from masculinity scripts about initiating sex; whenever their female partner initiated sexual activity, for some men it was the ultimate expression, or reassurance of a "we" feeling.

Ménard et al. (2015) examined aging men's and women's "very pleasant and welcome surprise" that their sexual experiences had steadily improved in quality over their lifetimes. The participants (age 60–82) had been in a relationship at least 25 years and credited their sexual experiences as something that they worked at. What "working at" involved was letting go of the negative beliefs about aging and sexuality they acquired much earlier in their lives; continuously cultivating new practices by being sensitive, attentive, and responsive to their partner; and resisting the easy route of settling into a personal comfort zone. As one man described his experiences with his wife, "A life of sexual exploration and adventure and excitement" (Ménard et al., 2015, p. 84). It was through narratives of intimacy that men expressed their continued interest in sexuality.

"Hold me" and the tenderness of touching sex are among the types of intimate sexuality that Linn Sandberg (2013) calls reciprocal "less selfish sex." Hinchliff and Gott (2004, p. 604) similarly characterize later-life couples' sexuality as more unselfish, particularly as they navigated health-related barriers to sexual activity. The argument we find easy to make is that for old men and women sexuality is about pleasurable sex, intimacy, and affirming feelings of connectedness.

SUMMARY

The intention of this chapter is to highlight key constructs and insights into gendered relationships in later life within the larger context of changing demographics and social expectations. While each topic introduced could well be a chapter in itself, we have attempted to provide an overview of some important areas of consideration to include gendered assumptions about men's and women's social relationships and opportunities, grandparenting as a unique site of socialization, and sexual intimacy and connectedness. If there is a general theme throughout the chapter, it is that the wide-scope lenses through which older age has traditionally been viewed has lacked the finer perspectives that are important when considering intersections of race, gender, age, class, and a variety of other layers. In addition, assumptions and perspectives drawing from and relying on such large lens approaches run the serious risk of stereotyping older persons.

REFERENCES

Arber, S., Davidson, K., & Ginn, J. (2003). Changing approaches to gender and later life. In S. Arber, K. Davidson, & J. Ginn (Eds.), *Gender and ageing: Changing roles and relationships* (pp. 1–14). Maidenhead, England: Open University Press.

Balaswamy, S., Richardson, V., & Price, C. A. (2004). Investigating patterns of social support use by widowers during bereavement. *Journal of Men's Studies, 13*, 67–84.

Barnett, M. A., Scaramella, L. V., Neppl, T. K., Ontai, L. L., & Conger, R. D. (2010). Intergenerational relationship quality, gender and grandparent involvement. *Family Relations, 59*, 28–44. doi:10.1111/j.1741-3729.2009.00584.x

Black, H. K., Groce, J. T., & Harmond, C. E. (2011). *From zero to eighty: Two African American men's narrative of racism, suffering, survival, and transformation.* Bloomington, IN: iUniverse.

Blieszner, R., & Roberto, K. A. (2004). Friendship across the life span: Reciprocity in individual and relationship development. In F. R. Lang & K. L. Fingerman (Eds.), *Growing together: Personal relationships across the lifespan* (pp. 159–182). New York, NY: Cambridge University Press.

Blieszner, R., & Roberto, K. A. (2012). Partners and friends in adulthood. In S. K. Whitbourne & M. J. Sliwinski (Eds.), *The Wiley-Blackwell handbook of adulthood and aging* (pp. 381–398). Malden, MA: Wiley-Blackwell.

Buchanan, A., & Rotkirch, A. (2016). *Grandfathers: Global perspectives.* New York, NY: Palgrave Macmillan.

Bullock, K. (2005). Grandfathers and the impact of raising grandchildren. *Journal of Sociology & Social Welfare, 32*, 43–59.

Calasanti, T. M., & Slevin, K. F. (2001). *Gender, social inequalities, and aging*. Walnut Creek, CA: AltaMira Press.
Carstensen, L. L. (1992). Social and emotional patterns in adulthood: Support for socioemotional selectivity theory. *Psychology and Aging*, 7, 331–338. doi:10.1037/0882-7974.7.3.331
Carstensen, L. L. (2006). The influence of a sense of time on human development. *Science*, 312, 1913–1915. doi:10.1126/science.1127488
Center for Medicare Medicaid Services. (2015). Nursing home data compendium 2015 edition. Retrieved from https://www.cms.gov/Medicare/Provider-Enrollment-and-Certification/CertificationandComplianc/Downloads/nursinghomedatacompendium_508-2015.pdf
Chatters, L. M., Taylor, R. J., Lincoln, K. D., & Schroepher, T. (2002). Patterns of informal support from family and church members among African Americans. *Journal of Black Studies*, 33, 66–85. doi:10.1177/002193470203300104
Cornwell, B. (2011). Independence through social networks: Bridging potential among older women and men. *Journals of Gerontology Series B: Psychological Sciences and Social Sciences*, 66, 782–794. doi:10.1093/geronb/gbr111
Cornwell, B., Laumann, E. O., & Schumm, L. P. (2008). The social connectedness of older adults: A national profile. *American Sociological Review*, 73, 185–203. doi:10.1177/000312240807300201
Cornwell, E. Y., & Waite, L. J. (2009). Measuring social isolation among older adults using multiple indicators from the NSHAP study. *Journals of Gerontology Series B: Psychological Sciences and Social Sciences*, 64 (Suppl. 1), i38–i46. doi:10.1093/geronb/gbp037
Davidson, K., Daly, T., & Arber, S. (2003). Exploring the social worlds of older men. In S. Arber, K. Davidson, & J. Ginn (Eds.), *Gender and ageing: Changing roles and relationships* (pp. 168–185). Buckingham, UK: Open University Press.
Dixon, P. (2009). Marriage among African Americans: What does the research reveal? *Journal of African American Studies*, 13(1), 29–46. doi:10.1007/s12111-008-9062-5
Dunifon, R., & Bajracharya, A. (2012). The role of grandparents in the lives of youth. *Journal of Family Issues*, 33, 1168–1194. doi:10.1177/0192513X12444271
Epstein, C. (1988). *Deceptive distinctions: Sex, gender, and the social order*. New Haven, CT: Yale University Press.
Erickson, R. J. (2005). Why emotion work matters: Sex, gender, and the division of household labor. *Journal of Marriage and Family*, 67, 337–351. doi:10.1111/j.0022-2445.2005.00120.x
Federal Interagency Forum on Aging-Related Statistics. (2016, August). *Older Americans 2016: Key Indicators of Well-Being*. Washington, DC: U.S. Government Printing Office.
Hammond, W. P., & Mattis, J. S. (2005). Being a man about it: Manhood meaning among African American men. *Psychology of Men & Masculinity*, 6, 114–126. doi:10.1037/1524-9220.6.2.114
Hanks, R. S. (2001). "Grandma, what big teeth you have!" The social construction of grandparenting in American business and academe. *Journal of Family Issues*, 22, 652–676. doi:10.1177/019251301022005007
Hinchliff, S., & Gott, M. (2004). Intimacy, commitment, and adaptation: Sexual relationships within long-term marriages. *Journal of Social and Personal Relationships*, 21, 595–609. doi:10.1177/0265407504045889
Jackson, D. (2016). *Exploring aging masculinities: The body, sexuality, and social lives*. London, UK: Palgrave Macmillan.
Johnson, C. L. (1999). Fictive kin among oldest old African Americans in the San Francisco Bay area. *The Journals of Gerontology Series B: Psychological Sciences and Social Sciences*, 54, S368–S375. doi:10.1093/geronb/54B.6.S368

Kemp, C. L. (2005). Dimensions of grandparent-adult grandchild relationships: From family ties to intergenerational friendships. *Canadian Journal on Aging, 24,* 161–177. doi:10.1353/cja.2005.0066

Kontula, O., &, Haavio-Mannila, E. (2009). The impact of aging on human sexual activity and sexual desire. *Journal of Sex Research, 46,* 46–56. doi:10.1080/00224490802624414

Kosberg, J. I. (2014). Rosalie Wolf Memorial Lecture: Reconsidering assumptions regarding men as elder abuse perpetrators and as elder abuse victims. *Journal of Elder Abuse & Neglect, 26*(3), 207–222. doi:10.1080/08946566.2014.898442

Kosberg, J. I., & MacNeil, G. (2003). The elder abuse of custodial grandparents: A hidden phenomenon. *Journal of Elder Abuse & Neglect, 15*(3–4), 33–53. doi:10.1300/J084v15n03_03

Kulik, L. (2002). Marital equality and the quality of long-term marriage in later life. *Ageing and Society, 22,* 459–481. doi:10.1017/S0144686X02008772

Lee, H. Y., Lee, S. E., & Eaton, C. K. (2012). Exploring definitions of financial abuse in elderly Korean immigrants: The contribution of traditional cultural values. *Journal of Elder Abuse & Neglect, 24,* 293–311. doi:10.1080/08946566.2012.661672

Leeson, G. W. (2016). Out of the shadows: Are grandfathers defining their own roles in the modern family in Denmark? In A. Buchanan & A. Rotkirch (Eds.), *Grandfathers: Global perspectives* (pp. 69–88). London, UK: Palgrave Macmillam.

Lindau, S. T., Schumm, L. P., Laumann, E. O., Levinson, W., O'muircheartaigh, C. A., & Waite, L. J. (2007). A study of sexuality and health among older adults in the United States. *New England Journal of Medicine, 357,* 762–774. doi:10.1056/NEJMoa067423

Lodge, A. C., & Umberson, D. (2012). All shook up: Sexuality of mid- to later life married couples. *Journal of Marriage and Family, 74,* 428–443. doi:10.1111/j.1741-3737.2012.00969.x

Mann, R. (2007). Out of the shadows?: Grandfatherhood, age and masculinities. *Journal of Aging Studies, 21,* 281–291. doi:10.1016/j.jaging.2007.05.008

Mann, R., &, Leeson, G. (2010). Grandfathers in contemporary families in Britain: Evidence from qualitative research. *Journal of Intergenerational Relationships, 8,* 234–248. doi:10.1080/15350770.2010.498774

Mather, M., Jacobsen, L. A., & Pollard, K. M. (2015). *Aging in the United States* (Population Bulletin, 70[2]). Washington, DC: Population Reference Bureau.

Ménard, A. D., Kleinplatz, P. J., Rosen, L., Lawless, S., Paradis, N., Campbell, M., &. Huber, J. D. (2015). Individual and relational contributors to optimal sexual experiences in older men and women. *Sexual and Relationship Therapy, 30,* 78–93. doi:10.1080/14681994.2014.931689

Mueller, M. M., & Elder, G. H., Jr. (2003). Family contingencies across the generations: Grandparent-grandchildren relationships in holistic perspective. *Journal of Marriage and Family, 65,* 404–417. doi:10.1111/j.1741-3737.2003.00404.x

Murray, S. H., Milhausen, R. R., Graham, C. A., & Kuczynski, L. (2017). A qualitative exploration of factors that affect sexual desire among men aged 30 to 65 in long-term relationships. *The Journal of Sex Research, 54,* 319–330. doi:10.1080/00224499.2016.1168352

National Council on Aging. (2015). The United States of Aging Survey: 2015 results. Retrieved from https://www.ncoa.org/news/resources-for-reporters/usoa-survey/2015-results

Neri, A. L., Yassuda, M. S., Fortes-Burgos, A. C. G., Mantovani, E. P., Arbex, F. S., de Souza Torres, S. V., . . . & Guariento, M. E. (2012). Relationships between gender, age, family conditions, physical and mental health, and social isolation of elderly caregivers. *International Psychogeriatrics, 24,* 472–483. doi:10.1017/S1041610211001700

Pinquart, M., & Sörensen, S. (2000). Influences of socioeconomic status, social network, and competence on subjective well-being in later life: A meta-analysis. *Psychology and Aging, 15*, 187–224. doi:10.1037/0882-7974.15.2.187

Pinquart, M., & Sörensen, S. (2001). Gender differences in self-concept and psychological well-being in old age: A meta-analysis. *The Journals of Gerontology Series B: Psychological Sciences and Social Sciences, 56*, P195–P213. doi:10.1093/geronb/56.4.P195

Reitzes, D. C., & Mutran, E. J. (2004). Grandparenthood: Factors influencing frequency of grandparent-grandchildren contact and grandparent role satisfaction. *The Journals of Gerontology: Psychological Sciences and Social Sciences, 59B*, S9–S16. doi:10.1093/geronb/59.1.S9

Riggs, A. (1997). Men, friends and widowhood: Toward successful ageing. *Australasian Journal on Ageing, 16*, 182–185. doi:10.1111/j.1741-6612.1997.tb01047.x

Roberto, K. A. (2016). Abusive relationships in late life. In L. George & K. Ferraro (Eds.), *Handbook of aging and the social sciences* (18th ed., pp. 337–355). New York, NY: Academic Press.

Roberto, K. A., Allen, K. R., & Blieszner, R. (2001). Grandfathers' perceptions and expectations of relationships with their adult grandchildren. *Journal of Family Issues, 22*, 407–426. doi:10.1177/019251301022004002

Rosenbloom, S. (2006, November 2). Here come the great-grandparents. *New York Times*, p. G1. Online version,. Retrieved from https://www.nytimes.com/2006/11/02/fashion/02parents.html

Sandberg, L. (2013). Just feeling a naked body close to you: Men, sexuality and intimacy in later life. *Sexualities, 16*, 261–282. doi:10.1177/1363460713481726

Silverstein, M., & Marenco, A. (2001). How Americans enact the grandparent role across the family life course. *Journal of Family Issues, 22*, 493–522. doi:10.1177/019251301022004006

Stafford, M., McMunn, A., Zaninotto, P., & Nazroo, J. (2011). Positive and negative exchanges in social relationships as predictors of depression: Evidence from the English Longitudinal Study of Aging. *Journal of Aging and Health, 23*, 607–628. doi:10.1177/0898264310392992

Stgeorge, J. M., & Fletcher, R. J. (2014). Men's experiences of grandfatherhood: A welcome surprise. *The International Journal of Aging and Human Development, 78*, 351–378. doi:10.2190/AG.78.4.c

Stroebe, M., Stroebe, W., & Schut, H. (2001). Gender differences in adjustment to bereavement: An empirical and theoretical review. *Review of General Psychology, 5*, 62–83. doi:10.1037/1089-2680.5.1.62

Teachman, J. D., Tedrow, L. M., & Crowder, K. D. (2000). The changing demography of America's families. *Journal of Marriage and Family, 62*, 1234–1246. doi:10.1111/j.1741-3737.2000.01234.x

Thompson, E. H. (2018). *Men, masculinities, and aging*. Baltimore, MD: Roman & Littlefield.

Umberson, D., Chen, M. D., House, J. S., Hopkins, K., & Slaten, E. (1996). The effect of social relationships on psychological well-being: Are men and women really so different? *American Sociological Review, 61*, 837–857. doi:10.2307/2096456

van den Hoonaard, D. K. (2009). Experiences of living alone: Widows' and widowers' perspectives. *Housing Studies, 24*, 737–753. doi:10.1080/02673030903203015

van den Hoonaard, D. K. (2010). *By himself: The older man's experience of widowhood*. Toronto, ON, Canada: University of Toronto Press.

Vespa, J., Lewis, J. M., & Kreider, R. M. (2013) America's families and living arrangements: 2012. *Current Population Reports*, P20-570. Washington, DC: U.S. Census Bureau.

Wentzell, E. A. (2013). *Maturing masculinities: Aging, chronic illness, and viagra in Mexico.* Durham, NC: Duke University Press.

Wierzalis, E. A., Barret, B., Pope, M., & Rankins, M. (2006). Gay men and aging: Sex and intimacy. In D. Kimmel, T. Rose, & S. David (Eds.), *Lesbian, gay, bisexual, and transgender aging: Research and clinical perspectives* (pp. 91–109). New York, NY: Columbia University Press.

Wright, R. (2015) *What a drag it is getting old: Awareness and appraisal of age related change in White men born between 1946 and 1955.* Unpublished PhD dissertation, Wichita State University. Retrieved from http://soar.wichita.edu/bitstream/handle/10057/11613/d15027_Wright.pdf?sequence=1

17

The Social Implications of Growing Old in Small Towns and Rural Communities

Kristina M. Hash, Deana F. Morrow, and Mandana R. Weirich

THE CASE OF MRS. ROGERS

Mrs. Florence Rogers is an 86-year-old African American woman who has resided in her small town for the past 70 years. She became widowed after providing care for her husband for almost 10 years. She considers herself to be healthy, despite her diabetes, rheumatoid arthritis, and macular degeneration that prevent her from being as active as she had once been. Mrs. Rogers moved into a senior housing unit after her husband passed away. Her only daughter moved out of state years ago for work and many in her family are already deceased or have their own health issues. Ms. Rogers' arthritis makes it very difficult to clean and take care of herself; she is on the waiting list to get in-home care. She hopes by next year she can receive services so that she doesn't have to go to the nursing home. Because she no longer drives, she relies on the van from the senior housing site to take her to the store. Many of the women in the building are widows and Mrs. Rogers has formed a few friendships with her neighbors; they get together every week to share dinner together to ease the loneliness.

INTRODUCTION

The rural community conjures up images of scenic landscapes, quiet living, and tight-knit relationships and people who take care of their own. It

---

The authors would like to acknowledge the lifelong work on rurality and rural social work of Dr. Barry Locke, Emeritus Associate Professor, West Virginia University, and one of the founding fathers of the Rural Social Work Caucus.

is sometimes assumed in these areas that people age with an abundance of family and other informal support persons on hand to provide assistance when needed. And given these connections, persons who age in rural areas are assumed to have rich and long-lasting relationships and social opportunities. Although social connections may be an advantage for some rural elders, many who age in rural communities may be at risk for loneliness and isolation (American Association of Retired Persons [AARP], 2014; Levasseur et al., 2015). This chapter offers insight into the context of growing older in small towns and rural areas, including the unique challenges faced by rural elders and the special strengths that they possess. Attention is given to the nature of social relationships, the roles of health and human services professionals, and effective interventions and programs in the rural context.

RURAL ELDERS

Before examining the characteristics and social networks and needs of rural elders, the term *rural* should be clarified. This is no easy task, as there are approximately 11 different ways in which an area might be designated as rural. This includes definitions originating from the U.S. Census Bureau, the U.S. Department of Agriculture, and the U.S. Office of Budget and Management, among others (Krout & Hash, 2015). For the purposes of this chapter, an ecological definition of rural is used, focusing on an area's size, population, and location in relation to other communities (particularly, urban areas). It is important to keep in mind, however, that rural and urban can also exist on a continuum from completely rural to completely urban and everything in between (Krout & Hash, 2015). It is also crucial to understand, as Chuck Fluharty from the Rural Policy Institute noted, "If you've seen one rural community, you've seen . . . one rural community" as these areas and their residents are very diverse (Lohmann & Lohmann, 2005, p. xxii).

A few statistics are helpful in understanding living and aging in the rural context. To begin, the rural population is shrinking in comparison to more urban areas (U.S. Department of Agriculture [USDA], 2017). The population is also older in rural areas. The average age is higher in rural areas as compared with urban communities and the United States as a whole—43.4 years in rural areas as compared with 36.4 in urban areas and 37.7 years for the entire United States (U.S. Census Bureau, 2012-2016a). Further, those age 65 and older account for a much larger percentage of the population in rural areas (17.5% compared with 13.8% in urban areas, and 14.5% in the United States as a whole) (U.S. Census Bureau, 2012-2016b). The older rural population is the result of a greater out-migration of young adults to larger communities, the decline of rural birth rates, and in-migration of older adults to rural areas with desired recreation and other amenities (Kirschner, Beery, & Glasgow, 2009). Just as we saw with Mrs. Rogers, these trends have created an "aging in place" concept of rural older populations (Colello, 2007).

In terms of ethnicity, rural areas tend to have fewer ethnic minorities as compared with urban areas as 89% of rural residents identify as White only. In comparison, 70% of urban residents and 73% of total U.S. residents are White (U.S. Census Bureau, 2012-2016c). These statistics on ethnic diversity, however, may not reveal the entire picture as ethnic minorities are not evenly distributed throughout rural America, and large groups of minorities are often clustered in specific rural regions (Hash, Wells, & Spencer, 2015).

Rural residents[1] over age 65 are more likely to be married (53.2%) than those in urban areas (40.3%), or in the United States as a whole (43%) (U.S. Census Bureau, 2012-2016g). In terms of family composition, a large percentage (47%) of grandparents living in rural areas are responsible for taking care of grandchildren under the age of 18 compared with 37% of the United States as a whole (U.S. Census Bureau, 2012-2016d). In terms of education, rural residents age 65 and older are less likely to have completed a bachelor's degree (19.2%) compared with their urban counterparts (26.8%) and the nation as a whole (25%) (U.S. Census Bureau, 2012-2016h). Rural areas also have slightly more veterans of all ages (10%) compared with urban areas (7.5%) and the United States (8%) (U.S. Census Bureau, 2012-2016f). Rural communities have a similar percentage of persons over age 65 who live in poverty (8.4%) as compared with urban areas (9.6%) and the United States (9.3%) (U.S. Census Bureau, 2012-2016e). Community-level poverty has been a decades-long issue in rural areas, as poverty levels are higher and employment rates lower than in metropolitan communities. In fact, rural median income has trailed that of urban median income by 25% since 2007 (USDA, 2017).

THE CASE OF RICHARD AND JERRY

Richard (68 years old) is very familiar with life in rural communities. He has recently returned to the small town that he grew up in after living in a nearby city for almost 20 years. He retired from public school teaching and has relocated back to his childhood home with his partner of 15 years and husband of 4 years, Jerry (74 years old). Following the death of Richard's mother, whom he had commuted to care for over the past several years, he and Jerry moved into her home. The couple decided to relocate to reduce

---

[1]Data used from the U.S. Census Bureau's 2012-2016 American Community Survey is based on the definition of rural as an area that is not considered urban (neither an urbanized area or cluster).

living expenses, have a more laidback lifestyle, have greater access to outdoor recreation, and to be closer to Richard's children and grandchildren who live in a nearby town. Since moving back, Richard has reconnected with some of his old friends and initially introduced Jerry to many of them as his "roommate." The couple is "out" to their family and they enjoy helping with five grandchildren who range in age from 2 to 15, including transporting the grandchildren to sports practices and hosting sleepovers at the couple's new home. They often spend time in the city they relocated from to socialize with friends and other gay couples, and to attend services at a gay-friendly church. Jerry also receives care from specialists from the Department of Veterans Affairs hospital in the nearby city after recently being diagnosed with early stage Parkinson's disease. Richard is taking medication for high blood pressure and cholesterol but is otherwise very healthy. The couple are happy in their new home but would like to become more socially connected and feel more a part of the close-knit community.

RURAL COMMUNITIES AND SOCIAL RELATIONSHIPS

We see in the case of Richard and Jerry that Richard is returning to his hometown with his husband after many years of living in a larger city. They believe this smaller town holds the promise of many advantages for them. Having a more leisurely lifestyle and closer proximity to, and strengthened relationships with, children and grandchildren are features that they value and enjoy in this rural community. In time, they will likely build social relationships with others in their new locale. The couple's view of rural retirement is consistent with research that supports the benefits of aging in rural communities. These benefits include a lower cost of living, lower crime rates, peaceful living, and opportunities to interact with nature (Butler & Cohen, 2010; Hawk, 2013; National Center for Victims of Crimes, 2014).

One obstacle to the couple's social inclusion might be the traditional values of the community. Rural communities tend to be more self-reliant, less trusting of government policies and programs, politically conservative, more likely to be religious and attend weekly church services, and less accepting of same-sex relationships (Dillon & Savage, 2006; Kellogg Foundation, 2001; Krout, 1986). Younger rural residents, however, tend to be more accepting of lesbian, gay, bisexual, and transgender (LGBT) people (Dillon & Savage, 2006). Although little research exists on the experiences of LGBT rural elders, a few studies suggest that these individuals may experience more isolation, have access to fewer LGBT-specific resources and less support from families of origin, and may be more reluctant coming out to professionals and others in the community (Comerford, Henson-Stroud, Sionainn, & Wheeler; 2004; King & Dabelko-Schoeny, 2009; Oswald & Culton, 2003).

Finding sensitive and supportive professionals is a significant concern for many older LGBTs living in rural communities (Hash, 2006). Richard and Jerry currently commute to the larger city that they relocated from for socialization and healthcare, but, as they become more immersed in their new community, they might choose to establish closer friendships and relationships with organizations and professionals closer to home. As a positive aspect, many older LGBT people in both rural and urban areas have built strong support networks that consist of friends, former partners, and even some family members (Grossman, D'Augelli, & Hershberger, 2000; Metlife Mature Market Institute, 2010). Given Richard's familial and other connections in this community, building this type of network is quite possible for Richard and Jerry.

FORMAL AND INFORMAL SUPPORTS

Rural communities tend to have a more limited range of medical and social services, something Richard and Jerry will have to consider for the future. Because of the difficulty accessing services, rural elders may rely on informal supports (family, friends, neighbors, etc.) to a greater extent (Mair & Thivierge-Rikard, 2010; Wedgewood, LaRocca, Chaplin, & Scogin, 2017). The out-migration of younger residents leaves fewer available caregivers and support persons for those who age in place in small towns (Kirschner et al., 2009). Access to transportation is a critical issue in rural communities and can restrict an older person's ability to get to medical appointments, to the grocery store, or to social events. This can be very isolating for many rural elders. Mrs. Rogers has experienced these challenges as she ages in her rural community. Since her daughter has moved out of the area, she must rely on friends and senior transportation services.

SOCIAL ISOLATION AND LONELINESS

Social isolation and loneliness can be challenges for older rural adults, especially when they have limited access to nearby family, friends, and social supports. Social isolation can be considered an objective state related to the number of social relationships (Jopling, 2015). Biordi and Nicholson (2009) describe social isolation as a loss of one's role relative to his or her group. Rural older adults can be at risk of reduced social relationships over the years owing to loss of work relationships, loved ones moving away, and the death of family and friends. This is the case for Mrs. Rogers, although she has been able to connect and socialize with other women in her building.

In contrast, loneliness is a negative emotional state associated with a person's perception of the gap between desired and the actual quantity and quality of relationships (Jopling, 2015). Loneliness is a subjective experience that is deeply personal. Loneliness is a serious health issue for older adults in that it is associated with a higher risk of disability and cognitive decline (Jopling, 2015). Social isolation may be accompanied by loneliness, but not all isolated people are necessarily lonely (Machielse, 2015).

There are a number of risk factors associated with isolation in older adults, including living alone, widowhood, emotional or psychological distress, addiction, poverty, deficits in social skills, cognitive impairment, health impairment, and membership in a minority group (AARP, 2014; Biordi & Nicholson, 2013; Machielse, 2015; Meeuwesen, 2006; Smith & Rosen, 2009; Victor, Scambler, & Bond, 2009). Older adults living in rural areas are also at risk for isolation owing to limited transportation access and limited social supports (AARP, 2014; Levasseur et al., 2015). Although Richard and Jerry are members of a minority group (lesbian, gay, bisexual, transgender, and queer [LGBTQ]), they are relatively young, healthy, and currently have close family in their new town and live close enough to a larger area in which to socialize.

Limited social support and isolation are also closely tied to elder mistreatment and share many of the same risk factors. In a recent study by the National Institute of Justice (NIJ), victims of elder abuse reported higher rates of major depressive disorder (MDD), generalized anxiety disorder (GAD), posttraumatic stress disorder (PTSD), and poorer self-reported health. However, the study also found that the level of perceived social support protected against the negative effects of mistreatment, particularly with health outcomes and GAD symptoms (Park & Mulford, 2018). This finding is encouraging for practitioners who are working with victims of elder abuse because it represents both a promising prevention target for elder abuse and a promising intervention to disrupt the negative effects for elders who have been abused (Park & Mulford, 2018).

RURAL PROFESSIONAL PRACTICE

Rural elders experiencing deficits in social support may seek formal support services from social workers and other professionals. Competencies have been developed to guide practice for professionals working with older adults and their families in healthcare and human service–related settings. These competencies center around knowledge and skills needed for working with older adults and their families. The Partnership for Health in Aging (PHA) offers a set of multidisciplinary competencies for entry-level healthcare professionals (including social workers, physicians and physician assistants, nurses, dietitians, pharmacists, dentists, physical and occupational therapists, and psychologists) (PHA, n.d.). These competencies include areas of health promotion and safety, evaluation and assessment, care planning and coordination, interdisciplinary and team care, caregiver support, and healthcare systems and benefits. Social work also delineated specific competencies related to work with older adults and their families (Social Work Leadership Institute & the Council on Social Work Education, n.d.). The Geriatric Social Work Competencies are similar to the PHA competencies but add the domains of values and ethics and leadership in the practice environment of aging.

Although specific competencies for working with rural elders have not yet been developed, there are unique issues that have been identified in this practice context, as rural practice presents both challenges and opportunities for professionals working in these communities. To begin, many health and human service professionals enjoy and value their work in rural communities with older residents and their families. Working in small towns and rural areas can provide a tight-knit service community and allow for long-term professional relationships with patients and clients (Neitch, Elliott, Nunley, & Weiner, 2015; Ullman, 2012). These relationships can be challenging, however. For example, if professionals live and work in the same community as their clients, they may encounter the ethical challenge of serving both as a service provider and a member of a shared community (Brownlee, Halverson, & Chassie, 2012). In such cases, social workers and other professionals may find themselves socializing in similar circles as their clients and encountering clients or families of clients at community events. Navigating professional and ethical boundaries is crucial when professional and social connections cross. Protecting client confidentiality and privacy are vital to professional practice. These ethical challenges and dual relationships are not uncommon and can be appropriately managed. Professionals serving in rural areas can and should expect to encounter clients in other realms of their lives. They should communicate openly and set clear boundaries with clients, and they should assess potential risks and harm to clients (Bosch & Boisen, 2011; Galbreath, 2005; Hash, Damron-Rodriguez, & Thurman, 2015; National Association of Social Workers [NASW], 2012). Mrs. Rogers has likely established long-term relationships with healthcare professionals in her community and may also have connections with them in other areas of her life, such as within her faith community.

It is also important to note that even professionals who work in urban areas will likely also work with older adults who reside in rural areas, as many times rural residents must seek care and services in larger communities that offer a wider range of services, large hospitals, and more specialized care. As noted by Hash et al. (2015, p. 254), "sometimes, urban practice can be rural." Because rural communities typically have larger proportions of older residents, all professionals should be prepared to work with this population (Hash et al., 2015). As Richard and Jerry must travel to a larger city for care through the VA, the professionals that work with them should be aware that the couple resides in an area with fewer resources.

POLICIES AND PROGRAMS

Professionals working with rural elders must work within the confines of available programs and policies. The Older Americans Act (OAA, 1965), one of the largest umbrellas for services, was established to address the lack of community social services for older adults. This policy established authority for states in the United States to initiate community planning and social services for older adults and their caregivers. The OAA also established the Administration on Aging (AoA) as the federal agency to administer new programs in support of older adults. The OAA has been a major initiative in providing social support and nutrition for older adults.

The passage of Medicare and Medicaid in 1965 created health insurance programs for adults age 65 or older and older adults who fall below the poverty line (Altman & Frist, 2015). The expansion of Medicaid services under the Patient Protection and Affordable Care Act (2016) further expanded health insurance for those with limited financial resources. These health insurance programs have benefited older adults in general, and particularly older adults in rural areas where poverty rates are higher. Programs initiated under the OAA (1965) and administered through the AoA include transportation support, adult day care, home care, nutrition programs and delivered meals, health promotion, long-term care ombudsman programs, and elder abuse and neglect services. Some services, such as delivered meals, are not always available in more rural areas as community delivery routes do not always extend to areas where fewer consumers reside. When faced with these challenges, practitioners have to be creative in identifying and utilizing community resources.

INTERVENTIONS

In order to develop interventions for addressing social isolation and loneliness among older rural adults, one must first begin with assessment. There are a number of instruments for assessing social isolation and loneliness in older adults including the Revised UCLA Loneliness Scale (Fukui, Koike, Ooba, & Uchitomi, 2003), the de Jong Gierveld Loneliness Scale (de Jong Gierveld & Kamphuis, 1985), and the Social and Emotional Loneliness Scale for Adults (DiTommaso & Spinner, 1993). In addition, the Hughes, Waite, Hawkley, and Cacioppo (2008) three-item loneliness scale is an easy-to-use brief instrument for assessing loneliness. The scale consists of three items with response choices of "hardly ever," "some of the time," or "often." The items are as follows:

1. How often do you feel that you lack companionship?
2. How often do you feel left out?
3. How often do you feel isolated from others?

This scale can easily be incorporated into assessment protocols in a variety of settings that serve older adults. It could certainly be used with Mrs. Rogers to determine if her current support system is sufficient to ward off feelings of loneliness or isolation. Validated instruments such as these can be used both for screening as well as for quantitative outcome measures to determine the effect of interventions.

Incorporating a life span perspective is also beneficial when assessing social isolation and loneliness in older adults. Charles and Cartensen (2010) highlight the importance of adaptive aging among older adults. As older adults cope with life challenges over time, they adapt and build resilience. Comprehensive assessment and effective intervention planning should incorporate client strengths and resilience whenever possible. Older LGBT people, like Richard and Jerry, are thought to have built great resilience as a result of coming out, dealing with lifelong discrimination, and building strong, alternative support networks (Hash & Rogers, 2013; Metlife Mature Market Institute, 2010; Morrow, 2001).

According to Jopling (2015), there are three key challenges to addressing loneliness and social isolation among older adults: (a) reaching, or accessing, individuals; (b) assessing the unique nature of a person's loneliness or isolation in order to develop a personalized intervention plan; and (c) facilitating access to services. Access can be particularly challenging in rural areas where public transportation is limited or nonexistent. Access is also a challenge for individuals who no longer drive and for those whose disabilities prevent them from readily leaving home. Mrs. Rogers is at a greater risk for loneliness and social isolation related to limited independence and access to her community.

One-on-One Intervention

Home visits from family members, neighbors, and volunteers are effective for reducing social isolation and loneliness in rural older adults. MacIntyre et al. (1999) found that weekly visits at mutually agreed-on times to clients' homes were beneficial for reducing loneliness. The visits were client centered in that clients identified discussion topics and activities that matched their interests. Similar to visitor programs are home healthcare visits that target loneliness and social isolation as part of the overall healthcare plan (Ciechanowski et al., 2004; Friedrich, 2008).

Greaves and Farbus (2006) developed a successful intervention for addressing depression and social isolation among older adults living at home. Mentors engaged in individually tailored activities with participants over a 12-month period. Outcomes included reduction in depression and social isolation and increases in self-confidence/self-efficacy.

The use of technology can be beneficial for reducing social isolation and isolation, especially in rural areas where face-to-face engagement may be more difficult logistically. Gellis, Kenaley, and Have (2014) utilized telehealth as a method for assisting 115 older adults coping with chronic illness and depression. Each participant was provided a small in-home computer monitor that connected to the provider's central station. Service providers also incorporated telephone calls to participants in order to provide healthcare and depression support. Participants demonstrated improvements with healthcare management, depression, and overall life satisfaction. Although the landscape is improving, rural areas still trail urban centers in broadband options. Thus, access to technology may be a challenge for Mrs. Rogers and Richard and Jerry (USDA, 2017).

As another technology-based intervention, Stewart, Barnfather, Neufeld, and Warren (2010) developed a telephone support intervention program for older adults who were serving as family caregivers. Experienced caregivers were paired with new caregivers. The experienced caregivers made weekly supportive phone contact with new caregivers. Results of the intervention were that the new caregivers reported increased satisfaction with support, coping skills, and caregiving competence. They also reported decreased feelings of loneliness and caregiver burden. This type of intervention can also facilitate shared connection and feelings of efficacy among experienced caregivers as they reach out to less-experienced caregivers going through similar life challenges.

SeniorNet (seniornet.org) is a technology-based resource to help older adults who have computer access feel more connected with resources and people. The focus of SeniorNet is to provide older adults "education for and access to computer technologies to enhance their lives and enable them to share their knowledge and wisdom" (seniornet.org 2017, para. 1). The program offers training support in computer skills, email usage, and Internet surfing.

Technology has the potential to expand possibilities in serving the ever-increasing aging population, especially in rural areas. However, lack of Internet access for seniors and the need for increased broadband access for rural areas can hamper implementation. Rural hospitals also face the challenge of financial resources needed to implement new technologies and training staff to operate telehealth technologies (Nelson, 2017).

Group Intervention

A number of group-based interventions incorporate the life experience and wisdom of older adults in giving back to their community. For example, Experience Corps (Rebok et al., 2011) promotes generative roles for older adults who are paired with elementary school children. The aim is to provide meaningful engagement and contributions for older adults while also improving academic and behavioral health outcomes in children. Another example is Lifestyle ReDesign (Mountain & Craig, 2010), which focuses on weekly group intervention to assist retired older adults in exploring meaningful occupational roles. This type of intervention is commonly led by occupational therapists in community-based sites. This would be a possibility and an appropriate program in the apartment complex where Mrs. Rogers and her friends reside.

The Virtual Senior Center (Larkin, Lerner, & DeCrow, 2010; Virtual Senior Center, 2017) is another technology-based group support intervention designed to reduce social isolation and loneliness. Using a computer, microphone, and video camera, older adults engage with other older adults in groups of approximately 25 individuals. The program promotes socialization and emotional support for participants and offers social activities on topics such as music, history, art, and medical information.

Community Intervention

The Village Model (Graham, Scharlach, & Stark, 2017) is designed for older adults who seek to age in their own homes and communities. Villages are funded primarily by membership fees. Members engage in a combination of providing and funding support services that enable aging in place. A variety of support services are typically available such as visitation, transportation, grocery shopping, house cleaning, and lawn work. The sustainability of villages is highly dependent on their capacity to continually recruit new members who can afford the membership fee. Thus, this model would be less suitable to lower income older adults.

Intentional Intergenerational Communities (Power, Eheart, Racine, & Karnik, 2008) is an intervention model that partners older adults with families who are in the process of adopting foster children. Older adults in the program have the opportunity to supportively engage with children and, in turn, children have the opportunity to experience relationships with older adults.

The Niagara Gatekeepers Program (Niagara Region, 2018) is a community-based program in Ontario, Canada, that supports community members helping older adults remain safe at home and in providing referral to social and medical services as needed. The program offers a phone referral line to facilitate connecting older adults with community agencies. The program also educates community members about at-risk conditions for which greater care assistance may be needed (e.g., memory loss, confusion, deteriorating home conditions, and neglect or abuse). The program is affiliated with a number of support service agencies in the Ontario region.

Support and Services at Home (SASH) is a program that began in Vermont in 2008 by the nonprofit housing provider Cathedral Square Corporation. The program provides a coordinator and a wellness nurse in congregate senior housing sites and some community sites. SASH helps seniors age 65 and over by connecting them with primary care doctors, specialists, and other services to improve wellness and quality of life, as well as reduce healthcare costs. Participants in the early panels experienced significantly slower growth in Medicare expenditures by an estimated $1,227 per beneficiary per year (U.S. Department of Health and Human Services, 2017). SASH currently serves over 5,000 people in Vermont and many states are implementing similar programs based on this model. A community program like SASH would provide the support that Mrs. Rogers needs while she waits for in-home services to start.

The World Health Organization (WHO) (2007) promotes the concept of "age-friendly cities." Age-friendly cities incorporate policies, services, and structures that support and enable positive and inclusive aging. WHO reports that age-friendly cities recognize and value the capacities and resources among older adults; anticipate and respond to the needs of older adults; respect the decisions of older adults; protect vulnerable older adults; and promote the inclusion of older adults in all facets of community life. Although the WHO age-friendly guidelines relate primarily to urban settings, many of the guidelines can be easily applied to rural communities and small towns. Practitioners in the field of aging should consider working collaboratively with community developers and planners. Such collaborations can improve accessibility not only for older adults but people of all ages and abilities.

While most older adults prefer to age in place in their own homes and communities for as long as possible, circumstances do arise where greater care and assistance are needed. When living independently is no longer possible and when family caregiving is unavailable or insufficient to meet the level of care needed, assisted living facilities, nursing homes, and memory care centers are utilized to provide care for older adults with significant care and medical needs. Institutional care is expensive, and the number of facilities is more limited in rural areas compared to urban areas. Older adults in rural areas are at higher risk of placement farther away from their home communities due to the limited number of beds available and their higher risk of institutional placement compared to urban older adults (Cohen & Bulanda, 2015). Moreover, given the very limited insurance coverage for institutional care, older adults can quickly become impoverished because of institutional care expenses. Affordable long-term care is a primary need for frail older adults.

SUMMARY

Like Mrs. Rogers and Jerry and Richard, many individuals choose to age in rural communities. They may encounter challenges to aging in place in these areas, such as limited access to needed healthcare and social services. Compounding these challenges is the risk of loneliness and social isolation for these rural elders. Informal support persons can help assuage these feelings and experiences as can professionals and formal programs based locally or in adjacent communities. If the population of older rural residents continues to grow, the demand for these supports will become even greater.

RESOURCES

Gerontological Association on Aging Rural Aging Interest Group
    https://www.geron.org/stay-connected/interest-groups#rural
HRSA Federal Office of Rural Health Policy
    https://www.hrsa.gov/rural-health/index.html
National Association of Rural Mental Health
    http://www.narmh.org
National Organization of State Offices of Rural Health
    https://nosorh.org
National Rural Health Association
    https://www.ruralhealthweb.org

National Rural Social Work Caucus
http://www.ruralsocialwork.org
Rural Health Information Hub
https://www.ruralhealthinfo.org
Rural Health Policy Network
http://www.rupri.org
Veteran Health Administration Office of Rural Health
https://www.ruralhealth.va.gov

REFERENCES

Altman, D., & Frist, W. H. (2015). Medicare and Medicaid at 50 years: Perspectives of beneficiaries, health care professionals and institutions, and policy makers. *Journal of the American Medical Association, 314*(4), 384–395. doi:10.1001/jama.2015.7811

American Association of Retired Persons. (2014). *Framework for isolation in adults over 50.* Washington, DC: AARP Foundation.

Biordi, D. L., & Nicholson, N. F. (2009). Social isolation. *Chronic illness: Impact and interventions* (7th ed.). Sudbury, MA: Jones & Bartlett.

Biordi, D. L., & Nicholson, N. F. (2013). Social isolation. In I. M. Lubkin & P. D. Larsen (Eds.), *Chronic illness: Impact and intervention* (pp. 85–115). Sudbury, MA: Jones & Bartlett.

Bosch, L. A., & Boisen, L. S. (2011). Dual relationships in rural areas. In L. Ginsberg, (Ed.), *Social work in rural communities* (5th ed., pp. 111–123). Alexandria, VA: CSWE Press.

Brownlee, K., Halverson, G., & Chassie, A. (2012). Multiple relationships: Maintaining professional identity in rural social work. *Journal of Comparative Social Work, 7*(1), 1–11. doi:10.31265/jcsw.v7i1.82

Butler, S., & Cohen, A. (2010). The importance of nature in the well-being of rural elders. *Nature and Culture, 5*(2), 150–174. doi: 10.3167/nc.2010.050203

Charles, S. T., & Cartensen, L. L. (2010). Social and emotional aging. *Annual Review of Psychology, 61,* 383–409. doi:10.1146/annurev.psych.093008.100448

Ciechanowski, P., Wagner, E., Schmaling, K., Schwartz, S., Williams, B., Diehr, P., & LoGerfo, J. (2004). Community-integrated home-based depression treatment in older adults. *JAMA: The Journal of the American Medical Association, 291*(13), 1569. doi:10.1001/jama.291.13.1569

Cohen, A., & Bulanda, J. R. (2015). Social supports as enabling factors in nursing home admissions: Rural, suburban, and urban differences. *Journal of Applied Gerontology, 35*(7), 721–743. doi:10.1177/0733464814566677

Colello, K. J. (2007). *Where do older Americans live? Geographic distribution of the older population.* Washington, DC: Congressional Research Service.

Comerford, S. A., Henson-Stroud, M., Sionainn, C., & Wheeler, E. (2004). Crone songs: Voices of lesbian elders on aging in a rural environment. *Affilia, 19*(4), 418–436. doi:10.1177/0886109904268874

De Jong Gierveld, J., & Kamphuis, F. (1985). The development of a Rasch-type loneliness scale. *Applied Psychological Measurement, 9,* 289–299. doi:10.1177/014662168500900307

Dillon, M., & Savage, S. (2006). *Values and religion in rural America: Attitudes toward abortion and same-sex relations.* Issue Brief #1. The Carsey Foundation.

DiTommaso, E., & Spinner, B. (1993). The development and initial validation of the Social and Emotional Loneliness Scale for Adults (SELSA). *Personality and Individual Differences, 14*(1), 127–134. doi:10.1016/0191-8869(93)90182-3

Friedrich, M. (2008). Programs bring care to homebound seniors. *JAMA: The Journal of the American Medical Association, 299*(22), 2618. doi:10.1001/jama.299.22.2618

Fukui, S., Koike, M., Ooba, A, & Uchitomi, Y. (2003). The effect of a psychosocial group intervention on loneliness and social support for Japanese women with primary breast cancer. *Oncology Nursing Forum, 3*(5), 823–830. doi:10.1188/03.ONF.823-830

Galbreath, W. B. (2005). Dual relationships in rural communities. In N. Lohmann & R. A. Lohmann (Eds), *Rural social work practice* (pp. 105–123). New York, NY: Columbia University Press.

Gellis, Z. D., Kenaley, F. L., & Have, T. T. (2014). Integrated telehealth care for chronic illness and depression in geriatric home care patients: The Integrated Telehealth Education and Activation of Mood (I-TEAM) Study. *Journal of the American Geriatrics Society, 62*(5), 889–895. doi:10.1111/jgs.12776

Graham, C. L., Scharlach, A. E., & Stark, B. (2017). Impact of the Village Model: Results of a national survey. *Journal of Gerontological Social Work, 60*(5), 335–354. doi:10.1080/01634372.2017.1330299

Greaves, C. J., & Farbus, L. (2006). Effects of creative and social activity on the health and well-being of socially isolated older people: Outcomes from a multi-method observational study. *Perspectives in Public Health, 126*(3), 134–142. doi:10.1177/1466424006064303

Grossman, A. H., D'Augelli, A. R., & Hershberger, S. L. (2000). Social support networks of lesbian, gay, and bisexual adults 60 years of age and older. *Journals of Gerontology: Series B: Psychological Sciences and Social Sciences, 55B*(3), P171–P179. doi:10.1093/geronb/55.3.P171

Hash, K. M. (2006). Caregiving and post-caregiving experiences of midlife and older gay men and lesbians. *Journal of Gerontological Social Work, 47*(3/4), 121–138. doi:10.1300/J083v47n03_08

Hash, K. M., Damron-Rodriguez, J. A., & Thurman, H. (2015). The role of the human service provider. In K. M. Hash, E. T. Jurkowski, & J. A. Krout (Eds.), *Aging in rural places: Programs, policies, and professional practice* (pp. 235–258). New York, NY: Springer Publishing.

Hash, K. M., & Rogers, A. (2013). Clinical practice with older LGBT clients: Overcoming lifelong stigma through strength and resilience. *Clinical Social Work Journal, 41*(3), 249–257. doi:10.1007/s10615-013-0437-2

Hash, K. M., Wells, R., & Spencer, S. M. (2015). Who are rural elders? In K. M. Hash, E. T. Jurkowski, & J. A. Krout (Eds.), *Aging in rural places: Programs, policies, and professional practice* (pp. 23–41). New York, NY: Springer Publishing.

Hawk, W. (2013, February). Consumer Expenditure Program, Expenditures of urban and rural households in 2011. *Beyond the Numbers: Prices & Spending, 2*(5). Retrieved from https://www.bls.gov/opub/btn/volume-2/expenditures-of-urban-and-rural-households-in-2011.htm

Hughes, M. E., Waite, L. J., Hawkley, L. C., & Cacioppo, J. T. (2008). A short scale for measuring loneliness in large surveys: Results from two population-based studies. *Residential Aging, 26*(6), 655–672. doi:10.1177/0164027504268574

Jopling, K. (2015). *Promising approaches to reducing loneliness and isolation in later life.* United Kingdom: Age UK, The Campaign to End Loneliness.

Kellogg Foundation. (2001). *Perceptions of rural America.* Battle Creek, MI: Author.

King, S., & Dabelko-Schoeny, H. (2009). "Quite frankly, I have doubts about remaining": Aging-in-place and health care access for rural midlife and older lesbian, gay, and bisexual individuals. *Journal of LGBT Health Research, 5*(1/2), 10–21. doi:10.1080/15574090903392830

Kirschner, A., Beery, E. H., & Glasgow, N. (2009). *The changing demographic profile of rural America*. Retrieved from https://wrdc.usu.edu/files-ou/publications/pub__3471631.pdf

Krout, J. A. (1986). *The aged in rural America*. Westport, CT: Greenwood Press.

Krout, J. A., & Hash, K. M. (2015). What is rural? In K. M. Hash, E. T. Jurkowski, & J. A. Krout (Eds.), *Aging in rural places: Programs, policies, and professional practice* (pp. 3–22). New York, NY: Springer Publishing.

Larkin, M., Lerner, A., & DeCrow, J. (2010). Program profile: Virtual senior center connects older adults to community and family. *The Journal on Active Aging, 9*(3), 36–43.

Levasseur, M., Cohen, A. A., Dubois, M., Genereux, R. L., Therrien, F., & Payette, H. (2015). Environmental factors associated with social participation of older adults living in metropolitan, urban, and rural areas: The NuAge study. *American Journal of Public Health*. Retrieved from https://docs.google.com/document/d/1qe95z3yrO9Zc5y0jOyx1LOISZXuS4pN_DOyWoHNwYdA/edit

Lohmann, R. A., & Lohmann, N. (2005). Introduction. In N. Lohmann & R. A. Lohmann, (Eds.), *Rural social work practice* (pp. xi–xxvii). New York, NY: Columbia University Press.

Machielse, A. (2015). The heterogeneity of socially isolated older adults: A social isolation typology. *Journal of Gerontological Social Work, 58*, 338–356. doi:10.1080/01634372.2015.1007258

MacIntyre, I., Corradetti, P., Roberts, J., Browne, G., Watt, S., & Lane, A. (1999). Pilot study of a visitor volunteer programme for community elderly people receiving home health care. *Health and Social Care, 7*(3), 225–232. doi:10.1046/j.1365-2524.1999.00178.x

Mair, C. A., & Thivierge-Rikard, R. V. (2010). The strength of strong ties for older rural adults: Regional distinctions in the relationship between social interaction and subjective well-being. *International Journal of Aging and Human Development, 70*(2), 119–143. doi:10.2190/AG.70.2.b

Meeuwesen, L. (2006). Life events and social isolation. In R. Hortulanus, A. Machielse, & L. Meeuwesen (Eds.), *Social isolation in modern society* (pp. 63–80). London, England: Routledge.

Metlife Mature Market Institute. (2010). *Still out, still aging: The Metlife study of lesbian gay, bisexual, and transgendered baby boomers*. Westport, CT: Author

Morrow, D. F. (2001). Older gays and lesbians: Surviving a generation of hate and violence. *Journal of Gay and Lesbian Social Services, 13*(1–2), 151–169. doi:10.1300/J041v13n01_11

Mountain, G. A., & Craig, C. L. (2010). The lived experience of redesigning lifestyle post-retirement in the UK. *Occupational Therapy International, 18*(1), 48–58. doi:10.1002/oti.309

National Association of Social Workers. (2012). Rural social work. In *Social work speaks* (9th ed., pp. 297–302). Washington, DC: Author.

National Center for Victims of Crimes. (2014). *Urban and rural crime*. Retrieved from https://ovc.ncjrs.gov/ncvrw2016/content/section-6/PDF/2016NCVRW_6_UrbanRural-508.pdf

Neitch, S. M., Elliott, D. P., Nunley, B. L., & Weiner, R. C. (2015). The role of the health care professional. In K. M. Hash, E. T. Jurkowski, & J. A. Krout (Eds.), *Aging in rural places: Programs, policies, and professional practice* (pp. 211–234). New York, NY: Springer Publishing.

Nelson, R. (2017). Telemedicine and telehealth: The potential to improve rural access to care. [Report]. *AJN, American Journal of Nursing. 117*(6), 17-18. doi:10.1097/01.NAJ.0000520244.60138.1c

Niagara Region. (2018). Niagara gatekeepers. Retrieved from https://www.niagararegion.ca/living/seniors/programs/gatekeepers.aspx

Older Americans Act, 42 U.S.C 3002 (1965).

Oswald, R., & Culton, L. (2003). Under the rainbow: Rural gay life and its relevance for family providers. *Family Relations, 52*(1), 72–781. doi:10.1111/j.1741-3729.2003.00072.x

Park, Y., & Mulford, C. (2018). *Social support can diminish negative effects of elder abuse.* Retrieved from http://www.napsa-now.org/wp-content/uploads/2018/01/R2P-Park-Mulford.pdf

Partnership for Health in Aging (2010, March). *Multidisciplinary competencies in the care of older adults at the completion of the entry-level health professional degree.* Retrieved from http://www.americangeriatrics.org/files/documents/health_care_pros/PHA_multidisc_competencies.pdf

Patient Protection and Affordable Care Act, 42 U.S.C 1800 (2016).

Power, M. B., Eheart, B. K., Racine, D., & Karnik, N. S. (2008). Aging well in an intentional intergenerational community. *Journal of Intergenerational Relationships, 5*(2), 7–25. doi:10.1300/J194v05n02_02

Rebok, G. W., Carlson, M. C., Barron, J. S., Frick, K. D., McGill, S., Parisi, J. M., . . . Fried, L. P. (2011). *Experience Corps: A civic engagement-based public health intervention in the public schools.* New York, NY: Springer.

Smith, M. L., & Rosen, D. (2009). Mistrust and self-isolation: Barriers to social support for older and adult methadone clients. *Journal of Gerontological Social Work, 52,* 663–667. doi:10.1080/01634370802609049

Social Work Leadership Institute and the Council on Social Work Education. (n.d.). Geriatric Social Work Competency Scale II with life long leadership skills. Retrieved from https://www.cswe.org/getattachment/Centers-Initiatives/CSWE-Gero-Ed-Center/Teaching-Tools/Gero-Competencies/Guidelines-and-Scales/GeriatricSocialWorkCompetencyScaleII-LifelongLeadershipSkills.pdf.aspx

Stewart, M., Barnfather, A., Neufeld, A., & Warren, S. (2010). Accessible support for family caregivers of seniors with chronic conditions: From isolation to inclusion. *Canadian Journal on Aging, 25*(2), 179–192. doi:10.1353/cja.2006.0041

Ullman, K. (2012, November). Practicing in rural settings offers slower pace, personal satisfaction for many rheumatologists. *The Rheumatologist.* Retrieved from http://www.the-rheumatologist.org/article/practicing-in-rural-settings-offers-slower-pace-personal-satisfaction-for-many-rheumatologists

U.S. Census Bureau. (2012-2016a). GCT0101 Median age of the total population. American community survey 5-year estimates. Retrieved from http://factfinder2.census.gov

U.S. Census Bureau. (2012-2016b). GCT0103 Percent of the total population who are 65 years and over. American community survey 5-year estimates. Retrieved from http://factfinder2.census.gov

U.S. Census Bureau. (2012-2016c). GCT0201 Percent of the Ttotal Ppopulation Wwho are White Aalone. American Ccommunity Ssurvey 5-Yyear Eestimates. Retrieved from http://factfinder2.census.gov

U.S. Census Bureau. (2012-2016d). GCT1001 Percent of the grandparents responsible for their grandchildren. American community survey 5-year estimates. Retrieved from http://factfinder2.census.gov

U.S. Census Bureau. (2012-2016e). GCT1703 Percent of people 65 years and over below poverty level in the past 12 months. Retrieved from http://factfinder2.census.gov

U.S. Census Bureau. (2012-2016f). GCT2101 Percent of the civilian population 18 years and over who are veterans. Retrieved from http://factfinder2.census.gov

U.S. Census Bureau. (2012-2016g). S1201 Marital status. American community survey 5-year estimates. Retrieved from http://factfinder2.census.gov

U.S. Census Bureau. (2012-2016h). S1501 Educational attainment. Retrieved from http://factfinder2.census.gov

U.S. Department of Agriculture. (2017). Rural America at a glance. Retrieved from https://www.ers.usda.gov/webdocs/publications/85740/eib-182.pdf?v=43054

U.S. Department of Health and Human Services. (2017). Support and Services at Home (SASH) evaluation: Evaluation of the first four years. Retrieved from https://aspe.hhs.gov/basic-report/support-and-services-home-sash-evaluation-evaluation-first-four-years

Victor, A., Scambler, S., & Bond, J. (2009). *The social world of older people: Understanding loneliness and social isolation in later life.* New York, NY: McGraw Hill/Open University Press.

Virtual Senior Center. (2017). Self-Help VSC: Where seniors connect, learn, and play online. Retrieved from http://vscm.selfhelp.net

Wedgewood, M., LaRocca, M. A., Chaplin, W. F., & Scogin, F. (2017). The role of interpersonal sensitivity, social support, and quality of life in rural older adults. *Geriatric Nursing, 38*(1), 22–26. doi:10.1016/j.gerinurse.2016.07.001

World Health Organization. (2007). Global age-friendly cities: A guide. Retrieved from http://www.who.int/ageing/publications/Global_age_friendly_cities_Guide_English.pdf

Appendix: Resources on Older Adult Isolation and Relationships

Lisa Dezso

AARP

888-687-2277
601 E St., NW
Washington, DC 20049
www.aarp.org
The AARP encourages members to "make the most of each day." To aid in that goal, they have published a list of 15 ways to make new friends. There is a "little more resistance" to forming new friendships in later life. With these tips and tricks, meeting and connecting with new people does not have to be difficult or uncomfortable.

A PLACE FOR MOM (SENIOR LIVING BLOG)

866-333-2174
www.aplaceformom.com/blog
A Place for Mom's Senior Living Blog is a resource that focuses on topics like senior living trends, aging and health news, retirement, finances, caregiving, and more. This site is a hub for information, connecting to other resources and agencies, and all things aging related.

ADMINISTRATION FOR COMMUNITY LIVING

330 C St. SW
Washington, DC 20201
202-401-4634
www.acl.gov
The Administration for Community Living understands the importance of living in and staying connected with the community. They work with other organizations and foundations to provide programs, grants, news articles, videos, blogs, and more to keep older adults and individuals with disabilities at home and thriving in their communities.

ALTERNATIVES FOR SENIORS

800-350-0770
Info@alternativesforseniors
www.alternativesforseniors.com/blog
This blog features an array of topics to guide seniors to live their best lives as they age. Information found on this site is aimed at seniors, providers, and their caregivers, focusing on topics such as health and safety, Medicare/Medicaid, senior housing, nutrition, legal information, and more.

AMERICAN SOCIETY ON AGING (ASA)

800-537-9728
575 Market St., Suite 2100
San Francisco, CA 94105
www.asaging.org
The ASA is a leading resource in strengthening the knowledge and skills of those who work for and on behalf of older adults. Their publications *Aging Today* and *Generations*, which provide information, education and training opportunities, and articles on various aging topics are available to members and nonmembers alike.

CAMPAIGN TO END LONELINESS

3 Waterhouse Sq.
138 Holborn
London, EC1N 2SW
England
www.campaigntoendloneliness.org

The Campaign to End Loneliness is an initiative out of the United Kingdom that has inspired thousands of organizations and community members to fight loneliness in older adults. Using research to fuel the change, the campaign provides information on the risk factors of loneliness and what can be done, information on the physical and mental effects of loneliness, and a blog with real stories from seniors who have faced and dealt with loneliness and isolation.

CENTERS FOR DISEASE CONTROL AND PREVENTION (CDC)

800-232-4636
1600 Clifton Rd.
Atlanta, GA 30329
www.cdc.gov/aging/pdf/healthy-aging-in-action508.pdf
In this document published by the CDC, the authors take a multifaceted approach at healthy aging, including increasing older adults' access to opportunities for social inclusivity and connectedness. Included is a plan to address healthy aging, including loneliness moving forward as well as a list of federal initiatives that are in place to empower older adults, keep seniors active and engaged in the community, and create the space for healthy aging.

CONNECT 2 AFFECT

www.connect2affect.org
Powered by the AARP, Connect 2 Affect's aim is to gain a deeper understanding of social isolation in older adults in an effort to end said isolation. Their goal is to create a network of individuals and resources that can meet the needs of any older individual to build social connections. In this website you can find places to turn for help, stories of individuals affected by isolation and loneliness, opportunities to get involved, and much more.

ELDERCARE LOCATOR

800-677-1116
www.eldercare.gov/eldercare.net/public/Resources/Brochures/docs/Expanding-Circles.pdf
This resource through Eldercare Locator offers facts about the effects of isolation and loneliness on an older adult, steps and ideas that can be used to help stay connected, self-assessment checklist to identify the risk of becoming isolated and lonely, as well as a list of national resources to turn to for more information and/or support for older adults.

THE GERONTOLOGICAL SOCIETY OF AMERICA (GSA)

202-842-1275
1220 L St. NW, Suite 901
Washington, DC 20005
www.geron.org
The GSA is a driving force behind advancing innovation in aging. Their website includes publications on the effects and prevention of isolation and loneliness, programs and services for interdisciplinary professionals on aging, webinars, and more. This site is a great resource for caregivers and scholars alike.

HEALTH IN AGING

212-308-1414
800-563-4916
40 Fulton St. 18th Floor
New York, NY 10038
info@health
www.healthinaging.org
Created by the American Geriatrics Society's Health in Aging Foundation, Health in Aging provides resources tailored for older adults, their caretakers, and providers. The site provides links to finding geriatric healthcare professionals, tip sheets for managing health, and aging and health topics.

KAISER HEALTH NEWS (KHN)

www.khn.org
Not to be confused with Kaiser Permanente, KHN is a nonprofit news source committed to covering all things healthcare. Supported by the John A. Hartford Foundation, KHN provides special information related to aging and improving the lives of older adults among other health-related topics.

MAYO CLINIC

www.mayoclinic.org
Committed to education and research, clinical practice, and providing expert care, the Mayo Clinic is a nonprofit organization with locations in Arizona, Florida, and Minnesota. Through their website and publications *Forefront* and *Mayo Clinic Magazine* you can find research articles, philanthropy efforts,

and the latest on best and holistic patient care practices and resources. All publications and newsletters are free and available in print and online.

MCMASTER OPTIMAL AGING PORTAL

905-525-9140
McMaster University
1280 Main St. West
Hamilton, Ontario L8S4L8
Canada
www.mcmasteroptimalaging.org
Powered by the Labarge Optimal Aging Initiative and McMaster University, the Optimal Aging Portal provides easy access to evidence-based information on how to stay healthy as you age. Blog posts, research, evidence-based summaries, and links to other web-based resources are all written and provided by professionals with expertise in aging.

MORNINGSIDE MINISTRIES

700 Babcock Rd.
San Antonio, TX 78201
www.mmlearn.org
mmLearn.org is an online training center for those who care about, and are caring for, older adults. With over 300 training videos on the site, it is a tool that can assist any caretaker, provider, or family member with helping the older adult in his or her life meet the individual's physical, emotional, and/or spiritual needs.

MY HEALTHEVET

www.myhealthevet.va.gov
Designed specifically for veterans and their families, this site provides access to resources to learn about benefits, healthcare, self-assessment tools, preventative techniques, prescriptions, and more.

NATIONAL ALLIANCE ON MENTAL ILLNESS (NAMI)

1-800-950-6264
www.nami.org
The NAMI is an organization that is dedicated to improving the lives of Americans who are affected with mental illness. Their primary publication,

The Advocate, a bi-yearly magazine, covers a variety of topics related to mental health, including research, arts, pop culture, and personal stories, and their digital newsletters, *NAMI Now* and *NAMI E-News*, feature blogs, information on mental illness, research, federal action alerts, and legislation and policy updates.

NATIONAL ASSOCIATION OF AREA AGENCIES ON AGING (N4A)

202-872-0888
1730 Rhode Island Avenue, NW, Suite 1200
Washington, DC 20036
www.n4a.org
The N4A is an organization whose aim is to build a society that values and supports individuals as they age by engaging in policy work in Washington; offering training and educational events; improving and expanding in the fields of transportation, volunteerism, and livable communities; and raising the visibility of Area Agencies on Aging and the individuals they help.

NATIONAL COUNCIL ON AGING (NCOA)

202-479-1200
1901 L St., NW, 4th Floor
Washington. DC 20036
www.ncoa.org
The NCOA's mission is to improve the health and economic security of older adults. They partner with many other organizations to help individuals improve their health, find careers, age in place, remain connected to their community, seek benefits, and more.

NATIONAL HOSPICE AND PALLIATIVE CARE ORGANIZATION (NHPCO)

703-837-1500
1731 King St. Suite 100
Alexandria, VA 22314
nhpco_info@nhpco.org
www.nhpco.org
Using advocacy and education, NHPCO is devoted to improving end-of-life care. This organization's searchable website provides articles and stories on the effects of isolation and loneliness and prevention strategies.

NATIONAL INSTITUTE ON AGING: PUBLICATIONS AND AGE PAGES

800-222-2225
Building 31, Room 5C27
31 Center Drive, MSC 2292
Bethesda, MD 20892
niaic@nia.nih.gov
www.nia.nih.gov/health
This website offers an extensive list of free publications, articles, and information on upcoming events on various health and aging topics including isolation and loneliness, diet, exercise, caregiving, sleep, and more.

NATIONAL INSTITUTES OF HEALTH, HEALTH TOPICS A–Z

www.nih.gov
This is a searchable website that provides the user with links to articles and other national organizations that address general health topics including those surrounding isolation and loneliness in seniors.

NEXT AVENUE

www.nextavenue.org
With content updated daily, Next Avenue is a one stop shop for all issues and perspectives surrounding aging. With articles contributed by providers, caregivers, and older adults, Next Avenue's content is easy to understand and implement at home and in the community.

OXFORD ACADEMIC PUBLIC POLICY & AGING REPORT

academic.oup.com/ppar
The *Public Policy & Aging Report* is published quarterly through the Oxford University Press. Each issue explores topics of importance to older adults, examines public policy, and highlights areas of emerging concern, end-of-life care, social connectedness, and more.

RURAL HEALTH INFORMATION HUB

800-270-1898
info@ruralhealthinfo.org
www.ruralhealthinfo.org

Formerly the Rural Assistance Center, the Rural Health Information Hub is committed to providing current and reliable information on the needs of individuals in rural settings across the country. Searchable by topic or by state, this site is a great tool for meeting the needs of the individuals in your area.

SCIENCE CARE

800-417-3747

www.sciencecare.com/tools-and-resources-that-help-seniors-lessen-loneliness-and-isolation

Although Science Care's business is in medical research and full body donation, do not let that scare you from their tools and resources list to help seniors lessen isolation and loneliness. In it, you will find information on local places to meet other seniors, ideas and opportunities to get involved with the community, other health-related activities, and links to other nonprofit organizations and resources working to fight senior isolation and loneliness.

SIXTY & ME

sixtyandme.com

Sixty & Me is a lifestyle website for individuals age 60-plus. It focuses on topics of interest to older adults ranging from community connectedness, brain health, nutrition, and retirement to cruises, dating, sexuality, and make-up. This website is easy to access and navigate. It is a perfect resource for those looking to learn more about aging-related topics while avoiding medical and technical jargon.

UNITED STATES GOVERNMENT GUIDE FOR SENIORS

844-872-4681

www.usa.gov/features/usagovs-guide-for-seniors

Published by USA.gov, the guide for seniors offers information focusing on topics important to older adults. This guide's aim is to empower seniors to face challenges head on and to make the most of life during the golden years.

UNITED STATES GOVERNMENT SENIOR CITIZENS' RESOURCES PAGE

www.hhs.gov/aging/index.html

The Senior Citizens Resources page is a searchable site with information on all things of interest to and for older adults. Resources on this page include information on fighting isolation and loneliness, government benefits, caregiving, retiring, housing, and much more.

U.S DEPARTMENT OF HEALTH AND HUMAN SERVICES (HHS)

877-696-6775
200 Independence Ave., SW
Washington, DC 20201
www.hhs.gov
The goal of the HHS is to protect the health and well-being of all Americans. This searchable site provides many resources regarding isolation and loneliness including research articles, programs, and services for seniors, as well as general information and links for social services programs, grant funding, health insurance, finding providers in your area, and education and training opportunities.

U.S. NATIONAL LIBRARY OF MEDICINE

8600 Rockville Pike
Bethesda, MD 20894
www.nlm.nih.gov
The U.S. National Library of Medicine, a part of the National Institutes of Health, is the world's largest medical library. With books and journals about all aspects of health and medicine on its shelves and Internet archives, this organization can provide you with information on many aging-related topics.

WORLD HEALTH ORGANIZATION

202-974-3000
North American Office
525 Twenty-Third St, N.W.
Washington, DC 20037
www.who.int
The World Health Organization's (WHO) goal is to build a healthier future for individuals across the globe. With offices in over 150 countries, WHO's website offers local and global perspectives on isolation and loneliness through research articles, news releases, videos, and fact sheets. Visit their health topics web page for more information.

Index

A Place for Mom's Senior Living (weblog), 271
AAIs. *See* animal-assisted interventions
AARP, 271
AARP Network of Age-Friendly Communities (NAFC)
 county plan, 94
 limitations, 98–99
 livability domain, 94
 Maine community, 93, 97–98
 social connectedness, 99
 social participation, 95
 3-year action plan, 92
 5-year planning cycle, 94
accessory dwelling units (ADUs)
 age distribution, 107
 caregiving aspects, 108
 empty nesters, 107
 housing arrangements, 107
 keys to success, 108
 "life cycle communities," 108
 Portland homeowners, 107
 and social connectedness, 107–108
 United States, 107
ACEs. *See* adverse childhood experiences
ACLU. *See* American Civil Liberties Union
active aging, 73
activity participation
 aging paradigm, 57
 background and health factors, 58
 condensed scale, 57
 mental state, 59–60
 scale score, 57
 SHARE dataset, 57
 and social connectedness, 58–59
 well-being indicators, 58
activity theory, 151
Administration for Community Living, 272
Administration on Aging (AoA), 260
ADUs. *See* accessory dwelling units
adverse childhood experiences (ACEs), 211–212
aerobic activities, 77
AFCIs. *See* age-friendly community initiatives
affectionate support, 37
age-friendly community
 AARP network, 92–93
 AARP Network of Age-Friendly Communities, 92–95, 97–98
 age-friendly action plans, 94–97
 age-friendly features, 89
 benefits, 90–92
 community characteristics, 90
 formal and informal social connections, 94
 free accessible transportation options, 93
 Maine initiatives, 95
 municipality, 90
 "social participation" domain, 93
age-friendly community initiatives (AFCIs), 106
Age-Friendly Pittsburgh plan, 96

281

Aging Project, 190
aloneness, 6
Alternatives for Seniors, 272
American Civil Liberties Union (ACLU), 183
American Pet Products Association (APPA), 163
American Society on Aging (ASA), 272
American Veterinarian Medical Association (AVMA), 165
AmeriCorps, 124
AmeriCorps State and National Program, 124
animal-assisted interventions (AAIs), 169
anxiety, 167–168
AoA. *See* Administration on Aging
APPA. *See* American Pet Products Association
appraisal support, 37
aquatic-based physical activity, 78
ASA. *See* American Society on Aging
attachment theory, 171
AVMA. *See* American Veterinarian Medical Association

Beloved Community Initiative, 202
Berlin Social Support Scale, 37–38
biophilia, 172
biopsychosocial model, 166
bisexual, 182

Campaign to End Loneliness initiative, 272–273
CAP study. *See* Caring and Aging with Pride study
cardiovascular aging, 10
Caring and Aging with Pride (CAP) study, 184
CCM plan. *See* Centro Civico Mexicano plan
CDC. *See* Centers for Disease Control and Prevention
Centers for Disease Control and Prevention (CDC), 170–171, 273

Centro Civico Mexicano (CCM) plan
  current mission, 111
  design, 112
  "Latinx new urbanism," 112–113
  livability, 113
  and social connectedness, 111–112
churches, 153–154
cognitive impairment, 44
cognitive training, 68
cohabitation, 224–225
communication, 97
companion animals, 163
Connect 2 Affect, 273
ConnectHomeUSA, 142–143
continuing bonds, 157
continuity theory, 152
Convoy Model of Social Supports, 103
Corporation for National and Community Service, 125
cybercrime, 144

dementia, 10
depression, 10, 169
developmental theory, 152
digital gap, 142–143
digital social networking, 135
discrepancy–attributional approach, 27
disengagement theory, 151, 152
disparate network indicators, 51
Duke-UNC Functional Social Support Questionnaire, 38

ego despair, 152
ego integrity, 152
Eldercare Locator, 273
emotional closeness, 61
emotional support, 37, 45
ENRICHD Social Support Inventory, 38
EURO-D scale, 52
Experience Corps, 127

faith communities, 153–154
federal programs, 125

FG program. *See* Foster Grandparents program
formal volunteering, 119, 120, 129
Foster Grandparents (FG) program, 125, 153, 201
friend power
　case study, 69–70
　casual friendships, 68
　dementia, 69
　genuine friendship and authentic connection, 69
　paid professionals, 68

GAD. *See* generalized anxiety disorder
GAS. *See* Gerontological Society of America
gay, 182
Gay Reunion in Our Times (GRIOT), 191
gendered nature of relationships
　aging women, 237–238
　instrumental or work-related interests, 239
　interactional exchanges, 239
　intergenerational relations, 242–246
　later-life relationships, 236
　life phases, 235
　married heteronormative couples, 239
　network size, 239
　postemployment lifestyles, 240–241
　rural/urban residency, 236–237
　sex difference perspective, 240
　social structural positions, 238–239
　socioemotional selectivity, 239
　widowers' social engagement, 240
　widows, 235–236
generalized anxiety disorder (GAD), 258
Gerontological Society Of America (GSA), 136, 274
Gierveld Loneliness Scale, 40
Global Network of Age-Friendly Cities and Communities (GNAFCC), 92
GNAFCC. *See* Global Network of Age-Friendly Cities and Communities

GrAND Voices initiative, 213
grandfamilies
　adversity and trauma, 210–214
　case example, 209–210
　child welfare system, 208
　legal relationship, 209
GRIOT. *See* Gay Reunion in Our Times

Health Aging and Body Composition (ABC) study, 170
Health and Retirement Study (HRS), 143
Health in Aging, 274
healthy places and social life
　environmental conditions, 104–105
　social connectedness and, 105–106
　social isolation, design and planning responses, 106–113
hearing loss, 44
heteronormative patriarch family system, 237
heterosexual men, 230
HHS. *See* U.S. Department of Health and Human Services
historical perspectives
　loneliness research, 24–28
　social disconnection, 20
　social epidemiology, 20
　social isolation research, 20–24
　social support, 28–31
　Solitude and Privacy: A Study of Social Isolation, Its Causes and Therapy (Halmos), 19–20
home-based passive sensing, 139
Housing and Urban Development (HUD)-assisted housing, 142
HRS. *See* Health and Retirement Study
HUD-assisted housing. *See* Housing and Urban Development-assisted housing
human–animal bond (HAB)
　animal's dependence on humans, 165
　anthropomorphism, 165
　attachment theory, 171

human–animal bond (HAB) (cont.)
  AVMA, 165
  biophilia, 172
  biopsychosocial model, 166
  cardiovascular disease, 166
  loneliness and depression, 168–170
  parent–child relationship, 171–172
  pet ownership, 166
  physical activity, 170–171
  psychosocial predictors, 166
  social supports, 171
  stress and anxiety, 167–168

I-CONECT. See Internet-Based Conversational Engagement Clinical Trials
immune function, 10
Inclusive Community Collaborative, 202
informal volunteering, 119, 120, 129
informational support, 37
insomnia, 10
instrumental support, 37, 45
Intentional Intergenerational Communities, 264
intergenerational relationships
  babies and toddlers, 199
  Beloved Community Initiative, 202
  Bridge Meadows, 202–203
  case studies, 198–199
  "Courageous Conversations," 203
  demographic diversity, 198
  demographic transformation, 197
  gendered nature, 242–246
  grandfamilies (see grandfamilies)
  human capital, 200
  Inclusive Community Collaborative, 202
  intentional engagement, 200
  intergenerational community, 200
  multigenerational families and grandfamilies, 205–207
  oral history project, 204–205
  programming in senior housing, 205
  programs, 200–201
  racial and ethnic diversity, 197
  sexual intimacy, 246–248
  social connectedness, 203
  social integration, 203
  young and middle-aged adults, 199–200
intergenerational volunteering, 98
Internet and social media
  adaptability and barriers, 137–138
  broadband accessibility, 138
  digital social networking, 135
  Gerontological Society of America, 136, 137
  psychological well-being, 143–144
  socially isolated seniors, 138–141
  TogetherTube, 137
Internet-Based Conversational Engagement Clinical Trials (I-CONECT), 140
interpersonal environment
  activity participation, 57–60
  interconnected phenomena, 49
  SHARE, 49
  social network, 50–57
Inventory of Socially Supportive Behaviors, 38

Kaiser Health News (KHN), 274
KHN. See Kaiser Health News
Kinship Care programs, 209

late-life social relationships
  cognitive impairment, 44
  data collection and interpretation, 43
  initial screening measures, 42
  measure selection, 43
  memory impairment, 44
  qualitative clinical interview, 42
  sensory impairment, 44
  structural and functional dimensions, 41–42
  two-step assessment, 42
  validated self-report measures, 42

Latinx Housing
   keys to success, 112–113
   and social connectedness, 60–61
LATs. *See* living apart together couples
lesbian, 182
lesbian, gay, bisexual, and transgender (LGBT) adults
   access to services, 188–189
   Aging Project, 190
   Alzheimer's Association, 189–190
   Caring and Aging with Pride study, 184
   Civil Rights movement, 182
   crisis competence, 184
   definition, 181, 182
   disclosure management, 188–189
   families of choice, 185–186
   historical context, 182–183
   issue of age, 182
   longitudinal NHAS study, 184
   Movement Advancement Project, 189
   National Health, Aging and Sexuality/Gender Study (NHAS), 181–182
   rural and urban communities, 256–257
   SAGE, 189, 191–192
   self-identified, 182
   Seniors Preparing for Rainbow Years, 190
   social isolation, 185
   social networks, 186–188
   social support, 186
   victimization and discrimination, 184–185
LGBT adults. *See* lesbian, gay, bisexual, and transgender adults
"life cycle communities," 108
Lifestyle Attributes for Pet Selection (LAPS) scale, 172
Lifestyle ReDesign, 263
livability, 113
living apart together (or LATs) couples, 225

loneliness
   age-related physical changes, 39
   Bowlby's research, 25
   cardiovascular risk, 39
   definition, 25–26
   depression, 39
   discrepancy–attributional approach, 27
   emotional isolation, 26
   lifestyle changes, 39
   objective–subjective distinction, 27–28
   perceived isolation, 39
   person-centered approach, 39–40
   risk factors, 41
   Rokach's model, 27
   self-report measures, 40–41
   shrinking social networks, 39
   social disconnectedness, 39
   social isolation (*see* social isolation and loneliness)
   treatment targets, 40
   Weiss's notes, 24–25
long-term care (LTC) facilities, 228–229
LSNS-6. *See* Lubben's Social Isolation Score, 6 items version
LTC facilities. *See* long-term care facilities
Lubben Social Network Scale, 38
Lubben's Social Isolation Score, 6 items version (LSNS-6), 140

macroenvironment, 103
MAP. *See* Movement Advancement Project
marital satisfaction
   baby boomers, 223
   cohabitation, 224–225
   late-life divorces, 224
   living apart together, 225
   remarriages, 224
Mather (More Than a) Cafés (MMC)
   keys to success, 110–111
   programming, 109
   quality of life, 114

Mather (More Than a) Cafés (MMC) (*cont.*)
   and social connectedness, 109–110
   tailored café menu, 109
   typical café options, 109
   wellness options, 109
Mayo Clinic, 274–275
McMaster Optimal Aging Portal, 275
meaning making, 155–156
Medical Outcomes Study Social Support Survey, 38
memory impairment, 44
mental health, 52, 60–62
mesoenvironment, 103
mHealth, 140
MMC. *See* Mather (More Than a) Cafés
Morningside Ministries, 275
Movement Advancement Project (MAP), 189
Multidimensional Scale of Perceived Social Support, 38
multigenerational families
   availability of kin, 206
   economic conditions, 206–207
   elongating life span, 206
   health and disability issues, 206
   immigration, 206
   making households work, 207
muscle strengthening, 77
My Healthevet, 275

name-generating social network inventory, 60
NAMI. *See* National Alliance on Mental Illness
National Alliance on Mental Illness (NAMI), 275–276
National Association of Area Agencies on Aging (N4A), 276
National Council on Aging (NCOA), 276
National Hospice and Palliative Care Organization (NHPCO), 276
National Indian Child Welfare Association (NICWA), 213

National Institute on Aging, 277
National Institutes of Health, Health Topics A-Z, 277
National Institutes of Healh–Veterans Administration (NIH-VA), 139
NCOA. *See* National Council on Aging
neuroplasticity, 68
Next Avenue, 277
N4A. *See* National Association of Area Agencies on Aging
NHPCO. *See* National Hospice and Palliative Care Organization
Niagara Gatekeepers Program, 264
NICWA. *See* National Indian Child Welfare Association
NIH-VA. *See* National Institutes of Healh–Veterans Administration
nondigital in-person interactions, 144
Norbeck Social Support Questionnaire, 38

OAA. *See* Older Americans Act
Older Americans Act (OAA), 260
one-on-one intervention, 262–263
ORCATECH. *See* Oregon Center for Aging and Technology
Oregon Center for Aging and Technology (ORCATECH), 139
osteoporosis, 77–78
outdoor spaces and buildings, 98
Oxford Academic Public Policy & Aging Report, 277

PACE model. *See* Program for All-Inclusive Care for the Elderly model,
PAR. *See* population attributable risk
Partnership for Health in Aging (PHA), 259
Patient Protection and Affordable Care Act, 260
Peace Corps, 124–125
perceived isolation, 7
Perceived Isolation Scale, 40

Perceived Support Scale, 38
Personal Reminder Information and Social Management (PRISM), 142
personal social network, 50–51
person-centered approach, 39–40
person–place transaction, 105
pets and elder well-being
  American Pet Products Association, 163
  case study, 161–162
  companion animals, 163
  depression, 163
  human characteristics, 164
  human–animal bond (see human–animal bond)
  pet ownership, 163–164
  pet selection, 172, 173
  risk factors for isolation, 163
PHA. See Partnership for Health in Aging
physical activity
  active aging, 73
  barriers to, 79–81
  case study, 84–85
  chronological age for social programs, 73
  considerations and guidelines, 75–77
  contraindications and modifications, 77–79
  exercise, 72
  habit systems, 75
  health promotion strategies, 71
  human–animal bond (HAB), 170–171
  multidimensional construct, 73
  opportunities, 81–82
  physician approval, 79, 80
  quality of life, 74
  resources on, 73–84
  social cohesion, 72
  social connectedness, 72
  social integration, 72–74
  "usual" and "successful" aging, 73
physical exercise, 68
pool-based physical activity, 78

population attributable risk (PAR), 141
PRISM. See Personal Reminder Information and Social Management
Program for All-Inclusive Care for the Elderly (PACE) model, 106
psychoeducation, 46
purposeful physical activity, 76

randomized controlled trials (RCTs), 140–141
RCTs. See randomized controlled trials
Retired and Senior Volunteer Program (RSVP), 121–123, 125
Retirees in Services to the Environment (RISE) program, 126–127
RISE program. See Retirees in Services to the Environment program
rural and urban communities
  case study, 253, 255–256
  ethnic minorities, 255
  formal and informal supports, 257
  interventions, 260–265
  policies and programs, 260
  professional practice, 258–260
  rural elders, 254–255
  rural residents, 255
  social isolation and loneliness, 257–258
  and social relationships, 256–257
Rural Health Information Hub, 277–278

SAGE. See Services and Advocacy for Lesbian, Gay, Bisexual and Transgender Elders
SASH program. See Support and Services at Home program
Science Care, 278
Senior Citizens Resources, 278
Senior Companion program, 125–126
Senior Corps programs, 125
SeniorNet (seniornet.org), 262–263
Seniors Preparing for Rainbow Years (SPRY), 190

sensory impairment, 44
Services and Advocacy for Lesbian, Gay, Bisexual and Transgender Elders (SAGE), 189, 191–192
sexual intimacy, 246–248
sexual intimacy post-50
  barriers, 225–229
  communication, 227
  isolated vs. single, 229–230
  long-term care, 228–229
  marital satisfaction, 223–225
  physical health, 227–228
  sexual longevity, 220–223
  social stigma and body image, 226–227
sexual longevity, 231
  AARP survey, 220, 221
  gay men and lesbians, 222–223
  men's sexual activity, 222
  multiple sociodemographic factors, 221
  older women's sexual activity, 221–222
  sexual frequency, 221
  sexual quality of life, 223
  sociological factors, 220
sexual quality of life (SQoL), 223
sexual satisfaction, 221
SHARE. *See* Survey of Health, Ageing and Retirement in Europe
Sixty & Me lifestyle website, 278
social capital, 168–169
social cohesion, 72
social connectedness, 72
  and accessory dwelling units (ADUs), 107–108
  downward trajectory, 4
  gendered nature (*see* gendered nature of relationships)
  healthy places and social life, 105–106
  intergenerational relationships (*see* intergenerational relationships)
  intimacy (*see* sexual intimacy post-50)
  and Latinx Housing, 60–61

LGBT adults (*see* lesbian, gay, bisexual, and transgender adults)
Mather (More Than a) Cafés (MMC), 109–110
  rural and urban communities (*see* rural and urban communities)
  trust and active involvement, 89
social disconnectedness, 7
Social Disconnectedness Scale, 40
social disconnection, 18
social health, 5–6
social integration, 36
  age-friendly community, 90–98
  friend power (*see* friend power)
  healthy places and social life, 103–116
  intergenerational relationships, 203
  pets and elder well-being (*see* pets and elder well-being)
  physical activity (*see* physical activity)
  spirituality and religion, 149–157
  volunteering (*see* volunteering)
social isolation and loneliness
  Berkman's model, 23
  "cause-and-effect" dilemma, 7
  "conceptual ambiguity," 22
  definition, 6–7
  demographic variables, 8, 9
  Durkheim's work, 20–21
  emotions and feelings, 21–22
  functional decline and death, 8
  geriatric care provider, 12
  health effects, 6
  ill-health, 8–9
  LGBT adults, 185
  Machielse's view, 23–24
  "organized society," 21
  relative risk ratio, 4
  rural and urban communities, 257–258
    assessment instruments, 261
    challenges, 261
    community intervention, 263–265
    comprehensive assessment, 261
    group-based interventions, 263

network characteristics, 21
one-on-one intervention, 262–263
social programming, 11–12
social support and health outcomes, 9–10
tripartite analysis, 22
underaddressed social issue, 4
"upstream" and "downstream" factors, 23
social network, 36
  interpersonal environment
    age interaction, 53
    CASP scale, 55
    disparate network indicators, 51–52
    "friend" network, 54–56
    health-related variables, 52
    mental health, 52, 53, 60–62
    "no network," 55
    "other family" network, 54
    "other" network, 55, 56
    personal social network, 50–51
    SHARE project, 51
    social isolation, 50
    sociodemographic controls, 52
    "spouse and children" network, 54, 56
    well-being, 52, 53
    well-being scores, 55–56
  lesbian, gay, bisexual, and transgender adults, 186–188
Social Network Index, 38
social opportunities, 98
social programming, 11–12
Social Provisions Scale, 38
social relationships. *See also* late-life social relationships
  individuals and families, 45–46
  loneliness and social isolation, 38–41
  qualitative elements, 35
  quantitative factors, 35
  self-report measures, 37–38
  social engagement and activity, 36–37
  social integration, 36
  social networks, 36
  social support, 36, 37, 45
  structural and functional factors, 44
  treatment planning, 45
social stigma and body image, 226–227
social support, 37, 45
  appraisal support, 30
  definition, 30
  emotional support, 30
  and health outcomes, 9–10
  information, 29
  informational support, 30
  instrumental support, 30
  Kraus's negative perceptions, 30
  lesbian, gay, bisexual, and transgender adults, 186
  small network size, 29
  source of strength, 31
  transmissibility of infectious disease, 29
Social Support Questionnaire, 38
socially isolated seniors
  in-home daily activities, 139
  morbidity and mortality rates, 4
  negative desirability biases, 138–139
  randomized controlled trials, 140–141
  wearable mobile technology, 140
sociodemographic controls, 52
sociodemographic proxies, 51
sodomy statutes, 183
spirituality and religion
  definition, 149
  faith communities, 153–154
  ministry of presence, 154–155
  soul, 150
  theoretical perspectives, 150–153
  transcendental connection, 155–158
SPRY. *See* Seniors Preparing for Rainbow Years
SQoL. *See* sexual quality of life
strengths-based framework, volunteering, 129–130
stress, 167–168
Support and Services at Home (SASH) program, 264

Survey of Health, Ageing and Retirement in Europe (SHARE), 49

technology and social health
digital gap, 142–143
Internet and social media (*see* Internet and social media)
user-friendly multifunctional devices, 141–142
technology-based intervention, 262
Three-Item Loneliness Scale, 41
transcendental connection, spirituality
assigning blame, 155–156
continuing bonds, 157
death or loss, 156
meaning making, 155–156
reconstruction of identity, 156
self-integrity and self-esteem, 158
transcendental reconstruction, 156
transgender, 182
transit-oriented development, 111–112
transportation, 97–98

UCLA Loneliness Scale, 41
unobtrusive in-home monitoring approach, 139
U.S. Government Guide for Seniors, 278
U.S. Government Senior Citizens' Resources Page, 278-279
U.S. Department of Health and Human Services (HHS), 279
U.S. National Library of Medicine, 279
U.S. Senate Special Committee on Aging, 3
user-friendly multifunctional devices, 141–142

Village Model, 263–264
Virtual Senior Academy, 142–143
Virtual Senior Center, 263
Visible Voices program, 126
VISTA program. *See* Volunteers in Service to America program
volunteering
benefits, 121
Christmas Bird Count, 127–128
Citizen science initiatives, 127–128
Experience Corps, 127
formal, 119, 120, 129
informal, 119, 120, 129
institutional barriers, 130
National Service programs, 123–126
nursing home residents, 121
personal and institutional barriers, 121
positive health and well-being outcomes, 120
practitioner strategies, 128–130
Retirees in Services to the Environment program, 126–127
RSVP, 121–123
Senior Companion program model, 126
strengths-based framework, 129–130
Visible Voices program, 126
Volunteers in Service to America (VISTA) program, 124

wearable mobile technology, 140
weight-bearing physical activity, 78
WHO. *See* World Health Organization
World Health Organization (WHO), 279